# British Cotton Textiles

This book examines the decline of the cotton textile industry, which defined Britain as an industrial nation, from its peak in the late nineteenth century to the state of the industry at the end of the twentieth century. Focusing on the owners and managers of cotton textile businesses, the authors examine how they mobilised financial resources, their attitudes to industry structure and technology, and their responses to the challenges posed by global markets.

The origins of the problems which forced the industry into decline are not found in any apparent loss of competitiveness during the long nineteenth century but rather in the disastrous reflotation after the First World War. As a consequence of these speculations, rationalisation and restructuring became more difficult at the time when they were most needed, and government intervention led to a series of partial solutions to what became a process of protracted decline.

In the post-1945 period, the authors show how government policy encouraged capital withdrawal rather than encouraging the investment needed for restructuring. The examples of corporate success since the Second World War – such as David Alliance and his Viyella Group – exploited government policy, access to capital markets, and closer relationships with retailers, but were ultimately unable to respond effectively to international competition and the challenges of globalisation. The chapters in this book were originally published in *Business History* and *Accounting, Business and Financial History*.

**David Higgins** is a Professor in Accounting and Finance at Newcastle University, UK. He has published widely in the field of business history, with particular reference to staple industries, corporate performance, and the protection of intellectual property. He has served on the editorial board, and acted as an associate editor, of the journal *Business History*.

**Steven Toms** is a Professor of Accounting at Leeds University, UK. He has published extensively in the field of business history, focusing on organisations' accounting and financial performance, with a particular interest in the history of cotton textiles. He is a former editor of the journal *Business History* and an editorial board member of the *Accounting History Review* (formerly *Accounting, Business and Financial History*).

# British Cotton Textiles

Maturity and Decline

*Edited by*
**David Higgins and Steven Toms**

Routledge
Taylor & Francis Group

LONDON AND NEW YORK

First published 2017
by Routledge

2 Park Square, Milton Park, Abingdon, Oxfordshire OX14 4RN
52 Vanderbilt Avenue, New York, NY 10017

*Routledge is an imprint of the Taylor & Francis Group, an informa business*

First issued in paperback 2020

*British Library Cataloguing in Publication Data*
A catalogue record for this book is available from the British Library

ISBN 13: 978-1-138-22388-2 (hbk)
ISBN 13: 978-0-367-59515-9 (pbk)

Typeset in Times
by diacriTech, Chennai

**Publisher's Note**
The publisher accepts responsibility for any inconsistencies that may have arisen
during the conversion of this book from journal articles to book chapters, namely
the possible inclusion of journal terminology.

**Disclaimer**
Every effort has been made to contact copyright holders for their permission to
reprint material in this book. The publishers would be grateful to hear from any
copyright holder who is not here acknowledged and will undertake to rectify any
errors or omissions in future editions of this book.

# Contents

# CONTENTS

# Citation Information

The chapters in this book were originally published in various issues of *Business History* and *Accounting, Business and Financial History*. When citing this material, please use the original page numbering for each article, as follows:

**Chapter 1**
*Windows of Opportunity in the Textile Industry: The Business Strategies of Lancashire Entrepreneurs, 1880–1914*
Steven Toms
*Business History*, volume 40, issue 1 (January 1998) pp. 1–25

**Chapter 2**
*Producer co-operatives and economic efficiency: Evidence from the nineteenth-century cotton textile industry*
Steven Toms
*Business History*, volume 54, issue 6 (October 2012) pp. 855–882

**Chapter 3**
*Financial constraints on economic growth: profits, capital accumulation and the development of the Lancashire cotton-spinning industry, 1885–1914*
John Steven Toms
*Accounting, Business and Financial History*, volume 4, issue 3 (1994) pp. 363–383

**Chapter 4**
*Firm structure and financial performance: the Lancashire textile industry, c.1884 – c.1960*
David Higgins and Steven Toms
*Accounting, Business and Financial History*, volume 7, issue 2 (1997) pp. 195–232

**Chapter 5**
*Financial distress, corporate borrowing, and industrial decline: the Lancashire cotton spinning industry, 1918–38*
David Higgins and Steve Toms
*Accounting, Business and Financial History*, volume 13, issue 2 (July 2003) pp. 207–232

**Chapter 6**

*Ownership, financial strategy and performance: the Lancashire cotton textile industry, 1918–1938*
David Higgins, Steven Toms and Igor Filatotchev
*Business History*, volume 57, issue 1 (2015) pp. 97–121

**Chapter 7**

*Public Subsidy and Private Divestment: The Lancashire Cotton Textile Industry, c.1950–c.1965*
David Higgins and Steven Toms
*Business History*, volume 42, issue 1 (January 2000) pp. 59–84

**Chapter 8**

*Financial Institutions and Corporate Strategy: David Alliance and the Transformation of British Textiles, c.1950–c.1990*
David M. Higgins and Steven Toms
*Business History*, volume 48, issue 4 (October 2006) pp. 453–478

For any permission-related enquiries please visit:
http://www.tandfonline.com/page/help/permissions

# Introduction – Lancashire cotton: A brief historical overview

David Higgins and Steven Toms

## The rise and decline of textiles

From the industrial revolution until well into the twentieth century, the cotton industry played a dominant role in the evolution of the British economy. Pioneering entrepreneurs developed the spinning mule and the power loom, which became the staple technologies of an industry that expanded enormously in the nineteenth century. The industry transformed the landscape of North West England, where factory chimneys dominated the skylines of its thriving mill towns. By 1914, the British cotton textile industry, located in mainly in Lancashire, dominated world textile production. Lancashire accounted for almost 40 per cent of global capacity in spinning, which, by far, exceeded any other nation. Over 80 per cent of its cloth production was exported, at a time when the industry accounted for around 70 per cent of world trade in cotton textiles.[1]

Notwithstanding the tremendous scale of the industry in 1914, Lancashire entrepreneurs faced some important challenges. International competition was always a threat, and access to world markets could not be guaranteed or sustained. To keep ahead of competition, investment in new technology was also a constant challenge. Entrepreneurs responded with refin ments to the spinning mule and power loom. An alternative to the intermittent mule spinning process was ring spinning, which was an adaptation of the continuous method originally developed by Sir Richard Arkwright. Investments in any of these technologies were costly and risky, and were made more so by the instability of demand for cotton goods. Indeed, since the earliest days of factory-based cotton production, the trade cycle had caused considerable uncertainty. Writing in the 1860s, Karl Marx used the history of the cotton industry to illustrate the cycle of boom and slump in capitalist production.[2] These swings in production continued throughout the later decades of the nineteenth century, but however serious the downturn, each was followed by a new boom and further expansion.

Few, therefore, could have predicted the precipitate decline of the industry after the First World War. In the slump of 1920, Lancashire's main export markets collapsed to a fraction of their pre-1914 levels.[3] The Indian market, in particular, accounted for a substantial proportion of these losses.[4] As with previous downturns, there was an expectation that normality would be restored, once world trading conditions stabilized. Winston Churchill's return to the gold standard in 1925, however, did nothing for the competitiveness of British exports, including cotton, and the decline continued. Only briefly, in 1950 and 1951, was there a short-lived return to boom conditions.[5] The longer-run downward trend resumed, as Lancashire lost further world market share to Western Europe, the United States and Japan.[6] In the 1970s, in particular, imports of cotton cloth into the United Kingdom from these locations increased dramatically, as one commentator contemplated 'the vanishing British cotton industry'.[7]

**Debates on the decline of Lancashire textiles**

Unsurprisingly, in view of its significance and scale, a substantial literature has emerged on the Lancashire cotton textile industry. The brief sketch in the previous section on the rise of and decline of textiles, has received its fair share of discussion and debate. Up until around 1990, such scrutiny reflected the wider contexts and symptoms of the decline of Britain as a manufacturing country.

Since 1990, the focus of investigation has broadened, with Lancashire figuring as one part of the story of a global industry. The forces of globalisation and the dramatic relocation of textile production to the global south have undoubtedly influenced the historiography. Contemporaries and academic researchers alike, have highlighted the loss of export markets as the key determinant of the industry's decline.[8] Although global competition and associated loss of markets has received considerable attention, it is not the focus of this book.

Instead, we concentrate on entrepreneurs and firm-level business strategies. As the earliest example of industrialisation, Lancashire cotton textiles have a special significance and a longevity that allows firm life-cycle dynamics to be all the better assessed. A particularly important aspect of this dynamic is the interaction of entrepreneurs with technology *and* systems of financial provision. Such an approach, adopted in this book, contrasts with economists, in particular, who have tended to stress monocausal explanations of decline. Alternative perspectives, as featured in this book, that examine the decisions of particular firms and entrepreneurs, can therefore shed further light on the extent to which entrepreneurs were, indeed, to blame for Lancashire's decline. Old-fashioned entrepreneurial attitudes, commitment to the wrong technology, or financial speculation, may, indeed, all be separate causes of economic failure and industrial decline. At the same time, each can be a consequence of apparently rational individual decision-making. History therefore matters. If mistakes were made, their sequencing and compounding effects are crucial.

Of direct relevance to our focus on entrepreneurs, technology and finance is the long-running and controversial debate among historians and economists about the adequacy of the industry leaders' response to the threat posed by international competition. Writing in 1990, Mass and Lazonick summarised the 'state of the debates' on this subject.[9] In part, these debates originated from a much broader enquiry about alleged 'entrepreneurial failure' in the late Victorian and Edwardian periods across the whole of British industry. Symptomatic of such failure was an apparent reluctance to invest in modern management structures and higher productivity technology.[10] According to some interpretations, Lancashire cotton, with its personally managed firms, atomised structure, and strong adherence to traditional mule spinning and power loom weaving, provided a compelling illustration of the more generic reasons for the loss of Britain's international competitive advantage.[11] Investments in such structures and technologies could, nonetheless, be represented as entirely rational, given prevailing factor cost conditions and the technical capabilities of mule spindles and power looms, relative to ring spindles and automatic looms.[12] In contrast, according to Lazonick's interpretation in a series of papers, the reason for the apparent failure to adopt alternative technologies was not factor cost, but the vertically specialised structure of the industry.[13] Specifically, the separation of the spinning and weaving branches prevented entrepreneurs from coordinating simultaneous investments in alternative systems of production in both branches of the industry.[14] In response to this argument, the technical feasibility of such improvements has been questioned in view of the superior technical characteristics of mule spinning before 1920.[15] Typically, these investigations have examined the industry as a whole and used industry data on exports, employment, import penetration, innovation and capacity utilisation, to support their arguments. As a consequence, as far as Lancashire was concerned, what began as a discussion of entrepreneurial failure became a debate about factor cost and industry structure, in which the behaviour of individual entrepreneurs was 'of little or no concern'.[16]

The focus of these academic debates up to 1990 was on the pre-1914 period, during which time Lancashire entrepreneurs allegedly made their crucial mistakes. However, comparatively less attention has been devoted to the interwar years, when dislocation of international markets and entrepreneurial shortcomings made Lancashire's problems more transparent. Writing during the latter period, John Maynard Keynes noted the relationship between unsound finance and surplus capacity, but also argued that the industry's problems lay in its atomised structure, and that the reason for its failure to restructure was that it would entail the dismissal of the managers required to endorse this strategy.[17] Keynes therefore called for government intervention as the only way of forcing through the required restructuring. Others argued for maintenance of the status quo: the sources of Lancashire's competitive advantage were indelible and the industry would recover, as before, once international conditions reverted to their pre-1914 norms.[18]

As the slump became more protracted, threatening insolvency for some banks, Keynes's arguments prevailed and were eventually endorsed by the Bank of England. It was instrumental in supporting a large amalgamation, which became the Lancashire Cotton Corporation (LCC) in 1929. Much of the subsequent historiography of the industry has endorsed the Keynesian analysis.[19] Certainly, the formation of the LCC had the potential to overcome the obstacles that had historically prevented entrepreneurs from making the 'correct' investments likely to secure the long-run future of the industry.

Since 1990, further investigation and analysis have tended to rehabilitate the Lancashire entrepreneur in the face of such criticisms. Research has again questioned the extent to which the industry's structure impeded technological choices and, therefore, productivity. The slow adoption of ring spinning made sense in view of the scarcity and expense of automatic, Northrop looms.[20] Leunig has shown that before 1914, in terms of output per spindle, Lancashire rings were superior to New England rings, and Lancashire mules were superior to New England mules. Moreover, the labour productivity of Lancashire mule spinners exceeded that of Lancashire ring spinners and of New England mules and ring spinners.[21] A likely reason for the superiority of mule spinning over ring spinning in Lancashire was the greater labour intensity of ring spinning.[22] Research for the post-1945 period has shown that vertical integration was not a necessary condition for the adoption of ring spindles. During this period, the decision to adopt rings by major specialised spinning firms, such as Combined English Mills, Crosses & Heaton's, Fine Cotton Spinners & Doublers and the LCC, was governed by taxation policy, shortage of mule labour and the superior profitability of ring compared to mule spinning.[23] Taken as a whole, this evidence provides some rational justification for the investment decisions taken by Lancashire entrepreneurs during significant phases of the industry's life cycle.

While recognising the value of these empirical results, new issues beyond the technological choice issue have become more prominent in recent debates, reflecting the acceleration of globalisation in the late-twentieth century. In considering the linkages between industry structure and international trade, new foci have thus included business networks, vertical linkages and survival strategies for textiles in industrial countries.[24] Lancashire has traditionally been cited as an example of an industrial district, comprising clusters of firms reliant on external economies of scale. As a source of competitive advantage, such economies persisted well into the twentieth century.[25] Prior to 1914, the industry benefitted from rapidly growing export markets facilitated by substantial external economies in the purchase of raw cotton, the manufacture of yarn and cloth and their subsequent processing and distribution. Merchants and their networks were pivotal to this growth. Additionally, merchants were crucial to the establishment of testing facilities to eradicate fraudulent transactions within the industry.[26]

Another prevalent feature of the Lancashire model of ownership and organisation was the evolution of networks of interlocked directors. These groupings provided access to finance primarily from within the Lancashire region, but also from sources further afield. Local and London-based finance imposed very different structures of accountability and also dictated the nature of strategic opportunity.[27] Ownership networks and governance structures impacted on entrepreneurial behaviour and had an important influence on how businesses responded to the challenges of industry decline.[28] A significant lesson of these more recent studies is that ownership and associated structures of governance and accountability can have important consequences for business performance.

Focusing on the decline phase in particular, several studies have considered the survival options for firms faced with globalisation. Some entrepreneurs responded by concentrating on niche markets.[29] Parsons and Rose have shown that the success of *Berghaus* and *Karrimor*, leading names in the outdoor and mountaineering clothing industry, depended on the networks established by their founders. They argued that the relationship between innovation and networks underpinned the focus on product design.[30] Similarly, these authors demonstrated that within the Lancashire textile industry, 'a segment of high-performance fabrics and technical textiles survived and developed, related to newly emerging demands from the outdoor trade and industrial customers'. For example, *Peter Storm*, *Mountain Equipment* and *Regatta* utilised the skills base inherited from Lancashire's traditional expertise in textile finishing and dyeing [31]

The studies referred to above have generated broader questions about the role and functions of entrepreneurs and how they adapted to pronounced changes in export markets. Beyond market niches, there were three broad strategic responses to the threat of global competition. One option, based on a literal interpretation of Ricardian trade theory, is that activities such as textile manufacture should be abandoned as labour costs increase in developed countries, in favour of lower cost imports from countries with an abundance of cheap labour.[32] In view of the long period of decline after 1920, which was in part driven by such considerations, Lancashire entrepreneurs could be criticised for not exiting quickly enough.[33] A second alternative, as advocated by Lazonick, building on his earlier arguments about Lancashire cotton, is that the direct alternative to such a cheap labour, 'sweatshop' orientated economy, is investment in capital intensive, automated production.[34] A third variant, accommodating aspects of both these models, is the design-led flexible network, which can be seen as a development of the literature on business and financial networks. In this model, dominant upstream firms, usually retailers, source selectively from high-tech and cheap labour producers.[35] As Beckert implies in his wide-ranging analysis of the global cotton industry, choices between these models have to some degree become constrained and enabled by national, and increasingly, international structures of regulation.[36]

Bypassing much of the intervening literature on the cotton industry, but engaging with the wider issue of globalisation and industrial strategy, Lazonick has recently returned to pick back up where he left off in 1990. He argues that cooperation between employers and employees and control of the shop floor by operatives resulted in productivity gains and a relatively equal share of returns between labour and capital. These arrangements suited Lancashire well, as the cotton industry continued to expand in the final decades of the nineteenth century. However, Lancashire failed because it did not respond to the challenge posed by overseas competitors, utilising technological combinations based on managerial, as opposed to shop floor, organisation.[37] Beckert, meanwhile, notes complaints about falling profits during this period, adding that for Britain at least, there was a decisive drop in the 1920s.[38] Beckert agrees with Lazonick, insofar as the working class was in a powerful position on the shop floor, but also points out that the consequence was not just an increase in wage costs, but also greater political influence, resulting in more welfare-oriented regulation and higher taxes.

The perspectives discussed in this introduction offer alternative interpretations of the decline of Lancashire cotton textiles in the face of increasing international competition, but can be complemented by the further perspectives offered in this book. The cyclical nature of the cotton trade means that it is easy to find complaints of falling profits at most times in the long-run history of the industry. Beckert is, therefore, correct also, to suggest that British cotton capitalists were 'spoiled by decades of enormous profits', including the pre-war boom of 1904–1910.[39] Neither Beckert nor Lazonick comment on how these profits were used, but we can assume they both agree that they were not invested productively. For Beckert, such investment would have made little difference, given rising national costs and global competitive pressures, at least until 1958, when the Greater Manchester Chamber of Commerce admitted defeat and called for protection.[40] For Lazonick, as noted earlier, the preferred solution to the problem of international competition before 1914 was to invest in integrated production using the new technologies of ring spinning and automatic weaving.[41] In other contexts, Lazonick is critical of institutions and ideologies that promote divestment, as opposed to financial commitment using 'patient capital', most notably, the 'shareholder value' driven buybacks in the US economy since 1970.[42]

Given their prominence in his general model, Lazonick's neglect of the *processes* of investment, divestment and reinvestment in his historical analysis of Lancashire is therefore surprising: these processes either constrained, or provided the opportunity for Lancashire entrepreneurs' adoption of vertically integrated structures. Instead, Lazonick views the stock market as a consequence of the rise of the large-scale industrial corporation in the United States; part of a process of wealth transfer from entrepreneurs to passive stock holders.[43] However, these arguments significantly underplay the historical role of the stock market in Lancashire. In contrast to Lazonick's portrayal of the financial system, Lancashire stock markets in the nineteenth century provided investment opportunities for diverse and active share ownership, with significant consequences for entrepreneurial behaviour

**The contribution of this book**

The above review has summarised a number of sometimes competing interpretations of the decline of the Lancashire cotton textile industry and highlighted several unresolved questions. The contrasting interpretations of Lazonick and Beckert suggest a trade-off between capital intensive and cheap labour-based strategies,[44] requiring far-sighted judgment by entrepreneurs and managers. The recently highlighted roles of business networks and associated access to markets and finance suggest that such judgments are not purely matters for isolated and unaccountable individual decision-makers. Related and unresolved issues concern the vertical structure of the industry and whether the integration of processes, or their separation, offer sustainable models for an industry that experienced pronounced cyclical variations in demand.

The chapters in this book provide details of the context and nature of these variations. They encapsulate a further strand of literature that has evolved since the 1990s: the role of financial systems, with a focus on how finance is raised, deployed, accumulated and reinvested. Such a focus permeates all the debates referred to above, particularly, entrepreneurial decisions concerning industry structure, technology and constraints on those decisions and their outcomes.

As the chapters in the present collection illustrate, the Lancashire stock market evolved and impacted on the industry at crucial stages in its development. Chapters 2 and 3 show that the stock market was an important vehicle for mobilising the savings of middle- and working-class investors in the spinning districts of Oldham and Rochdale. Public stock markets coexisted with networks of private capital in late nineteenth-century Lancashire. Entrepreneurs were therefore faced with a portfolio of opportunities arising from technological investments, restructuring and integration, and access to different sources of finance. Chapter 2 sets out these opportunities and examines the differential impact of ownership structures on business behaviour and performance.

Chapter 3 explores the origins of the system of finance that played a dominant role in investment and hence, the structure of the industry before 1914. Firms that began as producer cooperatives evolved into groups of connected firms through cliques of directors. Their modus operandi was the flotation of new and larger mills, with each further expansion of the export market before 1914 (chapter 3). In this context, their choice of mills of appropriate scale and technology was rational, and the financial performance of mills with differing structures and technologies confirmed this view (chapter 4). New firms generated significant profits, providing opportunities for reinvestment (chapters 2–5)

In the next, crucial, stage of the business cycle, the close relationship between the stock market and fixed investment became even more decisive. As chapters 6 and 7 demonstrate, the stock market boom of 1919–1920 and its subsequent collapse saddled firms with high fixed charges and deprived them of the financial resources needed for new investment. These chapters also show that ring spinning and automatic weaving only represented a source of competitive advantage in the 1920s, after the crash had curtailed the financial capacity of the industry, and once certain technical breakthroughs in intermediate processes were achieved. When these were in place, as shown in chapters 8 and 9, profits from post-war booms and the development of the market for corporate control created further opportunities for reorganisation and reinvestment.

Although crucial, the stock market by itself offers only a partial explanation of firm performance. Historical analysis of the Lancashire cotton industry is important because it reveals the interplay between technological and financial developments, as mediated by the role of exogenous events. As chapters 2–5 demonstrate, before 1914, Lancashire firms made significant investments in alternative technology, especially ring spinning, which was well suited to the production of certain specialised fibres. Specialised spinning firms were typically very profitable and prompted new investment in similarly specialised, but much larger factories, particularly in the boom years, 1904–1907. Amalgamated firms emerged during the merger wave of the late 1890s, and were typically less profitable than smaller, specialised spinning firms. Similarly, firms combining spinning and weaving were also less profitable before 1914, albeit enjoying more stable returns. It should be stressed, however, that few of these larger organisations were vertically integrated in terms of process.[45] They certainly incorporated more managerial resources, as Lazonick's model would have demanded, but rarely integrated production processes in single factory units. Specialised production and factor cost conditions militated against this, confirming Leunig's evidence, but so too did the lack of automation in winding and intermediate processes. High draft spinning and crucial automations in preparatory and intermediate processes, for example, were not commercially viable until the 1920s, which meant, as noted earlier, that investment opportunities occurred at precisely the moment when Lancashire firms were starved of finance in the post-1921 crash environment.

Chapter 5 confirms that whatever theoretical advantages have been claimed for vertical integration, the financial incentives for adopting this organisational form were rather poor. Using returns to capital for a large sample of specialised spinning and vertically integrated firms, the chapter shows that the former achieved higher rates of return during the periods of 1884–1913 and 1946–1960. Vertically integrated firms achieved superior returns to capital during the interwar period only. The chapter also demonstrates that claims about entrepreneurs' failure to achieve higher levels of integration were misplaced due to the symbiotic relationships between each type of firm. For example, specialised spinners supplied additional yarn when there was a shortfall between yarn supply and cloth production requirements in integrated firms

Taken together, these early chapters provide evidence of strong financial performance of publically owned, specialised firms. Profits were reinvested in new mills on a larger scale, rather than necessarily modernising existing factories. These new mills contained whichever technology was most suited to their specialised function. Consequently, specialist mule spinning mills performed as well as ring spinners and in some cases better. Vertical integration, as manifested in the common ownership of spinning and weaving plants, did not of itself enhance financial performance, nor did it provide a rational basis for the simultaneous adoption of alternative technologies in spinning and weaving.

The performance benefits of different patterns of ownership, technological adoption and vertical structure were, however, largely temporary. Even before 1914, these depended crucially on the trade cycle, which was reflected in share values and the associated timing of new investment and mill construction. The traditional, disaggregated, Lancashire model worked well in an expanding market, but after 1920, overcapitalisation became an absolute constraint on investment at a time when technological advantage began to shift away from the traditional Lancashire mule.

Chapters 6 and 7 show the effects of this technological shift in combination with a detailed analysis of the impact of finance on the business strategies of individual firms, that followed directly from the reflotation boom, 1919–1920, and persisted throughout the interwar period. These chapters therefore revisit the prevalent Keynesian interpretation of the finaning and structure of the industry. Specifically, chapter 6 examines the relationship between asset misvaluation, the post-crash illiquid market for cotton shares and the profit distribution policies of a sample of quoted firms, and shows that re-financing strategies were used to exploit the potential for systematic wealth transfers. Moreover, when the technical dominance and commercial feasibility of adopting high-throughput technology were established in the 1920s and 1930s, the majority of recapitalised spinning firms simply did not have the cash flow to invest in these projects, even if the probability of success was high

Chapter 7 re-examines Keynes' view that banks impeded exit during the interwar period, as a consequence of overcommitment to the industry. This chapter establishes that local, not external, syndicates predominated in the recapitalisation boom and also inhibited exit. Where external syndicates were involved in reflotation they had a deleterious effect on third party investors, for example the Beecham and Sperling Trusts with the Amalgamated Cotton Mills

Trust and Crosses & Heaton's recapitalisations, respectively. Ownership was therefore crucial, promoting exit or turnaround in some cases and restricting them in others. In particular, the financial involvement of a core of interlocked investors, drawn mostly from cliques previously involved in pre-1914 flotations, restricted exit, notwithstanding the absence of opportunity for these incumbent firms

The slump of 1921, therefore, signalled the start of a protracted decline in the fortunes of the industry. Although there were attempts to restructure supported by the Bank of England, there were few strategic opportunities in difficult international markets. The changed conditions identified by Beckert, to which we would add the increased cost base of Lancashire firm arising from fixed financial charges, and the role of incumbent ownership interests, rather than the managerially inspired counter-factual of Lazonick, appeared to prevail in this new era.

The financial burden inherited from the interwar period reinforced the need for government intervention in the industry, after 1945. Chapter 8 discusses the industry's response to the *Cotton Industry Act*, 1959. This act represented a new attempt to address the surplus capacity problem that had arisen in the interwar period due to the burden of fixed charges and the failure of 'inefficient' firms to exit. The chapter highlights a fundamental disjuncture between entrepreneurs' private assessment of the future, revealed by their divestment and investment activities, and those of successive governments, manifested by the use of tax-based investment incentives and the provision of public subsidy. Strikingly, companies with the greatest capital requirements were also those paying out the highest proportion of profits in dividends. By committing companies to higher fixed costs (because of re-equipment), but without guaranteeing stability of demand, the *Cotton Industry Act* increased capital market pressure on corporate cash flows and encouraged greater dividend payments to compensate for the higher risk incurred by re-equipment. Moreover, the uncertainty generated by growing competition in export markets encouraged firms that did not re-equip to accelerate their dividend payments.

For remaining firms and willing investors, the development of the market for corporate control in the 1960s provided one further and final significant opportunity to restructure. Alternative strategies are contrasted in chapter 9, which compares the exploits of David Alliance and his construction of the Coats Viyella textile conglomerate through a series of mergers, with other large firms, such as Courtaulds and Imperial Chemical Industries (ICI), which retained significant textile interests, including cotton. Alliance utilised his close relationships with Rothschild's merchant bank to finance the acquisition of incumbent textile firms at significant discounts. The acquired companies were willing to accept the bids made by Alliance because the illiquid market for cotton shares and depressed trading conditions meant it was the only viable exit option. The funds obtained from these discounted purchases allowed Alliance to 'pyramid' his acquisitions, using one transaction to prepare the way for the next. Additionally, Alliance, with the assistance of the Rothschild's network, was able to exploit political channels to secure the business finance offered by the Industrial Reorganisation Corporation. However, unlike Courtaulds and ICI, Alliance did not focus on scale-based economies. Rather, his acquisition policy was motivated by the realisation that he could revitalise famous, but dormant, brands, the owners of which were often locked-in to supplying Marks & Spencer (M&S). The net results of Alliance's activities were twofold: the consumer textile industry thrived, albeit comprising only a small rump of cotton-based firms; secondly, by making textiles shares 'hot', market liquidity in these shares improved. Although this created some success in the short run, inability to secure access to stable, sustainable markets, even through M&S, undermined the longer run prognosis.

This theme is returned to in the concluding chapter, which forms a short epilogue telling the story of the final years of decline and abortive survival plans of the remaining firms. Problems that had emerged in the 1920s, in particular the divergence between financial priorities and capital investment as undermined by unstable markets, doomed all but niche producers. At the strategic level of the industry, large-scale production was problematic in view of the lack of integration between production and marketing functions. Indeed, production decisions increasingly originated with powerful retailers, which meant the vertical control of the textile industry itself became a potential source of instability for manufacturing firms, creating a persistent deterrent to further investment.

In sum, the chapters in this book represent a reinterpretation of the maturity and decline of the Lancashire textile industry, in which the accumulation and circulation of capital investment, and the activities of financial networks are the overarching themes. Interpreting the financial and investment cycle as a process places an emphasis on path dependency, thereby placing history at the centre of the analysis, as opposed to mono-causal economic models. The contrast between the scale of the industry, at its zenith in 1914 and its disappearance in the 1960s and 1970s, was summarised by James Longworth: 'Were it not for the reality [of such contrast] . . . it would be seen as a fiction of monumental proportions'.[46] Taken together, the chapters in this book demonstrate the key characteristics of that reality and represent a substantial contribution to debates seeking to interpret it.

## Notes

1. Robson, *Cotton industry in Britain*, p.4, Table 15, p.354; PEP, *Report on the British cotton industry*, pp.23–24. Although these data refer to the UK, the cotton-textile industry was predominantly Lancashire-based. For example, by the late 1890s, Lancashire accounted for 75.8 per cent of the cotton operatives employed in the UK (Broadberry and Marrison, External economies of scale in the Lancashire cotton industry, p.55).
2. Marx, *Capital I*, 1976, pp.583–584, *Capital III*, 1984, pp.124–137.
3. During the 1920s and 1930s, exports of cotton piece goods were 58 and 29 per cent, respectively, of their 1913 levels (calculated from Robson, *Cotton industry in Britain*, p.333).
4. Burnett Hurst, Lancashire and the Indian market.
5. Keynes, *Economic consequences of Mr Churchill*; Rooth, *British protectionism*.
6. Robson, *Cotton industry in Britain*, London, pp.6–26. Between 1950 and 1970, cotton cloth exports declined by 83 per cent. Calculated from Singleton, *Lancashire on the scrapheap*, p.116.
7. Blackburn, Vanishing British cotton industry. Comparing 1979–1980 with 1971–1973, Blackburn found that the United Kingdom's imports of cloth from these three locations increased by 257 meter square yards, while imports from all other countries increased by 40 meter square yards in the same period.
8. For respective examples, see: Burnett-Hurst, Lancashire and Indian market; Singleton, *Lancashire on the scrapheap*.
9. Mass and Lazonick, British cotton.
10. Aldcroft, Entrepreneur and British economy.
11. Chandler, *Scale and scope*; Landes, *The unbound Prometheus*.
12. Sandberg, American rings and English mules, 26; McCloskey and Sandberg, From damnation to redemption; Sandberg, *Lancashire in decline*.
13. Lazonick, Competition, specialization and industrial decline; Lazonick, Factor costs and diffusion; Lazonick, Industrial organization and technological change.
14. Mass and Lazonick, British cotton industry.
15. Saxonhouse and Wright, National leadership and technological paradigms.
16. Sandberg, *Lancashire in Decline*, p.10

17. Keynes, *Return to Gold*, p.631.
18. Drummond, *British economic policy*; FMCSA, *Lancashire cotton industry*.
19. Keynes, *Return to gold*, pp.601, 605; Bamberg, Rationalisation of British cotton industry, pp.26–30. Porter, The commercial banks; Marchionetti, Keynes and the collapse; Bowden and Higgins, Short-time working and price maintenance.
20. Ciliberto, British cotton entrepreneurs.
21. Leunig, A British industrial success, pp.101–104. Leuning, Myth of corporate economy.
22. Toms, Growth, profits and technological choice
23. Higgins, Rings, mules, and constraints.
24. Rose, *Firms, networks and business values*; Chapman, *Merchant enterprise*; Jeremy, Survival strategies; Filatotchev and Toms, Corporate governance, strategy and survival; Toms and Filatotchev, Corporate governance, business strategy and the dynamics.
25. Marshall, *Industry and trade*; Broadberry and Marrison, External economies of scale; Popp, Toms and Wilson, Industrial districts as organizational environments.
26. See, for example, Chapman, *Merchant enterprise*; Broadberry and Marrison, External economies of scale; Beckert, *Empire of cotton*; Higgins and Velkar, Spinning a yarn?
27. Contrast the examples in Toms, The rise of modern accounting, with: Filatotchev and Toms, Corporate governance, strategy and survival and Toms and Filatotchev, Corporate governance, business strategy and the dynamics. Using modern metrics, there is evidence that the Lancashire stock market of the nineteenth century operated to a high level of relative efficiency before c.1890, see: Toms, Information content of earnings.
28. Filatotchev and Toms, Corporate governance and financial constraints
29. Farnie and Jeremy, *Fibre that changed the world*; Parsons and Rose, Communities of knowledge; Parsons and Rose, Neglected legacy.
30. Parsons and Rose, Communities of knowledge.
31. Parsons and Rose, Neglected legacy, p.684.
32. Heckscher and Ohlin, *Heckscher-Ohlin trade theory*.
33. Singleton, *Lancashire on the scrapheap*.
34. Lazonick, Innovative enterprise or sweatshop economics?
35. Toms and Zhang, Marks & Spencer.
36. Beckert, *Empire of cotton*.
37. Lazonick, Innovative enterprise or sweatshop economics? pp.19–20; Mass and Lazonick, British cotton industry.
38. Beckert, *Empire of cotton*, p.390.
39. Ibid.
40. Ibid, p.428.
41. Mass and Lazonick, British cotton industry.
42. Lazonick, *Innovative enterprise or sweatshop economics*? p.13.
43. Ibid.
44. Higher capital intensity reduces *total* labour costs because less labour is employed. Simultaneously, the productivity of retained labour increases; this might result in higher wages for those employed after the move to more capital-intensive techniques of production.
45. There were exceptions. Ashton Brothers were vertically integrated by process and, so too, were Tootal, Broadhurst & Lee. Lazonick, *The cotton industry* 41; Longworth, *The cotton mills of Bolton*, pp.64.
46. Longworth, *The cotton mills*, p.99.

## Bibliography

Aldcroft, D. H. (1964). The entrepreneur and the British economy. *Economic History Review*, *17*(1), 113–134.
Beckert, S. (2014). *Empire of cotton: A new history of global capitalism*. New York: Vintage.

# INTRODUCTION

Blackburn, J. A. (1982). The vanishing UK cotton industry. *National Westminster Bank Quarterly Review* (November), 42–52.

Bowden, S., & Higgins, D. M. (1998). Short - time working and price maintenance: Collusive tendencies in the cotton - spinning industry, 1919–1939. *Economic History Review*, 51(2), 319–343.

Broadberry, S., & Marrison, A. (2002). External economies of scale in the Lancashire cotton industry, 1900–1950. *The Economic History Review*, 55(1), 51–77.

Burnett-Hurst, A. R. (1932). Lancashire and the Indian market. *Journal of the Royal Statistical Society*, 95, 395–440.

Chapman, S. D. (2003). *Merchant enterprise in Britain: From the Industrial Revolution to World War I*. Cambridge: Cambridge University Press.

Ciliberto, F. (2010). Were British cotton entrepreneurs technologically backward? Firm-level evidence on the adoption of ring spinning. *Explorations in Economic History*, 47(4), 487–504.

Drummond, I. (2006). *British economic policy and empire, 1919–1939*. Abingdon: Routledge.

Farnie, D., & Jeremy, D. (2004). *The fibre that changed the world: The cotton industry in international perspective, 1600–1990s*. Oxford: Oxford University Press.

FMCSA (Federation of Master Cotton Spinners' Associations) (1936). *Measures for the revival of the Lancashire cotton industry*. Manchester: FMCSA.

Filatotchev, I., & Toms, S. (2003). Corporate governance, strategy and survival in a declining industry: A study of UK Cotton textile companies. *Journal of Management Studies*, 40(4), 895–920.

Filatotchev, I., & Toms, S. (2006). Corporate governance and financial constraints on strategic turnarounds. *Journal of Management Studies*, 43(3), 407–433.

Heckscher, E. F., & Ohlin, B. G. (1991). *Heckscher-Ohlin trade theory*. Cambridge, MA: The MIT Press.

Higgins, D. M. (1993). Rings, mules, and structural constraints in the Lancashire textile industry, c. 1945–c. 1965. *Economic History Review*, 46(2), 342–362.

Higgins, D. M., & Velkar, A. (2017). Spinning a yarn? Institutions, law, and standards, c.1880–1914. *Enterprise & Society* (forthcoming).

Jeremy, D. J. (1993). Survival strategies in Lancashire textiles: Bleachers' Association Ltd to Whitecroft plc, 1900–1980s. *Textile History*, 24(2), 163–209.

Keynes, J. M. (1981). *The return to gold and industrial policy II*, collected works. Cambridge: Cambridge University Press, pp. 578–637.

Keynes, J. M. (2010). The economic consequences of Mr Churchill (1925). In *Essays in persuasion*. Basingstoke: Palgrave Macmillan UK, pp. 207–230.

Landes, D. (1969). *The unbound Prometheus*. Cambridge: Cambridge University Press.

Lazonick, W. (1981). Competition, specialization and industrial decline. *Journal of Economic History*, 41(1), 31–38.

Lazonick, W. (1981). Factor costs and the diffusion of ring spinning prior to World War One. *Quarterly Journal of Economics*, 96(1), 89–109.

Lazonick, W. (1983). Industrial organization and technological change: The decline of the British cotton industry. *Business History Review*, 57(2), 195–236.

Lazonick, W. (2015). Innovative enterprise or sweatshop economics? In search of foundations of economic analysis, *Institute for New Economic Thinking Working Paper Series* (25). (October).

Leunig, T. (1998). The myth of the corporate economy: Factor costs, industrial structure and technological choice in the Lancashire and New England cotton textile industries, 1900–1913. *Journal of Economic History*, 58(02), 528–531.

Leunig, T. (2003). A British industrial success: Productivity in the Lancashire and New England cotton spinning industries a century ago. *Economic History Review*, 56(1), 90–117.

Longworth, J. H. (1987). *The cotton mills of Bolton, 1780-1985: A Historical Directory*. Bolton: Museum and Art Gallery, Department of Education and Arts.

Marchionatti, R. (1995). Keynes and the collapse of the British cotton industry in the 1920s: A microeconomic case against laissez-faire. *Journal of Post Keynesian Economics*, 17(3), 427–445.

Marshall, A. (1919). *Industry and trade: A study of industrial technique and business organization*. London: Macmillan.

Mass, W., & Lazonick, W. (1990). The British cotton industry and international competitive advantage: The state of the debates. *Business History*, 32(4), 9–65.

Marx, K. (1976). *Capital*, Vol.1. Harmondsworth: Penguin.

# INTRODUCTION

Marx, K. (1984). *Capital*, Vol.3, London: Lawrence and Wishart.

McCloskey, D. N., & Sandberg, L. G. (1971). From damnation to redemption: Judgments on the late Victorian entrepreneur. *Explorations in Economic History* 9, 89–108.

Owen, G. (2010). *The rise and fall of great companies: Courtaulds and the reshaping of the man-made fibres industry*. Cambridge: Oxford University Press.

Parsons, M. C., & Rose, M. B. (2004). Communities of knowledge: Entrepreneurship, innovation and networks in the British outdoor trade, 1960–90. *Business History, 46*(4), 609–639.

Parsons, M., & Rose, M. B. (2005). The neglected legacy of Lancashire cotton: Industrial clusters and the UK outdoor trade, 1960–1990. *Enterprise and Society, 6*(04), 682–709.

PEP (Political and Economic Planning) (1934). *Report on the British cotton industry*. London: London Industries Group.

Popp, A., Toms, S., & Wilson, J. (2006). Industrial districts as organizational environments: Resources, networks and structures. *Management & Organizational History, 1*(4), 349–370.

Porter, J. H. (1974). The commercial banks and the financial problems of the English cotton industry, 1919–1939. *The International Review of Banking History, 9*(1), 1–16.

Procter, S., & Toms, J. S. (2000). Industrial relations and technical Change: Profits, wages and costs in the Lancashire cotton industry, 1880–1914. *Journal of Industrial History, 3*(1), 54–72.

Robson, R. (1957). *The cotton industry in Britain*. London: Macmillan.

Rooth, T. (1993). *British protectionism and the international economy: Overseas commercial policy in the 1930s*. Cambridge: Cambridge University Press.

Rose, M. B. (2000). *Firms, networks and business values: The British and American cotton industries since 1750*. Cambridge: Cambridge University Press.

Sandberg, L. G. (1969). American rings and English mules: The role of economic rationality. *The Quarterly Journal of Economics*, 25–43.

Sandberg, L. G. (1974). *Lancashire in Decline: A study in entrepreneurship, technology, and international trade*. Columbus, OH: State University Press.

Saxonhouse, G. R., & Wright, G. (2010). National leadership and competing technological paradigms: The globalization of cotton spinning, 1878–1933. *The Journal of Economic History, 70*(03), 535–566.

Singleton, J. (1991). *Lancashire on the scrapheap: The cotton industry, 1945–1970*. Oxford: Oxford University Press.

Toms, S. (1998). Growth, profits and technological choice: The case of the Lancashire cotton textile industry. *Journal of Industrial History, 1*(1), 35–55.

Toms, S. (2001). Information content of earnings in an unregulated market: The co-operative cotton mills of Lancashire, 1880–1900. *Accounting and Business Research, 31*(3), 175–190.

Toms, S. (2002). The rise of modern accounting and the fall of the public company: The Lancashire cotton mills 1870–1914. *Accounting, Organizations and Society, 27*(1), 61–84.

Toms, S., & Filatotchev, I. (2004). Corporate governance, business strategy, and the dynamics of networks: A theoretical model and application to the British cotton industry, 1830–1980. *Organization Studies, 25*(4), 629–651.

Toms, S., & Zhang, Q. (2016). Marks & Spencer and the decline of the British textile industry, 1950–2000. *Business History Review, 90*(01), 3–30.

# Windows of Opportunity in the Textile Industry: The Business Strategies of Lancashire Entrepreneurs, 1880–1914

Steven Toms

*University of Nottingham*

The decades immediately preceding the First World War offered important opportunities to businesses in Britain's vanguard export industry. The challenges of the second industrial revolution and the rise of overseas competition were, according to Chandler, during this 'window of opportunity', to fashion the new large corporate organisation and its associated managerial hierarchy.[1] Economic historians have given much attention to the failure of Lancashire entrepreneurs to follow the prescribed route of the 'strategy structure' school of thought. This has been attributed to the dominance of 'personal capitalism' and the inhibiting effect of individual control of businesses on investment and growth.[2] Also a significant amount of attention has been given to 'institutional constraints' on entrepreneurial behaviour[3], although this has been achieved without giving too much attention to many important institutions of Lancashire capitalism.

There are several reasons to suppose that the recent historiography of the industry has created a misplaced agenda that has stood in the way of deeper understanding. As argued below, the most important of these is the neglect hitherto of the process of capital accumulation, particularly regarding the emergence of family and local commercial elites. Economic and financial performance measures at the level of the individual business, as relative success indicators, and as signals influencing entrepreneurial strategies, have also been largely neglected. Furthermore, in a highly fragmented industry, linkages between firms are important and critics of Lancashire industrialists have examined only one of these, namely the relationship between the spinning and weaving branches. Far less has been said about linkages between producers and markets, especially the roles of intermediaries in Liverpool and Manchester. Less still has been said about the role of culture; the belief systems and common values which underpinned the development of businesses and institutions. Individual business strategies and the motivations of families, cliques and federations have also been absent from both sides of the 'institutional constraints' debate, which have concerned themselves only narrowly with entrepreneurial rationality and entrepreneurial failure. Ironically, these rival schools of thought have ignored entrepreneurs as individuals and historical actors. Although there are some important exceptions, which have a bearing on the data presented below,[4] for an industry supposedly weakened by 'excessive individualism', the absence of evidence dealing with examples of individual behaviour is surprising. Consequently, Lancashire cotton, even more so than general British business history, has witnessed a neglect of entrepreneurial history. It is only in the context of a broader investigation of the institutions within which entrepreneurs had to operate that a genuine understanding of Lancashire capitalism can be obtained.

In presenting the collective business histories of 20 Lancashire companies, the objective of this article is to address the above omissions. The principal findings of an empirical survey based on archive and other contemporary sources are reported. Two comparative measures are used as benchmarks for the entrepreneurial strategies pursued by the sample companies. These are financial performance (return on capital employed) and capital accumulation (increase in capital employed).[5] It is acknowledged that both measures rely heavily on accounting data and that there are possible resulting distortions, especially in shorter sub-periods. Nonetheless, the investigation is concerned with actual signals transmitted to investors through markets, and not with reified accounting accuracy. Whereas much has been written about the reliability of accounts in the late nineteenth century, it is beyond the scope of the current article to enter these discussions.[6] Instead, in concentrating on the business histories of these companies, accounting data is assessed by reference to its fit with other sources.

The structure of the sample allows variations in behaviour and performance to be made between firms with differing governance structures. Thus larger firms that sought capital on a national basis are contrasted with the smaller publicly owned limited liability firms of the Oldham district, which in turn are compared with family firms

To examine such contrasts, it is useful to construct a theoretical framework within which entrepreneurial behaviour can be formally analysed. Where industry concentration and large corporate hierarchies are avoided, it might be expected instead that entrepreneurs would place more reliance on trust and informal networks as a response to local conditions and with a view to minimising uncertainty in the business environment,[7] a phenomenon particularly likely where family connections are important.[8] Trusting behaviour of this sort, in a conventional economic framework, could be viewed as a more effective method of reducing transaction costs, and so improving resource allocation, than the alternative investment in formal organisational hierarchies, especially where monitoring costs are high.[9] It also constitutes a business environment likely to work to the advantage of well connected family groups.[10] Transaction cost economics, however, provides only a limited framework for analysis, given its a historical and static equilibrium tendencies.[11] In applying these models it is important to consider also the impact of shifts in wealth and power. This allows the examination of a further hypothesis; that private, family controlled companies tend to be more orientated towards the short term and adopt policies of higher dividend pay-outs, thereby damaging the long run economic performance of the economy.[12] For this reason the process of capital accumulation is placed at the centre of the analysis.

To achieve this, an examination of the relationship between the entrepreneur and capital market is presented with reference to the profit signals communicated by the market and to consequent investment and divestment behaviour of individual enterprises and contrasting sections of the industry. Local capital market conditions are then related to the rise of loose federations, cliques and family groupings. These linkages created horizontal and vertical overlaps within the structure of the industry and it is therefore necessary to consider them with reference to commodity, product, local labour and capital equipment markets. Reliance on informal relationships partly explains the development of further specialisation which is added to when the experiences and problems of companies relying on formal integration are contrasted. Conclusions are then drawn. Data sources are detailed in an appendix.

## II

Recent histories dealing with the British economy have emphasised the social nature of capitalist institutions.[13] One aspect, so-called 'personal capitalism', has been identifie as an important feature of British business. By this, it is understood that entrepreneurs viewed businesses in personal rather than organisational terms; as estates to be nurtured and passed onto heirs.[14] In such an economic system, the distribution of profits, corporate saving and capital accumulation are vital yet largely neglected issues.[15] Table 1 illustrates the rates of capital accumulation by category of ownership and Table 2 details their respective fina - cial performances. Two important trends are apparent. First, that private companies were more profitable and grew faster than public companies in Lancashire; second, those companies that raised public capital outside Lancashire grew faster than those that did not.

Table 1.   Fixed asset and capital growth

**(1) Growth in spindleage** (compounded growth rates, 1884–1911)

| | Growth per annum (%) |
|---|---|
| Spinning firms, Oldham are | 2.29 |
| Cotton spinning industry (excluding Oldham) | 1.03 |

**(2) Growth in capital** (compounded growth rates)

| | Period | Growth per annum (%) |
|---|---|---|
| **Oldham quoted** | | |
| Crawford | 1884–1913 | −1.02 |
| Dowry | 1885–1912 | −4.24 |
| Haugh | 1884–1913 | −0.92 |
| New Ladyhouse | 1884–1913 | −0.78 |
| New Hey | 1887–1913 | −1.52 |
| Moorfiel | 1884–1912 | −2.00 |
| Sun Mill | 1884–1912 | −1.56 |
| Wemeth | 1889–1912 | 0.30 |
| *Average* | | *−1.47* |
| **Private** | | |
| Fielden | 1891–1913 | 1.42 |
| Horrockses | 1887–1913 | 2.93 |
| Osbome | 1890–1913 | -3.50 |
| Tootals | 1888–1913 | 1.78 |
| T. & R. Eccles | 1897–1913 | 1.46 |
| Whiteley | 1898–1913 | 2.82 |
| *Average* | | *1.15* |
| **London quoted** | | |
| Armitage (Sir Elkanah) | 1892–1913 | 0.34 |
| Ashton Brothers | 1899–1913 | 3.43 |
| Barlow and Jones | 1900–1912 | 0.90 |
| FCDSA | 1899–1913 | 6.70 |
| Rylands and Sons | 1884–1913 | 1.63 |
| *Average* | | *2.60* |

**(3) Economy as a whole** (rate of growth of manufacturing and commercial capital)

| | Growth per annum (%) |
|---|---|
| 1882–1914 | 2.38 |

*Sources*: (1) Calculated from S.J. Chapman and T.S. Ashton, 'The Size of Businesses, Mainly in the Textile Industries', *Journal of the Royal Statistical Society*, Vol. LXXVII (1914), pp.469–555. (2) As per Table 5 and calculated by compounding the difference between total capital employed for each company for the specified period. (3) Calculated as a compound growth rate from C.H. Feinstein, *National Income, Expenditure and Output of the United Kingdom, 1855–1965* (Cambridge, 1972), p. 194.

Table 2.   Average returns to capital, by company and by period

| | Average Return to Capital (per cent) | | | | |
|---|---|---|---|---|---|
| | 1886–92 | 1893–1903 | 1904–1910 | *Whole period* | |
| | | | | Average | Std Dev. |
| **Specialised coarse mule spinners** | | | | | |
| Sun Mill | 2.14 | 1.06 | 12.01 | 4.60 | 6.92 |
| Werneth | 4.56 | 2.25 | 8.35 | 4.60 | 4.60 |
| Dowry | 5.51 | 4.13 | 5.24 | 4.70 | 7.44 |
| Moorfiel | 3.61 | 3.87 | 8.18 | 4.96 | 6.11 |
| Crawford | 6.36 | 4.67 | 7.07 | 6.30 | 5.83 |
| Osborne | 6.47 | 6.57 | 9.98 | 7.19 | 7.84 |
| *Average* | *4.78* | *3.76* | *8.47* | *5.39* | *6.46* |
| **Specialised coarse ring spinners** | | | | | |
| Haugh | 6.79 | 5.52 | 12.48 | 8.07 | 6.40 |
| NewLadyhouse | 13.88 | 12.03 | 17.10 | 13.79 | 4.86 |
| New Hey | 8.19 | 6.71 | 13.98 | 9.37 | 7.70 |
| *Average* | *9.62* | *8.09* | *14.52* | *10.41* | *6.32* |
| **Specialised fine mule spinners** | | | | | |
| FCSDA | N/A | 7.61 | 5.08 | 6.17 | 1.95 |
| Barlow & Jones | 7.43 | 6.43 | 6.30 | 6.75 | 1.39 |
| *Average* | *7.43* | *7.02* | *5.69* | *6.46* | *1.67* |
| **Specialised weaver** | | | | | |
| T. & R. Eccles | N/A | 17.17 | 14.58 | 16.66 | 8.26 |
| **Vertically integrated companies** | | | | | |
| E. Armitage | 10.04 | 8.80 | 6.81 | 8.73 | 4.01 |
| Ashton | N/A | 6.91 | 7.91 | 7.41 | 3.21 |
| Rylands | 6.50 | 8.18 | 6.58 | 7.12 | 1.17 |
| Whiteley | N/A | 4.01 | 6.55 | 6.19 | 5.04 |
| Horrockses | 12.83 | 13.69 | 10.40 | 12.33 | 3.80 |
| Tootal | 3.51 | 3.02 | 5.84 | 4.67 | 3.60 |
| Fielden | 1.03 | 0.44 | 5.94 | 2.19 | 5.51 |
| Healeywood* | 10.92 | 17.57 | 10.92 | 13.44 | 8.13 |
| Average (all companies) | 4.99 | 6.39 | 8.24 | 7.76 | 3.72 |
| Average (all specialised) | 7.46 | 6.28 | 10.20 | 7.76 | 5.17 |
| Average (all integrated) | 7.47 | 7.83 | 7.62 | 7.76 | 2.24 |
| Average (all private) | 8.65 | 8.55 | 9.47 | 10.45. | 3.92 |

*Notes*: * years 1884–1906 based on estimates only.
N/A no data available for these years.
*Sources*: Calculated for each company from the sources listed in Table 5 and incorporated into a simple average
for each sub-period.

Before analysing these aspects in detail, it is useful to sketch some trends which had an important impact on the Lancashire economy before 1914. Most importantly, the coarse trade lost some of its dominance in the Indian market and then recovered it in the 1900s.[16] In particular, close relationships between the rise and fall of gold values, and market share in India, influenced the large losses, then profits, of the Oldham district companies.[17] This had several important consequences. First, in the difficult years of the early 1890s there was a collapse in share values on the Oldham stock exchange.[18] A direct consequence was that many middle- and working-class investors were forced to sell shares at low values. With the demise of democratic investment came the rise of a new class of entrepreneurs ahead of the boom of 1904–7.[19] Meanwhile, the loss of the Indian market had other important effects. Increased tension between labour and capital culminated in the Brooklands lock out and augured the institutionalisation of industrial relations. Certain Liverpool market institutions also became a source of mistrust, especially the futures market which facilitated the activities of speculators. The 'corners' of Ranger and Steensrand of the late 1870s and the 1880s led the spinners of south-east Lancashire to form a cotton buying company in response.[20] Finally the attitude of the Indian government to Lancashire imports and the exigencies of Gold Standard economic orthodoxy, as manifested in the rise of real prices of Lancashire exports, created the need for association at national and local political levels.[21] Thus as the economic crisis reached its nadir in 1896, a new class of promotional entrepreneur arose from the old system whose strategy was increasingly determined by an organised federal collective.

In the Oldham district the slump of the 1890s ended the system of 'democratic limiteds' based on wide shareownership and created opportunities for representatives of this new class. They confined their significant investments to new concerns in the 1900s, and through generous dividend policies allowed capitalisation to wither in established companies.[22] The divestment tendency in Oldham meant that Werneth was the only company in Table 1 to show any growth in capital during the period, primarily due to its construction of a new mill.[23] The Sun Mill Company, despite undertaking extensive re-equipment in the period 1899–1907,[24] still showed a net decline in capital employed. For the Dowry Spinning Company, the downward trend was more dramatic, as there were very few years when the company managed to spend even its depreciation charges on new plant and equipment.[25] In 1913, individual Oldham District companies, including the ring spinners at Milnrow, had about the same number of spindles as they had in 1889.[26] Capital increasingly accumulated to individuals, a notable example being John Bunting (1839–1923), whose promotional activities facilitated the circulation of divested and reinvested capital.[27] Other entrepreneurs who could accumulate private capital were able to replicate his method of business empire building.[28] This contrasted with the period 1860–90 in the Oldham District, where ownership had been more diffuse and individualistic, and based on participatory traditions of cooperation.[29]

Elsewhere in Lancashire, William Birtwistle (1855–1936) of Blackburn and his emergent group of companies provided another example of personal empire building via loose federations of companies. Assembled in the late 1890s and early 1900s,[30] these companies shared Birtwistle's proprietorship but little else. Neither goods nor cash were transferred between businesses and there were no other signs of mutual interdependence.[31] Any integration was within the business units, for example Geo. Whiteley Ltd, which combined spinning and weaving, rather than for the enterprise as a whole. The remarkable feature of the Birtwistle 'empire' was the rapidity with which it was constructed. Treated collectively, the business in 1913 was on a par with the largest Lancashire enterprises,[32] and contemporaries recognised Birtwistle as a significant entrepreneur: 'William was a notability on the Manchester Royal Exchange, where his constantly growing group of spinning and weaving mills made him, by the beginning of World War One, one of the most powerful men in the trade.'[33] Unlike the Oldham empire builders such as Bunting, Birtwistle was less a share dealer or promoter, but drew his expertise from merchanting and familiarity with the Liverpool and Manchester markets. Directors of the companies in the group were drawn mostly from Liverpool cotton broking interests.[34]

Of the Birtwistle companies specifically investigated here, Whiteley was an indifferent performer, and, like other integrated firms such as Horrockses, Tootal, Ashtons, Barlow & Jones, and Rylands, missed the very high returns of the 1907 boom uniformly enjoyed by the Oldham companies, including those of the Bunting group. Another, Eccles, the only specialised weaving company examined, was a strongly performing company (Table 2). The recovery of the Indian market after 1896, the connections of Birtwistle on the Manchester exchange, and the reinvestment of profits in working capital, were the decisive success criteria.[35] That the company's performance was markedly different from Whiteley, given they shared the overall direction of William Birtwistle, reveals influences wider than entrepreneurship.

As for growth, the dynamism of Birtwistle as an individual was the driving force behind the rapid emergence of the group. The growth of the entity if considered collectively was quite remarkable, with spinning growing at a rate of 250 per cent and weaving at more than 700 per cent between 1895 and 1913 via personal acquisition.[36] Yet the businesses, once acquired, as typified by Whiteley and Eccles, did not expand their productive capacity.[37] Personal holding structures, exemplified by Birtwistle's companies, provided the ideal vehicle for individualistic entrepreneurs whose profits or losses depended on the judgement of market prices.[38] As in Oldham, capital growth and accumulation accrued to the individual, not to the managerially controlled hierarchical organisation.

In contrast, the managements of other firms, such as Preston and Manchester-based Horrockses and Tootals, despite private ownership, pursued less individualistic and more managerially orientated strategies, financed largely through the reinvestment of profits within the corporate balance sheet. For the former the decisive developments, initiated and orchestrated by Sir Frank Hollins, were the intensive merger period of 1885–87 leading to the formation of the company, and the developments of the Centenary Mill and a new Manchester warehouse.[39] Besides direct investment of this kind, some of the growth of the firm during this period came from the acquisition of Swainson Birley in 1900 and Fishwick mills.[40] At Tootals growth was slower (Table 1), reflecting repositioning in some markets. Withdrawal from the sewing cotton trade in the mid-1890s allowed the divestment of Lee Spinning Company to the English Sewing Cotton Company Ltd.[41] Sales of other parts of the business, such as Dan Lane mills, Atherton and the Bradford branch, also formed part of a reconcentration strategy in the 1890s.[42] Such asset sales helped finance important aspects of new strategies. Like Horrockses, the strategic centrepiece was the construction of a new Manchester warehouse for the merchanting arm of the business; as for Horrockses, the building would have been a source of considerable prestige. Work on Tootals' Oxford Street warehouse commenced at about the same time, and was completed much quicker than the Horrockses building.[43]

On a smaller scale, Fielden Brothers also adopted a refocusing strategy; the partnership divested older mills on or before incorporation in 1889, and financed re-equipment in ring spindles, and a small experiment in automatic looms, from depreciation and accumulated profits [44] Privately controlled companies, like Fielden, Horrockses and Tootals, retained more and divested slightly less than the Oldham limiteds, and when divestment did occur it was via directors' salaries rather than dividends.[45]

Companies seeking capital at national level, although a small minority of firms, followed a more conventional pattern of capital accumulation. Rylands & Sons, already the largest Lancashire firm, increased its capital dramatically between 1884 and 1895, but by a much slower rate after that.[46] The company expanded its capital base in 1886 through the issue of debentures, although the money came from immediate family. Expansion of the export business, combined with selected withdrawal from certain markets, took up some extra funding. Reinvested profits from these activities boosted reserves and contributed to further capital accumulation.[47] Surprisingly for a public company, Rylands thus raised most of its capital privately or internally. In contrast, Ashton Brothers grew rapidly, and, following its reconstruction in 1899, could mobilise a large capital base via the London and Manchester stock markets. In the early 1900s the accumulation of profits added to that capital[48] and assisted investment in expensive automatic looms. Investment in large corporate structures was thus a function of dependence on national capital markets; a dependence the majority of Lancashire entrepreneurs consistently sought to avoid.

A further interesting feature of all companies was their reluctance to depend on borrowing from the commercial banks. Long term finance came primarily from retained profits, divestment from other concerns, and, in Oldham, via the circulation of dividends and accumulated private wealth into new flotations. Promoters such as Bunting were able to raise large amounts of loan capital on the basis of personal reputation and without the use of intermediaries.[49] As Table 3 illustrates, Oldham companies shunned debentures and preference shares and instead used the depositors' loan account. Instant access, combined with a belief that a proportion of lending individuals would view their investment as long term, led most Oldham companies to adopt the sometimes risky strategy of financing both fi ed and working capital investments using such funds.[50] The pay-off was that, apart from difficult years in the mid-1890s, they generally escaped dependence on the banks, even for the financing of working capital. Private, and some of the larger public, companies were similarly able to escape dependence on the banks. Family capital allowed William Birtwistle to raise loans for two of his new companies by obtaining mortgage loans on inherited property.[51] The large public companies used debentures and preference shares for long term loans, usually in equal proportion from the flotation date. Thus only in a minority of cases, and in insignificant amounts, did cotton companies rely on commercial banks and then only for working capital. Financial independence from external stakeholders of all kinds became culturally well rooted in the Oldham district, and in the boom of 1907 became even more pronounced through massive dividends and capital reductions.[52] As capital accumulated to individuals, personal contacts and individual fortunes became the main sources of low transaction cost capital. When profi signals were positive, these private funds were easily attracted back into the industry; only when negative, after 1920, did the dependence of Lancashire on the banks become an important issue.

Table 3.   Financial strategies of lancashire companies

| | Period | Average External Funding as % of Total Capital | | Financing method |
|---|---|---|---|---|
| | | Bank Borrowing | Other Debt Capital | |
| Armitage | 1891–1913 | Nil | 11.66 | Debentures |
| Ashton Bros. | 1899–1913 | Nil | 46.35 | Debentures and Preference Shares |
| Barlow & Jones | 1900–1913 | Nil | 64.00 | Debentures and Preference Shares |
| Crawford | 1884–1913 | Nil | 41.83 | Depositors' Loan Account |
| Dowry | 1884–1913 | Nil | 35.85 | Depositors' Loan Account |
| Fielden Bros. | 1891–1914 | 1.89 | Nil | Bank overdraft |
| FCDSA | 1899–1913 | Nil | 62.47 | Debentures, Preference Shares and Depositors' Loan Account |
| Haugh | 1884–1914 | Nil | 51.90 | Depositors' Loan Account |
| Healey Wood | 1907–1913 | 1.32 | Nil | Bank overdraft |
| Horrockses | 1887–1914 | Negligible | 46.00 | Bank overdraft, Bills of Exchange, Loan Account, Preference Shares, Debentures |
| Moorfiel | 1884–1013 | Nil | 16.81 | Depositors' Loan Account |
| New Hey | 1887–1914 | Nil | 30.20 | Depositors' Loan Account |
| New Ladyhouse | 1884–1914 | Nil | 39.69 | Depositors' Loan Account |
| Osborne | 1890–1913 | 6.35 | 37.16 | Bank Overdraft, Mortgage Loan |
| Rylands | 1884–1913 | Nil | 17.18 | Debentures |
| Sun Mill | 1863–1912 | Nil | 36.76 | Depositors' Loan Account |
| T. & R. Eccles | 1897–1914 | 15.9 | 24.51 | Bank overdraft, Mortgage |
| Tootal | 1888–1914 | 1.23 | 59.62 | Bank overdraft. Debentures, Preference Shares |
| Wemeth | 1889–1912 | 2.94 | 42.41 | Bank overdraft, Depositors' Loan Account |
| Whiteley | 1898–1914 | 8.49 | 35.87 | Bank overdraft, Morgage |

Notes: External funding is defined as bank borrowings and other debt capital. Total capital is defined as external funding plus called up share capital plus reserves.
'Negligible' is defined as less than one per cent of total  verage capital.
'Full accounting analysis of working capital not available. Absence of overdraft inferred by reference to other cash fl w indicators, i.e. profit levels and absence of significant additions to fi ed assets and to net working capital.
Sources: Per Table 5.

## III

Lack of dependence on banks contrasted with the growth of alliances based on mutual trust in other areas of business activity. Thus in their relationships with cotton market institutions Oldham entrepreneurs chose intermediation as a method of reducing transaction costs and uncertainty. Despite a problematic relationship with Liverpool cotton brokers, and an inability to police the quality of cotton supplied effectively, Oldham entrepreneurs derived great benefits from building long term relationships within the importers' institutions. Dependence on Liverpool warehousemen as raw material stock holders was partly the price paid for independence from bank finance. These relationships allowed the spinner to operate effectively a 'just in time' system, holding only enough raw cotton stock at the mill to cover current orders.[53] The great value of the system was demonstrated in the early years of the operation of the Manchester Ship Canal. Despite a great antipathy towards Liverpool speculators, Oldham Spinning companies continued to favour distant Liverpool over the new port of Manchester. Monetary problems, the decline of cotton prices and Oldham share values in the early 1890s reinforced established and family connections with Liverpool Brokers as the Spinners sought to ride out the crash on the basis of minimal stock holdings.[54] Although shunned as an import market, a similar interdependence for finished goods had grown up with Manchester traders, specifically based on relationships with traders in the Royal Exchange yarn market.[55]

Linkages between local entrepreneurs and capital equipment manufacturers, together with the developing process of geographical specialisation, explain some important developments in the Rochdale area. In the early 1880s, a group of three companies was formed around the New Ladyhouse Spinning Company that became known as the 'Milnrow Ring Spinners'.[56] These small but highly significant firms operated in a geographically concentrated cluster, and shared cross-directorship structures increasingly characteristic of the industry.[57] The data in Table 2 suggest that superior performance arose from specialisation in ring spinning. The pioneering Milnrow ring spinners outperformed mule spinners in nearby Oldham in all periods, and those fine spinning companies later under the control of the Fine Cotton Spinners and Doublers Association. Two important questions arising are, first, why did the ring spinners sustain superior performance in all periods, and, second, given the clear and acknowledged premium to ring spinning,[58] why were these early concerns not more widely emulated in later decades?

The answer to both questions lies in the association of ring spinning with product and geographical specialisation and the history of the relationship between profit signal and investment decision. It was embraced more enthusiastically in some districts, notably Rochdale, than in others, notably Oldham. As in the Philadelphia area, cultural characteristics and the technical competence of local skilled workers provided a basis for fl xible specialisation.[59] In Rochdale, traditions of throstle spinning, an earlier continuous spinning technology, facilitated the introduction of ring spinning.[60] In this context local labour was a relatively expensive resource. Annual wages per hand and wages per spindle in 1890 averaged £30.90 and £0.3261 respectively for the three Milnrow ring companies, compared with averages of £26.13 and £0.1270 for four typical Oldham mule companies.[61] Rochdale entrepreneurs justified their investment by savings in raw material without any loss of quality, low breakdown and maintenance cost, and the relative cheapness of the machinery, but did not refer to labour cost.[62]

The role of capital equipment suppliers and their acquisition of patents reinforced such tendencies towards specialisation. Despite the early date of patent registration in the USA and in Britain, it was only the development of the Sawyer and Rabbeth spindles from the 1870s, and their associated increase in productivity, that created a significant shift to rings from mules in the former country.[63] In Britain, the first company to use the new method was the New Ladyhouse Cotton Spinning Co. Ltd, registered on 26 April 1877, Lancashire's first major vertically specialised, dedicated ring spinning mill.[64] It replaced an older mill that had previously burned down and was reconstructed on a shed pattern, a style emulated by later larger ring mills, notably Cromer at Middleton (1906).[65]

A distinctive feature of the Milnrow companies was the close relationship with the capital equipment manufacturer, Howard & Bullough.[66] Samuel Tweedale (1846–1928) was a founding director of the New Ladyhouse company and, as a trusted lieutenant of John Bullough (1837–91), also played a leading role in the management of Howard & Bullough & Co. Ltd.[67] Tweedale sent a relative on the visit to America in 1872, and from then on was closely involved in the ring spinning experiments at Milnrow. Such support would have helped offset early commercial and technical uncertainties; the Rochdale experiments were described as a 'leap in the dark, involving great risk'.[68] Of the few other mills promoted at this time capital equipment suppliers were also important: for example, Samuel Brooks supported the Burns Ring Spinning Co. Ltd at Heywood (1891).[69] In addition to support from connected larger firms, risk was also offset by the relatively small scale of new ring mills.[70] As mule mills exploited economies of scale, for ring spinners product specialisation and market niches were more important: for example, the Palm Mill in Oldham (1884) specialised in strong rope yarns.[71] In general, however, the capital equipment manufacturers' relationships with the spinning companies were crucial in the diffusion process.

Despite their distinctiveness, the Milnrow companies illustrate a more common phenomenon; the increased tendency of entrepreneurial groups to shun localism and paternalism in favour of dependence of industry federations. James Heap (1828–92), like all the other directors and shareholders, a local man, was the chairman of all three companies until his death in 1892. Like John Bullough in Accrington, he was a prominent Conservative and, as the main employer, a dominant figure in the locality.[72] However, instead of using the adoption of ring spinning to pursue individualistic strategies, local employers sought the greater certainty of solidarity with employers elsewhere in the industry.[73] As elsewhere, Milnrow had hitherto shared many characteristics of a 'company town', and, like the Ashtons of Hyde and the Fieldens of Todmorden, the Heaps exercised a good deal of local deferential and political influence [74] From the 1890s, however, local entrepreneurs, as industrial relations began to centralise, increasingly acted at the behest of the Masters' Federation.[75]

Another clique of entrepreneurs, also previously noted for a paternalist management style subsequently abandoned, formed the driving force behind the introduction of automatic weaving. Those involved were primarily Henry Philips Greg, to a lesser extent Henry Lee of Tootals, and others in the family connected group. Cross-directorships between equipment supplier and manufacturer provided some connections; for example, Henry Philips Greg (1865–1936), a director of Ashtons, and Edward Tootal Broadhurst (1858–1922) both held directorships with the British Northrop Loom Company (BNLC).[76] Ashton Brothers, Gregs of Styal and Tootals were therefore the scenes of most of the early experiments in new production methods.[77] Other weaving companies received little support from the capital equipment manufacturer, the monopolistic BNLC. Consequently prices of looms were set high and may have deterred adoption by British manufacturers.[78]

Of those which experimented, only one company, Ashton Brothers, adopted automatics on any significant scale, which it used with ring spindles.[79] In 1899, the company was restructured and went public, with quotations at London and Manchester.[80] Contemporaries would have thus monitored its progress with great interest. Yet despite an innovative strategy, overall performance was similar *vis-à-vis* vertically integrated competitors, and dismal when compared with those companies specialising in ring spinning alone (Table 2). Fellow entrepreneurs considering the model of vertical integration combined with ring spindle and automatic loom adoption would not have felt an urgent need to emulate the company.

The major problem facing entrepreneurs in companies where new weaving methods were tried was labour relations. Two strikes occurred at Ashtons in 1904 and 1908.[81] However, profitability was not affected by either dispute. In the first strike, the buoyancy of trade helped guarantee the union easy concessions within a week, whereas in the depressed times of 1908 the strike was more protracted. Management used the 13-week 1908 strike to unload surplus stock, but also wanted to test, and if possible break, the strength of the union.[82]

In doing so, here and elsewhere they had significantly departed from their previously paternalist management style,[83] a trend reflected elsewhere. Strike problems experienced at Ashtons were paralleled by a dispute at Styal over speed-ups, six loom working and attempts to introduce 'American methods'. Industrial relations remained problematic, as typified by the subsequent disputes in 1907 and 1908 [84]

Of all the cases of weaving automation developments, Tootal's Sunnyside mill, part of the Rumworth Mills complex at Daubhill, Bolton, witnessed the longest and most bitter strike in 1906. Harold Lee, the son of Henry and the man responsible for the management of Sunnyside, did not consider Northrop looms to be suitable for the mills' high quality patterned output. Instead he proposed to introduce 'drop wires', or automatic warp stop motions, and this became the specific cause of the strike.[85] The length of the strike, failure to recruit 'knobsticks',[86] and favourable trading conditions placed the Tootal board under considerable pressure. The directors' report to shareholders acknowledged that 'profits would have been higher but for a weavers' strike at Rumworth Mill . . . This created considerable difficulty in meeting demands at a time of prosperity' [87]

To put an optimistic gloss on the outcome of the strike the same report stated: 'new workers have been gradually introduced to replace those who have left the company's service'.[88] It was true that Lee had attempted this, but his failure to do so led to acceptance of union list terms two weeks later. A side effect of the strike was that the arbitrators persuaded Lee to join the Masters' Federation.[89] The lessons of the strikes at Bolton and Hyde were thus twofold; traditional management styles had to be severely compromised, and automation at a time of industry prosperity meant generous concessions to the labour force. Only the second effect had a direct impact on profit, but as the industry recovered in the 1900s restored profitability elsewhere raised opportunity cost creating a disincentive to investment in automatic looms.

## IV

Local cliques of businessmen were able to reduce uncertainty and transaction costs through the development of informal linkages which in turn influenced investment and resource allocation and offered an alternative to the formal monitoring systems of integrated companies. In some cases, linkages were more formally developed through integration. This section explores the special problems encountered by such companies, which may explain why in general entrepreneurs placed more faith in specialisation.

Integrated companies were more market-led and were able to avoid reliance on intermediaries in product markets. This reduced risk and associated wide product ranges provided access to several markets.[90] Consequently, they had better financial results than specialised concerns before 1896, and had lower risk, the returns to capital demonstrating lower variation (Table 2). Of the large vertically integrated companies, Horrockses was by far the most successful in the 1890s (Table 2). Product quality, branding and dealing directly with retailers became important elements in marketing strategy and were highly innovatory at the time.[91] Tootal failed to match the marketing-driven successes of Horrockses. Although the company also marketed branded products domestically, it remained more exposed to problematic overseas markets. Difficulties were attributable to worthless debts taken over from the previous partnership, in particular arising from the failed chartered corporation, the North West Africa Company, and an endemic bad debt problem affecting trade in the West Indies through the early 1890s.[92] The latter problem was so bad that the company became technically insolvent.[93] The subsequent debt write-off failed to satisfy the auditor, who qualified the accounts again in 1897, arguing that the measure was insufficient. New York was now the problem; the auditor hinted at both poor trading position and a lack of management control by pointing out that 'serious losses had occurred which required further investigation'.[94] Such difficulties explained the poor performance of the company in the 1890s. Private company status meant it was easier to hide these problems, and, unlike the Oldham limiteds before and during the depression of the mid-1890s, there was no threat from external financial stakeholders' loss of confidence

Tootals' management thus gained a breathing space. By the early 1900s, profits reached higher levels than previously. The management described the recovery as a turnaround; aggressive marketing, coupled with withdrawal from the Coats-dominated sewing thread market, represented important components of the strategy.[95] Tootals retained its important North American markets by establishing channels for the sale of branded products direct to the retailer, a policy similar to that of Horrockses.[96]

Nonetheless, for integrated companies, efficient marketing and efficient production worked in opposite directions.[97] At Tootals, imposition of short production runs created inefficien y in manufacturing,[98] a problem compounded by the 1906 strike. However, despite such liaison difficulties, integration created strategic marketing opportunities for some companies and benefited the investor before 1900. However, the large returns available to specialised companies in the boom of 1907 eluded them and new investment reinforced the industry-wide tendency towards specialisation.

## V

Perhaps the most significant institutional feature of pre-1914 Lancashire capitalism was the transformation of ownership. This occurred through the creation of business empires via personal shareholdings and simultaneous individual management of similar firms. Their entrepreneurs relied on price and intermediation rather than organisation structure as a coordinating mechanism. Loose federations helped orchestrate collective responses where necessary, for example to the rise of organised labour, which in turn reinforced the decline of paternalistic managerial styles. Apart from some private firms, and the handful of those who sought funds elsewhere, Lancashire became dependent on the circulation of capital via the individual from previously established companies to the newly floated. Few corporations achieved the scale required to justify significant investment in personnel, marketing and finance specialisms, while most remained highly vulnerable to market fluctuations. For these reasons, levels of reported profit, upon which this survey has relied, were very important to the contemporary investor.

Such relationships show that neither the advocates of big firm restructuring nor the proponents of neoclassical rationality can fully explain all the forces that shaped Lancashire's destiny. An exemplification has been provided of the circumstances where 'personal capitalism' based on small, specialised business units can work successfully if necessary conditions are met; most importantly external economies of scale and collective entrepreneurial activity across commodity, product, capital and labour markets. In response to the classical school, while much was apparently rational about investment responses to market signals, ownership and local capital markets were important determinants of resource allocation. Accordingly, the industry supported large capitalists, but not managerial hierarchies, the only exception being in the big private companies, where ownership and control remained unified. Notwithstanding family control, these companies limited their dividends and placed greater emphasis on corporate growth than the public companies of Oldham. Accumulation by individuals and a highly localised system of financial stake holding meant that the fate of the industry was bound up with a special form of personal capitalism which supported small owner-managers along with emergent federations and individual-dominated precursors of holding company structures. While divestment rates were high, this did not prevent individual capitalists making significant reinvestments when external conditions were buoyant. Nevertheless, in a growing industry investors remained undiversified and managements remained unprofessionalised.

Characterised by easy access to financial resources, emergent groups of capitalists might have chosen to restructure their businesses or make major investments in the corporate hierarchy on the American model. In Lancashire, significant corporate growth of this kind was associated primarily with the large private company. Public companies which became dependent on national capital markets also exhibited these characteristics. All other companies became dependent less on local capital and more on the personal fortunes of entrepreneurs. Trade cycle effects, in particular the depression of the 1890s, dampened the commercial incentives for the expansion of the corporate organisation and replaced a prosperous investing middle class with cliques of promotional entrepreneurs. Meanwhile, coordination difficulties in integrated production and marketing, external economies and local characteristics forced entrepreneurs down existing, channels of specialisation. Financial signals gave further encouragement to these processes; all specialised companies, whether ring spinners, mule spinners, or weavers, performed better than vertically integrated companies in the period after 1900.

In the above analysis, an attempt has been made to link the development of an industry with the process of capital accumulation. Lancashire was highly vulnerable to the world market and that vulnerability was accentuated by the way in which capital was created and divested. It is this social nature of capital accumulation, rooted in the discipline of business history, that is crucial to our understanding of the progress of an industry that became prosperous in the wake of the first Industrial Revolution, but that ultimately failed to respond to the challenges of the second.

## Appendix

### Data and sources

The companies chosen for detailed study with their attributes are listed in Table 4. An indication is also provided of sample size in relation to total industry capital. The main objective in sample selection was to achieve sufficient representation of different firms to address the dominant issues in Lancashire cotton historiographies, subject to the constraint of surviving archives. Profit and capital series, unique to the analysis of Lancashire textiles history, were constructed where possible from original accounting records.[99] Table 5 shows the principal archive or other source used for each sample company. With archival and secondary sources, local newspapers, in particular the *Oldham Chronicle*, were also used, which disclosed detailed financial statistics for many local companies.[100] Availability of press data meant that companies of importance *vis-à-vis* the historiography of the industry could still be chosen even if archival material was lacking.[101] Stock exchange records were used as a further data source.[102] Certain companies, such as those specialising in thread manufacture and finishing processes, were excluded, being beyond the scope of the investigation.[103] For the weaving sector, the dominance of the private company meant very few archival records and published results were available.

Table 4.   The companies and their characteristics

### (1) Sample companies

| Company | Description | Capital in 1890 (£) |
| --- | --- | --- |
| Armitage (Sir Elkanah) | VI; M,PL; Q; Ma | 255,600 |
| Ashton Brothers of Hyde | VI; M,R,AL; Q; Ma | 325,948 |
| Barlow & Jones | VI; M; Q; Bo | 500,002 |
| Crawford Spinning Company | VSS; M; Q; Ro | 155,970 |
| Dowry Spinning Company | VSS; M; Q; Ol | 44,726 |
| Fielden Brothers | VI; R; PL,AL; P, To | 130,169 |
| FCDSA | VSS; M; Q; Ma, Bo | 5,748,879 |
| Haugh Spinning Company | VSS; R; Q, Ro | 44,238 |
| Healey Wood Mill | VI; M; PL,P; Bu | 15,000 |
| Horrockses Crewdson | VI; M,R,PL; P; Pr & Bo | 1,067,620 |
| Moorfield Spinning Compa y | VSS; M; Q, Ol | 75,699 |
| New Hey Spinning Company | VSS; R,Q; Ro | 58,521 |
| New Ladyhouse Spinning Company | VSS; R; Q; Ro | 30,361 |
| Osborne Spinning Company | VSS; M; P; Ol | 23,960 |
| Rylands and Sons | VI; M; PL,Q; Ma | 4,196,994 |
| Sun Mill Company | VSS; M; Q; Ol | 99,270 |
| T. & R. Eccles | VSW; PL; P; Bl | 28,885 |
| Tootal, Broadhurst & Lee | VI; M,R,PL,AL; P; Bo, Ma | 830,130 |
| Wemeth Spinning Company | VSS; M; Q; 0l | 135,885 |
| Whiteley & Company | VI; M,R,PL; P, Bl | 38,976 |
| *Total* | VI; M,R,PL; P, Bl | *13,806,833* |

## (2) Lancashire textile industry as a whole

| | | |
|---|---|---:|
| Number of firms (1890 | | 1801 |
| Capital employed, £m (1886): | Total | 108 |
| | Spinning | 58 |
| | Weaving | 14 |
| | Finishing | 22 |

*Key*

Structure: VSS, vertically specialised, spinning company; VSW, vertical specialised, weaving company, VI, vertically integrated company.

Technology: M, mule spindles; R, ring spindles; PL, plain looms; AL, automatic looms.

Ownership: Q, quoted; P, private.

Location: Ol, Oldham; Ro, Rochdale; Bl, Blackburn district; Pr, Preston; Bo, Bolton; Ma, Manchester; To, Todmorden; Bu, Burnley.

*Notes*: A useful rule for the conversion of money values to modem equivalents is to multiply the above figures, and those used throughout the text, by a factor of 60. It should also be borne in mind that, relatively, these values compare to 1890 Gross National Product. Where 1890 figures were not available, for example, for companies formed after then, the earliest alternative date was used.

*Sources*: (1) See Table 5; (2) Number of firms, G.T. Jones, *Increasing Return* (Cambridge, 1933), p.277; capital employed, T. Ellison, *The Cotton Trade* (London, 1886), p.70; and analysis by industry branch based on M. Blaug, 'The Productivity of Capital in the Lancashire Cotton Industry during the Nineteenth Century', *Economic History Review*, Vol. XIII (1961), p.111 (where the capital of each branch is the cited figure, plus a proportion of the £25m floating capital of the whole industry allocated *pro rata*).

Table 5.    Data and sources

| Company | Source |
|---|---|
| Armitage (Sir Elkanah) | LGL, Commercial Reports, Yearly Balance Sheets, 1891–1913. |
| Ashton Bros | LGL, Commercial Reports, Half Yearly Balance Sheets, 1899–1913. |
| Barlow & Jones | LGL, Commercial Reports, Half Yearly Balance Sheets, 1900–1913. |
| Crawford | 'Commercial Reports', Oldham Chronicle (Saturday issues, published summaries of quarterly reports detailing profits, d vidends, share and loan capital) April 1884–December 1913. |
| Dowry | CAC, LCC/Dowl, Nominal Ledger; June 1885–December 1912; 'Commercial Reports', *Oldham Chronicle*, April 1884–December 1913. |
| Fielden | WYRO C353/475, December 1891–December 1914; 1884–1889, Law, *Fieldens of Todmorden*, Table XVII, p. 129. |
| FCSDA | LGL, Commercial Reports, Half-Yearly Balance Sheets, 1899–1913. |
| Haugh | 'Commercial Reports', *Oldham Chronicle*, April 1884–December 1913; *Rochdale Observer*, 28 June 1890, and Quarterly Reports April 1892–June 1914 inclusive. |
| Healey Wood | Rossendale Museum, BB614, Balance Sheets, Quarterly Trading and Profit and Loss Accounts and Balance Sheets, April 1907–December 1914; Dividends Ledger, April 1882–December 1914. |
| Horrockses | CVR, Detailed Accounts, Half-Yearly Balance Sheets and Profit and Loss Accounts, November 1887–October 1905; LCRO, DDHs/53, Balance Sheets, Half-Yearly Balance Sheets and Profit and Loss Accounts, October 1905–april 1914. |

*(Continued)*

Table 5.   Data and sources (*Continued*)

| Company | Source |
| --- | --- |
| New Hey | 'Commercial Reports', *Oldham Chronicle*, September 1886–June 1913; *Rochdale Observer*, 28 June 1890 and April 1892–June 1914. |
| New Ladyhouse | 'Commercial Reports', *Oldham Chronicle*, April 1884–December 1913; *Rochdale Observer*, 28 June and April 1892–June 1914. |
| Moorfiel | 'Commercial Reports', *Oldham Chronicle*, April 1884–December 1913; Smith, 'An Oldham Limited Liability Company', pp.34–53. |
| Osborne | LCRO, DDX/869/3/1, Trade, Capital, and Profit and Loss Accounts, June 1889–June 1914. |
| Rylands | LGL, 'Commercial Reports', Half Yearly Balance Sheets, 1884–1913; Farnie, John Rylands of Manchester', pp.71–2. |
| T. & R. Eccles | LCRO, 868/7/1, September 1897–September 1914. |
| Sun Mill | 'Commercial Reports', *Oldham Chronicle*, April 1884–December 1913; Tyson, thesis, appendices 1 and 2. |
| Wemeth | OLSL, Misc. 42/17 and 18, Quarterly Reports to Members, April 1889–October 1912; 'Commercial Reports', *Oldham Chronicle*, April 1884–December 1888. |
| Whiteley | LCRO, DDX/868/21/5, September 1898–September 1914. |

*Notes*: The above show the primary sources from which profit and capital series were constructed; aggregate data from these 20 companies have been used to construct financial indices which are used throughout the text. CVR is an unlisted archive, previously held by the Coats Viyella, recently deposited at Lancashire County Record Office (LCRO). Full titles of secondary sources are given in the notes.

## Notes

Financial support from the Pasold Fund assisted in the preparation of this article. I should like to thank the participants at the Association of Business Historians workshop at Leeds University Management School on 28 September 1996. I am also grateful to Stanley Chapman, Douglas Farnie, David Jeremy, Brian Law and Mike Wright.

1.  A.D. Chandler, *Scale and Scope: The Dynamics of Industrial Capitalism* (Cambridge MA, 1990), p. 286.
2.  Ibid., pp.240–86.
3.  For a summary of these contributions, see A.V. Marrison, 'Indian Summer', in M.B. Rose (ed.), *The Lancashire Cotton Industry: A History Since 1700* (Preston, 1996).
4.  In particular these include R.E. Tyson, 'Sun Mill: A Study in Democratic Investment' (unpublished M.A. thesis, University of Manchester, 1962); R. Smith, 'An Oldham Limited Liability Company', *Business History*, Vol.4 (1961), pp.34–53; G. Saxonhouse and G. Wright, 'New Evidence on the Stubborn English Mule and the Cotton Industry', *Economic History Review*, 2nd Series, Vol. XXXVII (1984), pp.507–18; M.B. Rose, *Gregs of Quarry Bank Mill: The Rise and Decline of a Family Firm*, 1750–1914 (Cambridge, 1986); S.D. Chapman, *Merchant Enterprise in Britain from the Industrial Revolution to the First World War* (Cambridge, 1992); D.A. Farnie, 'John Rylandsof Manchester', *Bulletin of the John Rylands Library*, Vol.75 (1993), pp.3–1 03; the collection of business histories in D. Jeremy (ed.), *Textile History*, Vol.24 (1993), J.S. Toms, 'Financial Constraints on Economic Growth: Profits, Capital Accumulation and the Development of the Lancashire Cotton spinning Industry, 1885–1914', *Accounting, Business and Financial History*, Vol.4 (1994), pp.363–83, B. Law, *Fieldens of Todmorden: A Nineteenth Century Business Dynasty* (Littleborough, 1986).
5.  Capital employed is defined as the balance sheet total of share capital, shareholders reserves and long term loan capital; return on capital employed is defined as profit before interest divided by capital employed. For examples of the use of these measures by contemporaries, see *Oldham Chronicle*, 3 Jan. 1889, and *passim*.

6. R. Brief, 'Nineteenth Century Accounting Error', *Journal of Accounting Research*, Vol.3 (1965), pp.12–31; G. Lee, 'The Concept of Profit in British Accounting, 1760–1900', *Business History Review*, Vol. XLIX (1975), pp.6–36. In specific industries, such as coal and iron, asset valuation and profit measurement might have been problematic, e.g., J. Wale, 'How Reliable were Reported Profits and Asset Values in the period 1890–1914? Case Studies from the British Coal Industry', *Accounting and Business Research*, Vol.20 (1990), pp.253–68; T. Baldwin, 'Management Aspiration and Audit Opinion: Fixed Asset Accounting at the Staveley Coal and Iron Company, 1863–83', *Accounting and Business Research*, Vol.25 (1994), pp.3–12; a broader based survey concluded that accounting reports were more reliable than previously thought, AJ. Arnold, 'Should Historians Trust Late Nineteenth Century Company Financial Statements?', *Business History*, Vol.38 (1996), p.50.
7. T. Corley, 'The Entrepreneur: The Central Issue in Business History', in J. Brown and M.B. Rose (eds.), *Entrepreneurship, Networks and Modern Business* (Manchester, 1993), pp.18–19.
8. M.B. Rose, *Family Business* (Aldershot, 1995), p.xviii.
9. M. Casson, *Economics of Business Culture: Came Theory, Transaction Costs and Economic Performance* (Oxford, 1991), pp.28, 238–9.
10. M.B. Rose, 'The Family Firm and the Management of Succession', in Rose and Brown (eds.), *Entrepreneurship*, p.28; idem, 'The Family Firm in British Business', in M.W. Kirby and M.B. Rose (eds.), *Business Enterprise in Modern Britain* (London, 1994), p.67.
11. L. Putterman, *The Economic Nature of the Firm* (Cambridge, 1986), p.16.
12. Chandler, *Scale and Scope*, p.390; R. Church, 'The Family Firm in Industrial Capitalism', *Business History*, Vol. 35 (1993), p.21.
13. Chandler, *Scale and Scope*, pp.240–42; B. Elbaum and W. Lazonick, *The Decline of the British Economy* (Oxford, 1986), p.2.
14. Chandler, *Scale and Scope*, p.286.
15. Ibid., p.390.
16. J.S. Toms, 'The Finance and Growth of the Lancashire Cotton Textile Industry' (unpublished Ph.D. thesis, University of Nottingham, 1996), Chapter II.
17. Ibid. Movements in the Oldham share index were strongly correlated with the price of gold; this had no impact on London prices of commercial and industrial companies which were driven instead by domestic gross national product.
18. A simple average index of 20 Oldham companies, selected from the *Oldham Chronicle* share listing and with a value of 100 at June 1890 had fallen to 50.2, its pre-war low, by March 1896. An index for companies quoted on the London stock exchange, calculated from the data in K.C. Smith and G.F. Home, 'An Index Number of Securities, 1867–1914', *London and Cambridge Economic Service*, Special Memorandum, NO.37 (1934), columns 1–10, pp. 14–15) showed corresponding figures of 100 and 128.3. See also, 'Is the Cotton Trade Leaving the Country?" *Textile Mercury*, 21 Jan. 1893, p.43.
19. Tyson, thesis, pp.294–5; Toms, 'Financial Constraints', pp.377; Toms, thesis, pp.90, 272.
20. Tyson, thesis, pp.25 1–2, 264.
21. E.E.H. Green, 'Rentiers versus Producers? The Political Economy of the Bimetallic Controversy, c.1880–1890', *English Historical Review*, Vol. CIII; 588–612; A.C. Howe, Bimetallism, c.1880–1890: a controversy reopened, *English Historical Review*, Vol.CV; pp.377–91.
22. Toms, 'Financial Constraints', pp.371–4.
23. Oldham Local Studies Library (hereafter, OLSL), Misc. 42/17, Werneth Cotton Spinning Co. Ltd, Quarterly Reports to Members, 1892; the Shiloh was another company which grew rapidly, constructing four new mills in this period, J. Worrall, *The Cotton Spinners and Manufacturers Directory for Loncashire* (Oldham, 1889 and 1913); DJ. Jeremy, TE. Gartside' in DJ. Jeremy (ed.), *Dictionary of Business Biography* (hereafter *DBB*) (1984–86), pp.495–8.
24. Tyson, thesis, pp.286–90.
25. Courtaulds Archives Coventry (hereafter CAC), LCC/DOW.I, Dowry Cotton Spinning Co. Ltd., Nominal Ledgers, 1886–1914.
26. Worrall, *Cotton Directory*, 1889 and 1913
27. D.A. Farnie, 'John Bunting', in Jeremy (ed.) *DBB*, pp.506–9; Toms, 'Financial Constraints', p.377.

28. Other examples in Oldham included Thomas Henthorn (1850–1913), Harry Dixon (1880–1947), William Hopwood (1862–1936), Ralph Morton (1875–1942), T.E. Gartside (1857–1941), John S. Hammersley (1863–1933), and Sam Firth Mellor (1873–1938), D. Gurr and J. Hunt, *The Cotton Mills of Oldham* (Oldham, 1985), pp.9–10.

29. D.A. Farnie, *English Cotton and the World Market*, 1815–1896 (Oxford, 1979); J.S. Toms, 'The Supply of and the Demand for Accounting Information in an Unregulated Market', *Accounting, Organisations and Society*, Vol. 22 (1997), forthcoming.

30. John Hawkins & Sons Ltd, Woodfold Mill Darwen (1895); Greenbank Mills, Preston (1898) Hartford Mill, Preston (1910); Abbey Mill, Withnell (1898); T. & R. Eccles, Lower Darwen Mill, Blackburn (1897); George Whiteley, Albion Works, Blackburn (1899); John Fish Ltd, Waterfall Mills, Blackburn (1906); Primrose Mill, Blackburn (1906). *The William Birtwistle Group of Mills* (privately published by the company) and Worrall, *Cotton Directory*, 1913.

31. T. & R. Eccles & Co. Ltd., Lancashire County Record Office (hereafter, LCRO), DDX/868/7/1, Profit and Loss Accounts and Balance Sheets; G. Whiteley & Co. Ltd, LCRO, DDX/868/21/5, Balance Sheets.

32. Taken together, the companies had 107,588 mule spindles, 96,588 ring spindles and 6,720 looms. Birtwistle's empire was thus approximately the same size as Horrockses, having slightly less spinning capacity, but slightly more weaving; Worrall, *Cotton Directory*, 1913.

33. *The William Birtwistle Group of Mills* (privately published by the company, undated), Birtwistle continued his acquisitive strategy into the 1920s, for example with the acquisition of Ewood mills in 1928, *Times*, 17 Dec. 1928 p. 11g, and by the time of his death in 1936 controlled 16 mills, 'forming one of the largest combinations under the same management in Lancashire', *The Times*, 15 June 1936, p. 17d.

34. Farnie, 'John Bunting', in Jeremy (ed.), *DBB*, pp.506–9; Whiteley and Eccles were both conversions from partnerships in the late 1890s, and Liverpool cotton brokers, such as Henry Eccles, continued to be significant shareholders, Whiteley, LCRO, DDX/868/21/l, and Eccles, DDX/868/20/l, Ledgers and Registers of Members, Minute Book, Directors' Minutes.

35. J.S. Toms, 'The Financial Performance of the Lancashire Cotton Industry, 1880–1914', in I. Blanchard (ed.), *New Directions in Economic and Social History* (Edinburgh, 1995), p.33. In the 1912 balance sheet stocks stood at 110 per cent of fi ed assets, compared to only 37 per cent in 1897, Eccles, LCRO, DDX/868/7/1. In the period 1897–1914 the company trebled its sales turnover, mainly for the Indian market, in the form of shirtings and 'dhooties', without needing to increase its capital.

36. Calculated from *The William Birtwistle Group of Mills*, and Worrall, *Cotton Directory*, 1913.

37. Eccles, LCRO, DDX/868/7/1, Whiteley, DDX/868/21/5.

38. Poor judgement in futures produced some dramatic losses in the early 1890s, for example, at Sun Mill in Oldham, the Eagle in Rochdale, and Fieldens at Todmorden, Tyson, thesis, p. 275, *Rochdale Observer*, 9 April 1892, Fielden Brothers, West Yorkshire Record Office (hereafter, WYRO), C353/475, Detailed Accounts, 1891–94.

39. Centenary mill was named for the centenary of the founding of the firm by John Horrocks in 1791, G. Pedrick, *The Story of Horrockses* (Nottingham, 1950), p.27, although the mill was not brought into full production until fi e years later, J. S. Toms, 'The Profitability of the First Lancashire Merger: The Case of Horrockses Crewdson, 1887–1905', *Textile History*, Vol. 24 (1993), p.135.

40. Chapman, *Merchant Enterprise*, p.318; Howe, 'Sir Frank Hollins', in Jeremy (ed.), *DBB*, p.315; Coats Viyella Records (hereafter, CVR), Detailed Accounts.

41. Manchester Central Reference Library (hereafter, MCRL), Tootal Broadhurst and Lee, M.461, Board Minutes Book No.2, 28 Dec. 1897.

42. MCRL, M.461, Board Minute Book No.2, 12 Sep. 1899 and Minute Book No.3, 9 Sept. 1902.

43. The warehouse was reported as due for completion in October 1898; MCRL, M.461, Board Minute Book No.2, 27 Sept. 1898.

44. WYRO, C353/475, 1890–1914; J.S. Toms, 'Integration, Innovation and the Progress of a Family Cotton Enterprise: Fielden Brothers Ltd, 1889–1914', *Textile History*, Vol.27 (1996), pp.79–80.

45. In 1912, ratios of directors' emoluments to sales ranged from 7.15 per cent at Fielden to 1.98 per cent at Eccles and 1.22 per cent at Horrockses (calculated from sources listed in the Appendix 1,

Table 5); in Oldham, Werneth at 0.34 per cent (calculated as above) was more typical, see B. Potter, *The Co-operative Movement in Great Britain* (Aldershot, 1891, reprinted 1987).

46. London Guildhall Library (herafter, LGL), Commercial Reports, Rylands & Sons Ltd., 1884–1895.
47. Farnie, 'John Rylands', pp.66–9.
48. LGL, Commercial Reports, 1899–1913.
50. In the depression of 1894–95; Sun Mill directors visited loan holders personally to persuade them to retain their investment, Tyson, thesis, p.281.
51. T. & R. Eccles, LCRO DDX/868/20/l, p.5; G. Whiteley Ltd, DDX/868/21/1, p.29.
52. *Oldham Chronicle*, 'Cotton Trade in 1907', 28 Dec. 1907, p.8(ii).
53. *Economist*, 23 Dec. 1848.
54. D.A. Farnie, *The Manchester Ship Canal and the Rise of the Port of Manchester*. 1894–1975 (Manchester, 1980), pp.74–5.
55. D.A. Farnie, 'An Index of Commercial Activity: The Membership of the Manchester Royal Exchange, 1809–1948', *Business History*, Vol. 21 (1979), pp.97–8; Rose, 'The Family Firm', p.76.
56. The mills were in the township of Milnrow south-east of Rochdale and north-west of Oldham. Ring spinning developed from the earlier throstle which in tum dated back to the continuous spinning of Arkwright's water frame. Mule spinning was intermittent, with twist inserted only on the outward movement of a wheeled carriage. For a more detailed explanation see L. Sandberg, *Lancashire in Decline* (Ohio, 1974), pp.18–20.
57. 'Milnrow Ring Spinning Companies', *Rochdale Observer*, 28 June 1890, p.4. Similar loose structures were beginning to emerge elsewhere in Lancashire, for example, the so-called 'Bunting group': see D.A. Farnie, 'John Bunting', in D. Jeremy (ed.), *DBB;* pp.506–9.
58. Commenting on the profit per spindle results for 1890, in a table showing the Milnrow group at 1st, 2nd and 4th positions out of a total of 68 mills, an *Oldham Chronicle* correspondent wrote: 'The ring spindle concerns lead the way as usual . . .', 3 Jan. 1891.
59. Rose (ed.), *Family Business*, p. xx; P. Scranton, 'Learning Manufacture: Education and Shop-Floor Schooling in the Family Firm', in Rose (ed.), *Family Business*, pp.303–25.
60. *Textile Recorder*, 13 May 1897. The spread of ring spinning in Rochdale was attributed to the previous tradition of throstle spinning (see also *Cot/on Factory Times*, 26 March' 1897) and in the 1870s coincided with an increased dependence on flannels and flannelettes, the latter being introduced in 1883; D.A. Farnie, 'The Cotton Towns of Greater Manchester', in M. Williams with D.A. Farnie (eds.), *Colton Mills in Greater Manchester* (1992), p.44.
61. These were the Hathershaw, Stanley, Lees Union and Dowry Spinning Companies; *Oldham Chronicle*, 1 Oct. 1889, *Rochdale Observer*, 28 June 1890 (for ring spinners). Oldham companies attempted to drive down labour cost by increasing capital intensity, S. Kenney, 'Sub-regional Specialisation in the Lancashire Cotton Industry: A Study in Organisational and Locational Change', *Journal of Historical Geography*, Vol.8 (1982), p.54.
62. 'Ring Spinning', *Rochdale Observer*, 4 Jan. 1890, p.6; 'New Flexible Flyer Spinning Frame, for Spinning Weft', *Textile Mercury*, 5 Dec. 1896.
63. G. Saxonhouse and G. Wright, 'Rings and Mules around the World: A Comparative Study in Technological Choice', *Research in Economic History*, Supplement 3 (1984), p.289. The US patent of John Thorp was adopted and patented in England within six months by George William Lee in 1829; DJ. Jeremy, *Transatlantic Industrial Revolution: The Diffusion of Textile Technologies between Britain and America. 1790–1830s* (Cambridge, MA, 1981), pp.214 and 243.
64. Rochdale Local Studies Library, New Ladyhouse Cotton Spinning Co. Ltd, Memorandum and Articles of Association; 'Milnrow Ring Spinning Companies', *Rochdale Observer*, 28 June 1890, p.4. The New Ladyhouse followed an earlier and smaller experiment at Bright Bros.
65. Farnie, *English Cotton*, p.230; Farnie, 'Cotton Towns', p.44.
66. Their sale in 1877–78 did not feature in the surveys by Saxonhouse and Wright, 'Rings and Mules', Tables 7 and 8, pp.282–3, and 'New Evidence', Table 1, p.509.
67. 'Ring Spinning and its Development; with Especial Reference to its Introduction into Rochdale', *Rochdale Observer*, 4 Jan. 1890; R. Kirk, 'John Bullough', in Jeremy (ed.), *DBB*, p.502.
68. 'Milnrow Ring Spinning Companies', *Rochdale Observer*, 28 June 1890.
69. I am grateful to D.A. Farnie for information on this mill.

70. Belgrave No. Two had only 43,200 spindles, although Iris (62,568), Moston Ring (59,796) and Royton Ring (64,176) were more typical. By contrast, the median mule specialist in the Oldham district was by this time of the order of 100–130 thousand spindles. The largest, Times No. Two, at 174,000 spindles, revealed the limits of economies of scale in the mule section; see Jones, thesis, p.88.

71. Worrall, *Colton Directory*, 1889; see the company's advertisement in the annual editions of the directory.

72. 'Funeral of Mr. James Heap', *Rochdale Observer*. 16 April 1892.

73. Such contradictions were keenly felt throughout Lancashire, especially where joint stock companies were prevalent; P. Joyce, *Work. Society and Politics: The Culture of the Factory in Late Victorian England* (Brighton, 1980), pp.339–40.

74. The mills, with one exception, closed on the morning of James Heap's funeral in 1892, and flags fl w at half mast above the mills, the school, the Educational Institute, and the Conservative club, 'Funeral of James Heap', *Rochdale Observer*, 13 April 1892.

75. For example, in response to events in the Stalybridge dispute in 1892, the hands employed at the Milnrow companies were placed on a week's notice, *Rochdale Observer*, 9 April 1892.

76. C. Simmons, 'Denis Machell Hollins', in Jeremy (ed.), *DBB*, p.308; A.C. Howe, 'Sir Frank Hollins', in Jeremy (ed.), *DBB*, p.316; M. Dupree, 'Edward Tootal Broadhurst', in Jeremy (ed.), *DBB*, p.452. Draper Corporation, the US parent, retained two-thirds of the shares; S.B. Saul, 'The Engineering Industry', in D. Aldcroft (ed.), *The Development of British Industry and Foreign Competition* (London, 1968), p.195.

77. The only other recorded instance of a pre-1914 experiment was at Fielden Brothers of Todmorden; J.S. Toms, 'Integration, Innovation, and the Progress of a Family Cotton Enterprise: Fielden Brothers Ltd, 1889–1914', *Textile History*, Vol.27 (1996), pp.77–100.

78. Sandberg, *Lancashire in Decline*, p.77.

79. In 1911, 34 per cent of all automatics in Lancashire were installed at Ashtons; calculated from A. Fowler, 'Trade Unions and Technical Change: The Automatic Loom Strike, 1908', *North West Bulletin of Labour History* (1980), p.43; and Worrall, *Cotton Directory* (1913), which recorded Ashtons having 98,594 ring spindles and 67,284 mule spindles and 4,445 looms.

80. LGL, Commercial Reports, Ashton Brothers & Co. Ltd; T. Skinner, *Stock Exchange Official Year Book* (London, 1900).

81. Fowler, 'Trade Unions', pp.45–6.

82. Ibid, p.53.

83. For examples of the paternalism of the earlier Gregs, see M. Rose, 'Henry Philips Greg', in Jeremy (ed.), *DBB*, pp.647–8. At Tootals, the Sunnyside Institute was an established hallmark of Victorian paternalism, J. Liddington, Z. Mumby and J. Seddon, 'There's no Room on Daubhill for me', unpublished working paper, Manchester Metropolitan University, p.31.

84. C. O'Mahoney, *Quarr Bank Mill Memoranda: A Journal of Everyday Life in a Nineteenth Century Cotton Mill* (Manchester, 1989), pp.66, 71 and 75; automatics were not introduced until 1909, Rose, *Gregs of Quarry Bank*, p.98.

85. Liddington, Mumby, and Seddon, 'Daubhill', pp.I-2. The attitude of Harold Lee led to an escalation into a bitter dispute; for a description of the warp stop motion; see Sandberg, *Lancashire ill Decline*, pp.81–2.

86. Replacement non-union labour.

87. MCRL, M46I, Board Minute Book No.3, Directors report to shareholders, 4 Sept. 1906.

88. Ibid.

89. Liddington, Mumby and Seddon, 'Daubhill'.

90. For example, Tootal sold into a broad range of international and domestic markets but without the dependence on India characteristic of many specialist coarse spinners; MCRL, Finance Committee, Minute Book No.1, 24 Nov. 1890.

91. Amalgamated Cotton Mills Trust Ltd., *Concerning Cotton* (published by the company, 1920); Howe, 'Sir Frank Hollins', in Jeremy (ed.), *DBB*, p.315. Brand names were applied to products from other producers such as the Hollins and Co. 'Viyella' brand, and the goods marketed on their behalf, F.A. Wells, *Hollins and Viyella: A Study in Business History* (Newton Abbot 1968), p.98.

92.  A.C. Howe, 'Henry Lee and Joseph Cocksey Lee', in Jeremy (ed.), *DBB*, p.708. In the West Indies, in June 1891, overdue accounts reached £34,900, or more than half the total outstanding, MCRL, M.461, Finance Committee Minute Book No.1, 22 June 1891. In 1894 and 1895, there was insufficient capital to pay a dividend, MCRL, M.461, Minutes of General Meetings, Minute Book No.2, Auditor's Reports, 9 Oct. 1894 and 22 Oct. 1895.

93.  A solution of sorts was found, through the implementation of a 'scheme' suggested by the Auditor. This involved the revaluation of property assets, thereby creating a reserve against which bad debts of over £69,000 could be written off without reducing reported and distributable profits to catastrophic levels, MCRL, M.461, Board Minutes; Minutes of Annual General Meetings, Minute Book No.2., 29 Sept. 1896.

94.  MCRL, M.461, Board Minute Book No.2, 21 Sept. 1897.

95.  Howe, 'Henry Lee and Joseph Cocksey Lee', in Jeremy (ed.), *DBB*, pp.708–9.

96.  MCRL, M.46I, Board Minute Book No.1, 8 March 1888.

97.  D. Higgins, 'Structural Constraints and Financial Performance in the Lancashire Textile Industry, c.1945–60', Management School Discussion Paper No. 92.51; University of Sheffield (1992); J.S. Toms, 'The First Lancashire Merger', pp.129–46.

98.  Toms, 'The First Lancashire Merger', p.133. At Tootals, family liaison helped overcome some of the conflict; H we, 'Henry Lee and Joseph Cocksey Lee', p.706.

99.  Per the listing in Royal Commission on Historical Manuscripts, *Records of British Business and Industry, 1760–1914: Textiles and Leather* (London, 1990). Firms with the longest continuous archive of accounting records and directors' minutes were given precedence.

100.  'Commercial Reports', *Oldham Chronicle*, 2 April 1884–27 Dec. 1913. Saturday issues published the quarterly reports of companies detailing profits, d vidends, share and loan capital.

101.  For example, certain Rochdale companies, namely the New Ladyhouse, New Hey and Haugh Spinning Companies, were particularly important as pioneers of ring spinning.

102.  Foremost among these was Ashton Brothers of Hyde, which, as a pioneer in automatic weaving, has attracted considerable comment; Sandberg, *Lancashire in Decline*, pp.80–81; W. Lazonick, 'Industrial Organisation and Technological Change: The Decline of the British Cotton Industry', *Business History Review*, Vol. VVII (1983), pp.211–2; Fowler, 'Trade Unions', pp.43–55.

103.  Notable examples of the former included J. & P. Coats, and the English Sewing Cotton company, and of the latter, the Bleachers' Association and the Calico Printers' Association.

# Producer co-operatives and economic efficiency: Evidence from the nineteenth-century cotton textile industry

Steven Toms

*The York Management School, University of York, York, UK*

The relative efficiency of producer co-operatives is investigated through an examination of the financial performance of a group of cotton spinning firms that emerged from the spread of co-operative ideals after the mid-nineteenth century. Reflecting such influences these firms adopted two particularly important aspects of democratic governance: use of low denomination partly paid shares to encourage wide share ownership among local working class operatives, and the use of a one shareholder one vote rule at company meetings. Prior literature, much of which predicts the failure of producer co-operatives due to incentive problems, has not specifically examined these aspects of democratic control. Moreover because the case study utilises samples of stock market quoted companies, there is an opportunity to quantify the financial performance effects of these governance mechanisms. The case study therefore offers a unique insight and important contribution to the wider literature. The results show that both aspects of democratic governance contributed to the economic success of the companies that adopted them, enabling them to satisfy the high demand for cash dividends that characterised investor requirements. However, the cyclical nature of the cotton industry and the stock market booms and slumps that resulted led to redistributions of wealth through time that in the long run undermined the co-operative project.

## Introduction

The paper examines the proposition that co-operatives are relatively inefficient, as argued in mainstream economic theory, due to incentive and collective action problems, particularly among producer co-ops where ownership is distributed among employees. According to Jensen and Meckling, these problems arise where firms control non-fungible or realisable intangible assets, have non-perpetual ownership claims, need to share equally in cash flows which, because they are contingent on employment with the firms, are non-marketable. All of these features are common in labour managed firms which also have the control problem, which Jensen and Meckling define as the specification of the political procedures within the firm by which the workers arrive at decisions and control the managers.[1] The proposition is based on theory and evidence that might be contradicted by a previously under-researched example of apparently successful co-operative performance. There is prima facie evidence that the producer co-operatives of nineteenth-century Lancashire, located in the Oldham cotton spinning district,[2] were relatively efficient. They survived for a fairly long period, c.1854–96, and were able to compete effectively with non-co-operative firms during that time.[3] The reasons for this have not been fully explored, notwithstanding the considerable contemporary press commentary that these companies attracted, partly as a result of their apparent efficiency.[4]

The paper also builds on previous research on the Oldham limited companies involved in cotton production. There has been limited work from a business history perspective, excepting Farnie's chapter[5] on the subject, which describes the Oldham business system, including the important aspects of co-operation. Other research has examined the financial policies of these firms and other firms in the wider cotton industry, and has also examined the use of accounting information in their governance and management and has investigated the effectiveness of the Oldham stock market.[6] None of this research however has examined the link between ownership and performance, and the paper will develop the literature by examining the ownership, performance and business strategies of individual companies.

In the nineteenth century co-operative ideas influenced the development of retail and producer co-operatives alike, although only the former enjoyed longer run success.[7] Perhaps as a consequence producer co-operatives have attracted relatively little attention. Even so, following the pioneering experiments in Rochdale and the Lowbands Farm tea party at Jumbo near Oldham,[8] producer co-operatives flourished as the cotton spinning trade developed in the south-east Lancashire industrial district. From the mid-nineteenth century until the mid-1890s, co-operatives dominated the important coarse section of the cotton trade,[9] utilising Companies Act legislation to adapt the Owenite ideals upon which they were founded.

The Oldham Mills might have utilised Industrial and Provident Societies legislation, but preferred the Companies Act for technical reasons. Mills required substantial fixed capital investment, but the Industrial and Provident Societies Act (IPSA) allowed the withdrawal of capital. Oldham firms therefore used share capital plus instant access loan accounts to finance their operations and provide investment opportunities for their members. Also, because cotton spinning firms produced only intermediate output (i.e. yarn), they could not supply finished goods direct to members as required by the IPSA 1862.[10] A further feature of the IPSA 1862 was that it allowed societies to federate, which facilitated backward integration of retail societies and the Co-operative Wholesale Society (CWS)[11] thereby limiting the possibility of vertical links with the co-operative cotton mills.

The Companies Act 1862 provided illustrative Articles of Association. The Act specified one member one vote[12] with some variation in the example articles of association provided in its supplementary tables. Table A of the 1862 Act specified graduated voting scales. Article 44, 'Votes of Members' stated that: 'Every Member shall have One Vote for every Share up to Ten: He shall have an additional Vote for every Five Shares up to One hundred, and an additional Vote for every Ten Shares beyond the First Hundred shares.'[13] Table C offered a more democratic option, specifying that: 'Every member shall have one vote and no more.'[14] Even companies following Table A used simple show of hands voting,[15] but a small number of members (five or more) could demand a poll, in which case Article 44 could be strictly applied. Graduated voting and a show of hands remained accepted practice until 1900, but legal handbooks increasingly advised their abandonment, especially for company promoters wanting to give power to the 'largest proprietors'.[16] Many co-operative companies' Articles stated that Table A of the Act did not apply and clauses were inserted stating that each member shall have one vote only.[17] These adaptations included shareholder democracy, promotion of the dividend and high standards of corporate accountability.[18] Such features were promoted by two particular aspects of corporate governance, the use of a one shareholder one vote, or 'show of hands' rule at company meetings, and low denomination shares to ensure diffuse ownership.

Paying particular attention to these variables, the paper will examine the extent to which they contributed to financial performance of the cotton spinning firms that adopted them, relative to benchmark indicators of firms using less democratic methods. Contemporary press sources, including local newspapers, such as the *Oldham Standard* and *Oldham Chronicle*, and co-operative publications, such as *The Co-operator* and *Co-operative News*, will be analysed together with business archives of case study companies and British Parliamentary Papers.[19] These sources will be used to identify samples of firms with particular governance characteristics and to obtain share price and dividend data so that their financial performance can be compared. The second section of the paper reviews the prior theoretical and historical literature, explaining the rationales and evidence for the predicted inefficiency and failure of producer co-operative experiments. The third section introduces the special features of the Oldham limiteds, including the economic and institutional context in which they operated to explain why they offer a useful test case for evaluating the efficiency of these variants of producer co-operative organisation. The financial performance of the Oldham limiteds is then compared to firms operating in the wider economy, other sectors of cotton textiles and sub-samples of firms within the coarse spinning sector, as differentiated by co-operative governance characteristics. Following this analysis, the paper examines the reasons for the decline of the co-operative firms. In a concluding section, it then summarises the factors likely to promote the success and survival of producer and other co-operative organisations.

## Producer co-operation and economic efficiency: theory and historical evidence

Mainstream economic theory makes three important and general predictions that are relevant to assessing the likely performance and success of co-operative organisations. The first is that ownership rights and governance arrangements matter. So, in addition to inputs of capital, labour and technology, according to the influential framework of economic analysis outlined by Jensen and Meckling, the output of a firm also depends on the specification of contracting and property rights. The second prediction is that because co-operatives and other forms of industrial democracy are rare, they conclude that these alternative organisational forms are less efficient than their conventional capitalist counterparts. Reasons might include the incentive to restrict output and raise wages in response to an increase in demand, and the horizon problem, which suggests that workers will be incentivised only to invest in capital investment projects with shorter lives than their expected period of employment with the firm. Employees also have an incentive to use long-term structured debt to fund shorter-term consumption of benefits and perquisites. Third, theorists hypothesise that producer co-operatives 'degenerate' over time as members are replaced by non-members.[20]

Mainstream economic theorists are confident of their predictions, based on the absence of successful real world models of producer co-operation and argue that the burden of proof of successful performance lies with the proponents of alternatives.[21] Nonetheless, the empirical studies that have been undertaken tend to reject the hypothesis that worker participation damages productivity. They also find that it does not cause sub-optimal allocation of labour in the form of employment maximisation, and reject the degeneration thesis.[22] Although these studies have addressed questions of economic efficiency, there is a scarcity of firm level financial data,[23] so that there are few studies that examine comparative financial performance.

Even so, there are further theoretical difficulties for co-operatives. An important one is that employee co-operatives suffer from the non-transferability problem, which arises because employees cannot sell their jobs. Retail societies, which can be controlled by their customers, therefore become more prevalent. The success of some co-operatives is also linked to the use of high initiation fees.[24] As a result, employee co-operators cannot use portfolio diversification to mitigate their risk. A further difficulty arises from the monitoring problem, which means that in the absence of a market in which claims on employees' wealth invested in the firm can be traded a market for corporate control cannot develop, so that the market has no mechanism for disciplining inefficient managers through takeovers. Managers will not therefore be incentivised to reduce shirking and wastage.[25] Such problems can be mitigated or overcome entirely where co-operative firms issue negotiable shares on the market, depending on the extent to which employee control is retained through non-negotiable shares.[26] A co-operative that does not retain such control cannot be a co-operative, but in the presence of non-negotiable employee shares the value of the firm to an outside investor is reduced due to the perceived risk of residual claims being neglected for the benefit of firm insiders. These problems are compounded by agency costs which prevail in all organisations.[27] With a stock market, and in the absence of asset diversification by the firm, efficiency of production decisions requires that control rights be vested with the shareholders.[28] In summary, as this discussion suggests, there are factors associated with corporate governance in particular that might enhance financial performance for producer co-operatives.

However, none of this literature has considered a further compromise solution in which all shares are negotiable but democratic rights for employees are promoted through one shareholder one vote arrangements for general meetings and governance rules designed to promote employee ownership of those shares (for example employee pre-emption rights, low share denominations). Jensen and Meckling's propositions that co-operative organisations are somewhat rare and that successful employee co-operatives are rarer still might be accepted if such cases of democratic governance are not considered. Because Jensen and Meckling accept that co-operatives might succeed as a consequence of special legal rules,[29] it would follow that the absence of a suitable legislative framework could be a reason for the apparent lack of successful producer co-operative experiments. Moreover, in a more permissive legislative environment there is no reason why one share one vote should be preferred to one shareholder one vote, in view of the potential benefits of the latter for overcoming problems associated with non-transferability.

Even so, the instances of such rules being allowed under corporate law are comparatively rare,[30] and the apparent failure of employee co-operatives might plausibly be a consequence of prescriptive legislation on shareholder voting, rather than inherent organisational inefficiency. To examine this hypothesis, the paper investigates a historical case study of the Oldham limited liability spinning companies in the nineteenth century. These firms operated in a period of permissive company legislation and as a consequence voluntarily adopted the one shareholder one vote rule, and for a period of around 20 years promoted a large and apparently profitable expansion of the already powerful Lancashire cotton industry. For the purposes of analysing the modern economy, these companies are an interesting case study because the protection of the shareholder interest via a voting rule of one share one vote has become near universal in the USA and UK. Present day regulators therefore have restricted access to evidence about the likely effects of modifying corporate governance regulations in favour of more democratic shareholding structures.

Where such evidence has been examined previously, it has tended to draw negative conclusions about the economic performance of co-operatives. Several reasons have been advanced, and these overlap to some extent with economic theory. In Marx's view, the transition from co-operative social relations based on what he regarded as utopian socialist principles to capitalist social relations was rooted in the development of the credit system and the inability of the co-operative organisations to set up durable alternatives to it.[31] For Bowles and Gintis, co-operatives failed because in the face of rising economies of scale, they could not accumulate sufficient capital.[32] In the cotton industry, scale economies were driven by lengthening mule spinning carriages, so that it paid to build new mills in times of boom rather than extend existing buildings.[33] The effect was to reduce the requirement for co-operators to accumulate capital in operational mills, but to create incentives for speculative investment in new mills.[34] Insofar as new mills were controlled by these speculative interests, older co-operatives would have faced competitive disadvantage.

Marglin argues that workers simply lacked the entrepreneurial knowledge and skill to manage successfully their own firms.[35] Clark endorses this view, citing the examples of Sun Mill in Oldham and the co-operatives of the Rossendale valley studied by Beatrice Webb in the 1880s and 1890s. So resentment towards managerial control in these organisations manifested itself in the form of egalitarian wage structures that extended to managerial functions.[36] Co-operatives cannot escape the mistrust between capital and labour that characterises capitalist organisation. In the general case, efficiency depends on how capital responds to the behaviour of labour as a social group and the mistrust that arises. These views were echoed in the co-operative movement itself, in which middle class supporters of profit sharing and co-partnership opposed employee involvement in management.[37]

A problem with this interpretation is that it only partially reflects the experience of Sun Mill and similar organisations. Where management itself is less of a scarce resource, the success of participatory organisations tends to be promoted.[38] This appears to have been the case in the cotton industry where shop floor hierarchy, oversight and control were well established.[39]

Clark also argues 'that if radical economists are correct (that giving control of production to workers is more efficient) then, ironically, the efficient organization disappeared because workers used control of production to drive up wages and limit output'. In other words, Clark believes that co-operative experiments in nineteenth-century Britain were unsuccessful for reasons of incentive problems similar to those suggested by Jensen and Meckling.[40] On the other hand, neither radical nor neo-classical economic historians have spent much time examining circumstances in which co-operatives have been successful and investigating the reasons.[41] For instance, Clark's citation of the example of Sun Mill above refers only to the mistrust of managers by operatives and not to the apparent commercial success arising from the involvement of operatives in financial management and control.[42] Further research into the actual economic performance of producer co-operatives such as Sun Mill is therefore well justified. The next section discusses the origin and development of this and similar companies examining the economic and institutional context that promoted their growth and apparent success.

### The development of co-operation in nineteenth-century Oldham

After the rapid process of industrialisation in Lancashire, the Oldham district, which included nearby Rochdale, was at the centre of the specialised cotton spinning industry. The Rochdale Co-operative Manufacturing Society, which became known as the Mitchell Hey Mill was formed on orthodox co-operative principles in 1854. All the promoters were members of the Society, all employees were shareholders and surpluses were paid as a bonus, or 'bounty', to labour.[43] The bonus was determined as a proportion of the profits, which allowed the Pioneers to command 'a choice of the best hands, who, by sharing the profits and also working by the piece, acquired a wholesome interest in the amount and quality of the work turned out'.[44] As a result of its success, the mill attracted outside investors, typically over-lookers, foremen and shopkeepers, who begrudged the labour bonus given the workers were paid the full value of their labour in wages. So, the 'bounty' to labour, which had been an important principle upon which the Rochdale Co-operative Manufacturing Society had been founded was abolished in 1862, and from then on all profits accrued to capital.[45]

The discussion over the bounty revealed some interesting tensions in the movement. 'Anti-bounteyites' (*sic*) argued that the bonus to labour rewarded lazy and indolent workers at the expense of thrifty working class savers, who should be encouraged to invest through issuing low denomination shares.[46] Pro-bounteyites attributed these new ideas to the new investors who had joined the society since its inception.[47] As late as 1880, pro-bounteyites such as William Marcroft tried but failed to introduce a labour bonus at Sun Mill. He believed that a standard dividend of 5% on share capital should be charged as a trade expense and that any remaining surplus should then be distributed as a bonus to labour.[48] Marcroft's views were increasingly marginalised as attracting local investment through new share issues became a dominant motive for mill promoters. Sun Mill directors resolved that shares to finance the development of the mill be advertised in the Manchester press and regularly in the local papers.[49] In this fashion, and reflecting the use of co-operative principles, new mills created large shareholder bases of working class investors and attracted investment from other co-operative societies.[50] At Sun Mill, once local investment had been mobilised, it was then resolved that shareholders should be the first to be employed in the mill.[51] As a consequence, these firms were an interesting hybrid of community and employee co-operatives and as such constitute a unique and interesting case.

With the resolution of these debates in favour of wider participation and against labour bounties, as co-operatives developed in Oldham, dividends became the most important feature of the system from the point of view of the working class investor.

Dividends were always paid in preference to retention of profits for reinvestment in the mill. Oldham thus earned the nickname 'diviborough', as a result of the perceived obsession of its people with dividends.[52] They were preferred to bonuses to labour, particularly where experiments were conducted, for example at Sun Mill, Central and Oldham Twist, which linked incentive payments to managers and senior employees to the size of the dividend paid. In the Sun Mill scheme, introduced in 1869, directors were offered a bonus on a sliding scale related to the dividend payment and two years later bonuses were extended to the mill manager, salesman, carders, spinning master and engineer.[53] In the years immediately following the introduction of these schemes the company paid record dividends, averaging 22.75% in 1870 and 29.75% in 1871.[54] It is easy to see why applying this might be opposed by some operatives at least, since the effect would be to fix the return to capital and place the return to labour entirely at the mercy of the trade cycle. A fixed wage, topped up by a dividend in good years might be the preferred combination for the cautious hard working employee. Managerial incentives meanwhile were considered to be better aligned with the investors where bonuses were not paid, for example because managers would be less inclined to manipulate lower quality cotton to receive a higher price for yarn.[55]

Following the apparently successful experiment at Sun Mill, the policy of incentivising directors to maximise dividends through bonus payments became more generalised. At the same time, it was vulnerable to a downturn in trade. At the quarterly meeting of the Croft Bank Spinning Company, shareholders objected to the level of dividend and passed a resolution discontinuing the directors' bonus and requiring money already paid to be returned, and in other cases resisted increases in directors' basic salaries.[56] At the Shaw Spinning Company, shareholders called for a reduction in directors' salaries commensurate with the proposed reduction in dividend.[57]

Shareholder groups also attempted to impose democratic mandates over operating decisions that would fall due to directors in the conventional limited company. Such involvement was facilitated by the typical use of quarterly meetings, which also reported detailed financial results.[58] It included demands for technical investigations into mill operations that might have restricted the dividend.[59] In a similar vein in 1877, at Commercial Mills, shareholders voted on whether or not to adopt a wage reduction of 5%.[60] At Higginshaw Mills during the Brooklands dispute of 1893, directors accepted reductions to half pay as a gesture of sympathy with the operatives.[61] Co-operators such as Marcroft provided leadership. When the Oldham Master Spinners' Association moved to impose a lock-out in the 1875 strike, Marcroft called a special meeting of the Central Cotton Spinning Company, proposing a resolution requiring shareholder approval for action in support of the Masters Association. Marcroft's resolution was rescinded on procedural grounds following an animated discussion, during which his opponents pointed out that he had advocated joining the Masters Association in the first place.[62] Participation by co-operative organisations in employer associations appears at first sight counter-intuitive, but there were important incentives to join, for example to prevent local railway companies charging excessive rates, enforce forward contracts on manufacturers or reduce vulnerability to speculative activity in cotton and yarn markets.[63]

The experiments at Rochdale, the subsequent commercial success of Sun Mill at Oldham and the explosion of joint stock flotations that followed, continued the debate about democratic governance and economic efficiency within the co-operative movement for several years. The correspondence columns of the co-operative press provide some illustration of the divergence of opinion.

The co-partnership movement favoured profit sharing, but the more middle class members opposed participation in management and argued for the maintenance of divisions between mental and manual labour.[64] Trade unions also distrusted profit sharing schemes, seeing them as a means of undermining union membership.[65] The greater risk of failure associated with productive organisations explained some of the difficulties of determining profit sharing schemes. As a result of the failure of the Ouseburn engine works in 1875 and the associated Industrial Bank in 1876, retail societies and the CWS lost financially.[66] These groups became more sceptical of independent producer co-operatives as a consequence and increasingly advocated control of production by the retail societies.[67]

For the 'bounteyites', the obsession with dividends, and the notion of all profits to the capitalists were held to be indistinguishable from the old system.[68] Edward Vansittart Neale proposed a compromise scheme of profit sharing such that capital received some reward for the risks of financing the enterprise.[69] Profit sharing was an important issue at this time elsewhere in the co-operative movement, for example it was tried by the CWS from 1874–86, and developments at Oldham would have been observed with interest.[70] The advocates of co-partnership, including Neale, believed that productive co-operation was achievable through the conversion of capitalist enterprises, with wage earners controlling their business through the right to become a shareholder, the right to share in the profits and the right to take part in management.[71] All of these features were consistent with the letter of the limited liability acts and were prominent features of the Oldham system.

These features likewise brought condemnation of Oldham 'joint stockism', from some co-operators because although flotation booms attracted working class investors, they also encouraged existing manufacturers to 'turn over' their concerns into public companies. Feverish speculation was mocked by quoting an example of 100 or so potential investors racing each other from the train station to the house at which new shares were being issued, and describing the process of flotation as a 'limited lottery'.[72] Apparently large profits, with Sun Mill being the leading case were cited as reasons for poor industrial relations, for example the 1871 strike which was motivated in part by the operatives perceiving most of the profits going to capital.[73] Notwithstanding these criticisms, there is no doubt that there was considerable support from the co-operative movement, particularly in the 'anti-bounteyite' tradition. Robert Kyle argued that the point, well illustrated by the success of Oldham, was not to use co-operation to raise wages, but to make operatives the masters or partners in the businesses where they worked. At Oldham this was achieved by the election of a committee of six shareholders chosen at the company meeting. Even so, Kyle conceded that this was not the ideal form of productive co-operation.[74] Malcolm Ross, another 'anti-bounteyite' writing in 1862, pointed to the 40 or so mills 'professing to be governed by Co-operative principles' in Lancashire alone 'owned, for the most part, by the working classes', that provided a splendid investment opportunity for those 'of a saving disposition'.[75] Local press commentators also commented favourably on the 'large co-operative companies' that 'teach the operative classes the habit of thrift and saving ... putting forth efforts, mental and otherwise, to meet calls as they fall due'.[76] These arguments were strongly underpinned by the financial performance of Sun Mill in the decade after the cotton famine, which paid large dividends as a result. 'Working men are learning to borrow at 5 per cent and make ten more by it', wrote William Nuttall in 1872, pointing at the same time to the 25% recent average dividend paid at Sun Mill. Nuttall also believed thrift encouraged sobriety.[77] Indeed there were several incidents where alleged drunkenness was used by directors to rule shareholders out of order on attempts to influence cotton buying policy and reduce directors' remuneration in line with dividend reductions.[78]

Although Nuttall conceded that some good came of these companies, he nonetheless advocated that the mills should fall under the control of the retail societies.[79] On the issue of vertical control, by retail or wholesale, there was further division. The people of Oldham were admonished for not consulting congress before launching new companies and for apparently regarding the wholesale society as an inefficient, irresponsible and tyrannical institution.[80] Another suggestion from the editors of the *Co-operative News* was that Oldham should control its supply by joining in the project for a cotton buying mutual with the Grangers co-operative of the Mississippi valley.[81]

Rather than integrate with the rest of the movement, either vertically or by association, the Oldham system began to develop unique and independent features. From the 1860s a new cycle of mill building activity developed, reflecting the use of the new limited liability provisions of the Companies Act 1862, the use of new mills as a vehicle to mobilise working class savings and the cotton industry's pronounced business cycle. Product market features and trends, and the skill of individual managers in manipulating them, were crucial determinants of economic success. By providing the opportunity for cotton spinners to buy at forward rates, the Liverpool futures markets allowed Oldham and other firms to fix their input costs, giving 'free insurance against price fluctuations'. Likewise the Manchester market allowed yarn to be sold at a fixed price even prior to the commencement of production. Unfortunately these markets also facilitated speculators that might be a trap for the ill-informed careless buyer. Liverpool markets responded to wires detailing the latest American crop movements, Manchester markets to demand shifts in Eastern export markets.[82] For this reason, shareholders were concerned about the oversight of buyers in Liverpool and the competence of directors to monitor these managers.[83] Shareholders realised that their dividends depended heavily on prices and positions in the Liverpool cotton spot and futures markets and the Manchester yarn and cloth markets.

A liquid market developed in cotton company shares, although much of the trading was conducted by informal means, for example in public houses. Market listing imposed no requirements on its constituent companies and attempts to formalise the exchange were largely unsuccessful.[84] Some companies were therefore able to use high share denominations and tended to be secretive.[85] Of the 100 or so companies that typically were quoted in the period 1875–1900, some 70%, usually those with the broader shareholder base, voluntarily subjected themselves to public and shareholder scrutiny. The usual practice was to invite the press to attend quarterly meetings and to issue them with the published balance sheet.[86]

Share ownership was diverse and, in the town of Oldham itself, may have been as large as a quarter of the adult population.[87] The small shareholder was the norm, although larger, concentrated shareholdings began to emerge through time.[88] Insider trading rules were non-existent, and such practices were possible and undoubtedly took place. On the one hand, insider traders might have included workers participating in quarterly stock-taking, on the other, market makers who were also company promoters and multiple directors. The most prominent example was John Bunting, who by 1890, was serving on the board of half a dozen companies and also writing a weekly report on share trading in the *Oldham Standard*. His column provided readers with details of those companies whose stocks were in or out of favour.

As a consequence of these developments the two defining characteristics of producer co-operation were the one shareholder one vote rule and the use of low denomination shares. Only the former genuinely differentiates these firms from the ordinary capitalist joint stock enterprise which might equally issue low denomination shares. In the case of the Oldham limiteds where the voting system was democratic, the use of low denomination shares encouraged participation by operatives and less wealthy sections of society.

There is considerable anecdotal evidence from contemporary and more recent literature that this system of democratic accountability had positive consequences for economic efficiency. Referring to cotton operatives and other working class shareholders, Farnie notes they

> proved to be the strictest of economists and were prepared to oust a whole board which failed to produce an acceptable balance sheet, displaying as much ruthlessness as the Athenian Ecclesia or the leaders of the French Revolution towards their unsuccessful generals.[89]

In the slump year of 1891, shareholder wrath at the scale of financial losses was expressed vigorously at many company meetings.[90] The expertise and scrutiny of these shareholders over their businesses was thought by some to contribute towards improved efficiency[91] and contrasted with the poor management of other companies which were run as 'investment unions' and owned by those who 'know nothing of the business carried on'.[92]

By 1866, Sun Mill had a reputation for producing the best 32s yarn on the Manchester market.[93] Private and unincorporated businesses, viewing the limited liability ventures as dangerous rivals, were prompted to set their own houses in order.[94] Ellison, quoting a contemporary report, provides testimony to the contribution of this governance structure to the promotion of economic efficiency:

> The daily discussions which take place amongst the shareholders as to why dividends are small or otherwise, have led almost every intelligent operative to become more economical with materials, more industrious and to see what effect his individual efforts have on the cost of the materials produced. In fact, the bulk of the working class operatives of Oldham have more knowledge of the buying of cotton, working it up, and selling the manufactured good than most private employers had ten years ago. .... The competition between the managers of one company and those of another, and also between the directors of different companies and the pride which each body of shareholders take in their own mill is leading to improvements ... so that *it is almost impossible for the management of any mill owned by working men to be seriously defective for any length of time.*[95]

At the Guidebridge Spinning Company quarterly meeting, reported in the *Oldham Standard* on 30 October 1886, a shareholder complained that they were being beaten by another local company by £94 9s 3d in oil and £45 7s 8d in tallow. Although apparently trivial, it is easy to see how analysis of these cash based expenses would have been symmetrical with the day to day experiences of operatives who were cognisant with the detailed productive workings of a cotton mill. Larger expenses, in particular wages and cotton costs were also disclosed as cash paid amounts in published balance sheets, so these figures could be more easily checked than in modern accounts, which by using accruals of costs, potentially facilitate manipulation. Such simple reporting formats encouraged disputes not about accounting manipulation but about amounts paid and relative efficiency (for example at the Hope and Hollinwood Spinning Companies).[96] Operatives' knowledge of the cotton economy and the workings of the mills helped form expectations about likely profits. Raw material prices were published in the local press and mill expenses were standard and well known. Hence operatives and other shareholders, assisted by press commentators formed expectations about the earning power of their investments. Almost all press share market reports and many company reports discussed expected results against actual.[97]

The extent of financial scrutiny by operatives lends further credence to Ellison's important point about efficiency being promoted by co-operative organisation. What then was the source of local belief at least regarding the superior performance of the Oldham co-operatives? It is possible to investigate such claims of efficient business operation by looking at the actual financial results of the co-operative companies. In the next section, these claims are examined in more detail.


**Co-operation and efficiency: empirical evidence**

Efficiency is measured in terms of shareholder return. This corresponds to economic profit, or internal rate of return where dividend rates are adjusted for opening and closing stock market values. It would also be possible to measure efficiency in terms of the ratio of output to total inputs, including both capital and labour. Such measures are problematic to obtain, particularly wages and employment data at the level of the individual firm. Because the financial results including dividends and share prices were widely published, the Oldham share list provides a unique opportunity to examine efficiency in terms of at least the return to capital. Table 1 provides some wages data for Sun Mill compared to the wages of cotton operatives in Oldham generally, other districts and Lancashire as a whole. According to the data, Sun Mill operatives appear to be relatively well paid, but not dramatically out of line with other non-co-operatively employed groups. If Sun Mill were paying typical wages at the going rate, it would therefore be reasonable to suppose that the residual surplus or profit is a reasonable proxy for economic performance.

Using financial variables alone, several levels of comparison can usefully be conducted. First, a comparison of stock returns between Oldham firms and the London stock market. Second, a comparison within the cotton textile sector of Oldham firms with privately owned cotton companies outside the district. Third, because dividends were such an important aspect of the Oldham system, it is useful to compare dividend yields of Oldham companies compared to firms elsewhere. Fourth, a series of comparatives for dividend yield and total shareholder return can be conducted between companies operating within the Oldham district. These companies can be grouped and differentiated in terms of their adoption or non-adoption of two 'democratic' governance principles: one shareholder one vote, and low denomination shares.

Figure 1 shows their performance in terms of the return to an investor in an index of the Oldham market compared to the returns available to an investor in a portfolio

# BRITISH COTTON TEXTILES

Table 1. Comparative wages, Sun Mill and wider cotton trade, 1866–74.

| District | Pence per week[a] | | | | |
|---|---|---|---|---|---|
| | 1866 | 1870 | 1871 | 1874 | Average |
| Oldham | 177.5 | 187 | | 201.5 | *188.667* |
| Manchester | 141.5 | 154 | 160 | 177 | *158.125* |
| Bolton | 160 | | 166 | 181 | *169.000* |
| Preston | 156 | | 166.5 | 177.5 | *166.667* |
| Blackburn | 166 | | 180 | 187 | *177.667* |
| Clitheroe | | 181 | | 188 | *184.500* |
| Bury & Rochdale | | | 153 | 146 | *149.500* |
| All Lancs districts (average, unweighted) | *160.200* | *174.000* | *165.100* | *179.714* | *169.754* |
| *Sun Mill* | | | | | |
| Wages at Sun Mill (£) | 9719 | 15088 | 15835 | 14930 | *13893.000* |
| No of operatives | 300[b] | 400 | 400 | 400 | *375.000* |
| Year wage per operative | *32.397* | *37.720* | *39.588* | *37.325* | *36.757* |
| Pence per week (d) | *155.504* | *181.056* | *190.020* | *179.160* | *176.435* |

Notes: [a]Gaps indicate missing data; [b]Estimate based on adjustment pro rata to spindelage asset value.
Sources: District data, Wood 'The Statistics of Wages', 587; Sun Mill, *Co-operator*, July 18, 1874, *Co-operator*, November 23, 1874, *Co-operator*, January 13, 1872.

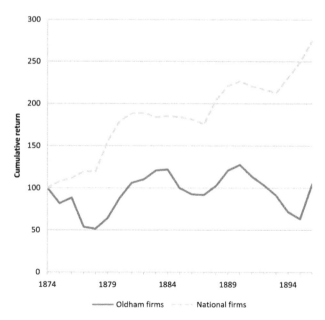

Figure 1. Comparative stock market performance, Oldham co-operatives and national firms, 1874–96.
Sources: Oldham co-operatives share price and dividend data calculated from a sample of 33 Oldham firms whose share price quotations were published in weekly editions of the *Oldham Standard*. National firms calculated using annual total return data weighted by share capital, Grossman, 'New Indices of British Equity Prices', Table 5.

of stocks of all quoted British firms for the period 1875–96.[98] The graph calculates these returns by adding dividends to the difference between prices at the beginning and end of each year and dividing the total by the opening share price. Annual returns are then cumulated into an index taking 1 January 1875 as the base = 100.

The results show that cumulative returns to national firms outpaced Oldham firms throughout the period and in all sub-periods. The average annual return to an investor in national firms was 4.97% per annum, whereas for the Oldham co-operative investor the return was 2.41% per annum, so that the index values of their investments in 1896 were 274.9 and 104.8 respectively. The underperformance of the Oldham companies is difficult to explain, if contemporary claims of relative efficiency are true. Of course the standard of comparison might be misleading, as nationally quoted stocks were dominated by utilities, infrastructure and overseas investments. Spinning and weaving companies are represented in the Grossman indices, which have been used for the purposes of this comparison, but carry relatively small weight.[99]

Figure 2 shows comparative accounting returns for Oldham companies compared to a sample of private spinning and weaving companies and a sample comprising all types of firms. Accounting data for a sample sufficient to carry out such a comparison are only available from around 1885 onwards. Even using other cotton firms as a comparator, the Oldham sector seems to do badly, at least after 1885. Returns on capital employed for Oldham firms averaged 3.09% in this period compared to 6.48% for private firms and 6.03% for the overall index of cotton

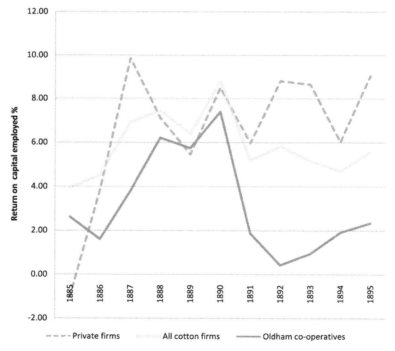

Figure 2.  Comparative returns on capital employed, 1885–96.
Source: Toms, 'Windows of Opportunity', Table 5, p. 19.

companies. It seems possible that whatever the efficiencies identified by Ellison, writing in the mid-1880s and reflected in the quotation earlier dissipated fairly soon thereafter. It is also possible that they were insubstantial in economic efficiency terms before then, looking at the evidence in Figure 1.

A further measure worth comparing is the dividend yield. As discussed above, dividends were an important part of the local culture of share-ownership, and although not successfully integrated into labour bonus payments, were nonetheless a significant source of income for operative shareholders. Figure 3 compares the dividend yield on Oldham co-operative investments with dividend yields in the national firm portfolio.

As Figure 3 shows, dividend yields were considerably higher in aggregate for Oldham companies when compared to the national average. Oldham co-operatives paid 5.63% over the period compared to 2.64% for firms nationally. The very important aspect of Figure 3 is the volatility of dividend payments made by the Oldham firms, and their tendency to pay out very high dividends when they were able, typically during boom years. Mill building booms coincided with upswings in the trade cycle and dividends played an important role in signalling the likely profit opportunities available to investors in the larger, more efficient mills which were developed in each new wave of construction. In the boom years of 1880–81, very high dividends were paid and yields of 17.86%, at Sun Mill, 23.80% at Albert and 18.37% at Borough in 1880 were typical.

To analyse performance differentials within the Oldham district, data were collected from the share price lists for the period 1875–96. The period start date coincides with the first publication of the share list and the end date corresponds to the de facto expiration of the co-operative experiment. All 12 companies with high denomination shares (defined as $>/= £20$) were included in the sample, along with a larger sub-sample of 21 firms with small denomination shares (defined as $</= £20$ but typically $<£5$) from a sample of 70 mills listed as operating in the following districts: Oldham; Ashton, Stalylbridge and Mossley; Middleton, Heywood and

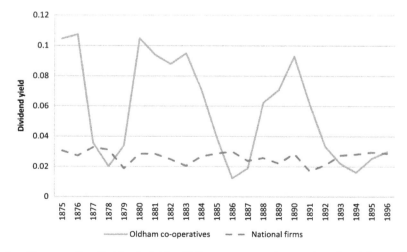

Figure 3. Comparative dividend yields, Oldham co-operatives and national firms, 1875–96. Sources: As for Figure 1.

Bury; Rochdale, Milnrow and Rossendale. The sampling process was non-random, and instead based on purposeful inclusion of pioneering co-operatives and firms whose organisation was known to be influenced by co-operative principles.[100] High denomination shares are indicative of a wealth qualification for ownership. Since the average wage of a cotton operative in 1872 was £37 7s per annum,[101] denominations higher than £20 would be beyond their means. Even so, firms that espoused co-operative principles nonetheless used such high denominations, for example at the Green Lane Spinning Company and Oldham Twist Spinning Company.[102] Grimshaw Lane Spinning Company shareholders numbered around 50 for most of period and typically consisted of professional classes such as architects, solicitors, estate agents and local small business owners. Shiloh Cotton Spinning Company by contrast had a large number of shareholders (295), including many operatives.[103] Not all firms used the one shareholder one vote (hereafter OSOV and firms not using this rule = NOSOV) and the sample was also stratified in order to select firms using OSOV ($N = 20$) and one share one vote ($N = 13$) rules, bearing in mind the availability of archival and press evidence.[104] Because firms combined different aspects of low denomination (LD) and OSOV, the sample was accordingly stratified varying from the most democratic (LD + OSOV) $N = 15$, to the least democratic (high denomination (HD) and NOSOV) $N = 7$, with the remainder featuring either LD or OSOV but not both. For each company in the sample the annual return was computed as described earlier for Figure 1. Using annual data, the total sample of 33 companies resulted in 550 firm year performance observations across the period of the study.

Constructing the sample in this way allows comparatives to be conducted through time between groups and differences in averages for specified periods to be measured for statistical significance. Performance is contrasted between LD and HD sub-samples by total shareholder return (Figure 4) and dividend yield (Figure 5) and between OSOV and NOSOV for the same measures respectively (Figures 6 and 7) and a summary table (Table 2) contrasts sample means.

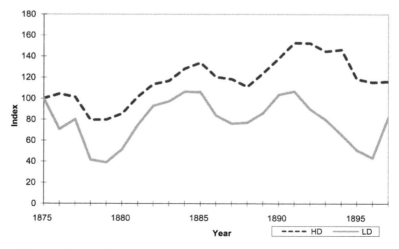

Figure 4.   Shareholder total return, 1874–96.

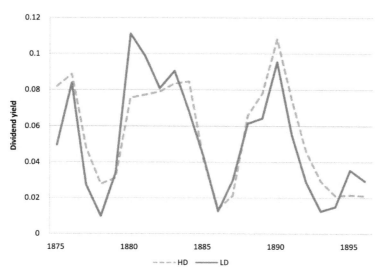

Figure 5.  Comparative dividend yields, high and low denomination Oldham firms, 1875–96.

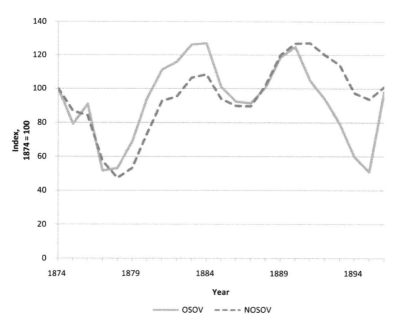

Figure 6.  Comparative total returns, OSOV versus NOSOV, 1874–96.

Figure 4 compares total shareholder return for LD and HD firms applied to a base index of 100 in 1875. The results show consistently higher total returns for the higher denomination shareholder group. The gap in performance is statistically significant (Table 2, column 1), bearing in mind that firms in both groups were similar age, product range (average yarn count) and size (spindleage). The difference is not significant before 1885 (Table 2, column 2), suggesting that in that period

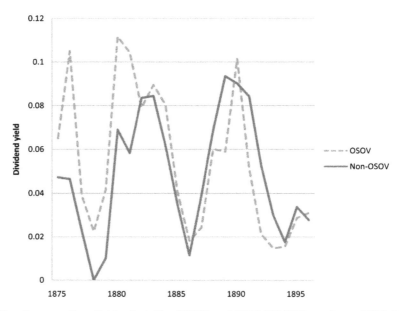

Figure 7.   Comparative dividend yields, OSOV and NOSOV Oldham firms, 1875–96.

working class involvement in corporate governance at least did not impair financial performance.

As noted earlier, working class investors were effective at pressurising boards and it is likely that they might have used their voting power to induce high dividend payments. To test this proposition it is possible to compare the dividends paid by two groups of company: those with high share denominations and those with low share denominations of less than £5 paid up capital. Only those firms with lower denominations would have been readily accessible to working class investors and such firms would have typically had more shareholders in numerical terms due to the lower entry qualification. Figure 5 shows the dividend yields of the two groups in the period 1875–96. Although the trends of the two groups track each other closely, the low denomination index of dividend yield is slightly more volatile, particularly before 1886, with a tendency to pay higher dividends during booms, for example in the boom of 1879–81.[105] Higher denomination firms in contrast seem to have a more conservative strategy. However with yields averaging 5.2% and 5.0% for the full period, these differences were insignificant (Table 2, column 3). In the period up to 1886, the difference was greater (6.2% vs 5.4%), but again not statistically significant. If these cash pay-outs did offer any reward to working class investors, however marginal, the consequence of higher dividends would be to reduce the capital value of the shares and investors' stock of wealth, assuming constant total shareholder returns. In other words, because LD firms matched if not bettered HD firms in terms of dividend yield, it is clear that investors in the HD group were more than compensated in terms of retaining the value of their investments. Indeed, the evidence in Figure 5 seems to suggest that HD share-ownership promoted better aggregate financial performance. Bearing in mind that most of the firms in Figure 5 were founded on co-operative principles, but differentiated only in terms of their

Table 2. Comparative shareholder mean returns.

| | Average total return, 1875–96 | Average total return, 1875–85 | Average dividend yield 1875–96 | Average dividend yield, 1875–85 |
|---|---|---|---|---|
| *All firms* | *1.015* | *0.998* | *0.051* | *0.059* |
| *Sub-group* | | | | |
| LD | 1.027 | 1.002 | 0.052 | 0.062 |
| HD | 0.992 | 0.990 | 0.050 | 0.054 |
| Difference | *0.035\** | *0.012* | *0.002* | *0.009* |
| OSOV | 1.027 | 1.019 | 0.055 | 0.069 |
| NOSOV | 0.997 | 0.964 | 0.045 | 0.044 |
| *Difference* | *0.030\** | *0.055\** | *0.011* | *0.025\*\*\** |
| *Combinations* | | | | |
| HD/NOSOV | 0.973 | 0.931 | 0.046 | 0.043 |
| HD/OSOV | 0.992 | 0.988 | 0.050 | 0.054 |
| LD/NOSOV | 1.021 | 0.992 | 0.044 | 0.044 |
| LD/OSOV | 1.030 | 1.006 | 0.056 | 0.070 |
| *Mean differences* | | | | |
| HD/OSOV-HD/NOSOV | 0.019 | 0.057\*\*\* | 0.004 | 0.010 |
| LD/OSOV- HD/OSOV | 0.038 | 0.018 | 0.006 | 0.016 |
| LD/NOSOV- HD/NOSOV | 0.048\* | 0.061\* | −0.002 | 0.001 |
| LD/OSOV- HD/NOSOV | 0.056\* | 0.075\* | 0.010 | 0.026\*\* |
| *Sample sizes* N | | | | |
| HD | 12 | 11 | 12 | 11 |
| LD | 21 | 21 | 21 | 21 |
| *Total* | *33* | *32* | *33* | *32* |
| NOSOV | 13 | 12 | 13 | 12 |
| OSOV | 20 | 20 | 20 | 20 |
| *Total* | *33* | *32* | *33* | *32* |

Notes: \*\*\**p* < .01; \*\**p* < .05; \**p* < .1, using one tailed tests of the hypotheses that co-operative democratic governance features (LD and OSOV) enhance returns and yields, reported as the lower of *t* tests on mean differences and Mann-Whitney-Wilcoxon sum of rank z tests.
LD = Low denomination (<= £5 paid up); HD = High denomination (=> £10 paid up) (no firms had paid up shares in the £5–£10 range). OSOV = One shareholder one vote; NOSOV = Not one shareholder one vote, i.e. one share one vote.
Sources: Returns are shown as decimal equivalents, standardised to 1 and together with dividend yields are calculated from weekly share price and dividend lists in the *Oldham Standard* and *Oldham Chronicle*.

openness to less wealthy investors, it would appear that it was wide participation and the associated demand for dividends, rather than the co-operative principle itself that was inimical to financial performance.

Figures 6 and 7 contrast the performance of the OSOV and NOSOV sub-sample groups, which can be interpreted with further cross-sectional comparisons in Table 1. Figure 6 shows the total cumulative shareholder return for the two sample groups, revealing a performance advantage to the OSOV group up to 1886, which reversed subsequently, particularly in the slump period of 1891–95. Before 1886, there was a statistically significant difference in performance averaging 5.5% for the OSOV group, and which notwithstanding the subsequent trend is still positive at 3% for the full period (Table 2 columns 1 and 2). Dividend yield was also higher throughout, and significantly (2.5%) higher for the OSOV group before 1886 (Table 2, columns 3 and 4 and Figure 7). These results support the hypothesis of democratic ownership generating superior profits and the propensity to pay those profits as dividends, albeit becoming less pronounced in the later period.

The discussion so far has considered only the separate effects of share denomination and voting mechanisms. Table 2 also reports means for combinations of these features. Firms with OSOV and LD combinations produced the highest returns of +3.0% compared to the lowest returns for the HD and NOSOV group of −2.7% (1.03 and 0.973 respectively in Table 2). The difference is marginally significant at the 10% confidence interval. The performance gap was higher before 1886 in terms of the mean difference (7.5%) at the same confidence interval, and of a statistically significantly higher dividend yield before 1886 (7.0% vs 4.3%). Table 2 also compares the marginal effects of specific governance mechanisms. Within the HD group, OSOV firms generated significantly higher total returns in the period before 1886 relative to NOSOV firms (+5.7%). For firms with OSOV the impact of LD was more marginal with only a 3.8% advantage in total return which was statistically insignificant. There were similar small and insignificant differences in the pre-1886 sub-period and for dividend yields. For NOSOV firms only, the effect of LD shares was to improve overall performance by 4.8% and by 6.1% in the pre-1886 period, with the differences marginally significant at the 10% confidence interval. These differences suggest that much of the superior performance in HD firms in Figures 4 and 5 is accounted for by those HD firms that also used OSOV. The message from Table 1 is that democratic voting and financial inclusivity both promoted financial performance, certainly before 1886 and that OSOV probably had the stronger effect.

In general the above evidence shows that the adoption of democratic governance structures enhanced financial performance to some degree and certainly did not seem to have detracted from it, at least before 1886. A residual question therefore is if these firms were indeed successful, why did they not survive during the further phase of expansion of the Lancashire textile industry up to 1914? With the working class of Oldham controlling over three million spindles in 1875,[106] and working co-operative factories to high levels of efficiency, it would be only a matter of time before they supplanted the privately controlled mills in Oldham and elsewhere in the industry. The issue has already been addressed in the prior literature to a large extent.[107] Trade union organisation created both economic and political opposition to co-operation, with collective bargaining emerging as the preferred mechanism to insure workers against the risks of the trade cycle.[108] As trade union membership increased, worker-shareholders were treated with suspicion on the shop floor.[109] In the slump of the early 1890s, the deepest since the cotton famine,[110] firms accumulated losses and prospects of future dividends became remote, so working class investors sold their shares as wages fell and savings were eroded.[111] Figure 6 shows that OSOV firms suffered particularly badly in this slump and Figure 7 that there was a dispro-portionate fall in dividend pay outs. By the mid-1890s shares had fallen to low values and provided an opportunity for investors to purchase control of the firms cheaply. By securing voting blocks in this way, investors were able to abolish democratic methods of control, for example the one shareholder one vote rule, shareholder audit and limitations of directors' salaries.[112] Company promoters, who no longer had anything in common with co-operative principles, were blamed for the depressed condition of the industry in the 1880s and for using laudatory prospectuses to guarantee high initial share prices and then selling their own holdings soon after flotation, which tended to defraud the longer-term investor, making large profits for themselves in the process.[113]

The use of the OSOV rule declined rapidly in the 1890s for several related reasons. Operatives faced hard times in the slump of 1891–96 and sold their shares. With the return of boom conditions in 1896, having purchased blocks of cheap shares, ownership became more concentrated among the wealthier classes.[114] Director-owners consolidated their control via the mechanism of extraordinary general meetings, which they used to adopt new articles of association. The voting rule became one share one vote, voting by proxy was allowed along with minimum shareholding qualifications for directors and the removal of the obligation to forward accounts to shareholders.[115] Such changes occurred prior to the reduction in scope of the one shareholder one vote rule in a 1906 Board of Trade amendment to the Companies Act 1862, in which companies were presumed to favour the more plutocratic one share one vote system.[116] The crucial reasons for the demise of the remaining co-operative features were therefore social changes and wealth effects, and transfers of ownership facilitated by stock market quotations. Share-ownership therefore centralised around cliques, accounting became secretive and the stock market became narrower as the proportion of listed companies fell.[117]

It was not purely the expansion of the credit system, as Marx suggested, but cyclical effects in production and related wealth redistribution effects of a cyclical stock market that undermined the co-operative experiment. As the empirical evidence above shows, the performance benefits of co-operation were stronger before 1886, which reinforces other evidence in the literature that the distinctions between co-operative and joint stock companies were increasingly blurred after that date.

**Conclusions**

The paper has addressed a gap in the literature by illustrating the potential success of producer co-operation when developed in conjunction with shares traded in a stock market. Such cases are rare today and difficult to replicate in the absence of experimental legislation, and consequently the evidence analysed above is all the more valuable to present day regulators and the promoters of co-operative organisations. It has specifically investigated the value of democratic shareholder voting rights in conjunction with working class investment though the use of low denomination shares.

The evidence shows that democratic voting rights promoted improved financial performance, at least until 1886, after which time co-operation began to lose its impetus. The evidence for low denomination shares is more equivocal. Firms using low denomination shares underperformed high denomination firms through time, although low denomination firms had a marginally better long run average. This discrepancy arose from the distribution of returns, since low denomination shares were more volatile.

In addition to the financial success enjoyed by one shareholder one vote firms there was also a successful sub-group of firms that combined high denomination shares with the one shareholder one vote rule. These firms were not strictly producer co-operatives since shareholders were typically middle class professionals and cotton entrepreneurs, rather than operatives. They owned small fractions of total capital and did not have significant blocks of shares but participated in company management. As a consequence, they appear to have been as effective as working class investors in promoting financial success.

High rates of dividend payment were associated with enthusiasm for participation in governance and management, and may have been self-reinforcing. At the same time, the excessive distribution of capital by the democratic participatory co-operatives tended to reduce their economic performance. Wide participation was also associated with reinvestment in new ventures, not capital accumulation in established concerns. However, although these new ventures attracted high initial participation through generous dividends, the increasing influence of speculative promoters undermined their value as investments and ultimately the participation of working class investors. The hypothesis that the apparent failure of employee co-operatives might plausibly be a consequence of prescriptive legislation on shareholder voting is only partially supported by this case. The evidence suggests that wealth effects and the social control of organisations tend to precede legislative changes that reinforce such control. Meanwhile, co-operatives that limit wider participation through higher entry qualifications and pay moderate dividends may be more effective under certain conditions.

The Bowles and Gintis hypothesis, that co-operatives failed because in the face of rising economies of scale they could not accumulate sufficient capital, appears well supported by the evidence in this case. Wider social ownership promoted demand for dividends, thereby restricting capital available for upgrading existing mills. Failure to accumulate capital for these reasons contrasts with retail and wholesale co-operative societies which acted as savings banks and used capital to integrate backwards into manufacturing and for social projects.[118]

The co-operative principles of democratic participation in cotton companies at first promoted economic growth and perhaps efficiency, and were assisted by certain factors that through time placed limits on co-operative production as a sustainable system. Most important was the effect of the trade cycle. World market conditions, including raw cotton and yarn prices were the fundamental determinants of this, but activities by co-operative and later speculative promoters accentuated it. Early co-operators, and later, speculative cliques both used the lure of high dividends to attract investment, the former to satisfy the demand for safe returns in cash from working class investors, the latter to profit at their expense through mis-priced share offers. A second factor was the improvement of mill technology, which meant that each successive wave of new mills was more efficient than the previous, so that the earlier mills where co-operation was more entrenched were at a competitive disadvantage to their better equipped and higher capacity competitors. The pressure to pay higher dividends in the working class co-operatives also meant there was less funding for reinvestment, and the re-equipment and extension of these mills. Whereas the analysis above compares firms of similar age, there is scope for further research offering more precise measurements of technology and product range.

A third factor was limited liability legislation. At first this provided co-operators an alternative to the Industrial and Provident Societies Act as a means of limiting liability while enshrining democratic principles. Later it was flexible enough for the cliques of local capitalists to undermine these principles and concentrate their control. Finally, there was the stock market. Like the trade cycle and technology, access to the stock market through the vehicle of joint stock organisation at first reinforced the dominance of producer co-operatives. Stock market share quotations reduced entry barriers for the promoters of newer, less co-operative and more overtly capitalist mills. Ultimately, the stock market was in contradiction to the co-operative principle, because the buying and selling of shares on the open market could not guarantee the replacement of principled shareholders with those sharing the same values. These firms were vulnerable to takeover and the advance of technology. Vulnerability to the trade cycle, rise of the labour movement and the ability of external profit maximising investors to use Companies Act legislation to their own advantage, destroyed their long-term future.

## Acknowledgements

I am grateful to Andrew Pendleton and the two anonymous reviewers for helpful comments on an earlier draft.

## Notes

1. Jensen and Meckling, 'Rights and Production Functions', 481.
2. The 'Oldham District' comprised a large area of south-east Lancashire and included Rochdale to the north, Ashton to the south and Middleton to the west.
3. Ellison, *The Cotton Trade*, 138; 'The Rise and Progress of the Rochdale Limiteds', *Rochdale Observer*, May 10, 1890. See also Toms, 'The Rise of Modern Accounting' for an account of the demise of the co-operatives in the slump of the early 1890s.
4. For example, see *Oldham Standard*, July 10, 1875, 8c; Jones, *Co-operative Production*, 284–5.
5. Farnie, *The English Cotton Industry*.
6. See respectively, Toms, 'Windows of Opportunity in the Textile Industry'; idem, 'The Supply of and Demand for Accounting Information'; idem, 'The Rise of Modern Accounting'; idem, 'Information Content'.
7. On the success of retail in northern England, see Purvis, 'Stocking the Store'.
8. Redfern, *The Story of the CWS*, 19–20. Producer co-operatives and limited liability dominated the agenda of this influential meeting on 12 August 1862, which was attended by 'a few friends from Rochdale, Oldham, and Middleton', including William Marcroft, the founder of Sun Mill Cotton Spinning Company.
9. The Oldham 'limiteds' constituted the most important group of joint-stock *manufacturing* corporations in Britain and were responsible for 12% of the *world's* cotton spinning capacity in 1890; Farnie, 'The Emergence of Victorian Oldham'. The 'Oldham District' comprised a large area of south-east Lancashire (much of present day Greater Manchester) and included Rochdale to the north, Ashton to the south and Middleton to the west.
10. Industrial and Provident Societies Act 1862, 25 & 26, Vict., c. 87. Yonekawa, 'Public Cotton Spinning Companies', 64–5.
11. Gosden, *Self-help*, 194, 199–200.
12. Companies Act, 1862, Part III, s. 52 Vic. 25 & 26, Cap. 89.
13. Companies Act, 1862, Table A, first schedule, s. 44, Vic. 25 & 26, Cap. 89.
14. Companies Act, 1862, Table C, second schedule, s. 19, Vic. 25 & 26, Cap. 89.
15. Dunlavy, 'Corporate Governance', 32.
16. Ibid., 30–1.
17. For examples see Toms, 'The Rise of Modern Accounting', 68.
18. Toms, 'The Supply of and Demand for Accounting Information'; idem, 'The Rise of Modern Accounting'.
19. For example: *Depression of Trade and Industry: Second Report of the Royal Commission Appointed to Inquire into the Depression of Trade and Industry*, 1886 [C.4715].

20. Jensen and Meckling, 'Rights and Production Functions'; Ben-Ner, 'On the Stability of the Co-operative'.
21. Ibid., see particularly, 473, 477, 482–3.
22. See respectively, Dow, *Governing the Firm*; Pencavel, Pistaferri and Schivardi, 'Wages, Employment, and Capital'; Estrin and Jones, 'The Viability of Employee-owned Firms'.
23. Arando et al., 'Assessing Mondragon'.
24. For example in the case of private clubs, see Jensen and Meckling, 'Rights and Production Functions', 500.
25. Ibid., 484, 500.
26. Dreze, 'Some Theory of Labor Management'.
27. Jensen and Meckling, 'Rights and Production Functions', 487–8.
28. Dreze, 'Some Theory of Labor Management', 1134. The cotton spinning industry in the second half of the nineteenth century was characterised by increasing asset and product specialisation, see Kenney, 'Sub Regional Specialization'.
29. Jensen and Meckling, 'Rights and Production Functions', 500.
30. Other voting systems, including dual class rights and cumulative voting for directors, have disappeared altogether from some states of the USA and are found infrequently elsewhere. The egalitarian decision rule of one shareholder one vote was sometimes used in corporate decision making in the early nineteenth century, but has subsequently disappeared. Dunlavy, 'Corporate Governance'.
31. Marx, *Capital III*, 440; Engels, *Anti-Duhring*, 284–98.
32. Clark, 'Authority and Efficiency'; Bowles and Gintis, *Schooling in Capitalist America*.
33. Wood, 'The Statistics of Wages', 612–13; Tyson, 'The Cotton Industry', 123.
34. In the regular boom/recession cycle of the period 1870–90, there were mill promotion booms in 1873–75, 1883–84 and 1889–90. Farnie, *The English Cotton Industry*, 250–1.
35. Marglin, 'Knowledge and Power'.
36. Clark, 'Authority and Efficiency', 1079. See also Potter, *The Co-operative Movement in Great Britain*; Jones, *Co-operative Production*, 288.
37. Gurney, 'The Middle-class Embrace', 260.
38. Putterman, 'Some Behavioural Perspectives', 157.
39. Lazonick, 'Industrial Relations and Technical Change'.
40. Clark, 'Authority and Efficiency', 1072, 1077, 1082–3.
41. An exception is Jones, 'British Producer Co-operatives', which shows that survival rates for co-ops are better than private sector equivalents.
42. Cf. Clark, 'Authority and Efficiency', 1079 and Ellison, *The Cotton Trade*, 138.
43. 'The Rise and Progress of the Rochdale Limiteds', *Rochdale Observer* May 10, 1890.
44. 'The Co-operator', *Quarterly Review* 114, no. 228 (October 1863): 432–3.
45. William Cooper, *The Co-operator* 31 (September 1862): 70.
46. 'Old Pioneer', *The Co-operator* 32 (October 1862): 84–5; F. Wilson, *The Co-operator* 18 (15 October 1861): 86.
47. William Cooper, *The Co-operator* 31 (September 1862): 70.
48. Marcroft, *The Companies Circular* (self-published pamphlet, Oldham, 1879). Marcroft was also an advocate of maximising dividend payments. Redfern, *The Story of the CWS*, 20.
49. Sun Mill Archive, John Rylands Library, Minutes of Directors Meetings, SM/1/1, 10 September 1861 and *passim*, e.g. 3 May 1864.
50. Belgian, Shiloh and Thornham were typical companies with large numbers of working class shareholders. Respectively these companies had 639, 295 and 406 shareholders and average shareholdings of 22, 17 and 18 (PRO BT31/14469/7869, 14486/8310 and 14494/8449). Oldham Equitable Co-operative Society took up 200 shares the Equitable Spinning Company and 100 in the Glodwick and Thornham Spinning Companies, while placing £3000, £3000 and £1000 respectively on deposit with the loan accounts of each company. Toms, 'The Rise of Modern Accounting', 67–8 and Table 2; Taylor, *The Jubilee History of the Oldham Industrial Co-operative*, 75.
51. SM/1/1, 6 January 1863.
52. 'Diviborough', see Farnie, *The English Cotton Industry*, 263, and for comparisons of dividend rates of Oldham companies see Toms, 'Financial Constraints on Economic Growth' and idem, 'Finance and Growth'.

53. SM/1/1, 7 August 1869 and 10 July 1871.
54. Calculated as a percentage of called up share capital from the table in *Co-operative News*, 'The Sun Mill', November 23, 1872.
55. Jones, *Co-operative Production*, 289–91.
56. 'Croft Bank Spinning Company Limited', *Oldham Standard*, April 17, 1875. See also 'Northmoor Spinning Company', *Oldham Standard*, December 23, 1876.
57. 'The Shaw Spinning Company', *Oldham Standard*, January 4, 1879. See also, 'Commercial Mills Spinning Company Limited', *Oldham Standard*, December 18, 1880.
58. The 'Rochdale plan' of the original pioneers of the 1840s advocated quarterly meetings and barred proxy representation; Jones, *Co-operative Production*, 23. For details of financial disclosures, see Toms, 'The Rise of Modern Accounting'.
59. 'Higginshaw Mills and Spinning Company', *Oldham Standard*, December 25, 1875.
60. 'Commercial Mills Spinning Company Limited', *Oldham Standard*, December 15, 1877.
61. 'Higginshaw Spinning Company', *Oldham Standard*, March 18, 1893.
62. 'The Central Mill Company and the Master Cotton Spinners Association', *Oldham Standard*, October 9, 1875. Marcroft described the directors as servants of the shareholders who could 'bag' them if they do not do as they ought to. Thomason (in the chair) replied, 'we are your servants; but for that man (Marcroft) I would not work a minute; he is a tyrant. (Sensation).'
63. See respectively for examples: 'The Shaw Spinning Company', *Oldham Standard*, January 4, 1879, 'Manchester Trade Report', *Oldham Standard*, May 30, 1891, 'Oldham Share Market', *Oldham Standard*, February 14, 1891.
64. Gurney, 'The Middle-class Embrace', 259–60.
65. For example the Briggs colliery scheme, ibid., 259.
66. Bonner, *British Co-operation*, 106–7; Cole, *A Century of Co-operation*, 164–5; Redfern, *The Story of the CWS*, 104–5.
67. Bonner, *British Co-operation*, 107.
68. W. Cooper, *The Co-operator*, October 15, 1861.
69. E.V. Neale, 'The Division of Profits', *The Co-operator*, October 1861, 86–7. See also W.R. Lemon, *The Co-operator*, October 1862, 86.
70. Bonner, *British Co-operation*, 113.
71. Ibid., 114.
72. 'Joint Stockism at Oldham', *Co-operative News*, February 20, 1875.
73. 'Co-operative Manufacture', *Economist*, May 6, 1871. See also criticism of excess profits at Sun Mill and implied labour exploitation in the *Preston Guardian*, cited in *Co-operative News*, July 18, 1874.
74. R. Kyle, 'Hindrances to Co-operative Production', *Co-operative News*, May 6, 1876.
75. M. Ross, 'The Capital and Labour Question', *The Co-operator*, October 1862, 69–70.
76. *Oldham Standard*, July 10, 1875, 8. Call risk was problematic for investors of all classes, and there is evidence that in some districts of Lancashire, shares were deliberately sold by third parties to minors who were not liable for calls, thereby precipitating bankruptcy. See Bennett's account of the Whittlefield and Calder Vale Self-Help co-operatives, *History of Burnley, Vol. 4*, 100–1.
77. W. Nuttall, *Co-operative News*, November 23, 1872, 598.
78. For example at the Thornham shareholders' meeting, held at Royton Temperance Seminary, two shareholders (Whitehead and Clegg) questioned the board's cotton buying, and received the riposte from Tetlow, a director, that they represented 'some taproom party'; 'Thornham Cotton Spinning Company', *Oldham Standard*, June 21, 1884; 'The Shaw Spinning Company', *Oldham Standard*, January 4, 1879. A shareholder shouting: 'All the board should be reduced 10 per cent. The Chairman: No one ought to come to the meeting unless he is sober (Hear hear, throw him out &c.)'. See also Gosden, *Self-help*, 206, on the positive stance of the co-operative movement on the temperance issue.
79. W. Nuttall, 'The Sun Mill', *Co-operative News*, November 23, 1872.
80. W. Bunton, 'On Some Co-operative Speeches', *Co-operative News*, November 23, 1872.
81. 'More Echoes from the Mississippi Valley' and 'Joint Stockism at Oldham', *Co-operative News*, February 20, 1875.

82. Under the operation of the Gold Standard demand for Lancashire goods in silver using markets was linked with the gold/silver price relationship. For example see the press commentary on role of these factors in the slump of 1891–92: *Oldham Standard*, February 7, February 14, February 28, May 23, 1891, March 12, 1892.

83. For example at the Thornham Cotton Spinning Company shareholders' meeting, held at Royton Temperance Seminary, two shareholders (Whitehead and Clegg) questioned such interference, and received the riposte from Tetlow, a director, that they represented 'some taproom party', *Oldham Standard*, June 21, 1884. According to one concerned shareholder of Albany Cotton Spinning Company, rumour had it that representatives of the limited companies did their Liverpool business in minutes and spent the rest of the time having picnic parties at New Brighton; *Oldham Standard*, December 26, 1891.

84. Thomas, *The Provincial Stock Exchanges*, 149–51.

85. In 1877, 59 companies had shares of £5 each and a further 11 had shares of $=> £10$, *Co-operative News*, April 7, 1877.

86. *Royal Commission on the Depression of Trade and Industry*, minutes of evidence, 4336 and 4586, *CWS Annual* 1884, quoted in Ellison, *The Cotton Trade*, 138.

87. Smith, 'An Oldham Limited Liability Company'.

88. For example in 1874, 772 shareholders held an average of 18 (£4) shares each in the Moorfield Spinning Company (calculated from Smith, 'A History of the Lancashire Cotton Industry', 188). When the Dowry Spinning Company was floated 10 years later, 127 shareholders held an average of 94 (£2 10s) shares each (calculated from form E Summary of Capital and Shares 1884, Dowry Spinning Company, PRO BT31/37928/16753).

89. Farnie, *The English Cotton Industry*, 266.

90. For example the losses at the New Earth and Boundary Spinning Companies, *Oldham Standard*, July 17, 1891, August 22, 1891.

91. Ellison, *The Cotton Trade*, 138.

92. *Royal Commission on the Depression of Trade and Industry*, q. 5275.

93. Jones, *Co-operative Production*, 284–5.

94. *Textile Manufacturer*, February 1877, 62.

95. Ellison, *The Cotton Trade*, 138, emphasis added.

96. *Oldham Standard*, January 17, 1885.

97. See *Oldham Standard*, and *Oldham Chronicle*, all Saturday issues, c.1875–1900; for a specific example see the report on the Stock Lane Spinning Company, *Oldham Chronicle*, December 25, 1897.

98. Grossman, 'New Indices of British Equity Prices', Table 5.

99. Ibid.

100. For example Mitchell Hey, Sun Mill, Central, Oldham Twist, Green Lane, Royton.

101. *Co-operative News*, January 13, 1872.

102. Jones, *Co-operative Production*, 292–3. Green Lane shares were called up at their £50 nominal values and Oldham Twist used £20 shares; Oldham share list, *Oldham Standard*, various issues.

103. Respectively, National Archives Form E Summary of Capital and Shares, PRO BT31, 14485/8274 and 14486/8310.

104. Mill building companies typically used OSOV, whereas 'turnover' companies tended to use one share one vote, reflecting their conversion from previously private companies, most commonly in 1873; Yonekawa, 'Public Cotton Spinning Companies', 67. Some companies, for example Grimshaw Lane Cotton Spinning Company, used a show of hands, and for this reason was classified as OSOV but members could under certain conditions force a ballot in which case a one share one vote ballot was used; National Archives, Articles of Association s. 74, BT31/14485/8274. In 1874, the company had 28 shareholders with an average holding of 16 shares with the largest shareholding of 40 shares (8.8% of the total), so ballots would have made little practical difference.

105. LD standard deviation = 3.05%; HD = 2.81%; pre-1886, LD = 3.26%, HD = 2.32%.

106. At the inauguration of the new Industry mill in 1875, the mill engine was christened the 'Oldham', as a tribute to the 3.375 million spindles now controlled by the working class of Oldham; *Textile Manufacturer*, June 1877, 180.

107. Toms 'The Rise of Modern Accounting'; idem, 'Information Content'.

108. Industry agreed wage lists negotiated by industry federation and trade unions became the norm from the mid-1880s onwards; Huberman, *Escape from the Market*, 136–9.
109. *Royal Commission on Labour*, Group C, Textiles (1892) qq. 190–3. Trade union leaders argued against the appropriation of profits by operatives, partly because it encouraged competition on the shop floor and created jealously and monitoring difficulties (evidence of William Mullin). See also evidence cited by Gurney, 'The Middle-class Embrace', 262, on trade union antagonism towards profit sharing and co-operators.
110. 'Is the Cotton Trade Leaving the Country?', *Textile Mercury*, January 21, 1893, 43. See also Figure 1.
111. A survey in the *Oldham Standard*, December 29, 1894 showed that the Belgian, Gladstone, Hope and Werneth Cotton Spinning Companies had adverse balances greater than £20,000 (the average subscribed equity capital per company in 1885 was £38,200 (calculated from the appendix data in Smith, 'An Oldham Limited Liability Company', 52–3). From a list of average profits per company for the last 10 years (*Oldham Standard*, ibid.), the average profit per company per year was £993 (based on 980 company/years).
112. Toms 'The Rise of Modern Accounting'; idem, 'Information Content'.
113. *Royal Commission on the Depression of Trade and Industry*, qq. 5041, 5117.
114. One firm of accountants promoted 12 mills in the period 1899–1914; Jones, 'The Cotton Spinning Industry', 13.
115. For examples, inter alia, see *Oldham Standard*, November 27, 1897, October 1, October 8, November 5, 1898.
116. S. 60. Order of the Board of Trade, substituting a new Table A for that contained in the first schedule to the Companies Act 1862, s. r. & o. 1906 no. 5961.15; July 30, 1906; http://www.companieshouse.gov.uk/about/tableA/comm1Oct06orderoftheboardoftrade 30July1906_P1.pdf.
117. Toms, 'Windows of Opportunity in the Textile Industry'; idem, 'The Supply of and Demand for Accounting Information'. In the longer run, these changes caused a mis-allocation of capital that undermined the international competitiveness of the industry from 1914 onwards; Toms, 'Growth, Profits and Technological Choice'; idem, 'The English Cotton Industry', 70–3; Higgins and Toms, 'Firm Structure and Financial Performance'.
118. Gosden, *Self-help*, 197–8; Bonner, *British Co-operation*, 106.

## Notes on contributor

Steven Toms is Professor of Accounting at the Leeds University Business School, University of Leeds.

## References

Arando, S., F. Freundlich, M. Gago, D.C. Jones, and T. Kato. 'Assessing Mondragon: Stability and Managed Change in the Face of Globalization'. William Davidson Institute Working Paper No. 1003, November 2010.

Ben-Ner, A. 'On the Stability of the Co-operative Type of Organization'. *Journal of Comparative Economics* 8 September (1984): 247–60.

Bennett, W. *History of Burnley, Vol. 4*. Burnley: Burnley Corporation, 1951.

Bonner, A. *British Co-operation: The History, Principles and Organisation of the British Co-operative Movement*. Manchester: Co-operative Union, 1961.

Bowles, S., and H. Gintis. *Schooling in Capitalist America*. New York: Basic Books, 1976.

Clark, G. 'Authority and Efficiency: The Labor Market and the Managerial Revolution of the Late Nineteenth Century'. *Journal of Economic History* 44, no. 4 (1984): 1069–83.

Cole, G.D.H. *A Century of Co-operation*. Oxford: Allen and Unwin, 1944.

Dow, G. *Governing the Firm: Workers Control in Theory and Practice*. Cambridge: Cambridge University Press, 2003.

Dreze, J.H. 'Some Theory of Labor Management and Participation'. *Econometrica* 44, no. 6 (1976): 1125–39.

Dunlavy, C. 'Corporate Governance in Late Nineteenth Century Europe and the U.S.: The Case of Shareholder Voting Rights'. In *Comparative Corporate Governance: The State of the Art and Emerging Research*, ed. K. Hopt, H. Kanda, M. Roe, E. Wymeersch and S. Prigge, 5–39. Oxford: Clarendon Press, 1998.

Ellison, T. *The Cotton Trade of Great Britain*. London: Frank Cass, 1886; reprinted 1968.

Engels, F. *Anti-Duhring*. London: Lawrence and Wishart, 1987.

Estrin, S., and D.C. Jones. 'The Viability of Employee-owned Firms: Evidence from France'. *Industrial and Labor Relations Review* 45, no. 2 (January 1992): 323–38.

Farnie, D. *The English Cotton Industry and the World Market, 1815–1896*. Oxford: Clarendon, 1979.

Farnie, D. 'The Emergence of Victorian Oldham as the Centre of the Cotton Spinning Industry'. *Saddleworth Historical Society Bulletin* 12 (1982): 41–53.

Gosden, P.H.J.H. *Self-help: Voluntary Associations in the 19th Century*. London: Batsford, 1973.

Grossman, R.S. 'New Indices of British Equity Prices, 1870–1913'. *Journal of Economic History* 62 (2002): 121–46.

Gurney, P. 'The Middle-class Embrace: Language, Representation, and the Contest over Co-operative Forms in Britain, c. 1860–1914'. *Victorian Studies* 37, no. 2 (1994): 253–86.

Higgins, D.M., and S. Toms. 'Firm Structure and Financial Performance: The Lancashire Textile Industry, c.1884–1960'. *Accounting Business and Financial History* 7, no. 2 (1997): 195–232.

Huberman, M. *Escape from the Market: Negotiating Work in Lancashire*. Cambridge: Cambridge University Press, 1996.

Jensen, M., and W. Meckling. 'Rights and Production Functions: An Application to Labor Managed Firms and Co-determination'. *Journal of Business* 52, no. 41 (1979): 469–506.

Jones, B. *Co-operative Production*. Oxford: Clarendon, 1894; Cass reprint, 1968.

Jones, D.C. 'British Producer Cooperatives and the Views of the Webbs on Participation and Ability to Survive'. *Annals of Public and Cooperative Economics* 46, no. 1 (1975): 23–44.

Jones, F. 'The Cotton Spinning Industry in the Oldham District from 1896–1914'. M.A. thesis, University of Manchester, 1959.

Kenney, S. 'Sub Regional Specialization in the Lancashire Cotton Industry, 1884–1914: A Study in Organizational and Locational Change'. *Journal of Historical Geography* 8, no. 1 (1982): 41–63.

Lazonick, W. 'Industrial Relations and Technical Change: The Case of the Self Acting Mule'. *Cambridge Journal of Economics* 3 (1979): 231–62.

Marglin, S. 'Knowledge and Power'. In *Firms, Organization and Labour: Approaches to the Economics of Work Organization*, ed. F.H. Stephen, 146–64. London: Macmillan, 1984.

Marx, K. *Capital III*. London: Lawrence and Wishart, 1984.

Pencavel, J., L. Pistaferri, and F. Schivardi. 'Wages, Employment, and Capital in Capitalist and Worker-owned Firms'. *Industrial and Labor Relations Review* 60, no. 1 (October 2006): 23–44.

Potter, B. *The Co-operative Movement in Great Britain*. London: George Allen and Unwin, 1891; reprinted 1930.

Purvis, M. 'Stocking the Store: Co-operative Retailers in North-east England and Systems of Wholesale Supply, *circa* 1860–77'. *Business History* 40, no. 4 (1998): 55–78.

Putterman, L. 'Some Behavioural Perspectives on the Dominance of Hierarchical over Democratic Forms of Enterprise'. *Journal of Economic Behavior & Organization* 3, no. 2–3 (1982): 139–60.

Redfern, P. *The Story of the CWS, Being the Jubilee History of the Co-operative Wholesale Society Limited, 1863–1913*. Manchester: CWS, 1913.

Smith, R. 'A History of the Lancashire Cotton Industry between the Years 1873 and 1896'. PhD thesis, University of Birmingham, 1954.

Smith, R. 'An Oldham Limited Liability Company, 1875–1896'. *Business History* 4, no. 2 (1961): 34–53.

Taylor, J.C. *The Jubilee History of the Oldham Industrial Co-operative Society Limited*. Manchester: CWS, 1900.

Thomas, W. *The Provincial Stock Exchanges*. London: Frank Cass and Co., 1973.

Toms, S. 'Financial Constraints on Economic Growth: Profits, Capital Accumulation and the Development of the Lancashire Cotton-spinning Industry, 1885–1914'. *Accounting, Business and Financial History* 4, no. 3 (1994): 363–83.

Toms, S. 'The Finance and Growth of the Lancashire Cotton Textile Industry, 1870–1914'. PhD thesis, University of Nottingham, 1996.

Toms, S. 'Windows of Opportunity in the Textile Industry: The Business Strategies of Lancashire Entrepreneurs 1880–1914'. *Business History* 40, no. 1 (1998): 1–25.

Toms, S. 'The Supply of and Demand for Accounting Information in an Unregulated Market: Examples from the Lancashire Cotton Mills'. *Accounting Organizations and Society* 23, no. 2 (1998): 217–38.

Toms, S. 'Growth, Profits and Technological Choice: The Case of the Lancashire Cotton Textile Industry'. *Journal of Industrial History* 1, no. 1 (1998): 35–55.

Toms, S. 'Information Content of Earnings Announcements in an Unregulated Market: The Co-operative Cotton Mills of Lancashire, 1880–1900'. *Accounting and Business Research* 31, no. 3 (2001): 175–90.

Toms, S. 'The Rise of Modern Accounting and the Fall of the Public Company: The Lancashire Cotton Mills, 1870–1914'. *Accounting Organizations and Society* 27, no. 1/2 (2002): 61–84.

Toms, S. 'The English Cotton Industry and the Loss of the World Market'. In *King Cotton: A Tribute to Douglas Farnie*, ed. J.F. Wilson, 64–82. Manchester: Crucible, 2009.

Tyson, R. 'The Cotton Industry'. In *The Development of British Industry and Foreign Competition, 1875–1914*, ed. D.H. Aldcroft. London: George Allen, 1968.

Wood, G. 'The Statistics of Wages in the Nineteenth Century Cotton Industry'. *Journal of the Royal Statistical Society* LXXIII (1910): 585–626.

Yonekawa, S. 'Public Cotton Spinning Companies and Their Managerial Characteristics, 1870–1890: A Comparative Study of Four Countries'. *Hitotsubashi Journal of Commerce and Management* 21 (1986): 61–90.

# Financial constraints on economic growth: profits, capital accumulation and the development of the Lancashire cotton-spinning industry, 1885–1914

John Steven Toms

## Abstract

Recent debates concerning the development of Lancashire cotton textiles to 1914 are addressed with reference to evidence from individual companies and a subsection of the industry. The industry is found to be relatively profitable and the investment decisions of entrepreneurs to be sensible in relation to profit indicators. Significantl , capital accumulation increasingly became a matter of individual priority rather than corporate strategy and the industry failed to concentrate in line with emerging overseas competition. The ultimate failure of the industry lay in its inability to adopt corporate structures capable of sustaining future growth and development.

## Introduction

Recent debates on the development of the Lancashire textile industry in the three decades before the First World War have concentrated on the investment decisions of entrepreneurs. As a class, entrepreneurs have been judged successful within certain structural constraints (Sandberg, 1974) and unsuccessful for failing to remove those constraints (Mass and Lazonick, 1990).[1] The controversy can be traced to quantitative analyses at the industry level with their attempts to rehabilitate the Victorian entrepreneur, (Sandberg, 1974) which in their turn were reactions to the debate on entrepreneurial failure initiated in the 1960s (Aldcroft, 1964). Participants in the debate have tended to rely on similar bodies of evidence, such as measures of output, quality growth and the marginal profitability of investment decisions (Sandberg, 1974), on world market share (Lazonick and Mass, 1984: 5–13), and estimates of efficien y based on measures of factor input in relation to output (Jones, 1933: 100–19; Phelps Brown and Handfield-Jones, 1952)

Such analyses of quantitative evidence form part of a literature which, although alive with controversy, has not dwelt heavily on case studies of individual organizations to inform its debates, an exception being Smith (1962). The investment decisions analysed in studies to date have dealt with the availability of different technologies and the constraints associated with those decisions, for example in the rings and mules alternative in the spinning section of the industry, and in the plain versus automatic looms alternatives in weaving.

The evidence is clear on attachments to traditional technologies, and the first section of this article examines the profitability of investment in traditional spinning technology from the standpoints of two different individual companies as compared with the general profitability of a significant sub-section of the industry. Conclusions on the investment behaviour of entrepreneurs are then drawn.

Another way to judge the pattern of entrepreneurial behaviour, and the institutional constraints thereon, is to consider the question of divestment as well as investment. The evidence on how the profits from Lancashire textiles were actually spent suggests some interesting conclusions on strategy and structure within the industry. The second part of the article will examine the evidence in this area.

The evidence upon which much of the following discussion is based was drawn from the surviving business and published records of spinning firms of south-east Lancashire. Companies in the Oldham district had a unique propensity to report their results to the general public, and the surviving copies of local, and to a lesser extent national, newspapers and journals form a valuable source of financial data.[2] Reliance upon these records limits the scope of this study to the 'Oldham District', consisting of Oldham itself, Rochdale and Ashton under Lyne. The district accounted for a significant proportion of the cotton-spinning industry of Britain (26 per cent) and of the world (12 per cent) in 1890 (Farnie, 1982: 42). With minor exceptions, the spinning of coarse to medium counts predominated during the period under consideration.

To complement the analysis from a micro perspective, archival material was also integrated into the study. Detailed records of internal company meetings and financial statements are important if the behaviour of managers is to be assessed adequately and the bias associated with publicly disclosed press information avoided. The survival of internal company records is, however, problematic and the evidence used was necessarily more selective, concentrating on the policies of two companies.[3] Conclusions based purely upon evidence from such a restricted number of cases must necessarily be tentative, and it is important that it is assessed in the wider context of the industry as a whole.

**Profitability of Lancashire firms**

Based on the above mentioned data sources, there follows an examination of the financial performance of the cotton-spinning industry in the Oldham area (hereafter 'the industry')· A comparison is then drawn with the cases of two individual firms from that area: Werneth Cotton Spinning Company Limited and Osborne Cotton Spinning Company Limited (hereafter 'Werneth' and 'Osborne').

*The industry as a whole*

Controversies surrounding the performance of the cotton industry to date have typically been based on the quantitative performance indicators already noted. Despite the intensity of the debates, the return on capital employed (ROCE) as an industry performance indicator has been largely neglected. This is surprising, since the rate of return on capital would have sent strong signals to entrepreneurs responsible for making the controversial investment decisions, and there is evidence it was used extensively by decision makers in the period under review.[4] If the rate of return from investment in existing technology was satisfactory, entrepreneurs could hardly be blamed for continuing to invest in such technology. For the purposes of the current investigation, the signalling function of the rate of return is analysed primarily for its likely impact on entrepreneurial behaviour and is defined as the percentage profit before interest to permanently invested loan and share capital as published in contemporary sources.[5]

Neglect of return on capital employed in the literature to date is also surprising given the availability of data from which an index can be constructed, at least for the spinning section of the industry.[6] The value of such a measure has been acknowledged in the construction of economic methods of performance measurement for the industry such as Total Factor Productivity (Lazonick and Mass, 1984: 33) and 'real cost' indices (Jones, 1933). Return on capital employed in conjunction with data on net output is of specific use for this approach. Yet, despite these criticisms, previous studies have ignored the available data.

Other measures of profit and profitability have been used in earlier work (Robson, 1957; Campion, 1934). However these either deal only in absolute measures or fail to relate the profits of the industry fully to the scale of capital investment responsible for their creation. Without such data, it is difficult to draw conclusions on the behaviour of management within the industry and their investment decisions, together with investment decisions made by external individuals and institutions. Our understanding of these issues is thus likely to benefit from the construction of a return to capital series. Figure 1 shows the return to capital for the two case- study firms and for the cotton-spinning industry for south-east Lancashire as a whole.[7]

The hypothesis of increasing returns and, with increasingly violent fluctuations in profits, increasing risk is suggested by the figures. Risk was high from an investor's point of view, the industry being very vulnerable to the trade cycle. The impact of the 1904–7 boom was particularly pronounced, and the industry clearly outperformed the previous peaks of 1890 and 1900. Given the orientation of the average producer to the manufacture of undiversified goods, such vulnerability to the trade cycle was partly to be expected. Table 1 shows the average return on capital and the standard deviation of the return in three periods. To control for trade-cycle effects, the returns were calculated as between respective troughs.

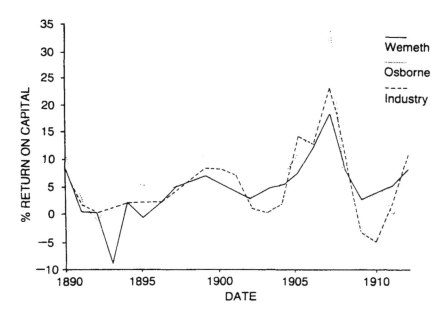

Figure 1.   Return on capital employed, 1890–1912
*Sources:* Werneth: Directors' Quarterly Reports to Members, OLSL, Misc/42/17 and 18; Osborne: Trade, capital and profit and loss accounts, LC O, DDX/869/3/1. Industry: calculated from various published sources (see notes 2, 6 and 7).

Table 1.  The rising trend of return to capital, 1886–1910

|  | Av. ROCE | Std. Dev. |
|---|---|---|
| 1886–1892 | 3.85 | 2.46 |
| 1893–1903 | 3.92 | 2.89 |
| 1904–1910 | 7.89 | 9.53 |

*Sources*: As for Figure 1.

As can be seen from Table 1, the history of profitability in the industry fell into distinct periods. The 1890s characteristically were years of low return and low risk. During this period the rate of profit was scarcely above the average official London discount rate (Williams, 1912). In the period immediately preceding the First World War, by contrast, the risks to investors were greater, but the premium over the risk-free rate was commensurately higher. In the context of recent debates, the rising trend is significant. The apparent improvement contrasts with the general consensus hitherto of no overall improvement in the performance of the industry during this period (Jones, 1933; Phelps Brown and Handfield-Jones, 1952). The explanation may lie in the treatment of profit in earlier surveys. For example Jones's real cost index assumes a constant 'normal' rate of profit throughout the period considered. This is in spite of the dramatic fluctuations caused by the trade cycle. It has been demonstrated that efficien y gains measured by the real cost index and the profitability of the industry were inversely related and the method thereby fl wed (Sandberg, 1974). Rising returns on capital noted here may also therefore suggest increasing returns to scale.

One important source of external economies of scale arose from access to cheap sources of finance. Local interest rates tended to be above the London discount rate, but at a typical rate of 4 to 5 per cent were lower than the average rate of profit on total capital invested. The high dependence on loan finance meant the return on share capital increased to an even greater extent than the return on total capital during a boom. For example, whereas the ROCE for 1907 was 23.6 per cent (per Figure 1), the return on the share capital employed was 35.2 per cent (Campion, 1934: 627). Conversely, recessions accentuated losses, but the general effect was beneficial g ven the underlying positive trend in ROCE.

Labour productivity figures tend to confirm the rising efficien y hypothesis. On the output per operative basis steep increases in productivity occurred during the upswing of the trade cycle, as acknowledged by Sandberg (1974: 97). For example in the upswing years of 1904–7, based on the figures of Phelps Brown and Handfield-Jones (1952: 294–7), there was a steep apparent annual average increase of 5.8 per cent. This can be confirmed from the figures presented by Lazonick and Mass (1984: 40), which show a 10.2 per cent increase during these years on the basis of their single year output data and 5.3 per cent when calculated on the basis of three-year average output. Corresponding falls occurred in the troughs of recessions, but over a longer period the increase in productivity is still apparent. Using the Lazonick and Mass data (1984: 40), productivity still shows an increase of 4 per cent between 1901 and 1912.[8] The use of labour productivity evidence from this period to prove stagnation in the industry is thus questionable, particularly given that the denominator in output per operative calculations is based on intermittent census data (Lazonick and Mass, 1984: 40). Indeed, when used in conjunction with return to capital the opposite conclusion may be drawn; that in the last uninterrupted boom before the decisive discontinuity of 1914, there was the highest level of investment and the largest increase in productivity recorded since the 1870s.

Output in relation to labour input, however measured, gives only one restricted view. The ROCE statistics allow a wider triangulation of the evidence on performance and there is evidence of more widely available economies of scale than the employment of labour. These have been discussed elsewhere (Farnie, 1979: 213–15, 244–51), and are confirmed by the statistics in Table 1.

*Individual companies: Werneth and Osborne Spinning Companies*

The above patterns of ROCE were replicated for individual companies within the industry. Werneth was in some ways typical of the industry as a whole. Originally floated in 1874, by 1890 it was owned and controlled by a diverse shareholder grouping, a pattern typical of companies floated in the Oldham area in the period 1870–90. In 1890, there were 451 shareholders with an average holding of fifty-three shares each (OLSL, Misc.42/17). It was a relatively large company compared to its neighbours and direct competitors, being slightly above the 85,000-spindle median observed at this time (Chapman and Ashton, 1914: 478). In 1884 the company had just less than 100,000 spindles with a book value of approximately £1 each and called up share capital of £72,000 (Smith, 1962: 53). The strategy of the company appears to have been to extend capacity at phased intervals in response to increases in demand for its product. The construction of a new mill was authorized in September 1890 by shareholder vote (OLSL, Misc/42/17) and evidence from company documents suggests the No. 2 mill was actually built in 1892–3 (OLSL, Misc/42/17). Extensions were added in 1904 and 1910 (Gurr and Hunt, 1985: 54).

Analysis of the trends in Figure 1 reveals a tendency for the company to under-perform against the industry in the earlier years and to outperform it in later years. The year 1893 was particularly disastrous, with the subsequent decade marking a gradual recovery. Along with most of the industry, Werneth suffered a nineteen-week closure during the 'Brook-lands' dispute in the early part of 1893 (OLSL, Misc./42/17). Problems were compounded later in the year following the perpetration of a major fraud against the company. The profit and loss account for the quarter ended 31 October 1893 showed an amount of £14,557 written off as a result of the fraud (OLSL, Misc./42/17). The manager, a Mr G. Ashton, was prosecuted on the active intervention of the shareholders for falsifying the books, but there is no evidence that any of the loss was recovered (OLSL, Misc./42/2, 28 November 1893). There was a strong recovery from the weak position of the 1890s and the effects of the trade cycle were less pronounced for the company than for the industry as a whole in the later years. The likely reason was that the company had expanded capacity by building the second mill. Size, and an expanded product range, would have constituted a useful hedge against the effects of the trade cycle, fire hazards and breakdown (Jones, 1959: 91). The investment in the second mill proved particularly worthwhile when No. 1 mill was destroyed by fire in 1899 and not reconstituted for the production of Egyptian yarns until 1901 (Hunt and Gurr, 1985: 54). As can be seen in Figure 1, the dampening effect on profit in that year was negligible, No. 2 mill presumably providing some reserve capacity for orders.

In contrast to Werneth, Osborne was a smaller and more narrowly controlled organization. Floated in 1889 to take over the running of a mill originally established in 1853 (Hunt and Gurr, 1985: 43), it was completely refitted with 45,000 Platt Brothers mule spindles

(LCRO, DDX/869/9/1). It was thus about half the average size for mills of this time. It remained under the control of the small group of promoters and directors, and, unlike Werneth, did not issue its shares to the local public. These individuals were perhaps wealthier than the average Werneth shareholder, requiring a down payment of £5 for each £100 share in contrast to 3/6d for each £5 share. Its strategy was to spin a range of counts with a bias towards higher quality Egyptian cotton at 60s and 70s counts (LCRO, DDX/869/9/1). It was a successful strategy, and Osborne out-performed both the industry and the larger Werneth company in terms of return on capital.

The policy of the Osborne management suggests that increasing returns to scale were not the only way to secure profits for Lancashire entrepreneurs. Specialization in the higher quality market on the basis of a small capital commitment produced relatively high profits. Apart from one minor refit, the directors made no significant investment in new equipment. As a result, the capital employed declined through the repayment of loan finance and the depreciation of fi ed assets throughout the period (LCRO, DDX/869/3/1). The variability of ROCE for Osborne compared to Werneth and the industry as a whole is partly explained by the very low capital denominator exaggerating the impact of fluctuations in absolute profit and loss. There is thus some evidence here of Lancashire entrepreneurs doing what they have often been accused of, continuing to run machinery long after it was written off for accounting purposes and resisting pressure to scrap and replace machinery in existing mills (Ryan, 1930). Osborne made good profits which could have been used to finance new investment, for example in ring spindles. The evidence suggests its management deliberately chose not to so invest, and not that they were constrained from doing so through lack of finance. Credence is thus given to the view of Saxon- house and Wright (1987), albeit from a financial, rather than industry structural, point of vi w.

The above-mentioned absence of investment in new technology was a feature of most of the industry. The proportion of ring spindles to total spindles in the Oldham area was 2.9 per cent in 1896, 5.8 per cent in 1905 and 9.3 per cent in 1914 (Jones, 1959: 5). Table 2 shows that the benefits of ring spinning were far from obvious in the whole period. If there was an opportunity it was in the 1890s when the relative lack of new investment meant existing machines were run at higher levels of capacity utilization. In the 1900s, when investment did occur in both types of technology and extra capacity was created, the advantages of ring spinning were less obvious in financial terms as high levels of capacity utilization were more difficult to guarantee. Figure 1 suggests the impact of the trade cycle was much more pronounced in the 1900s, and such guarantees were even more elusive as a result, despite the higher average returns available.

The final influence which may have confirmed the rationality of investment behaviour was the adequacy of rates of return *vis-à-vis* those available in the wider textile industry and in the economy as a whole. In the late 1890s there was a series of amalgamations leading to the creation of large horizontally integrated firms mainly in the finishing section. Being much larger than the typical Oldham company, these organizations might have been expected to produce higher rates of return. However, a contemporary observer noted that many of these concerns, for example the Fine Cotton Spinners' and Doublers' Association and the Calico Printers' Association, failed to produce the returns that might have been expected, given their size (Macrosty, 1907: 139–40,147–8). For another Association, the Bleachers', the return to capital averaged 5.39 per cent for the period 1903–14.[9] For returns available in the economy as a whole, Table 2 illustrates that an investment split equally between British equities and risk-free loan stocks would have yielded substantially less than in cotton-spinning companies which tended to depend on loan and equity finance in roughly the same proportions.[10]

Table 2. Example rates of return for different types of investment activity, 1890–1912

*(1) Company and industry returns*

| | Rate of return | | | Industry capacity utilization average % |
|---|---|---|---|---|
| | *Werneth* | *Osborne* | *Industry* | |
| Whole period | 4.75 | 6.84 | 5.25 | 78.6 |
| 1890–1899 | 2.09 | 5.74 | 3.60 | 82.2 |
| 1900–1912 | 6.80 | 7.70 | 6.51 | 76.0 |

*(2) Returns from replacement of mules by rings (for 10s yarns)*

| *Capacity utilization* | *Percentage return* |
|---|---|
| 90% | 10.3 |
| 75% | 8.0 |
| 50% | 3.3 |

*(3) Average return to an investor in the British economy as a whole, 1887–1914*

| | *Percentage* |
|---|---|
| Equity return | 4.88 |
| Risk free return | 2.97 |
| Average | 3.92 |

*Sources*: (1) Returns, as for Figure 1. Capacity utilization calculated from cotton consumed per spindle (Mitchell and Jones, 1971: 179, 186), and standardizing the series at 70 per cent capacity utilization for 1904, as noted in Sandberg (1974: 63). (2) Sandberg (1974: 50–7). (3) Calculated from Edelstein (1981: 79).

## Patterns of divestment in Lancashire textiles

Secular trends of increasing ROCE and increasing returns to scale have been identified. This section addresses two issues: the extent to which the rate of profit was matched by the rate of growth of individual companies and the industry, and how the cash from trading surpluses was actually spent. These issues are related since a rate of profit well above the rate of capital accumulation would be evidence of significant divestment: a phenomenon which may have influenced the development of the industry and the economy as a whole if divested cash was used unproductively. There follows an analysis of the pattern of divestment by reference to the relationship between the ownership and management groups as measured by propensities and pressures for profits to be paid out as dividends. The general approach suggested here is based on agency theory, which has gained wide recognition in contemporary financial and economics literature, for example, Jensen and Meckling (1976). Similarly well-established historical analysis presupposed the ownership/control split, for example, Chandler (1977). The difference in the current approach is the proposal of a financial agency variable, dividend policy, to explain the historical and institutional evolution of the relationship.

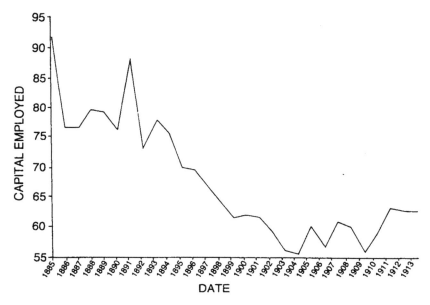

Figure 2.   Average capital employed per company, 1885–1913
*Sources:* see notes 2, 6 and 7.

*Growth and profit patterns: evidence*

The pattern of growth demonstrates some surprising characteristics; in particular, a trend towards the divestment of capital from existing concerns. Figure 2 shows the average capital employed in those companies publishing balance sheets and hence appearing in the *Economist* sample. Some distortions would result from yearly differences in those companies publishing balance sheets, but the general trend shows a decline to 1900 and a plateau in the ensuing years.

The statistics suggest a very significant hypothesis: that corporate saving, at a time when overseas competitors were developing large organization structures under corporate umbrellas, was absent from the leading export sector in the British economy. However, Figure 2 is at variance with other evidence pointing to a general growth trend and this must be considered before such an argument can be developed. Table 3 shows the growth rate of different sections of the textile industry in terms of spindleage compared to growth in terms of capital for a selection of companies.

The trend suggested in Figure 2 is confirmed by the record of capital growth for the two Oldham companies considered. There is, however, a contrast with the industry as a whole, which was growing in spindleage terms, and some companies in other cotton textile sectors and the wider economy, which were growing through the accumulation of capital. Some of the growth noted in Table 3 would have been as a result of the 1904–7 boom in the construction of new mills and the installation of new capacity. The number of spindles installed in Lancashire increased from 46m in 1905 to 55.3m in 1908 (Robson, 1957: 340), and in the Oldham area forty mills were floated in 1905, twenty-three in 1906 and thirty-nine in 1907 (Thomas, 1973: 154). A likely positive relationship between rates of return and investment decisions can thus be inferred. The data published in the Economist, upon which the

Table 3.   Fixed asset and capital growth in the textile industry

*(1) Growth in spindleage (compound growth rates, per cent per annum, 1884–1911)*

| | |
|---|---|
| Spinning firms, Oldham are | 2.29 |
| Cotton-spinning industry (excluding Oldham) | 1.03 |

*(2) Growth in capital: selected companies (compound growth rates)*

| | *Period* | *Growth per annum %* | |
|---|---|---|---|
| Osborne | 1896–1914 | –2.9 | Small Oldham spinning company |
| Werneth | 1889–1912 | 0.3 | Large Oldham spinning company |
| Fielden | 1880–1914 | nil | Large textile spinners, weavers and merchants |
| John Rylands | 1880–1914 | 0.59 | Large textile merchants and manufacturers |
| Horrocks | 1887–1914 | 2.78 | Large textile spinners, weavers and merchants |
| Whiteley | 1898–1914 | 2.87 | Small textile spinner and manufacturer |
| T.R. Eccles Ltd | 1897–1914 | 1.37 | Small textile manufacturer |

*(3) Economy as a whole (rate of growth of manufacturing and commercial capital)*

| | |
|---|---|
| *1882–1914* | *2.38%* |

*Sources*: (1) Calculated from Chapman and Ashton (1914). (2) Osborne, Trade, capital and profit and loss accounts LCRO DDX/869/3/1; Werneth, Directors' reports to members, OLSL Misc./42/17 and 18; John Rylands, Farnie (1993: 72); Fielden, Chapman (1992: 317–18); Horrocks, Balance sheets, 1890–1919, LCRO, DDHs/53; Whiteley, Balance sheets, LCRO, DDX/868/21/5; T.R. Eccles Ltd, Trading accounts, profit and loss accounts and balance sheets, 1897–1931, LCRO, DDX/7/1. (3) Calculated as a compound growth rate from Feinstein (1975: 194).

index of capital in Figure 2 depends, were derived from those companies publishing balance sheets. It is likely that these companies tended to be established rather than new companies. Significantl , many of the new companies floated in the 1904–7 boom tended to be private, showing a reluctance to disclose financial data to the public, presumably including the *Economist*. These newer companies would have accounted for a significant proportion of the new capital invested in the industry, but were excluded from the *Economist* samples. The trends in Figure 2 do not therefore give a fully representative view of the industry as a whole.[11] However, Table 3 tends to confirm that growth in capital accumulation was below potential growth suggested by the rate of profit in the industry as highlighted in Table 1. Capital therefore must have left the industry during this period in preference to reinvestment. The question thus remains as to why entrepreneurs in some established companies took the seemingly irrational decision to allow their capital bases to decline at a time of apparent optimism and expansion, while others chose not to reinvest available surpluses fully back into profitable concerns. The divestment pattern can be traced through the regular dividend payments made to shareholders and to a series of capital restructurings.

*Dividend behaviour*

As a matter of general policy for the companies considered, profits were paid as dividends to shareholders rather than reinvested for growth. High dividends can be confirmed by reference to the absence of accumulated profits. For the industry as a whole in the period 1902–11, credit balances on shareholders' reserves averaged 11 per cent of total capital invested, the trend following the trade cycle with no secular increase.[12] In 1912, total accumulated reserves for the whole British textile industry were only £8m (Cairncross, 1953: 98). Assuming capital was divided equally between spinning and the rest of the industry, accumulated reserves were 1s 3d per spindle. This compares with a ratio of 14s 6d of total capital employed per spindle as calculated based on figures per the *Economist* and Mitchell and Jones (1971: 186). Accumulated reserves thus represented only 8.6 per cent of total capital employed. Table 4 shows the average percentage of available profits paid out as dividend by Osborne, Werneth, and those firms in the industry as a whole regularly included in the *Economist*.

Documentary evidence supports the immediate conclusions drawn from the statistical analysis. There was a local perception that the companies existed primarily for the purpose of paying dividends and nothing more, earning Oldham the nickname of 'Diviborough' (Farnie, 1979: 263). Blatant examples of this were well publicized and attracted critical comment from contemporary observers. A correspondent to the *Oldham Chronicle* wrote (4 April 1887):

> I thought all limited companies had at last got a lesson for life. I was wrong. Evidently they will not learn. Leesbrook declares thirty per cent, dividend. To do so now seems to be insanity. If they *show* thirty per cent, when their mill is brand new, and weft exceptionally good, why not *pay* 10 per cent, and depreciate the rest? By declaring 30 per cent they deceive the public and, I think, themselves, for at their start they are going into the old error of not depreciating enough and paying away every available farthing in dividend. Every shareholder should surely know by now that depreciating more, and dividing less, makes any concern richer.

Another aspect of this trend, which tended to accentuate further the haemorrhaging of capital from established companies, was a series of capital reductions, repayments and reconstructions. The companies featured in the *Economist* sample repaid £1.38m outstanding loan capital in the period 1893–1907. So much money was made in the boom of 1907 by the existing mills that shareholders benefited from a bonanza of divested funds. Record dividends were to be expected during a record boom and the boom was far more pronounced in textiles than the rest of the economy (Jones, 1959: 10–11).

Table 4. Percentage of available profits paid as dividends

|  | % of profit |
|---|---|
| Osborne | 95.5 |
| Werneth | 73.0 |
| Industry | 94.0 |

*Sources*: As for Figure 1.

Paradoxically, record profit also signalled a wave of capital reductions throughout the limited liability sector. Capital was repaid in large bonus dividends, and a series of conversions to private companies were made. Thus Windsor Mill Spinning Company Ltd and Oldham Twist Co. Ltd were granted permission by the court to reduce capital in 1907, and Moorfield made a repayment to its shareholders of £1 per £5 share.[13] Werneth made a series of capital reductions. The first, in 1899, allowed the large debit balance on reserve arising from fraud and poor trading to be written off against share capital. Further reductions in 1908 and 1912 were responses to large profits and constituted straight cash repayments to shareholders, making up for the low dividends of the previous decade (OLSL, Misc./42/18). For established companies, there was thus a clear pattern of divestment.

A contrast can be established between the divestments and restructurings of the 1900s and the norms that had governed the industry previously. Much of the impetus came from the influence of the Companies Acts of 1900 and 1907 which gave auditing and financial reporting exemptions to private companies (Cornish and Clark, 1989: 262). In 1904, for example, 3068 of the 3477 new companies registered in London were private (Lavington, 1921: 201). The above divestments were part of a wave of public to private restructurings affecting a large section of the cotton industry. It is surprising to note that, at a time of growing overseas industrial concentration, the basic unit of British enterprise in a leading export sector became the smaller private company, capable of raising capital only from restricted sources, instead of the public company with much greater potential for growth.

To analyse the causes of divestment in more detail, the term 'entrepreneur' as used hitherto is temporarily put to one side. Separate managerial and shareholder interest groups existed in the 1890s and the motives of each must be examined. Conclusions may then be drawn on why divestment occurred and whether it constituted evidence of 'investor failure' (Kennedy, 1987) or 'managerial failure'. Broadly, two different types of company can be identified: the open public company as typified by Werneth and dominant in the 1890s, and the closed private company as typified by Osborne and more in vogue in the 1900s. In the former category there is some evidence for strong shareholder influences on the management of companies. They were highly participative with democratically structured quarterly meetings. These were on a 'one member one vote' basis. Norms of shareholder participation and democracy were evidenced by the strong resistance to proxy voting, for example, at a quarterly meeting of Leesbrook Spinning Co. Ltd (*Oldham Chronicle*, 19 January 1889: 6(iv)). The quarterly published balance sheet for Werneth, issued to all shareholders, gave the result of one such vote on the construction of the extension to the mill (OLSL, Misc./42/17). Shareholders were ruthless in removing the entire board where the balance sheet was found unacceptable. They were well aware of the financial and technical issues involved (Ellison, 1967: 137–8) and control was exercised very closely through quarterly meetings and balance sheet publication (Farnie, 1979: 266). An example of shareholders' power at Werneth was their active intervention concerning the fraud of 1893 and the publication of its effect on the front page of the quarterly report (OLSL, Misc./42/2 and 42/17). The general pattern was of active shareholdings with very close policing of directors' activities. The modem argument of 'dividend irrelevance' as founded on the assumptions of diversified investment portfolios in efficient capital markets (Miller and Modigliani, 1961) was not applicable in these circumstances. Shareholders preferred high and frequent dividends, presumably as compensation for their undiversified risk and out of a reluctance to incur the agency costs of giving the directors too much of a free hand.

The high levels of divestment noted above thus appear to have been motivated by the demands of powerful shareholder groups. If this tended to delay the emergence of managerial élites, and left financial power concentrated in the hands of the wealthier shareholders, it is perhaps unsurprising that the custodians of the industry have been left open to accusations of failure to make innovative investments or to utilize and develop productive resources (Mass and Lazonick, 1990: 9).

However, for a closely controlled company such as Osborne the profit retention rate was also very low, suggesting that shareholder power was not the only factor at work. The management of this company still preferred to hold wealth as individuals rather than allow capital to accumulate within the corporation. The directors of Osborne received a total of £17,200 in dividends between 1889 and 1903 (LCRO, DDX/869/3/1). This represented 107.5 per cent of the original equity capital invested, thus allowing the promoter/directors to more than recoup the initial investment. It is probable that they used some of this money for reinvestment in other concerns. Their flotation of Gresham Mill Spinning Co. Ltd to take over an existing concern in 1903 at a capital of £30,000 may have absorbed past profits from Osborne and helped to cement cross directorships. Although a separate company, the directors were essentially the same (LCRO, DDX/869/1/4; DDX/869/10/2). The power of this élite, as a group of individuals, tended to cut across the development of a concentrated corporate identity. Although there was no pressure to pay large dividends, limited companies were not seen as engines of accumulation, implying that the continued growth of the industry was dependent on the reinvestment of profits by ind viduals.

The structure and ownership of capital was an important constraint and has not been fully considered in the debate on Lancashire textiles to date. As the industry evolved, the earlier principles of co-operation and working class participation (Farnie, 1979: 255–6) began to disappear and the accumulation of individual wealth became more important. The financia restructurings of the early twentieth century and the large bequests of corporate wealth in favour of individuals underlined this trend. Wealthy individuals became vital middlemen between the earned profits of existing firms and investment in new concerns. Unlike the former, the latter were closely controlled and independent of equity markets and other fina - cial institutions. Promoters operated freelance and took their own chances on new issues, with no assistance from the banks (Thomas, 1973: 154–5). One such individual was John Bunting, who became the leading share broker in the area and ploughed his profits back into the promotion of new mills. Of the fourteen or so promotions with which Bunting is known to have been involved (Farnie, 1985), three were notable and innovative for different reasons. He assisted with the Palm, promoted in 1884, then the largest ring mill in Lancashire (Farnie, 1985: 507; Hunt and Gurr, 1985: 43). Iris, built in 1907 at the height of the boom, typified the apparently extravagant financial arrangements of many flotations with a very high degree of dependence on loan finance (Thomas, 1973: 155). Such borrowings were out of all proportion to the asset base of the new company and it seems highly probable that it was the financial standing of Bunting himself which was responsible for attracting the loan finance. The final flotation of note, Times No. 2, came in 1907. This attracted an enormous amount of publicity at the time, since at 160,000 spindles it was half as large again as its nearest competitors. The capital requirement was large at £1 per spindle but Bunting was again able to attract loan finance on the strength of his wider empire (Jones, 1959: 88).

The activities of individuals such as Bunting were facilitated by the structure of local capital markets, which gave ready access to cheap capital. Transaction costs associated with the issue of new capital were low. Share dealing was on the basis of cash-only deals and an absence of contract notes and official regulation. Loan finance, raised directly from the public via press advertisements, independently of the banks, was generated similarly on the basis of low transaction cost (Farnie, 1979: 253–5). High dividends provided confidence for lenders and shareholders, thereby facilitating the raising of new capital, and ensuring its circulation via a rising class of wealthy individuals (Thomas, 1973: 155–6).

Bunting was outstanding as a beneficiary of the system and performed a crucial function in the circulation of divested and reinvested capital. His method of business empire building was replicated by other successful managers who were able to accumulate private capital such as T.E. Gartside (Jeremy, 1985) and J.B. Tattersall (McIvor, 1985). The growth of the influence of such individuals manifested itself simultaneously in the concentration of shareholder wealth and the emergence of multiple directorships. The earlier predominance of active but diverse shareholder groups was in terminal decline by 1900. A Shareholders' Protection Association was formed in 1889 to protest against the rising power of multiple directors, but failed to stamp out the practice (*Oldham Chronicle*, 9 February 1889:8). Other methods of reducing shareholder power were explored in the newer companies set up in the 1890s and 1900s. These tended to issue less marketable higher denomination shareholdings, had limited shareholding and did not issue published balance sheets. Werneth ceased to issue published balance sheets to the public in 1912 (OLSL, Misc./42/18), hence the lack of surviving detailed data for the company beyond that date. Bunting also adopted a policy of minimum disclosure with his companies at about this time (Farnie, 1985: 507). Such retreats from shareholder scrutiny helped reduce dependency on external financial stakeholders, and may have removed constraints on decision making for powerful individual directors and promoters. Diversificatio of risk may have been a motive, but from the point of view of managerial élites rather than investors. Thus these individuals failed to utilize the corporate form to concentrate financia resources but left their individual wealth scattered across otherwise independent companies.

The trend in Figure 2 of declining capital accumulation for some firms in an industry still experiencing overall growth can thus be explained by the willingness of local promoters to launch new concerns. When capacity was expanded, typically existing companies were not enlarged through the plough back of profits. Instead, new companies were floated, usually with a heavy dependence on fi ed interest loan finance. As these companies traded profitabl , surplus cash fl w was used to repay loans rather than invest in new equipment. Established companies could therefore be expected to show a decline in capital employed as equipment depreciated and loans were repaid. New share issues were rare for companies not being newly promoted. Takeovers and mergers using holding company and subsidiary relationships were equally scarce.

Limitations were placed upon the emergence of the large, diversified organization, since the diversification function was left to the individual accumulator of distributed profits. These individuals had emerged as a result of promotional, rather than functional, management expertise. By 1900, they commanded a power over the accumulation and distribution of capital which had been much less evident in the days of shareholder dominance of the 1890s and to that extent represented a newly emergent entrepreneurial class.

**Conclusions**

Two areas have been dealt with: the rate at which surpluses were earned, and how they were spent by their recipients. The aggregate level of profit was high relative to the wider economy, suggesting that, if incorrect investment decisions were being made, the signals from the market were unsatisfactory in providing any indication. Indeed the investors in the mill building boom of 1904–7 would have been highly satisfied with the rate of return from predominantly traditional mule-spinning technology.

It has been argued elsewhere that pre-war commitments to traditional technologies were the principal cause of the post-war collapse of the industry (Lazonick and Mass, 1984: 9). The above analysis confirms the broad hypothesis in the financial, rather than the technical, dimension. Furthermore, it could be said that the former dimension represents a framework for the analysis of the latter. Entrepreneurs were unsurprisingly happy to invest in traditional technology as long as it was profitable for them to do so, effectively until 1911 when the number of installed mule spindles reached its peak. By 1920 investment was more problematic as entrepreneurs were without the concentrated corporate financial power necessary to restructure the industry, regardless of market signals hinting at its profitability. Without the guarantee of profits and dividends in a stable expanding market, share issues and new loan finance were ruled out. The only potential source of funding left to entrepreneurs wishing to reposition the industry through investment in new, cost-reducing technology, would be to draw on accumulated reserves from previously profitable trading or, as individuals, to draw on private savings. As the former were minimal, the fate of the industry depended on the willingness of individuals to reinvest previously accrued profits at a time when there was insufficient certainty to guarantee such i vestment.

These seeds of ultimate failure are detectable by analysis of the patterns of profit distribution. Much of the wealth was reinvested locally; there was no apparent integration with London capital markets (Lavington, 1921: 208) and no desire for access to overseas investment opportunities. Structurally, the framework of ownership and control of manufacturing assets tended to encourage individual rather than corporate capital accumulation. The powerful individual, contrasted with weak corporate organization, provides interesting evidence for some of the hypotheses advanced recently to explain the pattern of Britain's industrial dominance and decline. Lazonick (1991: 44–5) has pointed out an important gulf between generalist and specialist managerial groups. The prevalence of small organization structures in cotton textiles would indeed have prevented the emergence of specialist managers in personnel, marketing and finance, with the preparation of product cost and management accounting information for decision makers limited accordingly. Financial accounting, with its concern for the monitoring of capital circulation between corporate and individual sectors of the economy, remained dominant. The implications of these issues are discussed in Kaplan and Johnson (1987).

The cotton industry was thus characterized by an individual capitalism, as identified by Chandler (1990). Contrasts can be made with emerging corporate concentration in overseas economies. In the British textile industry such concentration as did occur in the spinning section was in the loosest possible form of holding company; financial empires, but without a corporate headquarters; multi-business units, but with all units producing similar products for the same markets; a business strategy based on the investment and divestment priorities of individuals. Increasing dependency of the industry on rich individuals for future investment returns the debate to the entrepreneurial failure hypothesis, albeit from a different perspective. Sensible investment decisions were taken on the basis of the profit signals that would have been received. However, Lazonick (1983: 204–5) has argued that there was a failure to remove constraints such as vertical specialization. Individuals to whom profits accumulated had the power to remove such constraints when diversifying their investments into new mills, but demonstrably failed to do so. From a profit point of view they had no need, but the instrument for such a strategy, the centralized corporation, could not be created due to the way in which the profits were spent. The lack of institutional capital accumulation in the industry was at least in part a function of the institutional development of the British economy as a whole. It became an important constraint on the development of the industry, and as such is worthy of greater recognition in the debates that have taken place hitherto.

*University of Nottingham*

## Notes

1.  Much of the debate hinges on the definition of an entrepreneur (Lazonick, 1983: 232). For the purpose of this discussion the Schumpeterian definition is used of an individual capable of removing constraints with a view to creating profitable opportunities. In addition, command of, or access to, capital resources is added as a necessary condition of entrepreneurial activity.
2.  The sources of published accounting data used are: *Oldham Chronicle*, financial reports (Saturday issues), 1885–1914. Listings by company of profit and dividend per quarter. Annual Review of the Cotton Trade, *Economist*, 1895–1914. Aggregate listing of paid-up share capital, loan capital, profit per company, aggregate dividend and aggregate reserve balances carried forward. Profits and dividends as ratios to share capital employed (not calculated for all years). In occasional years, the ratio of profit (before interest) to total capital empl yed.
    Both sources published the same cumulative table of profit per company showing the trend over time from 1884.
3.  The principal sources used were:
    Werneth Spinning Company Ltd: Directors' Quarterly Reports to Members, 1890–1912, Oldham Local Studies Library (hereafter OLSL), Misc./42/17 and 18. Directors' Minute Book, 1890–1912, OLSL Misc./42/2.
    Osborne Spinning Company Ltd: Financial Records, Lancashire County Record Office (hereafter LCRO) DDX/869/3; Plans and Tenders, LCRO, DDX/869/9; Share and Loan Books, LCRO, DDX/869/1; Records of Gresham Mill Co. Ltd, LCRO, DDX/869/10.
4.  *Oldham Chronicle*, 2 October 1888; a league table was published ranking all local companies by return on capital employed for the previous quarter; a feature common in other issues of the newspaper around this time.
5.  More formal economic definitions are the subject of academic debate and will not be examined here. The definition used deals exclusively with loan and share capital as disclosed in the *Economist* and *Oldham Chronicle* surveys. Loan capital does not include bank loans since such loans were rare, typically short term and used to finance working capital. The usage of return on capital in this paper is consistent with that referred to periodically by the *Economist* and *Oldham Chronicle*.
6.  The *Economist* Annual Review of the Cotton Trade typically contained between 75 and 105 spinning companies operating in Oldham, Ashton and Rochdale out of a total of around 320 in Oldham alone in 1914. The number of companies issuing balance sheets varied from year to year and the data from these was published in aggregate form in the *Economist* as part of its annual review of the cotton trade. Because the Economist based its own survey on information published in the *Oldham Chronicle* it is possible to identify individual firms in the sample from the listings in the latter. From this it can be established that from 1885 the sample consistently included a core of around seventy companies which issued balance sheets. These companies were all in the Oldham district and hence predominantly in the coarse to medium section of the industry. The sample in the *Economist* tended to increase in the 1900s to include typically around twenty-fi e newer companies. While issuing balance sheets, these companies were not on the sharebrokers' lists and were thus more closely controlled by their promoters and owners. The ranges of counts spun also tended to be predominantly coarse to medium see Jones (1959: 221–3, Table 5).
7.  No single source contains a complete picture of the return on capital employed. However, by combining data from several sources it is possible to construct an index: data on profits for all

years and capital employed for some is available in the 'Annual Review of the Cotton Trade' *Economist*, 1895–1914; a collation of some data from various sources for various years is provided in Farnie (1979: 213–15, 244–51). From these sources it is possible to estimate a return on capital index if assumptions are made about the rate of interest on loan capital. A figure of 5 per cent was used to 1888 and 4 per cent from then on, being an approximation to the average rate used throughout the period and as noted by Thomas (1973: 153) and Farnie (1979: 257).

8. Lazonick and Mass (1984: 21, Table 8), using the same data, show a decline of 1.51 per cent in output per operative for the period 1901–13. Conclusions thus depend heavily on the year selected for measurement.
9. Calculated using the figures in Jeremy (1993: 188)
10. The following ratios of loan to total capital were calculated from the annual Review of the Cotton Trade, *Economist*: 1898: 35 per cent, 1902: 32 per cent, 1906: 32 per cent, 1910: 40 per cent, 1914: 41 per cent. It should be borne in mind that the *Economist* survey relied on established companies, most of whom repaid significant amounts of loan capital, but excluded the more secretive and higher geared newer concerns.
11. The ROCE series may be extrapolated to the industry as a whole. Given low entry barriers, production of a relatively homogeneous commodity and intense competititon, it is unlikely that there was any significant deviation in the rate of profit between new and established companies.
12. Calculated from the *Economist*, Annual Review of the Cotton Trade, 1902–12.
13. *Oldham Standard*, for each company respectively, 15(iii), 31 August 1907; 15(ii), 27 November 1907; 14(v), 26 October 1907.

## References

Aldcroft, D.H. (1964) 'The entrepreneur and the British economy, 1870–1914', *Economic History Review*, 2nd Ser., 17(1): 113–34.

Caimcross, A.K. (1953) *Home and Foreign Investment, 1870–1913*, Cambridge: Cambridge University Press.

Campion, H. (1934) 'Pre-war fluctuations of profits in the cotton spinning industry', *Journal of the Royal Statistical Society*, VI: 626–32.

Chandler, A.D. (1977) *The Visible Hand: The Managerial Revolution in American Business*, Cambridge, Mass.: Harvard University Press.

Chandler, A.D. (1990) *Scale and Scope: The Dynamics of Industrial Capitalism*, Cambridge, Mass.: Belknap Press.

Chapman, S.D. (1992) *Merchant Enterprise in Britain from the Industrial Revolution to the First World War*, Cambridge: Cambridge University Press.

Chapman, S.J. and T.S. Ashton (1914) 'The size of businesses, mainly in the textile industries', *Journal of the Royal Statistical Society*, LXXVII(5): 469–59.

Cornish, W. and G. Clark (1989) *Law and Society in England, 1750–1950*, London: Sweet & Maxwell.

Edelstein, M. (1981) 'Foreign investment and empire, 1860–1914', in R. Floud and D.N. McCloskey (eds) *Economic History of Britain since 1700*, Vol. 2, Cambridge: Cambridge University Press.

Ellison, T. (1967) *The Cotton Trade of Great Britain*, London: Frank Cass.

Farnie, D.A. (1979) *The English Cotton Industry and the World Market*, Oxford: Clarendon Press.

Farnie, D.A. (1982) 'The emergence of Victorian Oldham as the centre of the cotton spinning industry', *Saddleworth Historical Society Bulletin*, 12: 41–53.

Farnie, D. (1985) 'John Bunting', in D. Jeremy (ed.) *Dictionary of Business Biography*, London: Butterworths, pp. 506–9.

Farnie, D. (1993) 'Rylands, John of Manchester', *Bulletin of the John Rylands University Library of Manchester*, 75(2): 3–103.

Feinstein, C.H. (1975) *National Income, Expenditure and Output of the United Kingdom, 1855–1965*, Cambridge: Cambridge University Press.

Hunt, J. and D. Gurr (1985) *The Cotton Mills of Oldham*, Oldham: Oldham Leisure Services.

Jensen, M. and W. Meckling (1976) 'Theory of the firm: managerial behavior, agency costs and ownership structure', *Journal of Financial Economics*, 3: 350–60.

Jeremy, D. (1985) 'T.E. Gartside', in D. Jeremy (ed.) *Dictionary of Business Biography*, London: Butterworths, pp. 495–8.

Jeremy, D. (1993) 'Survival strategies in Lancashire textiles: Bleachers' Association Ltd to Whitecroft pic, 1900–1980s', *Textile History*, 24(2): 163–209.

Johnson, H.T. and R. Kaplan (1987) *Relevance Lost: The Rise and Fall of Management Accounting*, Boston, Mass.: Harvard Business School Press.

Jones, F. (1959) 'The cotton spinning industry in the Oldham District from 1896–1914', unpublished MA thesis, University of Manchester.

Jones, G. (1933) *Increasing Return*, Cambridge: Cambridge University Press.

Kennedy, W.P. (1987) *Industrial Structure: Capital Markets and the Origins of British Economic Decline*, Cambridge: Cambridge University Press.

Lavington, F. (1921) *The English Capital Market*, London: Methuen.

Lazonick, W. (1983) 'Industrial organization and technological change: the decline of the British cotton industry', *Business History Review*, LVII: 195–236.

Lazonick, W. (1991) *Business Organization and the Myth of the Market Economy*, Cambridge: Cambridge University Press.

Lazonick, W. and W. Mass (1984) 'The performance of the British cotton industry, 1870–1913', *Research in Economic History*, XI: 1–44.

Mclvor, A. (1985) 'J. B. Tattersall', in D. Jeremy (ed.) *Dictionary of Business Biography*, London: Butterworths, pp. 444–53.

Macrosty, H.W. (1907) *The Trust Movement in British Industry: A Study of Business Organisation*, London: Longman.

Mass, W. and W. Lazonick (1990) 'The British cotton industry and international competitive advantage: the state of the debates', *Business History*, XXXII(4): 9–65.

Miller, M.H. and F. Modigliani (1961) 'Dividend policy, growth and the valuation of shares', *Journal of Business*, 34: 411–33.

Mitchell, B. and H. Jones (1971) *Second Abstract of British Historical Statistics*, Cambridge: Cambridge University Press.

Phelps Brown, E.J. and S. Handfield-Jones (1952) 'The climacteric of the 1890s: a study in the expanding economy', *Oxford Economic Papers*, 4(3): 266–307.

Robson, R. (1957) *The Cotton Industry in Britain*, London: Macmillan.

Ryan, J. (1930) 'Machinery replacement in the cotton trade', *Economic Journal*, 40: 568–80.

Sandberg, L.G. (1974) *Lancashire in Decline*, Columbus: Ohio State University Press.

Saxonhouse, G. and G. Wright (1987) 'Stubborn mules and vertical integration: the disappearing constraint', *Economic History Review*, 2nd Ser., XL(1): 87–94.

Smith, R. (1954) 'A history of the Lancashire cotton industry between the years 1873 and 1896', unpublished PhD thesis, University of Birmingham.

Smith, R. (1962) 'An Oldham limited liability company, 1875–1896', *Business History*, IV(1): 34–53.

Thomas, W.A. (1973) *The Provincial Stock Exchanges*, London: Frank Cass.

Williams, T. (1912) 'The rate of discount and the price of consols', *Journal of the Royal Statistical Society*, LXXV(IV): 380–400.

# Firm structure and financial performance: the Lancashire textile industry, c.1884 – c.1960

David Higgins and Steven Toms

## Abstract

Recent business history has been much concerned with the relationship between organization structure and competitive advantage. Using an archetypal case, the decline of the export-led British cotton industry, the contention that the vertically integrated, professionally managed firm has been an important pre-condition for the creation of international competitive advantage during the twentieth century is subjected to scrutiny. This is achieved by a long-run comparison of accounting-based financial performance indicators. Evidence suggests that vertical specialization was a superior form of business organization. Explanations for this lie in the evolution of technology, a conflict between production and marketing in integrated firms, but, above all, in market signals which repeatedly informed entrepreneurs that specialization worked. In drawing such conclusions we differ fundamentally from previous interpretations of the rise and fall of Lancashire textiles.

## Introduction

Debates on the development of the modern corporate firm have occupied a central role in the recent British business history and for no industry is this more true than Lancashire textiles. There has been a widespread concern that the slow emergence of the large-scale, fully vertically

integrated enterprise placed the industry at a serious competitive disadvantage and a strong suspicion that a major explanation for this was to
be found in the narrow-minded interests and individualistic attitudes of
mill owners (Chandler, 1990; Lazonick, 1983, 1986). This paper challenges
these arguments and offers an alternative explanation of why the vertically
integrated firm was not more widely adopted during this period. Our
explanation focuses on the rate of return as a signalling device informing
entrepreneurs of the most profitable type of firm structure. In only one of
the sub-periods encompassed by this study, 1920–38, do we find evidence
which would support the idea that the vertically integrated firm was, in
fact, the most profitable type of firm structure. One of the major
implications which emerges from our findings is that, far from being
irrational, or narrow-minded, entrepreneurs when adopting the specialized
type of firm may have been rather more successful than has been
thought.

This paper is in four parts. In the first part we provide data on the
extent of vertical specialization which existed within the industry during
the period c.1880–c.1960, and discuss the various advantages and disadvantages which have been claimed for this structure. The second part
describes the methodology used in this study and presents the findings
which have emerged. Our study is unique because we have constructed a
very long time series showing movements in the rate of return of capital for
a sample of integrated firms and specialized spinning firms. The third part
discusses the implications of our findings for the current debate on the
alleged weaknesses of entrepreneurs in the textile industry. In the final
section we draw conclusions

## Industrial structure in the Lancashire textile industry, 1880–1960

Table 1 shows that specialized spinning and specialized weaving firms have
accounted for the greater share of the industry's spinning and weaving
capacity for much of the period 1880–1960. Any assessment of the net
advantages which have been claimed for the integrated and specialized firm
must bear two considerations in mind. The first is that some of the
advantages which have been claimed for each type of firm structure have
varied according to the overall state of the Lancashire economy (for
example, whereas there is agreement that the high levels of vertical
specialization were advantageous prior to 1914, thereafter high levels of
vertical specialization have been thought to be disadvantageous). The
second consideration is that there have existed more fundamental
differences between the relative strengths of the two types of firm
structure. An illustration of this is provided by the argument that
specialization impeded co-ordinated investment decision making. Because
the degree of vertical specialization within the industry remained largely

Table 1 Ownership of spinning and weaving capacity by type of firm in the UK textile industry, 1878–1960.

| | Ownership of spindles (%) | | Ownership of looms (%) | |
|---|---|---|---|---|
| | Spinners | Spinner-weavers | Weavers | Spinner-weavers |
| 1878 | 65 | 35 | 46 | 54 |
| 1911 | 77 | 23 | 65 | 35 |
| 1946 | 90 | 10 | 86 | 14 |
| 1956–1960 | 44 | 56 | 64 | 36 |

Source: data for the years 1878, 1911, and 1946 were taken from Jewkes and Jewkes (1966). Data for the period 1956–60 were calculated from sources supplied by the British Textile Employers Association.

unaltered between 1880 and 1960, problems of uncoordinated decision making would have been as acute in 1960 as they were in the 1880s.

During the nineteenth century, expanding markets stimulated a high degree of specialization in Lancashire, which reinforced its competitive position. In other words, in conditions of expanding markets vertical specialization and competitive strength were mutually reinforcing. The existence of a large and diverse market allowed spinning firms to concentrate on the production of particular counts. This, in turn, enabled Lancashire to produce a wider range of goods at a lower cost. Increasing specialization also generated important external economies for firms in the industry. These external economies took the form of, for example, large pools of spinning and weaving labour, highly developed commercial facilities for the purchase of raw materials, the delivery of intermediate goods and the export of the final product (Farnie, 1979; Lazonick, 1983; McPhie, 1965).

However, the advantages of vertical specialization were dependent on the size of the market. After 1914, Lancashire's share of the international textile market decreased rapidly. In such an environment, the advantages of vertical specialization became less obvious. Thus external economies became less important as a source of Lancashire's competitive strength. One solution to contracting markets and declining industry size was for firms to rely less on the market for competitive advantages and more on their internal organization. Specifically, greater adoption of the vertical form has been espoused because this type of firm structure has been thought most suitable for the realization of technological and organizational economies.

For British manufacturing as a whole, the issues of technology, co-ordinated, high-throughput operations, vertical integration and managerial structure have received critical comment from Chandler who has forwarded the argument that the majority of firms failed to make the necessary three-pronged investment in manufacturing technology, marketing and management (Chandler, 1990: 235). As far as the textile industry was concerned, Chandler has long recognized that it was unlikely that high-throughput, capital-intensive methods of production and sophisticated managerial structures would emerge in this industry:

> In these industries, until well into the twentieth century, the relatively labour intensive and simple mechanical technology created few pressures or opportunities to develop new types of machinery.... Small incremental improvements continued in technology and organisation.... As a result neither the technology nor the organization of the modern factory evolved out of the production processes in the older mechanical industries of textiles, apparel and other clothing industries.
>
> (Chandler, 1977: 248)

However, particularly during the inter-war years, when foreign competition had become more severe, the industry was unable to change because, 'Neither the needed organisations nor the essential organisational capabilities existed' (Chandler, 1990: 334). For Chandler, as for other writers (such as Lazonick, 1983, 1986, 1990), antiquated technology, vertical disintegration and the stultifying effects of individualism combined to prevent rationalization, the achievement of economies of scale, and, as a consequence, the international competitiveness of the industry was reduced (Chandler, 1990: 333).

There were, of course, exceptions to this general picture. The large firms which had integrated spinning and weaving and established their own marketing networks – for example, Tootal Broadhurst & Lee, Ashton Bros, Horrockses, and Joshua Hoyle – have generally been perceived to have been in a more favourable position than the smaller, specialized spinning and weaving firms which dominated the industry until the 1950s (Chandler, 1990: 333; Clay, 1931: 25; Lazonick, 1983: 41). But what precisely were these advantages? And, perhaps more importantly, did these presumed advantages reveal themselves in terms of superior rates of return compared to those of specialized firms?

As far as technology was concerned, it has been alleged that the high levels of specialization prevented Lancashire firms making a sufficiently rapid move out of low-productivity technologies (the spinning mule and the Lancashire loom) into what became higher-productivity technologies (ring spinning and automatic looms).[1] It has been thought that the structure of the industry prevented a sufficiently rapid response in three ways. First, specialization presented problems for co-ordinated investment between spinning and weaving firms (Lazonick, 1986). Second, the geographical separation of spinning and weaving firms meant heavy transport costs would be incurred by firms adopting the new technologies (Lazonick, 1981, 1987). Third, only vertically integrated firms had the necessary structure to permit intensive utilization of machinery and the co-ordinated processing of products. Each of these constraints has been assessed in great detail (Lazonick, 1983, 1986), so here we shall discuss them only briefly.

Investment in ring spindles was not a decision that could be left entirely to a specialized spinning firm because the type of yarn produced by mule and ring spindles required different types of weaving machinery: the Lancashire loom was better suited for weaving the yarn produced by mule spindles and the automatic loom was better suited for weaving the yarn produced by ring spindles. Because of this complementarity it has been alleged that the ease with which the specialized spinning firm and the integrated firm could adopt ring spindles differed. Specifically, the specialized spinning firm could not know what the investment decisions of its weaving customers would be, and so was constrained to retain mule spindles because it could not be certain that weaving firms would take up the output of its ring yarn; weaving firms were reluctant to adopt automatic looms because they were uncertain whether they would be able to obtain sufficient supplies of ring yarn (Lazonick, 1986: 24). By contrast, a vertically integrated spinning and weaving firm has a clear advantage over specialized spinning and weaving firms, because the investment decisions of its spinning and weaving plant are co-ordinated by one firm.

A peculiar aspect of the specialization which existed in the Lancashire textile industry was the geographical separation of spinning and weaving firms. By the late nineteenth century, the spinning trade was highly concentrated in the south of Lancashire at Bolton, Leigh, Manchester, Oldham and Stockport. The weaving trade was highly concentrated in the north and north east of Lancashire at Burnley, Blackburn, Nelson and Preston (Farnie, 1979; Kenny, 1982). The consequence of this geographical specialization was that transport costs were incurred when yarn was supplied to weaving firms. However, the size of these transport costs appears to have differed according to the type of spinning machinery being used (Lazonick, 1983, 1987; Saxonhouse and Wright, 1984, 1987). Mule yarn was spun onto lightweight packages or onto lightweight paper tubes. Ring yarn, by contrast, had to be spun onto relatively heavier wooden bobbins which meant the transport costs of ring yarn were higher than for mule-spun yarn. In this case, firms which had integrated their spinning and weaving operations at the *plant* level had a clear advantage over specialized firms in adopting ring spinning because they need not incur such transport costs.

The adoption of more productive technologies was not in itself sufficient to improve the competitiveness of Lancashire textile firms after 1945. What was also required was the intensive use of this equipment so that unit costs were minimized and flows of intermediate goods between the various textile processes co-ordinated so that high and stable levels of capacity utilization were maintained (Great Britain, Ministry of Production, 1944: 26–32; Productivity Team Report, 1950: 15). If we focus on specialized spinning and weaving firms, it can be suggested that these firms faced greater risk compared to integrated firms in two major respects. First, there could be no guarantee that the production schedules of spinning and weaving firms would always coincide: variations in the quality and quantity of the yarn delivered by spinning firms made it very difficult for weaving firms to plan their work flow and operate their machinery intensively. A vertically integrated firm, however, has a strong interest in ensuring that machinery in all its processes is used intensively, and is able to co-ordinate internally the output of its spinning operations with the uptake of yarn in its weaving operations. Second, specialized spinning and weaving firms need not have any concern for the stable operation of each others' activities. Weaving firms need worry only about maintaining their own levels of operation, irrespective of the consequences of this for capacity-utilization levels in spinning. Such a divergence was clearly illustrated by the difference in the severity of the impact of the 1952 recession on spinning and weaving firms (Turner and Smith, 1953; Turner, 1953). By contrast, the integrated firm cannot ignore the impact of its spinning plant on changes in the level of activity of its weaving plant.

In order to address the issues raised above we compiled a sample of firms which highlights the basic characteristics of textile firms during this period. These characteristics are shown in Table 2. It is clear from Table 2 that our sample of textile firms contains three distinct firm types: small, specialized spinning firms, many of which operated one or two mills only; very large, multi-plant or combine specialized spinning firms, which owned numerous mills, often distributed over a wide geographical area; and vertically integrated firms.

Within the sample there are wide variations in size between firms. To some extent, these variations are inevitable. For example, comparing a single-mill spinning firm with a vertically integrated firm, we would expect the latter to be bigger. However, it would be dangerous to assume that, therefore, all vertically integrated firms were bigger than all spinning firms. In fact, the biggest spinning firms were substantially bigger than the verticals during our period (see Table 2). These very large spinning firms – or combines – were the result of the amalgamation of numerous independent spinning firms. The Fine Cotton Spinners & Doublers Association was formed in 1898 and initially comprised forty-six firms; Crosses & Heatons, formed in 1920, originally comprised twelve firms; Combined English Mills and the Lancashire Cotton Corporation, both formed in 1929, initially comprised fourteen and one hundred firms respectively. However, as we have already indicated, in debates on the performance of the Lancashire textile industry, it has not been size *per se* which has attracted attention but rather the issue of firm structure.

We have now indicated three ways by which integrated firms could be more favourably positioned for achieving higher levels of internal economies compared to specialized firms. Given the rapid decline in the size of Lancashire's export market, and the inroads being made into its

**Table 2** Structural characteristics of firms in the sample.

| | Small, specialized spinning firms | Large (combine) spinning firms | Vertically integrated firms |
|---|---|---|---|
| Multi-plant operation | No | Yes | Yes |
| Multi-stage processing | No | No | Yes |
| Integration of production and distribution[1] | No | No | Yes |
| Sample size, 1884–1913 | 10 | 1 | 8 |
| Sample size, 1920–1938 | 8 | 4 | 10 |
| Sample size, 1946–1960 | 14 | 4 | 11 |
| Capital employed by firm type (averages), 1884–1913 | £67,437 | £8,198,860 | £800,258 |
| Capital employed by firm type (averages), 1920–1938 | £379,667 | £8,823,333 | £2,002,043 |
| Capital employed by firm type (averages), 1950–1960 | £756,000 | £14,217,000 | £6,260,000 |

*Notes*
Within the sample of vertically integrated firms not all firms had integrated forward into merchanting. Of the firms in this sample, those that did not integrate into merchanting were: Eccles, Fielden Bros, Jackson Steeple, and Whitely.

domestic market after 1914, it might be expected that internal economies and not external economies would be vital for the survival of firms. If vertically integrated firms were in a better position to achieve higher levels of internal economies compared to specialized firms, then we should expect integrated firms to have achieved higher levels of profitability compared to specialized firms after 1914. In periods of market expansion prior to 1914, however, we should anticipate that specialized spinning firms would have superior levels of profitability compared to integrated firms.

**Methodology**

To establish a suitable measure for the comparison of profitability, an index of return to capital employed was derived for each sample firm which was then aggregated into simple averages for sub-groups of vertically specialized and integrated firms. Return to capital employed (ROCE) is a commonly used measure of financial performance. It is defined here as profit after tax and before interest and dividends divided by the total long-term capital employed (after Singh and Whittington, 1968). In turn, capital employed was defined as equity share capital, plus distributable reserves, plus outstanding long-term loans. In this section, we describe the advantages and limitations of such data, the sample data used and the method of calculation.

The great advantage of use of return on capital employed is that it facilitates comparison between the performances of different firms regardless of size. However, there are also shortcomings, and it is important to be aware of these when calculating and interpreting the resulting data. Because the measure relies primarily on externally reported accounting data, there is inevitably some subjectivity in the numbers used. Accountants, under pressure from external interest groups, such as banks, shareholders, and government, may have manipulated components of both profit and capital employed.

While it is beyond the scope of the current paper to address fully the wider debate on 'accounting error', it is none the less important to acknowledge its potential implications for the accuracy of the data used. In doing so, it is not necessary to deny that accountants may have manipulated the reported figures. Rather, it is sufficient for our comparison of the performances of two particular sub-samples of firms to establish that any bias was unsystematic both through time and across the two major sub-samples used. For example, it would be true that systematic bias existed if the overstatement of the depreciation charge by accountants ocurred in specialized companies but not in vertically integrated ones. It is also sufficient to establish that any manipulations which may have occurred were unlikely to have a material impact either on the figures reported for a single company or on the sample as a whole.

To begin with, therefore, it is useful to attempt to quantify the likely impact of variation in accounting practice on the reliability of the numbers used, rather than to quantify the extent of such variation *per se*. The most important threat to reliability of accounting numbers in the late nineteenth and first half of the twentieth centuries arose from the use of secret reserves (Marriner, 1981), as typified by the Royal Mail case (Arnold, 1991). In the case of cotton companies, most of the balance-sheet value was typically accounted for by reasonably standard production machinery and stocks and work in progress. It was here that the principal opportunities lay for cotton-company accountants to boost profit on the one hand or create secret reserves on the other, in the deliberate over- or under-valuation of these assets. As in other surveys (Arnold, 1996; Edwards and Boyns, 1994), the best way to test the extent of such activities is to examine the management accounts of the companies concerned. For the current sample, partly because only scant management accounting records were available (RCHM, 1990), but also because of the scope of the paper defined above, we tested the sensitivity of putative changes in accounting policy based on the financial accounts to changes in the calculated ROCE.

An example of the sensitivity of changes in depreciation policy to changes in ROCE for a typical company, Barlow and Jones Ltd, are shown in Appendix 2. Other sample companies, for the same period, showed similar results.[2] Thus variations in depreciation policy could have had only limited effects on the overall reported ROCE. As far as stock was concerned, rising or falling prices may have created opportunities to boost or depress profit by means of the stock valuation. To assess the sensitivity of our data to such manipulations, we examined a year of extreme price rises, the boom of 1907, in which coarse yarn prices advanced more than 15 per cent, and by reference to the half yearly balance sheets of one company, quantified the effect of the stock-holding gain. This accounted for only 2.55 per cent of total profits and a difference of 0.3 per cent in return to capital.[3] Even such a small difference could produce only short-term distortions. Under accruals accounting, which had generally been adopted by cotton companies in the 1880s,[4] these manipulations tend to even out over a longer period. Thus, while the use of accounting data might fail to withstand criticisms of inaccuracy in certain circumstances, the appeal of the data set used in this article is that it presents a very long-run data series, and that any short-run deviations were likely to have been immaterial.

In contrast, other recent business histories which have used return on capital employed as a performance measure have examined much shorter time periods (for example, Lewchuk, 1985) or concentrated on the period before 1914 (for example, Church et al., 1994). Those who have been most critical of the unreliability of accounting data either contained their conclusions within specific time periods – for example before 1900 (Brief, 1965; Lee, 1975) – or were concerned with specific industries, such as coal and iron, where asset valuation and profit measurement might indeed be said to be problematic (Baldwin, 1994; Edwards, 1986; Wale, 1990). In a recent survey, Arnold broadened the base of comparison by including, *inter alia*, an analysis of the archival records of eight commercial and industrial companies, and concluded that accounting reports were more reliable than previously thought (Arnold, 1996: 50), thereby confirming the view that the accounting-error debate has been biased by its over-concentration on certain industries. Perhaps rather more so than the above single-industry studies, the sample described below included a larger cross-sectional number of observations. Hence any inaccuracies for one particular firm would be more likely to be cancelled out across the sample as a whole. Also, unlike the heavier industries considered elsewhere, the cotton industry, which has thus far been excluded from the 'accounting error' debates, possessed relatively uniform units of production, the mills, and relatively standard machinery types, spindles and looms. Aggregate valuations on a per spindle or loom basis were well known and publicized in the trade, and standard depreciation and stock valuation methods were widely adopted (Moss, 1905: 34; Ryan, 1930). In such an industry, attempts at creative accounting were likely to have been highly transparent and therefore less common than elsewhere; a feature made even more likely given the collective vulnerability of these comparatively small companies to the trade cycle (Toms, 1996a, 1996b). For all these reasons, it was concluded that some trust could be placed on the underlying accounting data used.

Despite the apparent advantages of using long-run data for a relatively large cross-section of companies, a further problem to be addressed beforehand was the possibility of bias arising from the use of different data sources and which companies to use in which periods. To simplify data collection, database information from the Companies Database Cambridge (CDC) and annual volumes collating the financial results of companies, such as the Stock Exchange Official Intelligence (SEOI), were used where possible in the first instance.[5] Generally these provided more data in greater detail over time. In earlier periods, data gathering was much more problematic, and the sampling base potentially much smaller, especially before 1926. Archival data and press reports were therefore relied upon far more extensively for the earlier years. A second use of archival data was to conduct a more detailed analysis, where appropriate, of the buying and selling policies of integrated and specialized firms.

The cotton industry prior to 1960 was typified by a large number of relatively small firms, and hence in all years there was a large population from which a sample could be selected. However, to use accounting data it was necessary to concentrate on those companies which typically published their annual results. Specialized weaving companies, which were overwhelmingly privately controlled and financially secretive, were thus excluded from the study. Companies with policies of more open disclosure tended to be those with quotations on the London, Manchester and Oldham stock exchanges. Those companies quoted at Oldham alone, all of which were vertically specialized spinning companies, numbered around 70 in 1884, rising to a maximum of 300 in 1927, before falling back to 45 by 1958 (*Oldham Chronicle*, 2 April 1884; *Skinner's Directory*, 1960: xxxv).[6] A feature of these companies, especially before 1914, was the publication of extensive accounting data in the local press. With the companies quoted at Manchester and London added, there was thus for all years a large sampling base.

Vertically integrated companies tended to be larger, and those which publicized their results comparatively few in number, particularly in the earlier years. Isolated cotton companies, such as Barlow and Jones, and Rylands, were quoted on the London Stock Exchange in the 1880s and had consistently filed their accounts. The wave of mergers and amalgamations of 1899–1900 and the financial reconstructions of 1919–20 increased further the population of companies from which a sample could be drawn. Thus the only period in which data access for a sufficient sample of companies was problematic was for the thirty years before 1914 (RCHM, 1990). Even with archival records, it was possible to identify only a very limited number of vertically integrated companies which also had consistently available accounting data throughout this period.

Subject to this limitation, our aim was to produce a minimum sample of sixteen observations for each year in the series, split as far as possible equally between vertically specialized and vertically integrated companies. Companies were selected in the first instance by reference to data availability for long and continuous periods. Amalgamations and bank-ruptcies, particularly in the difficult 1920s and 1930s, meant that few companies were included in the sample throughout the total period. Individual vertically specialized companies, which typified the sample before 1929, sometimes tended to be superseded by combines, such as the giant Lancashire Cotton Corporation. Those that did feature in the sample for long periods tended to be vertically integrated – for example, Ashton Brothers of Hyde, Horrockses, Rylands and Tootals – and also happened to be those which provide useful exemplification of the corporate firm issues referred to above.

Exact data on the number of each type of firm in our sample are shown in Table 2. Despite the shortage of archival material there are, in fact, three strong reasons for believing the sample of firms we have compiled is representative of the industry and does allow us to make valid comparisons between firm structures. First, as Figure 1 shows, comparison of the rates of return achieved by our sample of spinning firms with those of a very much larger sample of spinning firms reveals that our sample tracks the industry average very well. Rates of return for the much larger sample of firms were calculated from *Skinner's Cotton Trade Directory of the World*, which contains data for between forty and one hundred firms between 1898 and 1958. Although *Skinner's* does not provide data to calculate ROCE on an entirely consistent basis with our study, the close movement of the two series in Figure 1 suggests that the trend in ROCE was not sensitive to measurement variations in profits or capital. Second, our sample of spinning firms has a disproportionate importance as far as ownership of spindleage is concerned. The four combines in our sample owned, approximately, thirty per cent of total spinning capacity from the 1930s. Finally, in relation to vertically integrated firms, even as late as 1930, of twenty-six firms which owned spinning and/or manufacturing facilities and owned merchanting facilities of their own, only eight such firms were publicly quoted and our sample includes six of these firms.[7]

A further element of potential inconsistency arising from the use of disparate data sources created some problems in the calculation of the return to capital statistic. For some years and for some companies, balance-sheet, but not profit and loss account, data were available. In the absence

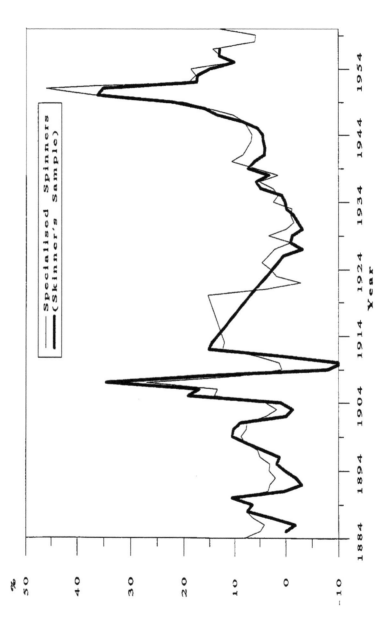

**Figure 1** Comparison of rates of return (%) for a sample of specialized spinning firms and Skinner's population of spinning firms, in the Lancashire textile industry, 1885–1958

of reported profit data, it was necessary to obtain an estimate. This was done by taking the difference between balances on revenue reserves at the beginning and the end of each year and adding back ordinary and preference dividends calculated according to the percentage rate to each class of capital, as published in Stock Exchange sources. The interest costs of fixed long-term loan capital were calculated and added back in the same way to arrive at an estimate of profit after tax, but before interest and dividends.[8]

For smaller companies, which tended to have relatively simple balance sheets and uncomplicated reserves, the calculation was straightforward and accurate. Larger companies, especially the amalgamations, were far more problematic, particularly given the frequency of capital reconstructions in the 1920s, 1930s and 1940s. In such circumstances it is necessary to take extreme care in dealing with reserve balances, especially when dealing with capital and revenue reserves. For normal years, it is relatively easy to observe such distinctions. In a reconstruction, often the consequences of years of unprofitable trading are recognized suddenly in a scheme which involves a significant write-off of capital. To deal with such effects, which, although occurring in isolated instances, did produce large negative outlying observations, two approaches were combined. First, the aggregate data and trend were examined and compared with the inclusion and exclusion of the outlier to assess its impact. Second, the impact of the reconstruction was averaged over two years instead of one. Neither of these adjustments changed the overall picture presented by the averaged data in a significant way. Thus the original data as computed are included in the data analysis presented below.

Overall, despite some data problems and limitations, it is felt that they are outweighed by the usefulness of such long-run time series and cross-sectional data and their ready comparability, not just within the industry, but also by sector, and for the economy as a whole. In general, perhaps, economic historians have been too cautious in their use of return on capital employed. Despite its weaknesses, the data presented below are probably less assumption driven, and at least as accurate, as economic-performance measures. In addition, they will be of use for future comparative studies. Most importantly for current purposes, by using and analysing return to capital data, it is possible to address and draw conclusions on the behaviour of managements and the corporate forms they adopted, their investment decisions and the allocation of capital by investors.

**The results**

Data on the rates of return on capital for our sample of specialized spinning firms and vertically integrated firms between 1884 and 1960, are presented in Figure 2. Two observations clearly stand out. First, the

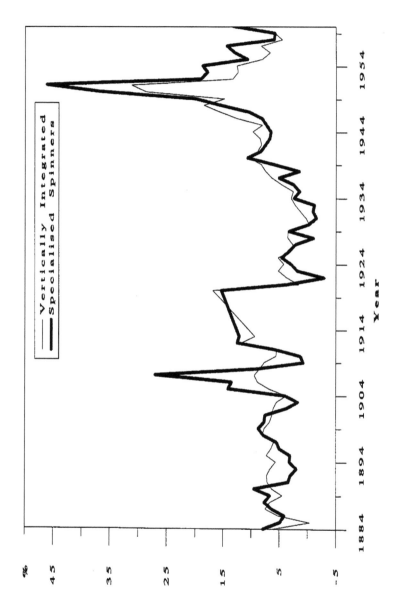

**Figure 2** Movements in rate of return (%) for a sample of vertically integrated and specialized spinning firms in the Lancashire textile industry, 1884–1960

relative superiority of each type of firm structure has varied during the period. Second, specialized spinning firms appear to have experienced far higher variability in their rates of return than integrated firms.

We suggested earlier that the superiority of each type of firm structure would vary according to the period in question and, specifically, that specialized firms would be superior prior to 1913 and that integrated firms would be superior thereafter. To examine this in more detail than Figure 1 allows, we divided the period 1884–1960 into three sub-periods, 1884–1913, 1920–38 and 1946–60,[9] and calculated the mean rates of return for both types of firm during each period. The results are presented in Table 3 which makes it clear that in two of the sub-periods, 1884–1913 and 1946–60, the rates of return achieved by specialized spinning firms exceeded those of vertical firms and it was only in the inter-war period that the advantages claimed for vertical firms revealed themselves. Of course, the preceding discussion has focused entirely on average rates of return which do not give information about the proportion of specialized and integrated firms which recorded relatively high or low profitability. This is an important consideration because the use of averages conceals the extent to which the typical or representative firm was able to achieve these rates of return. To consider this issue in more detail we calculated the mean rate of return for all firms in our sample for each of the sub-periods and then calculated the proportion of spinning firms and integrated firms which exceeded this mean. The results are shown in Table 4. Taking the period 1884–1960, approximately 50 per cent of spinning and integrated firms in our sample achieved rates of return in excess of the sample mean. This is important because it indicates that the sample averages were not unduly affected by 'outliers', that is, one or two firms in each sample which achieved rates of return greatly below or in excess of the sample average. This result also indicates that, taking the period 1884–1960 as a whole,

**Table 3** Rates of return (%) and their variability for a sample of specialized spinning firms and integrated firms, 1884–1960

| Period | Specialized spinning firms | | Integrated firms | |
| | Mean profitability | Standard deviation | Mean profitability | Standard deviation |
| --- | --- | --- | --- | --- |
| 1884–1898 | 5.4 | 2.2 | 6.0 | 2.0 |
| 1899–1913 | 8.6 | 6.7 | 7.3 | 2.0 |
| 1884–1913 | 6.9 | 5.2 | 6.7 | 2.1 |
| 1920–1938 | 2.2 | 3.8 | 4.1 | 3.7 |
| 1946–1960 | 16.9 | 11.0 | 13.6 | 7.6 |
| 1884–1960[1] | 7.9 | 8.5 | 7.5 | 5.6 |

*Source*: calculated from the *Stock Exchange Intelligence Official Yearbook*, companies data-bank held by the Faculty of Economics, Cambridge University, and Appendix 1.
*Notes*
Excludes the years 1914–1919 and 1939–1945.

**Table 4** Proportion of spinning firms and vertically integrated firms achieving rates of return (%) in excess of the sample average, 1884–1960.

| Period | Spinning firms | Standard deviation | Vertically integrated firms | Standard deviation |
|---|---|---|---|---|
| 1884–1898 | 40 | 21 | 58.6 | 15.7 |
| 1899–1913 | 56.5 | 17 | 46.3 | 22.4 |
| 1920–1938 | 44.4 | 12.5 | 59.8 | 10.2 |
| 1946–1960 | 49.4 | 13 | 37.5 | 16.2 |

there was a very similar proportion of specialized and integrated firms capable of exceeding the sample average. This does not, of course, apply to individual sub-periods, especially the inter-war years and the post-1945 period. We have already outlined our reasons for believing that specialized spinning firms would achieve superior rates of return prior to 1913, and in that period the profitability of specialized firms was correlated with the expansion of export markets, but their poor performance during the inter-war years and their superior performance post-1945 deserve further comment.

**The inter-war years**

Table 3 makes it abundantly clear that in both historical and relative terms the performance of the specialized spinning firms during the inter-war years was their worst ever. On average, between 1920 and 1938, our sample of specialized spinning firms achieved rates of return which were almost two percentage points below those achieved by the integrated firms. Further, the superior performance of the integrated firms was maintained for 84 per cent of this sub-period. Table 1 shows clearly that during the inter-war years the relative importance of specialized spinning and weaving firms, in terms of their ownership of the industry's capacity, increased. In other words, although financial signals were indicating that the integrated firm was the superior type of firm, the industry's entrepreneurs appear to have ignored these signals and increased the importance of the specialized firm.

To some extent the data presented in Table 1 are slightly misleading because one of the dates given, 1911, is two years before the industry recorded its greatest ever export figures and expansion of mills was still being completed. None the less, a number of new mills belonging to specialized spinning firms were established after 1918. For example, in 1926, Shiloh Spinning Co. Ltd built 'Elk', a new mill comprising 107,240 spindles (Shiloh, 1974: 16). During the same year the 'Sir John Holden' mill was built comprising 125,000 mule spindles and 30,000 ring spindles (Longworth, 1986: 95).

During the inter-war years the spinning section of the industry was badly affected by 'weak selling' (selling goods at a price which is below cost in an attempt to secure business). This 'weak selling' occurred because the industry suffered from substantial amounts of excess capacity brought about by the collapse of its export markets. The principal explanation for this collapse was the loss of the Indian market and Japanese competition in Third World markets. India was by far the greatest single market for Lancashire's goods. Of a total British production of approximately 700m yards of cotton piece goods in 1913, 43 per cent by quantity and 36 per cent by value was exported to India (Burnett-Hurst, 1932: 398). However, during the inter-war years, stimulated by the disruptive effects of the First World War, nationalism and tariff barriers, Indian production of cotton manufactures increased: from a pre-war average production of 647m pounds (weight) of cotton piece goods and 1,105m pounds of cotton yarn, production was 719m and 1,970m pounds respectively by 1924–5, and 867m and 2,561m pounds by 1930–1 (Burnett-Hurst, 1932: 411). In other words, India was becoming increasingly self-sufficient in cotton goods.

Compounding matters were the inroads being made in Lancashire's export markets by Japanese competition. For example, between 1914 and 1930, Japan increased her share of Indian imports of cotton piece goods from 0.3 per cent to 36 per cent, (Burnett-Hurst, 1932: 422) and in the Chinese market it was estimated that Japanese penetration was wholly responsible for the decline in Lancashire's exports (Bowker, 1928: 53).

There were two possible responses to the problem posed by rapidly contracting export markets: one was a substantial reduction in the capacity of the industry and the other was a greater adoption of more productive, high-speed technologies which would improve competitiveness. The two responses need not, of course, have been mutually exclusive: greater concentration of capacity and greater rationalization, by making the environment more certain, may have stimulated investment. We shall see, however, that neither was forthcoming on a sufficiently large scale.

Such contraction as did occur materialized very slowly and was confined almost entirely to the mid-1930s (Kirby, 1974: 158). A series of investigations into the state of the industry revealed that greater amalgamation in the spinning section and greater integration throughout the industry were essential prerequisites if competitiveness and profitability were to be restored to the industry (Economic Advisory Council, 1930: 19–21; Political and Economic Planning Industries Group, 1934: 10–11). Greater combination in the spinning industry, for example, would mean that a higher proportion of the industry's capacity would be controlled by a smaller number of firms. Such firms would be in a better position to reduce capacity in the industry, compared to a situation where capacity was more widely dissipated. Indeed, such combinations had a bigger incentive to reduce capacity because they would be in a better position to internalize the benefits. Moreover, greater combination in each section of the industry (spinning, weaving, merchanting) would facilitate better co-ordination of capacity between each section and would thereby allow a better balance to be achieved between the outputs of the spinning and weaving sections.

However, greater combination was not forthcoming. One of the major reasons for this was that individual owners put their own vested interests before those of the industry. This was rational from their own perspective, but very damaging for the industry because it meant excess capacity and its consequences in terms of 'weak selling', lower profits and low rates of re-equipment were prolonged (Bamberg, 1988: 84, 90, 98; Chandler, 1990: 333–4; Lazonick, 1986: 32–3). Even where combinations were formed as a vehicle for reducing capacity, the results were not always quickly apparent. The Lancashire Cotton Corporation (LCC), for example, rid the industry of 4.5m spindles by 1939, but the problems it encountered in the early years of its formation together with the resultant poor financial performance (between 1930 and 1935 the company achieved a rate of return of only 0.13 per cent) may have minimized in the eyes of the industry the advantages of further combination and actually discouraged it (Bamberg, 1988: 97; Political and Economic Planning Industries Group, 1934: 105).[10]

Various attempts were made to initiate price-fixing agreements, especially in the 'American'[11] section of the industry. Price agreements were tried in 1923, and 1926, but both ended in failure. In the latter case, the scheme was initiated on the suggestion by John Maynard Keynes to the Federation of Master Cotton Spinners Associations, and a Cotton Yarn Association was formed to fix production quotas and set minimum prices in the American section. But, as demand continued to fall through the late 1920s, outsiders succeeded in cutting prices and the scheme collapsed (Singleton, 1991: 14; Kirby, 1974: 154–5). In fact, it was only during the 1930s that successful price-fixing schemes such as the Royton Agreement (1933) were established (Porter, 1979: 42; Singleton, 1991: 17–18).

As far as technology and re-equipment were concerned, ever since the Industrial Revolution Lancashire firms had always used both intermittent and continuous spinning methods.[12] At some point between 1880 and 1960, the latter established its superiority. However, there has been remarkably little discussion as to when the superiority of ring spinning became an established fact. Both systems improved gradually between 1880 and 1920 (Table 5), but the race was indecisive, technology was in a state of flux, and the choices facing decision makers were far from clear. Between 1893 and 1915, improvements in both methods were almost identical, but not spectacular, with ring-spinning productivity beginning to accelerate only after 1915. Speed was a production constraint for rings and mules but the former, being independent of the wheeled carriage, was less restricted in terms of technical possibilities. Lack of automation in drafting[13] and winding[14] (Winterbottom, 1921: 261; Jewkes and Gray, 1935:

Table 5 Annual average rates of growth (%) in output (hanks per spindle)1866–1920

| Period | Mule spinning | Ring spinning |
|---|---|---|
| 1866–85 | 1.69 | na |
| 1885–93 | 1.33 | na |
| 1893–1915 | 0.08 | 0.08 |
| 1915–20 | 0.14 | 1.01 |

Source: calculated from Thornley (1923: 302).

129), especially before 1914, may have meant the introduction of the ring did not necessarily displace labour.

The invention of high-speed drafting in 1914 was decisive in the development of faster throughput techniques. By overcoming speed constraints it created the possibility of much higher efficiency in ring mill preparatory processes. Early drafting mechanisms, responsible for the attenuation of yarn in processes prior to spinning, placed limitations on speed, in terms of impaired quality and irregularity, for both ring and mule systems (Noguera, 1934: 20). To ensure correct quality, several stages of intermediate drafting were required in traditional systems. Like all important inventions, the high draft was based on a simple idea: the use of a grip device to ensure even pressure and attenuation. Cotton of uneven staple could thereby be regularized by a single process and at high speed (Noguera, 1934: 22–3). Although attempts were made to apply the new system to mules, high drafting destroyed the rationale of the intermittent carriage-based spinning system. Carriage speed rather than roller speed was now the constraint, and, whereas there were few technical obstacles to further speed increases for the latter, there were obvious problems in trying to accelerate the speed of a large wheeled carriage. Moving the frame instead of the material would increasingly look like fitting a light bulb by revolving the ceiling.

However, these new methods were not fully developed commercially until the 1920s (Catling, 1970: 189). Although at this time some contemporary writers still regarded the mule as superior (see, for example, Thornley, 1923: 137; Taggart, 1925: 331–2), its supremacy was now being seriously undermined. A survey in 1932 noted three cases of ring mills replacing traditional systems with high-draft spinning, resulting in improvements in labour productivity of 42 per cent, 56 per cent and 50 per cent (Board of Trade, 1932: 135). Most of the gain came from the elimination of intermediate roving stages (Tippett, 1969: 60). A further important development was the automation of the intermediate processes of doffing and winding. In view of the labour intensity of ring spinning in earlier years and compared with the improvement in ring-spinning efficiency prior to 1920 (Table 5), such gains were of great significance. For the first time spinning became capital, and not labour, intensive.

Furthermore, the automation of doffing and winding might have given a new impetus to integrated manufacture, since efficient throughput and compatibility between spinning and weaving machines could be more easily guaranteed.

The pre-1920 ring spindle has been overrated as a technical competitor to the mule under British conditions.[15] Saxonhouse and Wright (1984: 519) stressed the importance of high-speed drafting as the major technical breakthrough for the ring. If, as is surely correct, we date the technical changes to the 1920s, there are important consequences when these are considered in conjunction with our profit data. As we have seen, this technical opportunity coincided with a period when profit signals would have suggested to entrepreneurs that vertical integration might be the favoured strategy. If we are to attribute blame for poor investment decisions, it was in this period that the industry failed either to innovate or to restructure. However, in a period of over-capacity, loss of overseas markets and declining profits in most sectors, these opportunities came too late for any significant redeployment of capital. As J. B. Priestley wrote in 1934, 'Lancashire needed a plan, a big plan'.[16]

For most of the inter-war period, the fragmented structure of the industry and the vested interest of mill owners combined to condemn the spinning section to very low rates of profitability. As for re-equipment, especially the adoption of high-throughput methods of production, we have argued that too much emphasis has been placed upon this in much of the recent literature. Such methods of production do not appear to have been perceived as having widespread technical viability until the 1930s and during this period, of course, the depressed state of trade hardly provided a conducive environment in which to undertake such potentially risky expenditures. By contrast, integrated firms, especially those that integrated manufacturing with merchanting appeared much more successful. Contemporary observers such as Clay noted that integrated firms which had control of their merchanting operations were among the most successful (Clay, 1931: 25). Of the seven publicly quoted companies identified by Clay as having integrated manufacturing and merchanting operations, six are included in our sample: Barlow & Jones; Amalgamated Cotton Mills Trust; Sir Elkanah Armitage; Ashton Bros; Joshua Hoyle & Son, and Tootal, Broadhurst & Lee.

## Post-1945 period

In the post-1945 period the relative performance of specialized spinning firms changes. In this period, specialized spinning firms achieved much higher rates of profitability compared to integrated firms (on average their rates of return were 3.3 percentage points in excess of the average achieved by integrated firms), and they were also more profitable for a greater period of the time (73.3 per cent during the sub-period 1946–60). This result is particularly interesting because it *suggests* that, while the relative superiority of the integrated firm was becoming apparent before 1945, this was not conclusively established until after 1960. The issue that now needs to be addressed is why integrated firms were unable to derive maximum benefits from the theoretical advantages which have been claimed for their structure. We will argue that the explanation can be found in the fact that vertically integrated firms confronted problems that were unique to their structure and which have not been fully appreciated in the literature. One conclusion which emerges from our discussion is that, if integrated firms were incapable of surmounting their own problems, then there could be no guarantee in the 1950s that greater verticalization would have secured Lancashire's future.

To be at its most efficient a vertically integrated firm must fully utilize its spinning and weaving machinery. This restricts the variety of cloths it can economically produce and, therefore, the range of markets in which it can compete. Ideally, the vertically integrated firm should aim for long runs of production at its balanced count.[17] Deviations from this balanced count can mean there is excess spinning and weaving capacity. Fundamentally, the problem confronting a vertically integrated firm is the reconciliation of stable, long-run spinning operations (in order to derive maximum economies from yarn production) with the ability to weave as wide a range of fabrics as possible (in order to cater for the maximum range of market demand). For 'in-house' production these two objectives are often irreconcilable. For an integrated spinning and weaving firm to offer as large a variety of cloths as an independent weaving firm, intolerable pressure is placed upon its spinning facilities. This places the integrated firm at a disadvantage compared to specialized spinning firms which can aggregate the numerous small demands of many weaving firms and thereby achieve long runs over a particular count range. The vertically integrated firm producing all the types of yarn required by its looms can frequently offer only small runs to its spinning machines. Thus, to maximize productive efficiency, the integrated firm needs to limit the variety of yarns it produces in its own mills and to supplement its requirements of certain yarns by buying them from specialized spinning firms.

By investigating the business records of integrated firms, it was possible to throw more light on their purchases of yarn from specialized spinning firms. Ideally, we should have compared the yarn-purchasing policies of a number of vertically integrated firms during a similar period. Unfortunately, of the integrated firms that existed in the Lancashire textile industry, only the yarn contract books of Horrockses appear to have survived for the post-1945 period, and even these exist solely for the three years 1959–62, so it has not been possible to investigate whether there was any change over time in the yarn-purchasing policies of this firm. To supplement the records of Horrockses, the yarn contract books and invoices of two specialized spinning firms have been used. The records of the specialized spinning firms reveal that the following vertically integrated firms purchased some of their yarns at various times from specialized spinners: Ashton Brothers Ltd., William Birtwistle (Allied Mills) Ltd., Barlow & Jones Ltd., Tootals and Vantona Ltd.

One way by which an integrated firm could reconcile the conflicting demands of its manufacturing and marketing operations was to rely on specialized spinning firms for part of its yarn requirements. Fundamentally, there are two types of relationship which could exist between a specialized spinning firm and an integrated firm. The integrated firm could use the specialized spinning firm infrequently – for example, when it needed extra spinning capacity in the short run to meet a large unexpected order, or when it required external supplies of yarn to bolster its stocks when there was insufficient time between orders to replenish them using its own spinning capacity. In this case the integrated firm, by varying the size of purchases it made in the yarn market, could transfer some of the fluctuations in demand for its own products to specialized spinning firms while maintaining stable levels of internal capacity utilization. In these situations, the yarn contracts placed with specialized spinning firms would tend to be highly irregular. Examples of these types of orders are provided in the yarn contract books of Robert Walker & Sons Ltd. They show that between 1949 and 1960 this spinning firm dealt with the following integrated firms: Ashton Bros., Barlow & Jones Ltd, Wm. Birtwistle and Vantona. Examples of such orders are shown in Table 6.

The second reason why a vertically integrated firm might buy yarn from specialist spinning firms was that it was a means of avoiding expenditure on spinning plant at times when trading conditions were highly uncertain and when, therefore, the integrated firm feared that there might be periods when additional spinning plant would be rendered idle or under-utilized. Where this was an important determinant of the integrated firms' entry into the yarn market we should expect to find that the pattern of orders placed with specialized spinning firms differed from that resulting from the use of specialized spinning firms to meet unusual demands with which their own spinning capacity could not cope. Specifically, where an integrated firm was using specialized spinning firms to avoid the fixed costs of building additional spinning capacity, it might be expected that the orders would be very large and limited to short periods of time.

Some idea of the importance of such large orders can be derived from the records of Richard Harwood & Sons,[18] which reveal that it dealt with three integrated firms (principally Ashton Bros, Tootals and, occasionally, Wm. Birtwistle) during the period 1958–60. In order to calculate the importance of orders placed by these three integrated firms during the period, the weights placed by these three firms were compared with the total weights placed with Harwoods each month. In the two years between January 1958 and January 1960, there was only one month in

**Table 6** Yarn contracts between Robert Walker & Sons and integrated textile firms.

| Contract date | Firm | Quantity (lbs) | Counts[1] |
|---|---|---|---|
| 11/4/1960 | Ashton Bros | 16,250 | 1.25s |
| 6/10/1960 | " " | 3,000 | " |
| | | | |
| 19/4/1950 | Barlow & Jones | 5,000 | 150yds. |
| 21/6/1950 | " " | 5,000 | " |
| 28/8/1950 | " " | 20,000 | " |
| 10/9/1951 | " " | 15,000 | " |
| | | | |
| 21/11/1957 | Wm. Birtwistle | 3,000 | 2.5s |
| 23/4/1958 | " " | 1,460 | 3s |
| 19/5/1958 | " " | 7,285 | 3s |
| 5/1/1960 | " " | 6,300 | 1.5s |
| | | | |
| 27/1/1949 | Vantona | 3,533 | 4s |
| 8/8/1949 | " | 500 | 100yds |
| 23/8/1949 | " | 6,000 | 4s |
| 11/10/1949 | " | 10,000 | 83yds |
| 30/11/1949 | " | 10,000 | 83yds |
| 19/4/1950 | " | 6,000 | 150yds |
| 19/12/1950 | " | 5,000 | 150yds |

*Source*: yarn contract books of Robert Walker & Sons Ltd. (Bolton Central Library.)
*Note*
Traditionally the fineness of yarn was denoted by the number of hanks of 840 yards that were needed to make one pound weight of yarn. In the case of condensor yarns, this normal rule did not apply. Firms which produced condensor yarns were extremely specialized spinning firms, and the placing of orders by integrated firms supports the view that over a wide range of counts an integrated firm could not hope to be self-sufficient.

which these three firms failed to place an order with Harwoods. The average size of order (by weight) per month placed by these three integrated firms was 13.7 per cent of the total weights ordered per month during the year 1958–59, and 11 per cent of the total weights ordered per month during the year 1959–60. These averages conceal the much greater importance of the orders placed by these integrated firms during particular months. For example, in August 1959, such orders accounted for 25 per cent of the total weights ordered from Harwoods; in June of the same year the figure was 31.5 per cent.

The preceding discussion has shown that, at various times, there was a strong trading relationship between integrated firms and specialized spinning firms. Given the quantitative importance of the orders placed by integrated firms with specialized spinning firms during particular periods it is possible that commercial ties were established between the two types of firm allowing each to obtain the benefits of the others' structure without fixed investment. For example, by relying intensively on specialized spinning firms, integrated firms were able to obtain greater supplies of yarn more quickly and more economically than their own internal spinning capacity allowed; similarly, by agreeing to supply large quantities of yarn to integrated firms at various times, specialized spinning firms were guaranteed a given 'up-take' of their yarn output without having to integrate forward by buying their own weaving plant. In other words, although integrated and specialized firms may have been formally independent, they were not commercially independent: contractual agreements may have allowed them to circumvent the disadvantages inherent in their own structures.

Such considerations are particularly important when we consider that some integrated firms may have decided to focus entirely on their marketing operations (by marketing as wide a range of fabrics and styles of clothing as possible) and devote little attention to the need for stable manufacturing operations. Indeed, as has already been suggested, the more diverse the range and styles of cloth produced, the more difficult it became to achieve stable internal operations and the greater the reliance, therefore, on specialized spinning firms. Horrockses provides a good example of such a relationship.

Their yarn contract books show that they dealt with thirty-two firms between 1959 and 1961. With the exception of two of these firms (Barlow & Jones Ltd. and Wm. Birtwistle), all the other firms were specialist cotton spinners. The range of counts and styles of cotton yarn purchased by Horrockses covered the whole spectrum of cotton yarn production: condensor yarns, coarse-medium yarns, medium-fine yarns and fine-super fine yarns. This wide range of yarn purchases is clearly illustrated by Table 7.

The explanation for Horrockses' reliance upon a large number of specialist yarn suppliers is that the company produced an enormous range of fabrics and styles of cloth for sale to a very large number of retailers. Horrockses' records show that, around 1910, the company had 35,441 designs on its pattern books. The last ordinary pattern book (Book No.101) ends in 1951, with pattern number 297,476. The number of Horrockses' 'special patterns' was also very large: by December 1947, the company had over 1,600 such designs and by 1956 (the date of the last surviving special pattern book) the number had risen to 2,799.

Because Horrockses was a fully integrated firm marketing its own brand products, it was imperative that it should be able to offer as wide a range of fabrics and styles as possible. Thus Horrockses were unable to produce all the required yarns themselves as efficiently as specialist yarn producers. The varieties of yarn bought by Horrockses makes us wonder whether the company was 'fashion led'. In other words, was the main aim of management to support the Horrockses' brand name at the expense of efficient manufacturing operations? Instead of producing such a wide

Table 7 Weight of cotton yarn delivered to Horrockses by principal firms, October 1959–July 1961

|  | Quantity (lbs) |
|---|---|
| *Condensor yarns* | |
| Rhodeson Ltd | 284,617 |
| S. Renshaw | 95,770 |
| Milnrow Spinning Co. Ltd. | 115,660 |
| | |
| *Coarse-medium yarns* | |
| Lancashire Cotton Corp | 179,257 |
| Belgrave Mills Ltd | 31,053 |
| | |
| *Medium-fine yarns* | |
| Barlow & Jones Ltd | 51,193 |
| Lancashire Cotton Corp. | 43,310 |
| S. Bourne | 28,120 |
| | |
| *Fine-super fine yarns* | |
| Fine Spinners & Doublers | 56,827 |

*Source*: Horrockses Collection, yarn contract books. (Lancashire County Record Office).

range of apparel and household textiles, it would doubtless have been more efficient for Horrockses to have concentrated on producing a narrower range of goods. One of the directors of Horrockses, Mr. Leadbetter, stated that he thought it was impossible for a fully integrated firm such as Horrockses to be completely self-contained given the need to produce a wide range of fabrics for retail: 'it is not entirely self balanced, as this would be practically impossible, and therefore from time to time it sells yarn to independent consumers outside the group, and also purchases cotton yarns from outside suppliers for its looms' (Leadbetter, 1955: 2)

The evidence from Horrockses, together with the earlier discussion on the contractual relationship between integrated firms and specialized firms, indicates that the adoption of the integrated firm was not in itself sufficient to achieve all the benefits of high-throughput, co-ordinated production methods. Reliance on specialized spinners meant that a transport cost would have been added to the cost of the yarn – a cost which a fully self-contained firm would not have had to incur. Moreover, what guarantee could there be that sufficient supplies of yarn would be delivered on time to ensure that the weaving plant of the integrated firm was fully utilized? Finally, and particularly in the case of Horrockses, if an integrated firm was committed to the marketing side of its operations, it would have been impossible for such a firm to achieve long runs of standardized yarn production internally. Ever since the 1930s, a strong body of opinion has emerged which has suggested that it was practically impossible for an integrated firm to be completely self-sufficient because of the conflicting demands of production efficiency and marketing diversity (Clay, 1931: 24; Jewkes, 1946a: 9–10, 1946b: 9–10; Political and Economic Planning Industries Group, 1934: 11, 53; Murray, 1956: 11; Robson, 1951: 1306, 1957: 111–12). Unfortunately, these problems have remained largely neglected in the current literature. Until further research is undertaken into the marketing policies of firms in terms of the diversity of the goods they produced, we cannot be certain that integration would have been sufficient to secure the benefits of co-ordinated throughput. Indeed, the fact that Horrockses consistently under-performed the sample of integrated firms used in our sample suggests that it concentrated too much on offering a comprehensive range of fabrics (marketing), and not enough on securing the maximum levels of efficiency.[19] Certainly, it is the case that Horrockses indicates that to emphasize the benefits which are alleged to accrue to vertically integrated firms (on account of their structure) may be very misleading if no account is taken of the range of marketing policies that the managements of such firms decided to pursue.

Thus far our analysis has indicated that, taking the period 1884–1960 *as a whole*, there is little evidence to suggest that vertically integrated firms were obviously a superior type of firm structure. Our findings appear surprising given the advantages that Chandler and Lazonick have claimed for the integrated firm. The validity of our findings is further bolstered when greater recognition is made of the views of contemporaries, not all of whom were convinced that the advantages claimed for the vertically integrated firm were as strong as Chandler and Lazonick would subsequently have us believe.

G. C. Allen, for example, was highly critical of the belief that greater vertical integration was the explanation for Japan's success in the inter-war years. Allen was very keen to emphasize the dual nature of the Japanese industry: on the one hand, there was an important vertically organized sector of the industry producing the cheaper standardized commodities; but, on the other, a large part of the industry was organized along lines very similar to that of Lancashire – a large number of specialist units. Allen argued that, whereas in the 1920s the major part of Japanese exports came from the vertically integrated section, by the 1930s this was no longer the case. In fact, argued Allen, during the 1930s, when Lancashire was being urged to reorganize along vertical lines, the Japanese were finding it increasingly necessary to imitate Lancashire's structure in order to resist Indian competition (Allen, 1959: 241–2; Saxonhouse and Wright, 1987: 92; Dore, 1986: 158–9, 208).

In the post-1945 period, especially with regard to the unfavourable comparisons made between Lancashire and America, both the employers' organizations and independent experts doubted whether adoption of greater integration was desirable because of the vastly different market conditions the two industries faced. The Oldham Master Cotton Spinners

Association (OMCSA) stated: 'it is important to note that the American market is practically self contained, whereas Lancashire spinners are dependent on overseas markets'.[20] John Jewkes was so opposed to the recommendations of the Board of Trade Report that the industry should reorganize in order to be better able to secure implementation of mass production and the implementation of bulk-selling methods of standardized products, that he submitted a Note to the Report. Jewkes laid much stress on the importance of Lancashire's ability to supply a wide variety of cloths and yarns (which her varied export markets demanded) and which the vertically specialized structure of the industry had shown itself unparalleled in meeting (Jewkes, 1946a: 242–9.) In addition, at various times both the Federation of Master Cotton Spinners Associations (FMCSA) and the OMCSA have doubted whether the structure of the industry could be held responsible for poor performance. As late as 1962, for example, the OMCSA stated: 'what needs to be said over and over again is that no matter how we reorganize ourselves along vertical lines . . . we shall still not be able to compete with cheap Asian or subsidised imports. Vertical firms have suffered just as much as horizontal firms under the recent trading conditions.'[21]

As far as technology is concerned, and especially for the post-1945 period, a number of observers doubted whether the adoption of ring spinning was the obvious solution to Lancashire's problems (Higgins, 1993a, 1993b). In the case of Combined English Mills, which advertised in the 1950s as a producer of counts up to 300s, the managing director stated, 'there is no doubt that for many years to come a market will be available for fine mule spun yarns, and that for all times certain specialised cloths will need the super quality yarns which Lancashire mule spinners have made so famous'.[22] The FMCSA, which received many deputations throughout the 1950s from the major operatives association, the Amalgamated Association of Operative Cotton Spinners and Twiners (AAOCST), would not recommend a wholesale changeover from mules to rings stating:

> It is as unreasonable to suggest that all mules should forthwith be replaced by ring frames as it would be to propose that all mules should be retained indefinitely and that no more rings should be installed. Each case must be considered on its economic merits by the firms concerned.[23]

Other commentators on the industry went even further in their support of the need for mule spinning. In a Memorandum of Dissent, the advantages of traditional Lancashire equipment were very fully enumerated. It was argued, for example, that, whatever the gains to be derived in the production of cotton products from the use of modern ring spinning, some part, perhaps a considerable part, of the traditional Lancashire machinery must be retained to produce goods which can be sold. Further, that it was widely held by both producers and merchants that a considerable number of mule spindles must be retained to provide types of yarn, essential for many of our high-grade cloths, which cannot be produced, or cannot be produced as satisfactorily, on ring spindles. Finally, that greater productivity could be achieved with *existing* equipment by, for example, altering workloads within mills (Clegg *et al.*, 1946).

## Conclusions

This paper has sought to assess the comparative performance of vertically integrated firms in the Lancashire textile industry between 1884 and 1960. Using a long-run series on rates of return on capital we found that over the period the performances of integrated firms and of specialized spinning firms were roughly comparable. In only one of the sub-periods encompassed by this study, 1920–38, do we find evidence which would support the idea that the individualistic attitude of spinning mill owners impeded the industry. Taking the period 1884–1960, as a whole, we find that, for thirty-four out of the sixty-four years (our study comprises three periods, 1884–1913, 1920–38 and 1946–60), specialized spinning firms achieved superior rates of return compared to vertically integrated firms. Our findings suggest the current state of the debate on the relationship between the type of firm and the decline of the Lancashire textile industry needs to be modified in a number of directions.

It is clear that the relative merits of each type of firm, in terms of the rate of return on capital, has depended on the state of the export markets facing the industry. Broadly speaking, during periods when the industry experienced buoyant exports – for example, between 1899–1913 and 1945–1955 – it was the specialized firms which achieved superior rates of return. By contrast, in depressed conditions – for example, 1920–1938 – the vertically integrated firm has been superior.

This paper has been critical of the view that greater vertical integration would have restored competitiveness and profitability to the industry because integrated firms were not always the most profitable type of firm in the industry. We have shown that the presumed benefits of vertical integration were not always easily achievable because of the fundamental conflict between production and marketing requirements. Horrockses is an especially good example of this conflict. Because vertically integrated firms confronted problems which were unique to their structure (problems which have not had the attention they deserve in the literature) it is misleading to place undue weight on their alleged efficiency compared to specialized firms, and it is misleading therefore to assume that greater vertical integration would have provided a panacea for the industry's ills.

In view of our findings, we do not believe that specialization was so prevalent because managers were incapable of altering the structure of the industry – indeed, at various times during the period under consideration, they have increased specialization in the industry. Viewed from this perspective, what Lazonick criticizes as failure is only partially so. For almost half of the period under consideration, the managements of spinning firms appear to have been responding rationally to market signals. In a sense, therefore, the issue might not be one of entrepreneurial failure but of market failure. Of course, it could be argued that this misses the point: managers reacted well given the constraints facing them but they were not able to change the structure of the industry in such a way as to make vertical integration a more desirable strategy. We disagree with this because we do not believe the individual businessman can always be expected to operate in such a way as to benefit the industry as a whole – only in such a way as to benefit his own firm. If the two interests – that of the individual firm and that of the industry as a whole – correspond, then the market has operated to ensure individual and collective interests coincide, but, if the two interests do not match, then the individual businessman cannot be expected to estimate external economies when deciding what is the best course of action for his firm. Such a view has been argued by other scholars for other industries (Richardson, 1968: 275), but as far as the Lancashire textile industry is concerned the clearest exposition of this view came from the Textile Council itself:

> the relevant question is not what sort of structure looks appropriate for the industry as a whole, given certain technical and market conditions, but what is the industrial logic determining the policy of any single firm that makes that firm act in such a way as to cause structural change.
>
> (Textile Council, 1969, Vol. I: 17)

Our findings suggest that market signals, in the form of rates of return, failed to persuade managers to pursue greater levels of integration. If there was 'failure' in the industry it was not on the part of individual owners, but due to the role of the market.

*Sheffield University*
*Nottingham University*

## Acknowledgements

We would like to thank Geoff Tweedale, the editors, and two anonymous referees for their useful comments.

## Notes

1   The mule spinning frame draws out and twists a length of yarn, then winds it onto a spindle. It is characterized by a backwards and forwards motion of the

equipment. The Lancashire loom was a weaving machine developed in the nineteenth century which uses a power supply to propel the shuttle. Ring spinning refers to a type of spinning developed in the mid-nineteenth century in which yarn is passed through a ring before being wound onto a spindle. Automatic looms are looms on which the supply of weft is automatically replenished.

2   In the case of Ashton Brothers Ltd, their depreciation allowances averaged 7.3 per cent of fixed asset net book values; had the rate used been 10 per cent instead, the ROCE would have fallen by 1.4 per cent in this period (LGL Commercial Reports, Balance Sheets 1920–3). A similar adjustment to the actual figures for Sir Elkanah Armitage Ltd, showed a fall in ROCE of 0.7 per cent (LGL Commercial Reports, Balance Sheets, 1921–4).

3   OLSL Misc. 42/17, Werneth Spinning Company, Reports to Members. This was estimated by taking a holding period increase in yarn based on the yarn price and the average day's sales held in stock, applied to the average value of stock held. The company accounting policy was to value stock using current prices (OLSL Misc. 42/12, Werneth Spinning Company, Directors' Minute Book). Price information was obtained from Robson (1957: 336).

4   This can be determined from company financial statements and underlying records. For example, Dowry (CAC), LCC/Dow1, nominal ledger, June 1885–December 1912; Horrockses, CVA, detailed accounts, half yearly balance sheets and profit and loss accounts, November 1887–October 1905; Werneth Spinning Company, OLSL, Misc. 42/17 and 18, quarterly reports to members, April 1889–October 1912.

5   Details of the companies included in the sample, together with data sources, are given in Appendix 1.

6   Annual survey data based on information published in the *Oldham Chronicle* was also adopted by *The Economist*: for example, 'Commercial history and review of 1900, VII-textiles: the cotton trade' (16 February 1901: 29). The aggregate table as published in *The Economist*, and later in *Skinner's Directory* has been used extensively by historians of the cotton industry: Smith, 'A history of the Lancashire cotton industry', p.179; Robson (1957: 338); Sandberg, Lancashire in Decline, p.105.

7   These firms were: Amalgamated Cotton Mills Trust, Sir Elkanah Armitage & Sons Ltd, Ashton Bros & Co, Barlow & Jones Ltd, Joshua Hoyle & Sons, and Tootal Broadhurst & Lee.

8   Prior to 1950, no adjustment was made to arrive at pre-tax profits. Rates of return after that date are thus not directly comparable, although any discrepancy can be expected to be small due to the low incidence of income tax in earlier years and the low rates of profits recorded after 1920. Most importantly, as taxation would have affected integrated and specialized firms equally, our comparison of the two types of firm structure is not invalidated.

9   We have excluded the years 1914–19 and 1939–45 because the exigencies of war would not accurately reflect the true performance of the two types of firm structure. In addition, with respect to the period 1939–45, concentration and subsequent deconcentration of mills, and the redeployment of some mills for war-related production would affect the representativeness of our data and results. We further divided the sub-period 1884–1913, because between 1884 and 1898 integrated firms tended to achieve higher rates of return compared to specialized firms, but from 1899 the opposite tended to be the case. Taking the sub-period 1884–1913 as a whole, the average rate of return achieved by specialized firms exceeded that of integrated firms.

10   Originally the LCC had acquired 20,000 looms and had considered integrating forwards into weaving. Unfortunately, the scale of managerial problems was such that even as early as 1929 the board of the LCC had recognized there was

no immediate prospect of integrating weaving activities on a scale commensurate with its spinning activities. Further, the LCC was well aware that its intrusion into the weaving industry would simply antagonize its existing weaving customers who were then reluctant to purchase yarn from a company which was competing with them in the production of cloth. In view of these problems, the LCC abandoned its policy of vertical integration in 1934 (Bamberg, 1988: 93).

11    'American' section refers to those mills which used principally American raw cotton in their spinning operations.

12    The former developed from Crompton's mule and the latter from Arkwrights' water frame.

13    Drafting refers to the process by which the yarn is 'stretched' before entering the spinning machine.

14    Winding refers to the process by which the weft is wound onto a bobbin ready for use in weaving.

15    It is noteworthy that Lazonick, in noting the compatibilty of ring spinning with the automatic loom and automation through high-draft preparation, cited authorities writing from the early 1930s onwards – for example, Economic Advisory Council (1930: 17); Clay (1931: 13–14); Board of Trade (1932: 16) – but argued that the adoption of these methods could have extended productivity at the end of the *nineteenth century* (Lazonick, 1979: 258).

16    Priestley, 1934: 285.

17    The balanced count is that count of yarn at which the output of the preparatory processes in spinning ensures full utilization of the spindles. In an integrated spinning and weaving firm, the balanced count can be taken as referring to that count of yarn which maintains balance between the spinning section's output of yarn and the weaving section's uptake of yarn to produce cloth.

18    The records of this company are located at Bolton Central library.

19    This conflict was one of the most important factors determining the wide variation in profit margins achieved by Horrockses prior to 1905 (Toms, 1993: 133–4). Between 1950 and 1959, Horrockses averaged a rate of return of 8.04 per cent, which is substantially below the average for other integrated firms in our sample (see Table 3). The problem confronting Horrockses may have been rather more complex than we have indicated. Horrockses possessed a very strong brand name and its heavy market orientation may have been a more desirable policy because, if its brand name and identity had been diluted, it might have lost market share and suffered even lower rates of return. We are grateful to one of the referees for making this observation.

20    OMCSA, Annual Report, 1944, p.5.

21    OMCSA, Annual Report (1962: 6); FMCSA, General Committee Minutes (28 September 1945: 5).

22    Shareholders' Minute Book, 24th AGM, 21 December, p. 73.

23    FMCSA General Committee Minutes, 1 October 1948. Similar views were expressed by the chairman of the Board of Trade Working Party report on cotton when he visited the OMCSA (OMCSA, Annual Report, 1955:15). The belief in the superiority of mule spinning for high quality yarn production was argued most vehemently by the Bolton branch of the AAOCST (69th Annual Report, 1948: 8; 70th Annual Report, 1949: 10; 73rd Annual Report, 1952: 11; 74th Annual Report, 1953: 5–6).

24    Horrockses was part of the Amalgamated Cotton Mills Trust for most of the inter-war period.

25    Since deposited at the LCRO, Preston, but, at the time of writing, not yet officially listed.

## References

Allen, G. C. (1959) *British Industries and their Organisation*, 4th edn., London: Longmans.

Arnold, A.J. (1991) 'No substitute for hard cash?: an analysis of returns on investment in the Royal Mail steam packet company, 1903–29', *Accounting, Business and Financial History*, 1: 335–53.

Arnold, A.J. (1996) 'Should historians trust late nineteenth century company financial statements?', *Business History*, 38: 40–52.

Baldwin, T. (1994) 'Management aspiration and audit opinion: fixed asset accounting at the Staveley Coal and Iron Company, 1863–1883', *Accounting and Business Research*, 25: 3–12.

Baldwin, T., R. Berry and R. Church (1992) 'The accounts of the Consett Iron Company, 1864–1914', *Accounting and Business Research*, 22: 99–110.

Bamberg, J. H. (1988) 'The rationalisation of the British cotton industry in the interwar years', *Textile History*, 19: 83–101.

Board of Trade (1932) *An Industrial Survey of the Lancashire Area (Excluding Merseyside)*, London: HMSO.

Bowker, B. (1928) *Lancashire under the Hammer–1*, London: Hogarth.

Brief, R. (1965) 'Nineteenth century accounting error', *Journal of Accounting Research*, 3: 12–31.

Burnett-Hurst, A. R. (1932) 'Lancashire and the Indian market', *Journal of the Royal Statistical Society*, 95: 395– 440.

Catling, H. (1970) *The Spinning Mule*, Newton Abbot: David & Charles.

Chandler, A. D. (1977) *The Visible Hand: The Managerial Revolution in American Business*, Cambridge, Mass.: Harvard University Press.

Chandler, A. D. (1990) *Scale and Scope: The Dynamics of Industrial Capitalism*, Cambridge: Cambridge University Press.

Church, R., T. Baldwin and R. Berry (1994) 'Accounting for profitability at the Consett Iron Company: measurement, sources, and uses', *Economic History Review*, 47: 703–24.

Clay, H. (1931) *Report on the Position of the English Cotton Industry*, confidential report for Securites Management Trust Ltd.

Clegg, C. B. and E. L. Hirst *et.al.* (1946) 'Memorandum of dissent on certain matters', *Board of Trade Working Party Reports: Cotton*, pp. 232–4.

Dore, R. P. (1986) *Flexible Rigidities: Industrial Policy and Structural Adjustment in the Japanese Economy, 1970–1986*. London: Athlone.

Economic Advisory Council (1930) *Report of the Committee on the Cotton Industry*, Cmnd.3615, London: HMSO.

Edwards, J. (1986) 'Depreciation and fixed asset valuation in railway company accounts to 1911', *Accounting and Business Research*, 23: 251–63.

Edwards, J.R. and Boyns, T. (1994) 'Accounting practice and business finance: some case studies from the iron and coal industry, 1865–1914', *Journal of Business Finance and Accounting*, 21: 1151–78.

Farnie, D. A. (1979) *The English Cotton Industry and the World Market*, Oxford: Clarendon Press.

Farnie, D.A. (1993) 'John Rylands of Manchester', *Bulletin of the John Rylands Library*, 75: 3–103

Great Britain, Ministry of Production (1944) *Report of the Cotton Textile Mission to the USA*, London: HMSO.

Higgins, D. M. (1993a) 'Rings, mules, and structural constraints in the Lancashire textile industry, c.1945–c.1965', *Economic History Review*, 46: 342–62.

**Higgins, D. M.** (1993b) 'Re-equipment as a strategy for survival in the Lancashire spinning industry, c.1945–c.1960', *Textile History*, 24: 211–34.

**Holden, R.** (1987) 'Pear Mill, 1907–1929: a Stockport cotton spinning company', *Manchester Region History Review*, 1: 23–9.

**Jewkes, J.** (1946a) 'Note by Professor Jewkes', *Board of Trade Working Party Reports: Cotton*, London: HMSO, pp. 242–9.

**Jewkes, J.** (1946b) 'Is British industry inefficient?', *Manchester School*, 14: 1–16.

**Jewkes, J.** and **E. M. Gray** (1935) *Wages and Labour in the Lancashire Cotton Industry*, Manchester: Manchester University Press.

**Jewkes, J.** and **S. Jewkes** (1966) 'A hundred years of change in the structure of the cotton industry', *Journal of Law and Economics*, 9: 115–34.

**Kenny, S.** (1982) 'Sub-regional specialisation in the Lancashire cotton industry, 1884–1914: a study in organisational and locational change', *Journal of Historical Geography*, 8: 41–63.

**Kirby, M. W.** (1974) 'The Lancashire cotton industry in the inter-war years: a study in organisational change', *Business History*, 16: 145–59.

**Law, B.** (1996) *Fieldens of Todmorden – a nineteenth century business dynasty*, Littleborough: George Kelsall.

**Lazonick, W.** (1979) 'Industrial relations and technical change: the case of the self acting mule', *Cambridge Journal of Economics*, 3: 231–62.

**Lazonick, W.A.** (1981) 'Competition, specialisation, and industrial decline', *Journal of Economic History*, 41:31–8.

**Lazonick, W.** (1983) 'Industrial organisation and technological change: the decline of the British cotton industry', *Business History Review*, 57: 195–236.

**Lazonick, W.** (1986) 'The cotton industry', in B. Elbaum and W. Lazonick *The Decline of the British Economy*, Oxford: Oxford University Press, pp. 18–52.

**Lazonick, W.A.** (1987) 'Stubborn mules: some comments', *Economic History Review*, 40: 80–6.

**Lazonick, W.A.** and **Mass, W.** (1990) 'The British cotton industry and international competitive advantage: the state of the debates', *Business History*, 32: 9–65.

**Leadbetter, F.** (1955) 'The Development and Organisation of Horrockses, Crewdson & Co. Ltd', *Seminar Problems in Industrial Administration*, 1954–55, London School of Economics, Misc. Collection, 312, Paper No. 174.

**Lee, G.** (1975) 'The concept of profit in British accounting, 1760–1900', *Business History Review*, 49: 6–36.

**Lewchuk, W.** (1985) 'The return to capital in the British motor vehicle industry, 1896–1939', *Business History*, 37: 3–25.

**Longworth, J. H.** (1986) *The Cotton Mills of Bolton, 1780–1985: A Historical Directory*, Bolton: Department of Education and Arts.

**Marriner, S.** (1981) 'Company financial statements as source material for business historians', *Business History*, 22: 203–35.

**McPhie, A.** (1965) 'The changing structure of the U.K. cotton industry', *Textile Weekly*, 28 May, 954–6.

**Moss, W.** (1905) *Cotton Spinning Companies' Accounts*, London: Gee.

**Murray, J.** (1956) 'A plan for cotton', *Fabian Research Series*, No.181.

**Noguera, J.** (1934) *Theory and Practice of High Drafting in Cotton*. Prestwich: private publication.

**Political and Economic Planning Industries Group** (1934) *Report on the British Cotton Industry*, London: PEP.

**Porter, J. H.** (1979) 'The cotton and woollen industries in the interwar years', in D. H. Aldcroft and N. K. Buxton *British Industries Between the Wars*. London: Scholar Press, pp. 25–53.

**Priestley, J. B.** (1934) *An English Journey*, London: Heinemann.

**Productivity Team Report** (1950) *Cotton Weaving*, London: Anglo-American Council on Productivity.
**Richardson, H. W.** (1968) 'Chemicals', in D. H. Aldcroft (ed.) *The Development of British Industry and Foreign Competition, 1875–1914*, London: Allen and Unwin, pp. 274–306.
**Royal Commission on Historical Manuscripts** (1990) *Records of British Business and Industry, 1760–1914: Textiles and Leather*, London: HMSO.
**Robson R.** (1951) 'Vertical integration', *Textile Weekly*, 48: 1300–06.
**Robson R.** (1957) *The Cotton Industry in Britain*, London: Macmillan.
**Ryan, J.** (1930) 'Machinery replacement in the cotton trade', *Economic Journal*, 40: 568–80.
**Sandberg, L.A.** (1974) *Lancashire in Decline: A Study in Entrepreneurship, Technology and International Trade*, Columbus: Ohio State University Press.
**Saxonhouse, G.** and **G. Wright** (1984) 'New evidence on the stubborn English mule and the cotton industry, 1878–1920', *Economic History Review*, 37: 507–19.
**Saxonhouse, G.** and **G. Wright** (1987) 'Stubborn mules and vertical integration: the disappearing constraint?', *Economic History Review*, 40: 87–93.
**Singh, A.** and **G. Whittington** (1968) *Growth, Profitability and Valuation*, Cambridge: Cambridge University Press.
**Singleton, J.** (1991) *Lancashire on the Scrapheap*, Oxford: Oxford University Press.
**Smith, R.** (1954) 'A History of the Lancashire Cotton Industry between the years 1873 and 1896, unpublished PhD thesis, University of Birmingham.
**Smith, R.** (1961) 'An Oldham limited liability company, 1875–1896', *Business History*, 4: 34–53.
**Taggart, W. S.** (1925) *Cotton Spinning*, London: Macmillan.
**The Textile Council** (1969) *Cotton and Allied Textiles: A Report on Present Performance and Future Prospects*, Vol. I, Manchester: The Textile Council.
**Thornley, T.** (1923) *Modern Cotton Economics*, London: Scott Greenwood.
**Tippett, L. H. C.** (1969) *A Portrait of the Lancashire Textile Industry*, London: Oxford University Press.
**Toms, J. S.** (1993) 'The profitability of the first Lancashire merger: the case of Horrocks, Crewdson & Co. Ltd, 1887–1905', *Textile History*, 24: 129–46.
**Toms, J. S.** (1996a) 'The finance and growth of the Lancashire cotton textile industry, 1870–1914, unpublished PhD thesis, University of Nottingham.
**Toms, J. S.** (1996b) 'The demand for and the supply of accounting information in an unregulated market: examples from the Lancashire cotton mills, 1855–1914', *Accounting, Organizations and Society*, forthcoming.
**Turner, H. A.** (1953) 'Unemployment in textiles', *Bulletin of Oxford University Institute of Statistics*, 15: 295–309.
**Turner, H. A.** and **R. Smith** (1953) 'The slump in the cotton industry', *Bulletin of Oxford University Institute of Statistics*, 15: 105–33.
**Tyson, R.** (1962) 'Sun Mill: a study in democratic investment', unpublished MA thesis, University of Manchester.
**Wale, J.** (1990) 'How reliable were reported profits and asset values in the period 1890–1914? Case studies from the British coal industry', *Accounting and Business Research*, 20: 253–268.
**Winterbottom, J.** (1921) *Cotton Spinning Calculations and Yarn Costs*, London: Longmans, Green.

## Appendix 1: Data and sources

| Company | Period of inclusion | Source |
|---|---|---|
| Ashton Bros | 1899–60 | London Guildhall Library (LGL), commercial reports, half yearly balance sheets, 1899–13 and annual balance sheets and profit and loss accounts, 1920–5; *Stock Exchange Official Intelligence* and *Stock Exchange Year Book* (hereafter, SEOI to denote both), 1920–50; Companies Database, Cambridge University (CDC), 1950–60. |
| Amalgamated Cotton Mills | 1922–60 | SEOI, 1921–50; CDC, 1950–60. |
| Armitage (Sir Elkanah) | 1891–49 | SEOI, 1891–50; commercial reports, annual balance sheets, 1920–29. |
| Asia Mills | 1934–52 | SEOI, 1934–50; CDC, 1950–52. |
| Barber Text. Corp. | 1950–60 | CDC, 1950–60. |
| Barlow & Jones | 1884–60 | LGL, commercial reports, half yearly balance sheets, 1900–13; SEOI, 1920–50; LGL, commercial reports, annual balance sheets, 1920–29; CDC, 1950–60. |
| Bee Hive | 1950–60 | CDC, 1950–60. |
| Belgrave | 1927–60 | SEOI, 1927–50; CDC, 1950–60. |
| Brierfield Mills | 1920–48 | SEOI, 1920–48. |
| Broadstone | 1922–49 | SEOI, 1922–49. |
| Butts Mills | 1921–58 | SEOI, 1921–50; CDC, 1950–8. |
| Coldhurst | 1951–60 | CDC, 1951–60. |
| Comb. Eng. (Egyptian) Mills | 1929–60 | SEOI, 1929–50; CDC, 1950–60. |
| Crawford Cotton Spinning Co. | 1884–13 | *Oldham Chronicle*, 'Commercial reports', Saturday issues, quarterly reports detailing profits, dividends, share and loan capital; LGL, commercial reports, quarterly balance sheets, 1885–1890. |
| Crosses and Winkworth | 1922–60 | SEOI, 1922–50; CDC, 1950–60. |
| Cromer | 1950–60 | CDC, 1950–60. |
| Dart | 1951–60 | CDC, 1951–60. |
| Dowry | 1885–12 | *Oldham Chronicle*, 'Commercial reports', Saturday issues, quarterly reports detailing profits, dividends, share and loan capital, April 1884–December 1913; Courtaulds plc archives department Coventry (CAC), LCC/Dow1, nominal ledger; June 1885–December 1912. |

| | | |
|---|---|---|
| Eccles Spinning & Manuf. Co. | 1920–28 | SEOI, 1921–31. |
| Era Ring Mill | 1950–60 | CDC, 1950–60. |
| Fielden Bros. Ltd. | 1884–13 | West Yorkshire Record Office, Wakefield, C353/475, detailed accounts, balance sheets and summary profit and loss accounts, December 1891–December 1913; Law, B., *Fieldens of Todmorden*, Tables XXV and XXVIII. |
| Fine Cotton Spinners and Doublers | 1899–60 | SEOI, 1900–50; CDC, 1950–8. |
| Haugh Spinning Company | 1884–13 | *Oldham Chronicle*, 'Commercial reports', Saturday issues, quarterly reports detailing profits, dividends, share and loan capital, April 1884–December 1913; *Rochdale Observer*, ditto, 28th June 1890 and quarterly reports April 1892–June 1914 inclusive. |
| Hollins Mill Co. | 1920–49 | SEOI, 1921–50. |
| Horrockses[24] | 1887–13 | Coats Viyella Archives (CVA),[25] accounts, half yearly balance sheets and profit and loss accounts, November 1887–October 1905; Lancashire County Record Office (LCRO), DDHs/53, balance sheets, half yearly balance sheets and profit and loss accounts, October 1905–April 1914. |
| Horrockses | 1950–60 | CDC, 1950–60. |
| Iris | 1929–58 | SEOI, 1929–50; CDC, 1950–58. |
| Jackson and Steeple | 1920–35 | SEOI, 1920–36. |
| Lancs. Cotton Corp. | 1931–60 | SEOI, 1931–50; CDC, 1950–60. |
| Mutual Mill Co. | 1926–49 | SEOI, 1927–50. |
| Moorfield | 1884–13 | *Oldham Chronicle*, 'Commercial reports', Saturday issues, quarterly reports detailing profits, dividends, share and loan capital, April 1884–December 1913; Smith, (1961) 'An Oldham limited liability company', pp. 34–53. |
| New Hey Spinning Company | 1887–13 | *Oldham Chronicle*, 'Commercial reports', Saturday issues, quarterly reports detailing profits, dividends, share and loan capital, September 1886–June 1913; Rochdale Observer, ditto, 28th June 1890 and April 1892–June 1914. |

| | | |
|---|---|---|
| New Ladyhouse Spinning Co. | 1884–13 | *Oldham Chronicle*, 'Commercial reports', Saturday issues, quarterly reports detailing profits, dividends, share and loan capital, April 1884–December 1913; *Rochdale Observer*, ditto, 28 June 1890 and April 1892–June 1914. |
| Osborne | 1890–13 | LCRO, DDX/869/3/1, trade, capital, and profit and loss accounts, June 1889–December 1913. |
| Pear Mill | 1920–28 | Holden, 'Pear Mill', p. 28 |
| Rylands | 1884–49 | LGL, Commercial reports half yearly balance sheets, 1899–13; SEOI, 1884–98; Farnie, 'John Rylands of Manchester', pp. 71–2. |
| Sun Mill | 1884–13 | *Oldham Chronicle*, 'Commercial reports', Saturday issues, quarterly reports detailing profits, dividends, share and loan capital, April 1884–December 1913; Tyson (1962), 'Sun Mill', appendices 1 and 2. |
| Tootal | 1888–60 | Manchester Central Reference Library, M.461, board minutes, yearly balance sheets and profit and loss accounts, July 1888–July 1914; SEOI, 1920–50; CDC, 1950–60. |
| Werneth | 1884–13 | Oldham Local Studies Library (OLSL), Misc. 42/17 and 18, quarterly reports to members, April 1889–October 1912; *Oldham Chronicle*, 'commercial reports', Saturday issues, quarterly reports detailing profits, dividends, share and loan capital, April 1884–December 1888. |
| Whiteley | 1898–13 | LCRO, DDX/868/21/5, balance sheets, annual balance sheet and profit and loss account summary, September 1898–September 1914. |

## Appendix 2: Sensitivity of ROCE calculations to variations in depreciation rates

| Year | Barlow and Jones Ltd ROCE (see Figure 2) | Revised ROCE |
|---|---|---|
| 1921 | 7.28 | 6.71 |
| 1922 | 12.74 | 12.27 |
| 1923 | 12.44 | 12.02 |
| 1924 | 10.79 | 10.35 |
| 1925 | 6.55 | 6.07 |
| 1926 | 7.57 | 7.13 |
| 1927 | 7.77 | 7.50 |
| 1928 | 7.49 | 7.27 |

*Source*: LGL Commercial Reports, Barlow and Jones Ltd., 1921–28
*Note on calculation*: revised ROCE derived by calculating a new depreciation charge based on 10% reducing balance. The difference in profit arising from the use of this charge and one based on 7.5% reducing balance was deducted from the reported profit; a revised capital employed calculation was then made to reflect increased accumulated depreciation. Revised ROCE was computed by taking the ratio of revised profit to revised capital employed.

# Financial distress, corporate borrowing, and industrial decline: the Lancashire cotton spinning industry, 1918–38

David Higgins and Steve Toms

## Abstract

The analysis presented is based on a case study of Lancashire cotton textile firms. It traces their financial history through the sharp boom of 1919–20, and the sudden crisis that followed. Using a sample of representative companies it is shown that firms unwittingly adopted inappropriate financial structures that acted as the decisive constraint on the adoption of recovery strategies in the subsequent slump. The paper explains how the relationship between indebtedness and asset values prevented subsequent internal financial retrenchment, restructuring and re-equipment, and dictated the competitive processes within the industry. It is demonstrated that financial constraints were the decisive factor determining the feasibility of competitive strategies available to the industry's leaders.

## Introduction

From the cradle of the Industrial Revolution to World War I the Lancashire cotton textile industry was a dominant force in world export markets. In the post-war period the industry entered a crisis so severe that it never recovered, although many firms survived for a protracted period. The cause of the crisis, it is widely agreed, was the loss of export markets (Burnett-Hurst, 1932; Dupree, 1996: 270–1; 283–90). However, there were other factors at work that accentuated the initial crisis, made even partial recovery of competitiveness impossible and led to accusations of ineptitude that were to taint the reputation of Lancashire entrepreneurs.

David M. Higgins is a lecturer in the Department of Economics, Sheffield University, Sheffield, UK, J. Steve Toms is Professor of Accounting at the University of Nottingham Business School, Jubilee Campus, Nottingham, UK

The primary concern here is to analyse the links between the financial structures generated during the re-flotation boom (1919–20), the financial distress caused by the collapse in product and stock markets, and how these forces accelerated industrial decline. Although previous studies have examined these issues, the relationship between them has not been fully explored. Further, they have emphasised the problem of debt rather than the more general financial problem of asset mis-valuation (Bamberg, 1984a, 1988; Dupree, 1996: 272–6). Central to our argument is evidence that asset valuation and restructuring of financial claims conclusively impeded *any* attempt at strategic restructuring.

In this respect this article both differs from, and complements, the previous literature in a number of respects. First, it differs by suggesting that too much emphasis may have been given to the argument that the causes of the industry's decline were present prior to 1914 (Lazonick, 1981: 31–8; 1983: 211–36; 1986: 39–45; Mass and Lazonick, 1990). Along with other commentators we recognise that, with *hindsight*, signs of the industry's long-term decline were becoming apparent pre-1914 (Marrison, 1996: 246–53; Singleton, 1991: 10). However, the view presented here is of an abrupt financial crisis after the re-flotation boom of 1919–20, followed by an explanation of failure to recover in the aftermath. In other words, we argue that much greater prominence should be given to the industry's financial problems following directly from the re-flotation boom.

Second, this article complements and extends the recent literature in two directions. In a previous paper it was demonstrated that whatever theoretical advantages have been claimed for vertical integration, the financial incentives to adopt this organisational form were rather poor (Higgins and Toms, 1997: 207–10). On the basis of a new financial data-set for the industry we demonstrate that, even if vertical integration had been a superior type of organisation (in terms of profitability), the re-flotation boom of 1919–20, and its aftermath, conclusively impeded any restructuring of this industry. Also, the new financial data set we employ offers new perspectives on the relationship between financial distress and collusive practices (Bowden and Higgins, 1998: 319–43). Using new financial evidence the paper analyses the financial structure of the industry through time, its impact on cash flow to key stakeholder groups, the role of wealth transfers during the re-flotation boom between those entering and exiting the industry, and their constraining effects on business strategy. In particular, the problem of asset valuation, the subsequent illiquid market for shares in cotton spinning companies and its knock-on effects for pricing and re-equipment are emphasised.

Thirdly there is a re-examination of contemporary debates about proposed solutions to the crisis facing the industry. In particular, the writings of John Maynard Keynes are re-assessed. The failure of proposed schemes of amalgamation and refinancing, advocated by Keynes and others, including the formation and subsequent performance of the Lancashire Cotton Corporation, are examined with reference to the constraints imposed by the *ex ante* structure of equity and other financial claims.

A final differentiating objective of the analysis is to provide insights at a more general level on how managers might respond to crises and how their capacity to respond might be limited by *ex ante* financial arrangements. A considerable number of studies have empirically investigated the common strategic actions of firms and industries when confronted with crisis conditions (Hambrick and Schecter, 1983; Robbins and Pearce, 1992; Zimmerman, 1991). However, despite the necessarily longitudinal nature of these investigations, none have applied the methodologies of systematic historical investigation. Nonetheless their analytical techniques contain instructive models which have potential historical applicability. This analysis of the Lancashire textile industry between 1919 and 1938 seeks to exploit that potential.

This article is organised as follows. The next section outlines the nature of the crisis that engulfed the industry in the years immediately following World War I and analyses the managerial options for responding to the problems facing the typical firm. The following two sections present and discuss the key empirical aspects of the argument. The first outlines the general financial characteristics of the 1919–20 boom and subsequent slump, and its differential effects at the firm and sector level. The second explains why the financial structure inherited from 1920 prevented the industry from developing its own schemes of financial restructuring without reference to external intervention, and explores the collective impact of persistent financial distress on firm strategy, concentrating on exit, restructuring, collusion and re-equipment. A further section shows how financial constraints impeded the process of re-equipment and integration. The final section draws conclusions on each of the empirical sections and evaluates the central claim of the paper, that *ex ante* asset valuations can impose rigid financial constraints on subsequent strategic decisions.

## Crisis and recovery options

As an indicator of external conditions and subsequent decline in financial performance, Figure 1 shows the pattern of exports by value (£m) and spinning margins for 32s yarns during the period of the study.[1] Few would dispute that the overwhelming and immediate cause of the Lancashire crisis, post-1922, was the collapse in demand in export markets. As Figure 1 shows, the boom of 1919–20 was dramatic, even by the standards of this heavily cyclical industry.

Unlike previous booms, for example, that of 1907, which had led to an expansion of capacity through mill building, the 1919–20 boom was driven by wider margins associated with shortages and temporary dis-equilibrium in world markets. There was no physical increase in demand for Lancashire textiles (Daniels and Jewkes, 1928: 170). Also, a new wave of mill construction was prevented by a shortage of equipment and building supplies. Consequently, money capital was invested through the re-capitalisation of existing mills with bonus issues and new loan finance (Thomas, 1978: 156). These aspects of the boom determined the subsequent financial characteristics of many Lancashire firms.

As the re-flotation process indicated, many Lancashire entrepreneurs believed that the industry had a bright future in 1920. These optimists included the financial syndicates and banks that invested in the re-floated companies. The resulting interdependencies between financial stakeholders and the companies, particularly the banks, have been analysed in prior research (Bamberg, 1984a: 20–30, 70–98).

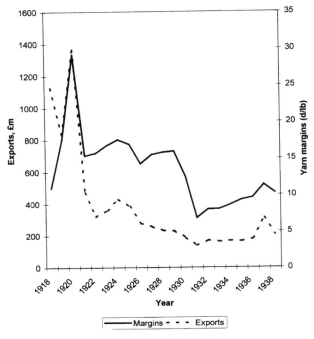

**Figure 1** Cotton exports and margins, 1918–38
*Source*: Robson (1957: 334–6)

However, although the debt mountain contributed to subsequent paralysis, there has been much less emphasis on the position of the equity stakeholder and the question of asset valuation. As will be demonstrated, equity holders were forced to take an optimistic view of the industry's future. So, even as it became apparent that overseas markets were lost, many in the industry did not doubt subsequent recovery and did not regard these losses as permanent. Parallels with the past boom and slump activity characteristic of the industry informed their opinions (*The Economist*, 20 September, 1930: 520; FMCSA, 1936). Also, some entrepreneurs did not follow industry trends. By keeping a cooler head during the re-flotation boom, Thomas Gartside was able to fund the new and ultimately successful Elk Mill project using distributable reserves and loan capital (Shiloh, 1949: 29–30). How-ever, there remains the possibility that cotton entrepreneurs were poor economists and, as historians of the industry have argued, should have foreseen the inevitability of decline in the face of increased world competition and exited the industry (Singleton, 1991: 231–2). If this hypothesis were accepted, re-flotation would have made little difference to the ultimate fate of the industry.[2] However, as the case of the wool textile industry illustrates, the absence of re-flotation placed the industry in a stronger position relative to cotton (Bowden and Higgins, 2000: 91–111). As in Lancashire, the Japanese cotton industry faced a similar recession in 1920, prompted by declining yarn exports and changes in world demand (Robertson, 1990: 89).[3] Despite these difficult conditions, certain firms survived because they had accumulated reserves of capital (Yamazaki, 1997). Consequently they were able to build successful interwar strategies based on forward integration into finishing and capital re-equipment. Not all firms re-floated in Lancashire and many of those that did not, also performed dismally. However, unlike in Japan, the scale of re-flotation prevented the exit of a sufficient number of firms to improve the competitiveness of the remainder. In other words, as will be demonstrated in detail below, the relationship between asset value, exit and firm performance also interacted with capacity utilisation in the Lancashire case and prevented the implementation of recovery strategies at the level of the individual firm.

The boom, followed by sharp decline in 1921, is consistent with common definitions of a turnaround situation (Hambrick and Schecter, 1983). The typical features of a turnaround process are particularly useful for beginning an analysis of the crisis. The first stage response, described as *retrenchment*, is usually directed towards the primary objective of survival and stabilising rapidly declining cash flow. The classic retrenchment strategy involves cost cutting, asset reduction, or a combination of both. Severe situations, usually driven by strategic or external factors, for example, low-cost foreign competition, technological change and a collapse in demand, require asset reductions to achieve stability (Robbins and Pearce, 1992: 308). These factors were present in the Lancashire case. Recovery strategies depend on the blend of causes of decline and retrenchment strategy. For example, external causes and asset reductions are matched with entrepreneurial expansion strategies. Thus, in the case of a recovery phase, firms might adopt growth-oriented strategies, for example, new investment, organisational changes and changes in product mix. Turnaround research considers retrenchment not only as a short-term emergency response to a crisis situation, but also as a powerful means to reverse decline and to secure survival and growth of firms in the long run (Robbins and Pearce, 1992: 296–7).

This general framework suggests several useful lines of enquiry for empirical investigation. First, was the crisis facing Lancashire the product of external rather than internal causes? Those concerned with the apparent problems caused by internal factors, such as the specialised structure of the industry, acknowledge the importance of changed conditions in export markets and look to internal structure as a reason why the industry failed to respond to changed circumstances (Lazonick, 1983, 1987; Mass and Lazonick, 1990). This hypothesis will be re-examined in more detail later in the discussion. Second, whatever the cause, in order to retrench, Lancashire entrepreneurs had to address their cash flow. Although previous studies of Lancashire textiles have examined the financial legacy of the 1919–20 boom, they have done so only at the industry level (Daniels and Jewkes, 1928: 167–82; Political and Economic Planning, 1934: 58–60; Clay, 1931a: 64; Committee on Industry and Trade, 1928: 36–8). The exception has been the focus by some on the financial experiences of the most prominent single company, the Lancashire Cotton Corporation (LCC), in the period 1929–31 (Bamberg, 1984a, 1988; Sayers, 1976; Sjogren, 1998). The analysis below examines the differential effects of the boom and subsequent slump on the strategies of *other* firms. The third and final issue was the influence of the causes of decline and retrenchment on subsequent recovery strategies. Previous studies have partially addressed this issue, for example, by tracing linkages between the cost structures of re-floated firms, disincentives to exit and subsequent attempts to organise short-time working and price maintenance schemes. According to this research, strategic response depended on sector, with the American section[4] having greater need but less ability than the Egyptian section to collude (Bowden and Higgins, 1998: 330). Also, it has been suggested that the best equipped firms prior to 1920 were also those facing the highest fixed costs and were hence incapable of exploiting their technical advantage (Bowden and Higgins, 1998: 326–7). However, as argued below, the refinancing process had significant and differential effects at firm level *within* each sub-sector. Also, because of the problems associated with retrenchment, the overwhelming majority of firms were unable to obtain the technical advantages associated with re-equipment.

**Financial characteristics of inter-war Lancashire**

To examine the financial strategies of specific firms, the study used a sample of quoted companies. The sample chosen was all firms whose financial details appeared in the *Stock Exchange Official Intelligence* (SEOI) and/or *Tattersall's Annual Review of the Cotton Trade*. To be selected, a firm had to be defined as belonging to the cotton industry and be included in either source continuously for at least a five-year period. Furthermore, sufficient financial details had to be available for it to be possible to calculate at least one of the two ratios that are particularly useful for measuring the financial structure of a business and confidence of market participants in its future prospects. These are, first, the ratio of book debt to total long term book capital (borrowing ratio) and, secondly, the ratio of book value of net assets (i.e. all assets minus all third party debt) to equity market value (book to market ratio). Both were used to measure the degree of financial stress and facilitate assessments of relative positions of financial stakeholders. The second ratio was only calculated where an equity share price quotation was available. Although the sample does not provide systematic coverage of the industry, it nonetheless includes all firms for which public domain information was available.[5] The firms for which details are available comprised approximately 48 per cent of re-floated spindleage and 20 per cent of the industry's total spindleage.[6] Table 1 shows the financial details described above for the sample of companies at three dates, 1920, 1930 and 1938. Significant firms are listed individually. Larger numbers of similar spinning mill companies are shown in aggregated sub-samples for 1930 and 1938, split into groups according to whether or not they were re-floated in 1919–20. The firms in Table 1 provide a useful cross section of the industry. Product range and firm size vary across the sample. Although necessarily biased towards spinning specialists, some vertically integrated firms are also included.

The re-financing strategy adopted by the typical firm in 1919–20 was to re-value fixed assets and offer new shares based on the higher values. An average book to market ratio of 0.98 across the sample (Table 1) is a consistent reflection of this strategy. On average, buildings, machinery and engines were re-valued by a factor of six. Working capital values were unaltered, so capitalisation of the typical company

**Table 1** Financial structure of Lancashire companies, 1920–38

| Company | Debt | Equity | Total | Debt/ Total | BM Ratio |
|---|---|---|---|---|---|
| **1920** | | | | | |
| ACMT | $3,391,127 | £ 5,225,609 | £ 8,616,736 | £ 0.39 | 1.23 |
| Ashton | 216.000 | 528,787 | 744,787 | 0.29 | 1.22 |
| Barlow + Jones | 553,000 | 648,839 | 1,201,839 | 0.46 | 0.79 |
| Brierfield Mills | 86,925 | 170,872 | 257,797 | 0.34 | nd |
| Crosses + Winkworth | 3,365,462 | 2,500,000 | 5,865,462 | 0.57 | 0.58 |
| Elkanah Armitage | 0 | 373,075 | 373,075 | 0.00 | 0.99 |
| FCSDA | 6,010,960 | 6,532,770 | 12,543,730 | 0.48 | 0.58 |
| Hollins Mill | 700,000 | 624,112 | 1,324,112 | 0.53 | nd |
| Jackson + Steeple | 0 | 358,291 | 358,291 | 0.00 | 1.64 |
| Joshua Hoyle | 1,391,810 | 1,248,476 | 2,640,286 | 0.53 | 0.81 |
| Rylands | 1,500,000 | 2,967,493 | 4,467,493 | 0.34 | 1.03 |
| Tootal Broadhurst | 700,000 | 1,587,597 | 2,287,597 | 0.31 | nd |
| **Averages*** | | | | **0.44** | **0.99** |
| **1930** | | | | | |
| ACMT | 3,264,313 | 4,653,683 | 7,917,996 | 0.41 | 22.88 |
| Ashton | 216,000 | 229,406 | 445,406 | 0.48 | 3.03 |
| Barlow + Jones | 553,000 | 855,060 | 1,408,060 | 0.39 | 0.90 |
| Brierfield Mills | 50,000 | 127,902 | 177,902 | 0.28 | nd |
| Combined Egyptian Mills | 6,338,637 | 1,791,207 | 8,129,844 | 0.78 | nd |
| Crosses + Winkworth | 937,359 | 578,463 | 1,515,822 | 0.62 | 59.09 |
| Elkanah Armitage | 0 | 300,546 | 300,546 | 0.00 | 3.56 |
| FCSDA | 7,254,321 | 5,829,095 | 13,083,416 | 0.55 | 0.96 |
| Hollins Mill | 710,195 | 573,476 | 1,283,671 | 0.55 | nd |
| Jackson + Steeple | 0 | 331,458 | 331,458 | 0.00 | 8.42 |
| Joshua Hoyle | 2,328,972 | 1,136,851 | 3,465,823 | 0.67 | 2.02 |
| Lancs Cotton Corporation | 2,014,291 | 1,377,029 | 3,224,595 | 0.62 | nd |
| Rylands | 1,500,000 | 2,618,994 | 4,118,994 | 0.36 | 1.23 |
| Tootal Broadhurst | 469,913 | 1,244,774 | 1,714,687 | 0.27 | nd |
| Refloated spinning cos.** | 44,701 | 145,816 | 190,518 | 0.23 | 10.85* |
| Non refloated spinning cos.** | 31,000 | 45,989 | 76,989 | 0.40 | 3.98* |
| **Averages*** | | | | **0.39** | **11.30** |
| **1938** | | | | | |
| ACMT | 1,981,713 | 4,263,119 | 6,244,832 | 0.32 | 17.88 |
| Ashton | 216,000 | 237,179 | 453,179 | 0.48 | nd |
| Barlow + Jones | 123,164 | 842,913 | 966,077 | 0.13 | nd |
| Brierfield Mills | 0 | 213,365 | 213,365 | 0.00 | nd |
| Combined Egyptian Mills | 10,123,845 | 1,146,908 | 11,270,753 | 0.89 | nd |
| Crosses + Winkworth | 1,396,215 | 301,154 | 1,697,369 | 0.82 | 13.55 |
| Elkanah Armitage | nd | nd | nd | nd | nd |
| FCSDA | 6,690,000 | 5,515,560 | 12,205,560 | 0.55 | 5.80 |
| Hollins Mill | nd | nd | nd | nd | nd |
| Jackson + Steeple | nd | nd | nd | nd | nd |
| Joshua Hoyle | 1,606,094 | 811,782 | 2,417,876 | 0.66 | 1.45 |
| Lancs Cotton Corporation | 2,877,500 | 2,123,273 | 5,000,773 | 0.52 | 2.47 |
| Rylands | nd | nd | nd | nd | nd |
| Tootal Broadhurst | nd | nd | nd | nd | nd |
| Refloated spinning cos.** | nd | 141,577 | nd | nd | 13.80* |
| Non refloated spinning cos.** | nd | 86,270 | nd | nd | 1.27* |
| **Averages*** | | | | **0.44** | **8.03** |

*Sources*: Calculated from the *Stock Exchange Official Intelligence*, 1921, 1931 and 1939.

*Notes*: * $y^2$ Calculated from Tattersall's *Directory of the Cotton Trade*, 1931 and 1939.

** Book to market ratios were calculated for sub-samples of smaller cotton spinning companies that were either refloated in the 1919–20 boom or whose capital structures were left unaltered. The sample included all companies for which data was available in the relevant volumes of Tattersall's *Directory*. The total number was: 1930–121 re-floated and 40 non-capitalized; 1938–92 re-floated and 17 non-refloated.

*** Averages are unweighted.

nd no data available.

increased by a factor of three. Consequently, the implied cost increase in fixed interest and depreciation charges was £43,233 for a typical 100,000-spindle mill. On the basis of average output, that translated into a 2.8d increase in the cost per pound on 30s yarns and a 12.2d increase for 100s yarns.[7] To put these figures into context, the average net profit per company, even at the height of the 1919–20 boom, was only £14,786. Margins for 32s yarns were 29.88d per pound in 1920, but then fell sharply at first and then steadily to 2.98d by 1931 (Robson, 1957: 336–8). It follows that, in general, the newer the assets, the higher the revaluation and the greater the increase in fixed costs. Hence, the best-equipped mills of 1920 became the most financially embarrassed by 1930 (*The Economist*, 11 October 1930: 667: Bowden and Higgins, 1998: 330) although, as Table 1 suggests, there was significant cross sectional variation among larger firms. In general *ex ante* financial structure had a large influence on loss of competitiveness after 1920. In subsequent sections this influence is evaluated against other causes, particularly economic and technical efficiency arising from *ex ante* industry structure.

Why, then, did Lancashire entrepreneurs invoke such a terrible nemesis on their industry through their financial activities between 1919–20? It is possible they genuinely believed that cash flows from future operations would stabilise at permanently higher levels in post-war conditions. More likely, they used their re-financing strategies to exploit the potential for systematic wealth shifts in their favour. Such strategies had been a common feature of pre-war booms. Promoters floated new mills during booms using their influence to attract new finance and then used liquid equity markets to realise their equity investments (Toms, 2002). In all booms, but especially that of 1907, they attracted outside investors via large amounts of loan finance (Jones, 1959: 87–8; Toms, 1998b: 228; Toms, 2001). In this sense, the boom of 1919–20 was no different from its predecessors. Samuel Firth Mellor and Frank Platt, men who had participated in, and profited handsomely from, previous flotation booms were typical entrepreneurs (Thomas, 1978: 157; Bamberg, 1984b: 6). High dividend pay outs to shareholders, and the prospect of even higher payments in the future, were a driving force in the re-flotation boom. At the height of the boom in 1920, it was reported, 'probably more money has been paid in dividends at the end of March by spinning companies than on any previous occasion in the history of the trade' (*The Economist*, 24 April 1920: 857). Reports of dividend payments in the region of 25 per cent of called-up capital were commonplace.[8] In some cases payments in excess of 50 per cent were reported.[9] Platt retired on the proceeds of the 1919–20 boom (Bamberg, 1984b: 6).

As in previous booms some individuals who sold at the right time benefited at the expense of the remaining stakeholders. However, as will be shown, the industry as a whole could only sustain wealth transfers in the absence of externally imposed crises and the requirement to re-adjust to new trading conditions. The fragility inherent in the boom was not lost upon contemporary observers. According to *The Economist*:

Very high prices are being paid, and shareholders are doing remarkably well. It is quite evident that many people believe that the Lancashire cotton industry will experience a prosperous state of trade for many years … . It is held, however, that the new companies that are now being floated stand at a much higher value per spindle than other mills in Lancashire, and when a lean time comes, as undoubtedly it will, the concerns that have just changed hands will feel the depression very severely.

*The Economist*, 16 August, 1919: 265–6)[10]

Although there were commonalties across the industry, re-financing strategies differed for individual firms. Some companies, for example, Barlow and Jones and the Fine Cotton Spinners & Doublers Association (FCSDA), when floated in the amalgamation boom of 1898–1900, raised large amounts of fresh capital from the metropolitan stock markets of London and Manchester (Macrosty, 1907). In the intervening profitable years up to 1920, they built up further reserves because they did not follow the high dividend strategies of Oldham companies in the American section of the industry (Toms, 1998a). Hence, the scale of their re-financing activities was lower than other companies. For example, the total equity and loan capital of the FCDSA was £9.633m in 1912. By 1921 this had increased to £12.633m.[11] Although a large increase of 30 per cent, this was small compared to the averages described above. Some entrepreneurs used the opportunity provided by the post-war boom to create new amalgamations. For example, the Amalgamated Cotton Mills Trust (ACMT) was formed in 1920 via an amalgamation of existing mills. The group was centred on Horrockses, Crewdson & Co. and smaller, previously independent, west Lancashire companies with reputations at the quality end of the market and relatively modern machinery (ACMT, 1920). Similarly, Crosses and Heatons' Associated Mills was a new group of mills formed under the auspices of the combine of Crosses and Winkworth (CAW). The latter consisted of nine pre-war mills, again with relatively modern equipment consisting of 709,000 mule-equivalent spindles. These mills were valued into the new combine at £2.456m (*Manchester Commercial Guardian*, 7 September 1922). Accepting an (optimistic) valuation of £1 per spindle pre-1914, this firm was dramatically overvalued. For these companies in particular, re-financing placed a heavy burden on competitiveness and, as will be shown, made subsequent retrenchment impossible.[12]

## Financial constraints on recovery schemes

The re-financing activities of 1919–20 placed impregnable constraints on the abilities of managers to respond to the subsequent crisis and re-structure the industry. Hence, by 1930, the industry's capacity and its competitive and financial structures were unaltered in all *major* respects since the re-flotation boom. This section examines the causes of paralysis with reference to the relationship between asset values and financing arrangements. It then goes on to explain why these financial relationships undermined industry level rescue schemes.

Had Lancashire followed the standard pattern of a speculative boom, debt levels alone might have been a sufficient condition for managers' failure to respond to the crisis. Previous studies have stressed the importance of debt (Dupree, 1996: 275; Sjorgren, 1998). A substantial economics literature shows how debt de-stabilises during speculative booms (Allen and Gale, 2000; Bernanke, 1983; Fisher, 1933; Kindleberger, 1990). In standard models of this process, the speculative bubble bursts because, at some point, the high levels of debt undermine confidence and this, in turn, leads to tumbling share prices, distress selling and business liquidations, thereby undermining confidence even further and so on.[13] Conversely, it has been suggested that high debt levels can lead to closer stakeholder scrutiny of managers, reduce the free cash flow available to them and hence improve their incentives in re-structuring situations (Maloney et al., 1993). In other words, as is well known, debt may be beneficial up to a point, but at extreme levels can become disproportionately damaging to the firm and its stakeholders. In Lancashire, because debt contracts were written in nominal terms, price falls greatly increased debt burdens. However, these apparent relationships depend on a further crucial factor, also illustrated in the Lancashire case: the valuation of assets.

The relationship between the valuation of assets and financial claims, including equity as well as debt, was important due to the requirement for retrenchment as a precursor for recovery strategies. Managers were faced with two options: either cut costs or reduce assets. However, the crucial consequence of redistribution of ownership rights in the boom of 1919–20 was that managers could do neither. Cost reduction was important, even though crisis severity suggested asset reduction might be more so. Re-floated companies were committed to high fixed costs, especially depreciation and interest charges arising from the boom. These costs were fixed in the true sense; they were unalterable without further re-ordering of the financial claims of equity and loan investors. Lenders are usually reluctant to forego interest payments, but will agree postponement to avoid the costs of liquidation. Such postponements are usually accompanied by asset sales (Berglof and Van Thadden, 1994). Financial claims are based on assets and to reorder them in the Lancashire case also meant asset sales. However, asset sales were the least attractive option to loan creditors. The main reason was that realisable values were low (Bowker, 1928). The collapse in export markets had created over-capacity and hence there was no second hand market. The assets involved were highly specific, especially machinery, and in many cases were of old vintage (Ryan, 1930; Political and Economic Planning, 1934: 54). As will be discussed below, new, but more expensive technology, was available. Book values were therefore well below replacement cost. Thus, the only alternative valuation available to financial claim holders was the economic value of the assets in use. As a correspondent wrote 'the real security for many outstanding loans in our depressed industries is little else but the earning power of the assets pledged' (*The Economist*, 30 August, 1930: 394). Such valuations require forecasts of future earning capacity. Where realisable values are low, forecasts of risk-adjusted present value cash flows need not be especially high for rational decision-maker's to continue investment in sunk capital. Moreover, these forecasts were imbued with a degree of optimism as a result of experience of the trade cycle. For example, some recalled the depression of the 1890s and argued that the causes of that depression (high world gold prices) were also causing the present difficulties. These commentators noted that when gold prices fell between 1897 and 1914, the industry had experienced its greatest boom (*The Economist*, 20 September, 1930: 520; FMCSA, 1936).

Notwithstanding the validity of any of these claims, optimism about world market conditions proved misplaced. Therefore, the important consequence was that Lancashire remained committed to an ageing and obsolescent asset base and the cumulative effects of fixed costs written against increasingly unlikely profit opportunities. It is important to stress, however, that even though the cotton employers' optimism exposed them to a certain amount of ridicule (Dietrich, 1928; Greaves, 2000), their wishful thinking was rooted in the realities imposed upon them by hard financial constraints. The removal of these constraints was an essential precondition for restructuring the industry. Industry leaders recognised this and looked to alter the financial claims of the main stakeholders.

To solve the financial problems without recourse to outside assistance, the main option was to call-up unpaid share capital. This had been a method of finance in the American section for many decades and was used again as security for debt- holders during the 1919–20 boom (Farnie, 1979; Thomas, 1978). If uncalled capital could be raised, the cash could be put to retiring fixed interest bearing debt created in the boom. Although there is limited evidence of some calls being unsuccessful,[14] Table 2 shows that taking the interwar years as a whole, the amounts raised through calls and their average incidence were at times substantial. These calls raised £20.9m in the period 1923–38, whilst the total debt of the industry can be estimated at around £33m.[15] On the surface, therefore, calling of equity capital might have been sufficient to eliminate a substantial portion of the debt.

However, the effect instead was to extend and deepen financial distress. There were two interrelated reasons for this. First, the unnerving effect on financial sentiment and share prices of calling-up unpaid shares and second, the network

**Table 2:** Amounts raised through calls on unpaid share capital by Lancashire spinning firms, 1923–38

| Year | Totals raised (£) | No. of companies | Averge per company (£) |
|------|------------------|------------------|------------------------|
| 1923 | 1,418,500 | 32 | 44,328 |
| 1924 | 939,375 | 28 | 33,549 |
| 1925 | 533,750 | 13 | 41,057 |
| 1926 | 1,999,750 | 42 | 35,328 |
| 1927 | 4,317,478 | 85 | 50,793 |
| 1928 | 3,230,279 | 80 | 40,378 |
| 1929 | 1,513,207 | 42 | 36,028 |
| 1930 | 3,638,620 | 78 | 46,648 |
| 1931 | 3,702,494 | 76 | 48,717 |
| 1932 | 663,083 | 24 | 27,628 |
| 1933 | 381,518 | 17 | 22,442 |
| 1934 | 173,340 | 11 | 15,758 |
| 1935 | 147,494 | 7 | 21,070 |
| 1936 | 20,000 | 1 | 20,000 |
| 1937 | 65,000 | 2 | 32,500 |
| 1938 | 48,225 | 2 | 24,112 |
| Total | 20,910,500 | | 33,771 |

*Source*: Calculated from *Tattersall's Cotton Trade Review* (various issues)

*Note*: The above figures refer only to spinning companies. Wherever possible, combined spinning and weaving firms were removed.

of financial interdependencies between shareholders, creditors and banks, created an industry specific problem of 'debt deflation'.[16] The direct consequence of calling-up unpaid share capital was to undermine the stock market further through forced sales, as the owners of partly-paid shares tried to sell them on to avoid call liabilities.[17] This reinforced the depression driven bear market in company shares.[18] Apart from a brief recovery following suspension of the Gold Standard,[19] activity on the Manchester market did not really begin to improve until 1936.[20] Another consequence was that to meet liabilities represented by partly-paid shares, shareholders withdrew loan monies from the same firms in which they owned partly-paid shares![21] Such companies then had to turn to their bankers to make good the loss of loan capital.[22]

Meanwhile the banks were confronted with the problem that their loans to spinning companies were becoming increasingly doubtful and less valuable because the collapse in trade meant that asset values of companies to which they had supplied loans were substantially reduced. In other cases, shareholders owning fully paid shares were forced to sell these in order to meet calls on partly-paid shares.[23] The situation was summed up as follows:

> It has been a depressing month in the cotton mill share market. The outlook with regard to finance is considered more serious. Rumours of a disquieting nature have been circulated, and pressure for the withdrawal of loan money has accentuated the difficulties of numerous mills. In the circumstances prices for shares have been weak, with selling pressure, and unexpected developments have occurred in connection with some mills that have a small amount of paid-up share capital and big loan accounts.
>
> (*Tattersall's Cotton Trade Review*, 18 May 1928)

Moreover, as Table 1 suggests, the typical debt to equity ratio did not fall as a result of calling-up unpaid capital. In part, this reflected the pressure to pay dividends, as illustrated by the tendency of dividend decline to lag behind the fall in profits (Figure 2). Even so, as share values declined, market to book ratios increased, reflecting accentuated financial distress on the basis of supposed asset values in the balance sheets of cotton firms. Dis-equilibrium and instability in capital markets constrained the ability of re-floated companies to retire their debt by calling-up unpaid share capital. To the extent that owners of partly-paid shares met calls by withdrawing loan money, the net position was no better, either for firms or for shareholders.

The practice of obtaining required money by calling in loans from the same or other spinning companies, in turn aggravated the prevalence of undercutting industry prices or 'weak selling'. The banks might have been expected to protect their loans by requiring that their spinning customers complied with price maintenance schemes. In the 1920s the Federation of Master Cotton Spinners' Associations (FMCSA) sought the banks' support to discourage individual firms from 'weak selling'. It was noted, for example, that 'It is understood that the employers associations are in negotiation with the leading banks in order to ascertain if some arrangement can be made to prevent forced selling of goods' (*The

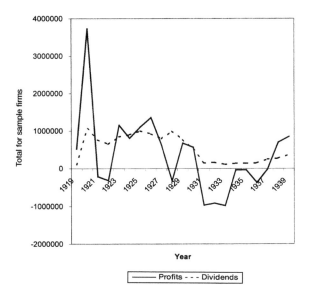

**Figure 2** Profits and dividends, 1919–39
Source: Calculated from the *Stock Exchange Official Intelligence*, 1919–39

*Economist*, 9 December, 1922: 1076). When the banks promised support, there was an immediate revival in demand for mill shares.[24]

However, disunity continuously undermined attempts to enforce price maintenance schemes. The Lancashire banking industry had a competitive structure that matched the cotton industry, so the banks were just as incapable of adopting a united front (Bamberg, 1984a: 26). Their excuse was that they could not 'be expected to support a policy when the spinners cannot apparently come to an agreement' (Shepherd, 192–8: 71). More importantly, *individual* banks recognised that it was in their interests to encourage mill customers to renege on price maintenance schemes. The Balfour Committee noted this pressure:

> A further effect was the creation of 'weak sellers' of yarns, consisting of mills which, in order to meet bank charges or other immediate requirements, were *forced* to sell their production and stocks of yarn at less than production costs. This also tended to weaken the commercial position of the American spinning section as a whole.
> (Committee on Industry and Trade, *Survey of Textile Industries*, part III: 37)[25]

In these circumstances, dis-equilibrium in financial markets helped generate disequilibrium in product markets and these, in turn, represented serious constraints on recovery strategies. High fixed charges at a time of depressed trade lowered profit margins and increased indebtedness to the banks. In order to meet bank charges, revenue of any sort, even from weak selling, was necessary. However, this weak selling further lowered yarn prices and necessitated even further weak selling if previous volumes were to be realised. Share prices, which were badly undermined by threats of further calls, were affected in turn: the collapse of prices undermined sentiment making it even more difficult to sell, thereby increasing pressure on shareholders to withdraw loans to meet calls. This increased the relative importance of bank loans.

In the absence of re-flotation, the normal operation of market forces would have removed excess capacity: the most inefficient firms would have become bankrupt and excess capacity and the incentive for weak selling would both have been reduced. However, the re-flotation boom and its consequences prevented this process. One problem involved identification of the 'inefficient' firm. Re-flotation resulted in a high degree of convergence between the interests of the technically strong (but financially weak) and technically weak (and financially weak) firms. Neither type of firm could afford the prospect of an all-out price war to determine which would survive (Bowden and Higgins, 1998: 327). The corollary of this was that all firms had an incentive to pursue collusive pricing and working agreements, which further interfered with normal market processes. Additionally, the re-flotation process encouraged very high prices to be paid for existing equipment (which had a very low resale value) which meant that 'exit' was not a realistic financial option. The new owners of the industry simply could not afford to walk away and accept the huge losses that exit implied. Indeed, so long as much of the equipment was fully depreciated, they had a powerful incentive to remain in the industry in the hope that the market environment might improve. Finally, as our discussion of the regional stock market has indicated, the highly illiquid and depressed market for cotton mill shares meant it was also impossible for the new owners to reverse the wealth transfers, the hope of which had brought them into the market in the first place.

Because industry leaders could not solve their problems with their inherited financial structure they began to lobby for outside support. It has long been recognised that financial claims and, implicitly, governance structures, had pernicious effects on short-term product market strategies at firm and industry level and prevented a united response to the crisis. Keynes accused the banks of abandoning their responsibilities, referring to the bankers as 'a species of deaf mutes' (Keynes, 1981: 601). More recently, historians have shown the competitive structure of bank lending to have been inimical to industry recovery (Bamberg, 1988: 26–30). The argument presented in this section is that whilst it is all well and good to blame specific institutions such as the banks, excess competition or 'individualistic' attitudes (Lazonick, 1984: 396; Saxonhouse and Wright, 1987: 89), the processes preventing industry turnaround were deeper. *Ex ante* financial claims, both debt and equity, and the relationship between them, decisively determined subsequent events, illustrating the vital path dependency of the process and the importance of historical analysis to understanding the economic problems of debt and over-capacity.

It is informative to begin by analysing the writings of Lancashire's most strident contemporary critic, J.M. Keynes. Keynes's attacks on all main interest groups, from obstinate directors to the paralysis of bankers and the uncooperative unions, are clearly documented (Keynes, 1981: 578–637; Skidelsky, 1992: 261–3). In particular, he argued that the industry leaders' strategy of short time working was flawed, because overheads were spread over a smaller output, driving unit costs to disadvantageous levels. Later, he argued that financial unsoundness was a bigger factor than short-time working. Later still, he argued that over-capacity was more important than financial unsoundness (Keynes, 1981: 583–4, 591). These arguments, whilst reflecting some change in position and learning about the industry and its problems, demonstrated his consistent and overriding concern to promote amalgamation as a solution, first via the Cotton Yarn Association and then via the Lancashire Cotton Corporation.[26]

However, there are several problems with this critique and, especially, its conclusion. Amalgamations had occurred before in the merger boom of 1898–1900, and again crucially in the boom of 1919–20. As demonstrated above, these were a cause of difficulty for the industry rather than a panacea. Keynes argued that the fine-spinning section was not problematic as world demand remained constant and there was little need for short-time working (Keynes, 1981: 581). Yet the combines formed by amalgamation in the fine section between 1919–20, such as CAW, and ACMT, under-performed other firms and suffered acute financial distress (especially compared to the FCSDA, see Table 1). The first two companies were re-floated in 1919–20, whereas FCDSA was not. Combined Egyptian Mills (CEM), formed in 1929, also performed badly in the 1930s. Although no data was available to calculate the book to market ratio, the rise in indebtedness, trebling of negative balances on reserves, and failure to pay dividends, strongly suggest that such amalgamations were ineffective, even in the fine section where external competitive pressures were less intense.[27] Jackson and Steeple, another re-floated company, had the third highest book to market ratio in Table 1 in 1930, behind CAW and ACMT, but no debt, suggesting that the causes of financial distress went beyond mere indebtedness. In contrast, for other firms that did not re-capitalise, such as Ashton Brothers, Barlow and Jones and Elkanah Armitage, the level of financial distress represented by the book to market ratio was less extreme. Similarly, there are striking differences between the aggregated book to market ratios for the smaller mills that re-capitalised and those that did not (Table 1).

Contemporaries such as Daniels and Jewkes (1928: 180–3) argued, as has been argued in this paper, that overcapitalisation had important consequences for the strategies of firms, especially the promotion of price-cutting or weak selling. Keynes disagreed. Instead, he argued that re-capitalisation had no effect on earnings and hence was irrelevant, the real problem being over-capacity (Keynes, 1981: 629–31). He was correct in the sense that associated costs were fixed and hence irrelevant to decisions about price. However, there was an important relationship between recapitalisation and over-capacity. Keynes only had half the story by making the link between governance structure and solutions to over-capacity via amalgamation. He called for the dismissal of the vast majority of cotton company directors, adding that the people required to vote on such a proposal were precisely those directors (Keynes, 1981: 631). As he acknowledged, many of these directors had risen to their positions of influence precisely as a result of re-flotations in 1919–20 (Keynes, 1981: 630). The missing part of his analysis was the link between re-flotation, governance and industry capacity.

It has been shown above that re-flotation prevented retrenchment and re-equipment, and distribution of ownership claims accentuated the problem. The final aspect of the present analysis is to establish a clear relationship between re-flotation and subsequent exit barriers, thereby linking the re-flotation boom directly to over-capacity. As suggested earlier, re-flotation created exit barriers since the economic value of assets in use was below replacement cost, a gap which increased with advances in technology, and above net realisable value. The banks, in particular, were forced to accept the economic value of earnings in order to salvage at least some of their advances. Under these conditions it was rational for firms to stay in the industry if the expected rate of return was equal to, or greater than, the required rate or cost of capital. As shown earlier, in an industry characterised by boom and slump throughout its history, it is not difficult to believe that industry decision-makers tempered their wishful thinking with rational expectations about the future return to profitability. At the same time the cost of the capital already committed to the industry was low, but not, as Keynes suggested, irrelevant. Lancashire hence provides an empirical verification of the theoretical framework suggested by Edwards *et al.* (1987), that links the decision to enter or exit an industry to the valuation of assets in use and expectations about future rates of profit. Further, the case shows the importance of path dependent consequences arising from *ex ante* valuation decisions and structuring of financial claims. This explanation also takes the analysis of Bowden and Higgins (1998: 319–43) one step further. The claims of the banks influenced competitive behaviour and presented an exit barrier, thereby helping to prevent industry agreement and perpetuating over-capacity. However, although bank debt made the situation much worse, it was not a sufficient condition to explain this behaviour. As a result of the asset mis- valuations of 1919–20, *all* financial stakeholders, whether debt or equity holders, had an incentive to encourage maximisation of return on capital in use. This follows from the analysis above, but can also be confirmed by comparing the situation after 1950. The industry remained reliant on sunk physical capital, but excessive debt had largely vanished during the war and post-war boom periods. Over-capacity and weak selling remained endemic, however (Singleton, 1991: 199–204), reflecting the incentives of residual equity holders.

Some contemporaries recognised the requirement for a cash injection as a pre-requisite for re-ordering financial claims. A good example was the scheme advocated by Hammersley. In view of the inter-relationship between the owners of shares, general depression in the Lancashire trade, incidence of short-time working, and market sentiment, it seemed inevitable to Hammersley that capital would have to come from outside Lancashire. He recognised that if the stock market was heavily depressed then owners of 'good' and 'bad' shares (i.e. shares with low values and subject to call risk) would be unable to liquidate the former in order to meet claims arising on the latter. Therefore, external capital was needed. In effect, Hammersely proposed a swap of cash for equity (Hammersley, 1931: 47–56). Unsurprisingly, the scheme failed to attract any institutional support. One reason was that the Bankers Industrial Development Corporation (BIDC) had a policy of not using its capital to relieve investors of existing financial burdens (Lloyds Bank, 1930: 268–70).[28] Consequently, assets could not be bought for cash and the BIDC would not countenance mergers involving cash acquisitions. The paramount objection to the scheme was that it involved persuading outside financiers that the industry had a prosperous future when existing owners wished to divest. This exposed the contradiction of financial stakeholders' enforced reliance on the future cash generation potential of assets in use. As one commentator put it,

> Had the existing owners and creditors of the businesses concerned so little faith in the future ... that they wished to get clear of it for good and for all? (For the prospective investor) this would immediately make him wonder whether in these circumstances he could prudently interest himself or advise his clients to take an interest.
>
> Lloyds Bank, 1930: 269–70)[29]

Without an external cash injection, other possible schemes involved the formation of large combines of indebted firms. However, to succeed, such schemes had to recognise that the owners taking over existing debt acquired by the combine would require interest payments just like their predecessors. In other words, rationalisation based on low realisable values was insufficient in itself to reduce fixed interest bearing debt. What was also required was writing-down of debts, or substitution of income bonds or ordinary shares for cumulative fixed interest charges. In this respect the LCC was unusual because, as part of the purchase consideration, 5.5 per cent convertible debenture stock was to be offered, such interest being contingent on earnings (*The Economist*, 26 January 1929: 155; Bamberg, 1984a: 71).[30] Hence the LCC intentionally comprised the most heavily indebted firms.[31] Consequently, its formation did eliminate some debt as it underwent a series of debt to equity restructurings during the 1930s. Of the firms that remained outside the LCC, debt levels were moderate. Table 1 shows that in 1930 average debt for re-floated firms outside the LCC was £44,701 against an asset base of £190,518, or a ratio of 0.23. This compares very favourably with the debt of the LCC and firms in the fine-spinning section such as CAW and the FCSDA. However, this analysis ignores the crucial relationship to asset values. Following from the discussion in section two above, although book values were a precise representation of financial claims, they bore little relationship to underlying economic or realizable values of the assets. The book to market ratio of 10.85 for the sub-group of re-floated spinning companies (Table 1) shows that the degree of mis-valuation was extreme. It also follows that the ratio of debt to market based asset values was also extremely high. In other words, formation of the LCC failed *directly* to relieve financial distress in firms remaining outside its control.[32] The LCC was also unsuccessful in overcoming indebtedness and financial distress for firms that it acquired, as the high ratios in Table 1 indicate.

In the absence of any successful restructuring, the combined effects of financial ownership constraints and the fall in export demand were to continue to generate catastrophic effects on company balance sheets. By 1930, the financial distress of many Lancashire companies had reached extreme levels that were maintained throughout the decade. Table 1 shows that borrowing levels had not reduced. Indeed, the average borrowing ratio was about the same as it had been in 1920. As suggested earlier, commitment of additional funds was not on the agenda for loan providers. The striking feature of Table 1 is that only two firms for which data are available had book to market ratios of less than one. In other words, market values had slumped to very low levels. For all other firms, the ratio had risen to high or extreme levels. Normally, where product and financial capital markets are efficient, such firms would expect to be taken over and be stripped of their assets (Manne, 1965). However, this did not happen due to poor realisable values available on asset disposal. Extreme book to market ratios also indicate that debt/equity ratios had reached extreme levels if expressed in market value rather than book value terms.

### Financial constraints on restructuring and re-equipment

The previous section established that there were no simple solutions to the financial problems arising from the flotation boom of 1919–20. However, retrenchment was an essential precondition for the re-structuring and re-equipment of the industry. In this section the link between financial constraints and re-equipment will be examined in more detail. Specifically, it is demonstrated that, given the financial difficulties of the industry, re-equipment programmes, although risky, were contingent upon higher capital expenditures, which could not be countenanced on the basis of *a priori* asset valuations.

There has been considerable debate about the relative merits of ring and mule spinning and plain loom and automatic weaving (Sandberg, 1969; Saxonhouse and Wright, 1984: 507–19; 1987: 87–94; Mass and Lazonick, 1990). That ring spinning and automatic weaving became dominant is, however, undisputed. The important facts are that technical dominance was not established until after 1914 and, in British conditions, investment in new technology only became a commercial option in the 1920s and 1930s. The new technologies were based on faster throughput and, in particular, the invention of high-speed-drafting in 1914. Prior to this breakthrough, before World War I, productivity in ring and mule spinning increased at approximately equal rates (Higgins and Toms, 1997: 213). Only in the spinning of very fine yarns did mule spinning retain its advantages, even after 1945 (Higgins, 1993: 350–1). From 1920, high-drafting and other improvements in intermediate processes, such as doffing and winding, provided opportunities to speed up production and offered savings in areas of traditional labour intensity (Catling, 1970: 189; Noguera, 1936: 20–3; Tippett, 1969; Saxonhouse and Wright, 1984: 519; Procter and Toms, 2000). A survey in 1932 noted three cases of ring-spinning mills replacing low-draft with high-draft spinning, resulting in improvements in labour productivity of 42, 56, and 50 per cent respectively (Board of Trade, 1932: 135). To benefit, Lancashire firms faced steep step costs for new capital equipment. As re-equipment decisions were delayed, the gap between book values of existing assets and replacement costs had become very wide by the 1930s.[33] From 1931, Japanese producers adopted these techniques. This, together with devaluations of the Yen, explained Lancashire's loss of traditional Far Eastern markets (Farnie and Abé, 2000). By now industry commentators recognised that 're-equipment was needed on a vast scale' (*The Economist*, 30 August,

1930: 394). Some have argued that the vertically specialised structure of the industry prevented re-equipment, notwithstanding recognition of the importance of change among managers (Lazonick, 1983). The apparent powerlessness of Lancashire managers in the face of crisis resulted in calls for their wholesale dismissal (Keynes, 1981: 631).

However, financial constraints rather than technological conservatism or vertical structure, dictated Lancashire's response. At first sight this argument appears counter-intuitive. A common theoretical view is that shareholders or owner–managers will accept riskier projects when such decisions cannot easily be monitored by outside debt-holders (Watts and Zimmerman, 1986). This is because if the project is successful (even with small probability) the debt and outstanding interest will be covered and the equity holders will gain from incremental cash flows and higher values of residual assets. Conversely, if the project is unsuccessful, all losses fall on the debt-holders.

The opportunity to re-equip was not taken because the Lancashire case illustrates an exception to the predictions of economic models of management and creditor behaviour. There is a direct relationship between conditions of financial distress and the supply of capital. The classical model of capital investment described by the separation theorem assumes no 'hard' capital rationing as a corollary of perfect markets,[34] but as demonstrated above, the allocation of capital to, or within an industry, depends on *ex ante* governance structures and lending conditions. In particular, these created a requirement to recover cash from the future operation of highly specific assets. Therefore, cash flow was not available to fund new projects, even if the probability of success was very high. Managers were faced with the option of re-equipment, a risky strategy involving a steep increase in fixed costs against uncertain future cash flows. With very high levels of debt to market values of equity (Table 1), high asset specificity and low resale values in external markets, the supply of financial and physical capital became highly inelastic. In other words, even projects with certain positive net present values could have been rejected. *Ex ante* debt to equity, asset specificity and low resale values, meant that Lancashire entrepreneurs could only ignore the re-equipment opportunity at a decisive moment in the evolution of the world textile industry.

## Conclusions

Previous sections have presented empirical evidence in favour of several time-dependent propositions which, taken together, suggest a new interpretation of the catastrophic decline of Lancashire textiles. First, it has been shown that the re-flotation boom of 1919–20 created a set of financial constraints that prevented the formulation of effective recovery strategies. Asset valuations, and the associated reordering of financial claims that followed, fixed these constraints. Debt and the paralysis of the banks were part of the problem, but less important than the assumptions of all investors about asset values and future profitability. Traditional remedies such as drawing on unpaid calls were ineffective and the requirement to further re-order financial claims limited the effectiveness of amalgamation schemes. Meanwhile, the disparity between replacement cost and the profit, or other cash realisations available from assets in use, acted as a barrier to reequipment. Those amalgamation schemes that were adopted, including the LCC and CEM, inherited the same financial constraints and were thus ineffective.

Several important conclusions emerge from the analysis. Prior literature has addressed the financial condition of the industry in this period and some studies have identified (non-financial) constraints. The empirical survey presented here synthesizes these strands of the literature. It has shown that financial structure represented the hardest constraint faced by Lancashire entrepreneurs. These financial constraints, and the governance structures that they implied, reduced the capability of industry leaders to respond to the crisis, regardless of their abilities as managers or the scope of their activities as entrepreneurs.

Financial constraints under conditions of financial distress present new theoretical insights. Retrenchment as a response to crisis, as advocated in strategic management research, is difficult under certain conditions of financial distress and may be made impossible by asset specificity and *ex ante* asset values and financial structure. Similarly, recovery strategies, even when the pay-off is certain in financial terms, will not be available to managers in circumstances of financial distress and *de facto* capital rationing. Previous studies on industry turnarounds have tended to concentrate on the board and its relationship with investors, rather than on financial constraints that suppliers of funds might impose. The Lancashire case demonstrates that such financial constraints can impose an absolute constraint on managers' ability to react to crisis and develop any kind of retrenchment strategy. Without retrenchment there can be no recovery strategy. This point is particularly pertinent to the prior literature that has argued that Lancashire needed to re-structure through vertical integration as a pre-requisite for re-equipment (Mass and Lazonick, 1990). However, as the above evidence demonstrates, it was the financial constraint that prevented autonomous solutions to the crisis being generated from *within* the industry. Where solutions cannot be found within the industry, its leaders must lobby for outside help. From 1929, outside help did arrive in the form of Bank of England intervention. The subsequent failure of this and other government inspired interventions is testimony to the tightness of the financial knot that strangled the Lancashire cotton industry.

## Acknowledgement

We would like to thank the participants at the 2001 ABFH conference, in particular Derek Matthews, for their constructive comments on an earlier version of this paper.

## Notes

1. The fineness of cotton yarn was traditionally determined by the number of hanks of 840 yards that were needed to make one pound weight. In the above example, 32s meant that it would have taken 32 hanks of 840 yards to make one pound. The coarser (heavier) the yarn, the smaller the number of hanks needed to make one pound weight.

2. Some commentators have argued that the decline of the industry was entirely inevitable, and that attempts to preserve it represented a serious mis-allocation of resources (Singleton, 1991: 232).

3. As far as the American cotton textile industry was concerned this, too, suffered from the effects of excess capacity and rapidly declining financial health (Rose, 2000: 210–14).

4. Within the Lancashire cotton textile industry, firms were generally divided into two sections: those primarily using American raw cotton and those primarily using Egyptian raw cotton.

5. The period 1918–26 was one of great secrecy in the disclosure of financial statistics by cotton firms (Farnie and Abé, 2000).

6. Data for firm spindleage (excluding Hollins Mill Co., Ltd., Jackson & Steeple, and Rylands), was calculated from Clay, (1931: 10; 22 and table Xva, p. 26a) and Bamberg (1984a: 268). Figures for the LCC taken from Bamberg are as at 1932, after taking into account spindles that were planned to be scrapped by the end of that year. Data for industry spindleage was taken from Robson (1957: 340).

7. Examples of these calculations can be found in Thornley (1923: 187–9).

8. See, for example, *The Economist*, 11 October 1919: 575; 24 April 1920: 857; 18 September 1920: 431.

9. In some cases, dividend pay-outs in excess of 100 per cent were reported (*The Economist*, 21 August 1920: 298). The Times Mill, Middleton, paid 600 per cent (Porter, 1974: 2).

10. See also the *The Economist*, 31 January 1920: 183.

11. The figures in this example are calculated from the annual accounts, Commercial Reports, Stock Exchange Records, London Guildhall Library.

12. Clearly, those firms which had not re-floated were in a relatively stronger financial position compared to those which had: they would have had more reserves to draw on as the depression deepened and had a smaller fixed interest burden (Porter, 1974: 6–7).

13. For example, it was noted that the failure of the Belgrave Group of mills in 1926, 'caused increased nervousness, with fears of other companies being compelled to go into liquidation. The mill share market is being affected, and now and again brokers report considerable selling pressure' (*The Economist*, 19 December 1925: 1042).

14. *Tattersall's Cotton Trade Review*, 16 May 1923; 20 June 1923; 21 April 1926; 15 May 1930; 18 June 1930.

15. Estimates of industry debt were calculated by taking the mid-point of debt for a sample of companies contained in Bamberg (1984a, appendix 4.1: 122).

16. The term appears to have been first coined by Irving Fisher (1933: 341).

17. *Tattersall's Cotton Trade Review*, 21 March 1923; 24 April 1923; 18 July 1923; 16 January 1924; 20 February 1924; 18 June 1924; 16 July 1924; 16 December 1925; 14 January 1926; 17 February 1926; 17 March 1926; 21 April 1926; 16 June 1926; 15 July 1926; 22 September 1926; 15 December 1926; 17 January 1927; 14 April 1927; 22 June 1927; 20 July 1927; 17 August 1927; 21 September 1927; 16 May 1928; 20 June 1928; 15 August 1928; 19 September 1928; 17 October 1928; 14 March 1929; 15 January 1930; 20 August 1930; 16 October 1930; 15 January 1931.

18. See monthly reports of activity in cotton mill shares quoted on the Manchester exchange. This is most vividly conveyed by reading the *Annual Reports* for the year end in *Tattersall's Cotton Trade Review*, 16 January 1924; 17 January 1927; 16 January 1928; 16 January 1929; 15 January 1930; 15 January 1931; 16 January 1932; 25 January 1933; 17 January 1934; 19 January 1935; 21 January 1936.

19. *Tattersall's Cotton Trade Review*, 21 October 1931; 18 November 1931.

20. *Tattersall's Cotton Trade Review*, 19 November 1936; 17 December 1936; 21 January 1937; 18 February 1937; 18 March 1937; 21 April 1937.

21. *Tattersall's Cotton Trade Review*, 16 February 1927.

22. In fact, the increase in bank advances to make good the loss of loans from shareholders actually encouraged further withdrawals by loan holders (Bamberg, 1984a: 25).

23. *Tattersall's Cotton Trade Review*, 16 January 1928.
24. *The Economist*, 12 April 1924: 782; 19 April 1924: 821. Keynes himself recognised that, in order to prevent mills breaking away from cartel schemes in the American section, coercion from banking interests would be necessary (*The Economist*, 27 November 1926: 910).
25. Committee on Industry and Trade, *Survey of Textile Industries* part III, p.37. Similar views were expressed by Keynes, 'All the spinners whom I have seen are agreed that this *involuntary* selling by financially necessitous mills is causing the final loss of blood' (Keynes, 1981: 598).
26. The precise cost savings that might have been generated from amalgamation and the obstacles to their realisation have been emphasised in prior research (Bamberg, 1984a: 39–72, 136–32; 1988: 88–97; Greaves, 2000: 106–9).
27. CEM failed to generate a sustained profit until 1937, and paid its first dividend only in 1948 (Farnie and Yonekawa, 1988: 183, Bamberg, 1984a: 134–8; 1988: 93–7).
28. The BIDC was established, on the initiative of the Bank of England, in 1929. Its primary aim was to devise schemes to re-equip and, where necessary, to amalgamate companies in the staple industries which were often in financial difficulties.
29. A series of other objections were raised by Henry Clay, a special adviser to the Bank of England (Clay, 1931b: 87–94).
30. The LCC was unusual but unique in this respect. In the case of CEM, the banks were also prepared to accept income debentures as security for a substantial proportion of the indebtedness of the constituent companies (*The Economist*, 25 May 1929:1176).
31. The percentage of companies entering the LCC for which financial information was available was, 21.3 per cent of those with debts ranging between ten and twenty shillings per spindle, 25 per cent of those with debts ranging between twenty and thirty shillings, 42 per cent of those with debts ranging between thirty and forty shillings, 70.3 per cent of those with debts ranging between forty and fifty shillings, 75 per cent of those with debts ranging between fifty and sixty shillings per spindle, and 61.5 per cent of those with debts exceeding sixty shillings per spindle (calculated from Bamberg, 1984a, Appendix 4.1, p. 122).
32. There is some evidence, though, that *indirectly* the LCC may have helped the financial position of firms that it did not absorb. The explanation for this was that the LCC was able to use its position as a 'price-leader' in the American section to enforce price maintenance agreements. According to this view, the LCC's financial position was sufficient to allow it, at the first signs of the break-up of price agreements, to flood the market with stocks. This appears to have acted as a sufficient deterrent (Bamberg, 1984a: 307–12).
33. For example, according to manufacturers' price lists in 1935, automatic winding systems had a capital cost of nearly six times those on the 'ordinary system' and automatic looms had a capital cost of nearly three times the cost of plain looms (Joshi, 1935: 10–11, 21).
34. In the subsequent literature the tradition has been to neglect empirical research into the existence of externally imposed or "hard' ('pure') rationing (Weingartner, 1977: 1403–5).

## References

*Official publications*

**Committee on Industry and Trade** (1928) *Survey of Textile Industries*, London: HMSO.
**Bard of Trade** (1932) *An Industrial Survey of the Lancashire Area (Excluding Merseyside)*, London: HMSO.

*Secondary sources*

**Allen, F.** and **Gale, D.** (2000) 'Bubbles and crises', *The Economic Journal*, 10: 236–55.

**Amalgamated Cotton Mills Trust (ACMT)** (1920) *Concerning Cotton: A Brief Account of the Aims and Achievements of the Amalgamated Cotton Mills Trust and its Component Companies*, Manchester: Amalgamated Cotton Mills Trust Ltd.

**Bamberg, J.H.** (1984a) The government, the banks, and the Lancashire cotton industry, 1918–1939', unpublished PhD. thesis, University of Cambridge.

**Bamberg, J.H.** (1984b) 'Sir Frank Platt', in D.J. Jeremy (ed), *Dictionary of Business Biography*, Vol. 4, London: Butterworths, pp. 716–22.

**Bamberg, J.H.** (1988) 'The rationalisation of the British cotton industry in the inter-war Years', *Textile History*, 19: 83–102.

**Berglof, E.** and **Von Thadden, E.-L.** (1994) 'Short-term versus long-term interests: capital structure with multiple investors', *Quarterly Journal of Economics*, 109: 1054–84.

**Bernanke, B.** (1983) 'Non-monetary effects of the financial crisis in the Great Depression', *American Economic Review*, 73: 257–76.

**Bowden, S.** and **Higgins, D.M.** (1998) 'Short-time working and price maintenance: collusive tendencies in the cotton spinning industry, 1919–1939', *Economic History Review*, 51: 319–43.

**Bowden, S.** and **Higgins, D.M.** (2000) 'Quiet successes and loud failures: the UK textile industry in the inter-war years', *Journal of Industrial History*, 3: 91–111.

**Bowker, B.** (1928) *Lancashire under the Hammer*, London: Hogarth.

**Burnett-Hurst, A.** (1932) 'Lancashire and the Indian market', *Journal of the Royal Statistical Society*, 95: 395–440.

**Catling, H.** (1970) *The Spinning Mule*, Newton Abbot: David and Charles.

**Clay, H.** (1931a) *Report on the Position of the English Cotton Industry*, Confidential Report for Securities Management Trust Ltd.

**Clay, H.** (1931b) 'Rationalisation: the cotton trade', *Lloyds Bank Limited Monthly Review*, 13: 87–94.

**Daniels, G.** and **Jewkes, J.** (1928) 'The post-war depression in the Lancashire cotton industry', *Journal of the Royal Statistical Society*, 91: 153–206.

**Dietrich, E.** (1928) 'The plight of the Lancashire cotton industry', *American Economic Review*, 17: 473–4.

**Dupree, M.** (1996) 'Foreign competition and the inter-war period', in Rose, M.B. (ed), *The Lancashire Cotton Industry*, Preston: Lancashire County Books, pp. 265–95.

**Edwards, J., Kay, J.** and **Meyer, C.** (1987) *The Economic Analysis of Accounting Profitability*, Oxford: Oxford University Press.

**Farnie, D.** (1979) *The English Cotton Industry and the World Market*, Oxford: Oxford University Press.

**Farnie, D.** and **Abé, T.** (2000) 'Japan, Lancashire and the Asian market for cotton manufactures, 1890–1990' in D. Farnie, T. Nakaoka, D.J. Jeremy, J. Wilson, and T. Abé (eds), *Region and Strategy in Britain and Japan*, London: Routledge, pp. 115–57.

**Farnie, D.** and **Yonekawa, S.** (1988) The emergence of the large firm in the cotton spinning industries of the world, 1883–1938', *Textile History*, 19: 171–210.

Fisher, I. (1930) *The Theory of Interest*, New York: Macmillan.

Fisher, I. (1933) 'The debt-deflation theory of Great Depressions', *Econometrica*, 1: 337–57.

FMCSA (Federation of Master Cotton Spinners' Associations) (1936) *Measures for the Revival of the Lancashire Cotton Industry*, Manchester: FMCSA.

Greaves, J.I. (2000) '"Visible hands" and the rationalisation of the British cotton industry, 1925–1932', *Textile History*, 31: 102–22.

Hambrick, D.C. and Schecter, S.M. (1983) 'Turnaround strategies in mature industrial-business product units', *Academy of Management Journal*, 26: 231–48.

Hammersley, S.S. (1931) 'Rationalisation: the cotton trade', *Lloyds Bank Limited Monthly Review*, 12: 47–56.

Higgins, D. (1993) 'Rings, mules and structural constraints in the Lancashire textile industry, c.1945–c.1965, *Economic History Review*, 46: 342–62.

Higgins, D. and Toms, J.S. (1997) 'Firm structure and financial performance: the Lancashire textile industry, c.1884–c.1960', *Accounting, Business and Financial History*, 7: 195–232.

Jones, F. (1959) 'The cotton spinning industry in the Oldham district from 1896 to 1914', unpublished MA thesis, University of Manchester.

Joshi, B. (1935) *Articles on Preparatory Machines, Cotton Weaving, Yarn Testing etc.*, Bombay: Times of India Press.

Keynes, J.M. (1981) *The Return to Gold and Industrial Policy II*, Collected works, Cambridge: Cambridge University Press, pp. 578–637.

Kindleberger, C.P. (1990) *Manias, Panics and Crashes*, London: Macmillan.

Lazonick, W. (1981) 'Competition, specialisation and industrial decline', *Journal of Economic History*, 41: 31–8.

Lazonick, W. (1983) 'Industrial organisation and technological change: the decline of the British cotton industry', *Business History Review*, 57: 195–236.

Lazonick, W. (1983) 'Stubborn mules: some comments', *Economic History Review*, 40: 80–6.

Lazonick, W. (1984) 'Rings and mules in Britain: a reply', *Quarterly Journal of Economics*, 99: 393–8.

Lazonick, W. (1986) 'The cotton industry', in B. Elbaum and W. Lazonick, *The Decline of the British Economy*, Oxford: Oxford University Press, pp. 18–50.

Lloyds Bank (1930) The banks and industry', *Lloyds Bank Monthly Review*, 1: 268 –70.

Macrosty, H. (1907) *The Trust Movement in British Industry*, London: Longman.

Maloney, M., McCormick, R. and Mitchell, M. (1993) 'Managerial decision-making and capital structure', *Journal of Business*, 66: 189–218.

*Manchester Commercial Guardian* (various issues).

Manne, H. (1965) 'Mergers and the market for corporate control', *Journal of Political Economy*, 73: 110–20.

Marrison, A. (1996) 'Indian summer', in M.B. Rose (ed), *The Lancashire Cotton Industry*, Preston: Lancashire County Books, pp. 238–64.

Mass, W. and Lazonick, W. (1990) 'The British cotton industry and international competitive advantage: the state of the debates,' *Business History*, 32: 9–65.

Noguera, S. (1936) *Theory and Practice of High Drafting*, privately published.

Pearce, J.A. and Robbins, K.D. (1993) 'Retrenchment remains the foundation of business turnaround', *Strategic Management Journal*, 19: 613–36.

Political and Economic Planning (1934) *Report on the British Cotton Industry*, London: PEP.

Porter, J.H. (1974) The commercial banks and the financial problems of the English cotton industry, 1919–1939', *The International Review of Banking History*, 9: 1–16.

Procter, S.J. and Toms, J.S. (2000) 'Industrial relations and technical change: profits, wages and costs in the Lancashire cotton industry, 1880–1914', *Journal of Industrial History*, 3: 55–72.

Robbins, K. and Pearce, J. (1992), 'Turnaround: retrenchment and recovery', *Strategic Management Journal*, 13: 287–309.

Robertson, A.J. (1990) 'Lancashire and the rise of Japan, 1910–1937', *Business History*, 32: 87–105.

Robson, R. (1957) *The Cotton Industry in Britain*, London: Macmillan.

Rose, M.B. (2000) *Firms, Networks and Business Values*, Cambridge: Cambridge University Press.

Ryan, J. (1930) 'Machinery replacement in the cotton trade', *Economic Journal*, 40: 568–80.

Sandberg, L. (1969) 'American rings and English mules: the role of economic rationality', *Quarterly Journal of Economics*, 83: 25–43.

Saxonhouse, G. and Wright, G. (1984) 'New evidence on the stubborn English mule and the cotton industry, 1878–1920', *Economic History Review*, 37: 507–19.

Saxonhouse G. and Wright, G. (1987) 'Stubborn mules and vertical integration: the disappearing constraint', *Economic History Review*, 40: 87–94.

Sayers, R.S. (1976) *The Bank of England, 1891–1944*, Cambridge: Cambridge University Press.

Shepherd, W.E. (1928) 'Banking in its relation to the cotton industry', *Journal of the National Federation of Textile Works Managers' Assocs*, 7: 68–77.

Shiloh (1949) *The Shiloh Story, 1874–1949*, London: Harley and Co.

Singleton, J. (1991) *Lancashire on the Scrapheap*, Oxford: Oxford University Press.

Sjogren, H. (1998) 'Financial reconstruction and industrial reorganisation in different systems: a comparative view of British and Swedish institutions during the inter-war period', *Business History*, 39: 84–105.

Skidelsky, R. (1992) *John Maynard Keynes: Economist and Saviour, 1920–1937*, London: Macmillan.

Thomas, W. (1973) *The Provincial Stock Exchanges*, London: Frank Cass & Co.

Thomas, W. (1978) *The Finance of British Industry, 1918–1976*, London: Methuen.

Thornley, T. (1923) *Modern Cotton Economics*, London: Scott Greenwood and Co.

Tippett, L.H.C. (1969) *A Portrait of the Lancashire Cotton Industry*, London: Oxford University Press.

Toms, J.S. (1998a) 'Windows of opportunity in the textile industry: the business strategies of Lancashire entrepreneurs, 1880–1914', *Business History*, 40: 1–25.

**Toms, J.S.** (1998b) 'The supply of and the demand for accounting information in an unregulated market: examples from the Lancashire cotton mills, 1855–1914', *Accounting Organizations and Society*, 23: 217–38.

**Toms, J.S.** (2002) 'The rise of modern accounting and the fall of the public company', *Accounting Organizations and Society*, 27: 61–84.

**Watts, R.** and **Zimmerman, J.** (1986) *Positive Accounting Theory*, Englewood Cliffs, NJ: Prentice Hall.

**Weingartner, H.M.** (1977) 'Capital rationing: n authors in search of a plot', *Journal of Finance*, 32: 1403–31.

**Yamazaki, H.** (1997) 'Competition and co-operation in the Japanese textile industries', in H. Pohl (ed), *Competition and Co-operation of Enterprises on National and International Markets*, Stuttgart: Franz Steiner Verlag.

**Zimmerman, F.M.** (1991) *The Turnaround Experience*, New York: McGraw-Hill.

# Ownership, financial strategy and performance: the Lancashire cotton textile industry, 1918–1938[1]

David Higgins[a], Steven Toms[b]* and Igor Filatotchev[c]

[a]Newcastle University Business School, University of Newcastle, Newcastle upon Tyne, UK; [b]Leeds University Business School, University of Leeds, Leeds, UK; [c]Cass Business School, City University London, London, UK; Department of Business Administration, Vienna University of Economics and Business, Vienna, Austria

This article assesses the validity of John Maynard Keynes' claim that the Lancashire cotton industry failed to restructure because the banks as debt holders prevented firms exiting the industry, creating persistent over-capacity. Using case studies from a substantial sample of Lancashire firms, the article explores archival evidence to establish their financial characteristics, to examine their equity and debt finance and the governance roles of directors and outside ownerhip groups. On the basis of this review the article develops hypotheses to suggest alternatives to the view that bank debt was the dominant explantion of firm level behaviour and industry failure. Applying these to a statistical dataset, results show that syndicates of local shareholders, *not* banks, were an important impediment to the exit of firms. Moreover, syndicates milked firms of any profits through dividends, thereby limiting reinvestment and re-equipment possibilities. Our results show that where laissez-faire fails in response to a crisis, incumbent investors, particularly block-holders, can be an important impediment to corporate restructuring.

## 1. Introduction

There has been a substantial debate about the benefits rationalisation might have conferred on British manufacturing during the interwar period.[2] One industry which has featured prominently is the Lancashire cotton-textile industry. In the *End of Laissez-Faire*, writing against the backdrop of the inter-war economic crisis, Keynes argued that the role of the government is not to try to do what is being done better, but to do what is not being done.[3] For Keynes, there was no better illustration of this point than the Lancashire cotton textile industry. As demand in overseas export markets collapsed, creating a serious problem of over-capacity, the industry's large number of relatively small firms competed intensely on the basis of marginal cost pricing. For Keynes the solution was the reorganisation of the industry. An important obstacle was the intractability of the incumbent management and financial stakeholders. The banks might have promoted reorganisation, but were 'professional paralytics', and it was 'against their tradition to do anything whatsoever in any conceivable circumstances'.

He also called for the dismissal of the vast majority of cotton company directors. However, Keynes was careful in his choice of scapegoats. In particular he sought to avoid implicating those responsible for the re-financing of the industry already carried out in the boom of 1919–20. Contemporary commentators who stressed the problems resulting from these events, were criticised by Keynes for finding easy solace and standing in the way of educating opinion as to what he saw as the correct diagnosis (Keynes, 1928, 199).[4]

In presenting new evidence to test the propositions that follow from Keynes's arguments, the article addresses the key aims and objectives of this special issue which are to examine the 'methodological issues, particularly the role and opportunities for empirical research in business history'; to 'explicitly address the development of theory and/or hypothesis testing'; as well as building 'generalisations [that help us to] understand and explain causal mechanisms', and, perhaps most importantly, we 'develop scientific knowledge by constructing theories which are subject to empirical testing [which] will develop knowledge about businesses and entrepreneurs in their *historical context and about their interactions with the environment*'[5] (emphasis added).

To achieve these objectives, the article uses archival evidence to demonstrate that investor syndicates, both internal and external to this industry, exerted powerful effects on the ability of heavily recapitalised firms to pursue exit strategies. These links between finance, ownership and strategic behaviour provide an opportunity to develop and test hypotheses concerning the *relative* impact of investment by different groups of financial stakeholders on firm strategy. They suggest that strategy, financial performance and long term survival will be determined by the governance characteristics of the firm. The hypotheses generate evidence useful in wider literatures by illustrating the role of ownership as a potential constraint on corporate restructuring and as a determinant of managerial performance.[6] For the cotton industry these results also indicate that Keynes was far too dismissive of refinancing and the problems it caused; that investor groups in particular were at least as important, if not more so, than the banks that subsequently kept indebted firms in the industry. The results are important because they show that the Keynesian panacea of reorganisation was insufficient and that financial restructuring, especially the radical variation of ownership rights, was also required.

Our analysis is also relevant for research on corporate restructuring and business turnaround within strategic management since it uncovers a complex interplay of governance conflicts associated with a combination of debt and equity financing. As a consequence, the article also contributes to more recent studies that question the universality of the governance-strategy-performance relationship associated with agency-grounded research and suggests that the impact of governance factors may also depend on organisational contingencies, such as the stage in the firm's life-cycle, industry environment, etc.[7] More specifically, we revisit the proposition that, in the context of organisational decline, governance factors, such as board directors' interlocks or the presence of concentrated institutional ownership in a situation of limited stock market liquidity, may impose severe constraints on possible turnaround strategies.[8] Our archival evidence helps to develop this theoretical framework further by combining firm-level data with more qualitative evidence obtained from the contemporary sources for individual cases and industry dynamics in general.

The article is organised as follows. In Section 2 we compare and contrast the key features of Keynes's analysis of the industry's problems with those of other informed contemporaries. Particular emphasis is placed on the observation that, unlike his contemporaries, Keynes was generally dismissive of the impact of re-flotation. In Section 3 the composition of investor syndicates is analysed. Notwithstanding contemporary and subsequent debates, there is no prior empirical evidence concerning the composition of these groups. Indeed there are only passing references to 'London' and 'Metropolitan' syndicates and our research shows that these references are partially and materially inaccurate. Section 3 examines the role of investor groups, both syndicates and banks, and their impact on firm level performance outcomes, using a financial data set and appropriate econometric models. The comparative impact of bank lending and financial syndicate investment is assessed. Discussion and conclusions are presented in Section 4.

## 2. Keynesian and other interpretations of the collapse

The fundamental feature of the Lancashire textile industry between the wars was the violent and, as it turned out, irreversible contraction in world demand for cotton goods. The broad facts of this collapse have been extensively documented. The salient points are that during the 1920s, and 1930s, exports of cotton piece goods were 58% and 29% respectively of their 1913 level. For yarn exports, the relevant figures were 80% and 66% respectively.[9] Of particular importance in this collapse were the loss of the Indian market and the growth of Japanese competition in third markets. In 1913, out of a total British production of approximately 700 million yards of cotton piece goods, 43% by quantity and 36% by value, were exported to India.[10] By the 1930s, Indian production of cotton piece goods and yarn was 34% and 131% greater, respectively, than its pre-war average. A number of factors, including the disruption caused by the war, reduced shipping facilities, growing nationalism and increasing tariff protection, account for India's reduced dependence on Lancashire exports. The reversal in the Indian market was exacerbated by Japanese competition. Between 1914 and 1930, Japan's share of Indian imports of cotton piece goods increased over a hundred-fold, and Bowker estimated that Japanese penetration of the Chinese market was responsible for 17.6% of the decline in Lancashire's exports.[11]

However, although these basic facts were well known to contemporaries, there was less agreement on what the industry should have done in order to restore its competitiveness. For convenience, we contrast two interpretations: one is Keynes' view that reorganisation was required but the banks and industry directors prevented this outcome. The second, advanced by other contemporaries, that world economic conditions were to blame and recapitalisation simply made matters worse.[12]

### 2.1 The Keynesian historiography

Keynes' analysis of the problems affecting the industry focused on excess capacity and its consequence, short-time working: 'The termination of the short-time policy is urgently called for, and the substitution for it of a "rationalising process" designed to cut down overhead costs by the amalgamation, grouping or elimination of mills.' Short-time working increased the costs of the industry, aggravated financial losses, and led to financial exhaustion. Keynes was adamant that while a policy of short-time working might be desirable to meet temporary disturbances in trade, it was absolutely disastrous as a long-term solution. In any case, as he pointed out, the actual practice of short-time working was very badly organised.[13]

The solutions to short-time working proposed by Keynes were threefold: the elimination of weak-sellers (those selling output below cost), the adjustment of surplus capacity and rationalisation to achieve appropriate economies.[14] Why, then, was the required contraction in capacity not forthcoming? Keynes position on this was clear: the banks had lent so much to the industry, particularly its financially weaker companies, that they were loath to let their debtor companies go bankrupt, even though this would have accelerated the adjustment of capacity in the industry.[15] In Keynes' perspective, the banks *could* have promoted change in the industry,[16] but *chose* not to (our emphasis). Whilst castigating the banks, Keynes dismissed the significance of the re-capitalisation boom:

> The industry is riddled with unsound finance; some of it the result of the over-capitalisation of the boom period. ... If high capitalisation and bad management were the essential troubles, reconstructions and bankruptcies might be the right solution. But they are only secondary troubles. The real trouble – and this is the beginning, the middle and the end of my argument – is surplus capacity.[17]

Keynes argued that the recapitalisations of the 1919–20 boom were irrelevant as they did not affect earnings, suggesting that even if this capital were written off the problem would persist without solving the underlying problem of over-capacity.[18] Therefore, as far as Keynes was concerned, the writing-off of capital was trivial and the important challenge was reorganisation.

In this respect, Keynes was not unique. Turning to the *general* problem of excess capacity, there was recognition that rationalisation and reorganisation could improve the competitive position of industry, but the existence of a large fringe of small producers hampered the efforts of big firms trying to secure these efficiencies.[19] John Ryan (Managing Director of the Lancashire Cotton Corporation [LCC]), argued that amalgamation and reorganisation would simultaneously help Lancashire to improve her international competitiveness and provide relief to the spinning section which was labouring under heavy financial losses.[20] In the specific case of the Lancashire cotton textile industry, the subsequent historiography strongly endorses the Keynesian interpretation, and most acknowledge that over-capacity was a root cause of the post war problems.[21]

Opinions differ somewhat as to who should have taken responsibility. Bamberg adds to Keynes' famous accusation that the bankers acted as 'a species of deaf mutes', abandoning their responsibilities, showing the competitive structure of bank lending to have been inimical to industry recovery. Indeed, as Bamberg has noted, the indebtedness of the industry *could* have provided the means for its salvation.[22] However, this had to await the formation of the LCC in 1929. Frank Platt, managing director of the LCC, realised that many firms in the American section were heavily indebted to the banks who might be able to coerce their mill customers to obey price maintenance schemes. The banks had an obvious reason for exercising this coercion: their own fortunes had become intricately and heavily tied up in the fortunes of the spinning industry. For example, the index of bank overdrafts for a sample of 145 refloated companies increased from 100 in January 1921 to 152 by January 1924.[23] The extent to which individual banks were exposed varied substantially: the Midland Bank's customers accounted for 34.7% of American spindles, but its total commitment was lower than Williams and Deacons which accounted for 13.8% of American spindles and whose total advances to 40 spinning companies was £3.7 million by the end of 1928.[24] Consequently, the banks had little option but to increase their overdrafts in order to try and protect previous loans to these firms. Periods of 'weak-selling', by increasing the operating losses of these firms, increased further the demand for overdraft facilities from the banks. Thus, in 1933, for example, Platt launched a price maintenance scheme to cover the medium 'American' section, which enlisted the support of a number of banks, all of which agreed to use their influence to force debtor spinning companies to observe minimum prices. However, even this option seems to have operated with only very limited success and was a 'dead letter' by 1934.[25]

Bamberg's evidence indicates that the most effective means for securing adherence to price maintenance schemes was completely independent of the banks and rested, instead, on the ability of the LCC to instigate a form of price leadership. Instead of following prices down in successive stages, as more firms abandoned existing price agreements, Platt proposed in 1934 that the LCC should undercut all its competitors by going directly to the 'rock-bottom' price.[26] This option was more than just an idle threat: the LCC had accumulated substantial reserves to protect itself against the breakdown of 'gentlemen's agreements'. Such was the success of this scheme that not only did it provide the basis for new and effective price maintenance schemes in the 'American' section for the rest of the 1930s but, also, in the 'Egyptian' section.[27] Obstinate directors, whom Keynes suggested should be dismissed, have nonetheless been subsequently criticised for their 'individualistic attitudes',[28] as have the unions for lack of co-operation.[29]

## 2.2 Contemporary opinion

For a second interpretation we need to consider contemporary opinion, since this view has attracted little support subsequently. Whiggish attitudes and hindsight make it difficult for historians to do other than condemn this view, since it is well known that the hoped for return to pre-1914 conditions never materialised. Indeed, contemporary opinion was far from a consensus, and such optimism attracted some ridicule.[30] However, unlike Keynes, many informed contemporary observers did place much greater emphasis upon the harmful effects of the recapitalisation boom. Daniels and Jewkes and the report by *Political and Economic Planning* argued that those firms that had recapitalised had stronger inducements to engage in price-cutting in order to secure the volumes required to cover their inflated costs.[31] Both of these authorities also suggested that the effects of recapitalisation worked against any effective joint action either regarding output restriction to raise prices, or to secure amalgamation.[32] Henry Clay, a special adviser to the Bank of England, supported these views. He also argued that the supply of loan capital, which should have been available to finance re-equipment and facilitate reorganisation, had been drained away by the need of re-capitalised companies to call-up unpaid share capital in order to meet interest charges and to replace withdrawn loans.[33]

In addition, contemporary observers were well aware of the disastrous effects that external syndicates could have on the fortunes of individual mills. James White established the London-based Beecham Trust[34] which was intimately involved in the flotation and re-flotation of famous British manufacturing companies such as Austin Motor Co. and the Dunlop Rubber Co.[35] In the Lancashire cotton industry, White, via the Beecham Trust, participated in the flotation of the Amalgamated Cotton Mills Trust (ACMT) in 1919.[36]

This year marked the start of the recapitalisation boom when the fortunes of the Lancashire textile industry appeared unlimited. During the first annual general meeting of ACMT – also in 1919 – the chairman of ACMT, Lord Fairfax, proudly proclaimed that:

> It would appear to me that certain gentlemen in Lancashire, who take an interest in the trade of that county, are agitated by the fear that the great cotton spinning and manufacturing trade may be in danger of becoming controlled by London financiers. I should like to recall to your memory that, so far as the Amalgamated Cotton Mills Trust (Limited) is concerned, our mills are in no sense of the word controlled by London financiers.[37]

At the same time, an extraordinary general meeting (EGM) was held at which the directors of ACMT were persuaded to create 1,300,000 new Ordinary shares of £1 which the Beecham Trust agreed to take at £3 a share, less a commission of £10,000. Subsequently, in 1920, the share capital was more than trebled. The consequences of this substantial – and unwarranted – increase in capital were clear for all to see: ACMT failed to pay a dividend on its ordinary shares from 1919/21 until 1937/38, when its capital structure was re-arranged.[38]

In addition, by 1930, the company's ordinary shares (nominal value £1), including those that the Beecham Trust agreed to purchase for £3, were quoted in the range 2s, 7.5d to 7.5d.[39] Unsurprisingly, therefore, the view of one commentator on White has been damning: 'the fact that he helped to saddle Lancashire with a disastrous load of 'watered' capital probably figured for as little in his calculations as the ruin caused to thousands of small investors who followed his star.'[40] White was a controversial figure, condemned by contemporaries for manipulating the share prices of companies that he floated.[41] Ernest Terah Hooley had a similar track record and attracted criticism for similar reasons. In 1920, Hooley promoted the Jubilee Cotton Mill in Oldham for the purposes of defrauding a wealthy Cardiff-based investor and was convicted for fraud.[42] On his release, Hooley wrote: 'Several people, with no more pretentions to honesty than myself, made millions of pounds, selling mill shares that were not worth a shilling apiece. ... If everybody had their just deserts there would have been a hundred other men put in prison.'[43]

Similarly, Sir Edward Mackay Edgar, who was a partner in the finance house, Sperling & Co., promoted the substantial amalgamation of Crosses & Winkworth Consolidated Mills (C&WCM) and Crosses & Heatons' Associated Mills Ltd., in 1920 and 1921, respectively.[44] Edgar was, significantly, chairman of both these companies during the early 1920s.[45] An important feature of the formation of the C&WCM was the sale of 11 million shares to the directors by Sperling at a substantial discount to the issue and subsequent market price. Twenty million ordinary shares of 1s were issued, of which 11 million were purchased by Sperling & Co., and resold to the directors 'and their friends' at par. Unlike the directors, the investing public were required to purchase in units of one £1 preference share and three ordinary shares for 33s. The preference shares were issued at a premium of 10s, so that the ordinary shares were notionally issued at par.[46] Although the preference share participated in a further 20% of profits after their fixed dividend,[47] a 50% premium, applied to the preference shares only, made little sense. Unsurprisingly, shortly after the issue the ordinary shares were trading at around 1s 11d (a 92% premium) whilst the preference shares traded at around 18s (a 40% discount).[48] The premium on the ordinary shares and the discount on the preference shares represented a risk free wealth transfer of just over £500,000 from the investing public to the directors.

Again, the subsequent financial performance of these companies was dire. C&WCM had to drastically restructure its capital in 1928, involving the writing-down of 3 million £1 cumulative preference shares to 6 shillings each, and the 20 million £1 ordinary shares to 2 million shares. The companies were bought for a total purchase price of £5 million, but for the purposes of this reconstruction, the company's land, building and machinery, were valued at just £1.2 million in 1928.[49] C&WCM paid a dividend on its ordinary shares in 1921, but no further dividends on this class for the rest of the inter-war period. Crosses & Heatons' appear never to have paid a dividend on ordinary shares.[50]

The evidence suggests therefore that recapitalisation impacted upon subsequent financial performance, which may explain why contemporary opinion referred to above concentrated on the relationships between re-capitalisation, over-capacity, individual firm behaviour, and weak-selling. The case also illustrates some important analytical relationships between principal and agent expectations and asset values.[51] However, the comparative influence of the banks and the syndicates on firm strategy, including the exit decision, has not been analysed. Indeed, until now, Keynes' views on earnings, re-capitalisation and capital write-offs have not been questioned much in the subsequent literature.[52] None have presented significant new empirical evidence. Even so, an empirical analysis of the composition of the syndicates and their relative impact on individual firm behaviour compared to the banks is important. This is in line with more recent research on the limitations of 'pecking order' hypotheses in corporate finance that suggest that net equity issues track financing deficit more closely than do net debt issues. Therefore, financial problems in a firm should be simultaneously attributed to the leverage and equity issues.[53] If the banks had an interest in preventing their clients exiting in order to avoid the consequent capital write-offs, then so too did the financial syndicates. Arguably the syndicates had more reason and greater ability to force firms to stay in the industry. Banks had the relative benefit of secured lending, albeit on reduced asset values and, even where these were minimal, stood to obtain any marginal benefit ahead of the unsecured equity syndicates. Where loan interest payments were deferred, they were allowed to accumulate so there was an expectation of higher payments in future years. Equity holders benefited only where the firm had sufficient earnings to depreciate the overvalued assets and meet fixed interest charges.[54] Unlike the banks, the syndicates had direct control over the board and the strategy of the firm through the control of voting shares. Corporate governance researchers have pointed out these potential differences between modes of financing and the associated control factors.[55] Although Keynes called for the removal of the company directors, adding they were unlikely to vote for their own dismissal,[56] it has not been empirically established that this was a realistic option. If outside syndicates were significant, such resolutions could only be carried with their support. Although it was well known that cotton directors had shareholdings, the scale of these and also the extent to which interlocks might have influenced directors to behave collectively have not been established empirically.[57] More specifically, it is not clear how controlling power associated with directors' interlocks and shareholdings was translated into majority voices at annual general meetings in companies they controlled.

Specifically, the role of cross directorships and shareholdings has not been examined for the crucial 1919–20 re-capitalisation boom. Unlike previous cotton booms, such as 1907 and 1911–13, the events of 1919–21, were without precedent, particularly with regard to the severity and duration of the ensuing depression.[58] Consequently, the presence of such network connections might impact on coalescence in the strategies advocated by the syndicates and any outside investor groups. Although convenient for the first interpretation of decline discussed above, the neglect of the role of the syndicates is therefore surprising, and the analysis below examines their effects, in contrast to the banks, more closely.

There is a further and potentially important consequence of the presence of these outside investors. Keynes and contemporaries seem to agree that they had little technical understanding or other useful knowledge of the industry other than perhaps its propensity to pay very generous dividends during periodic booms.[59] In addition to the question of whether the syndicates forced firms to stay in the industry, there is the further question of their impact on business and financial strategy. Specifically it is likely that they would have forced the cotton companies to repay any profits as dividends, so that the capacity for recovery through new investment could not be sustained. More recent strategic management research indicates that different types of institutional investors may have different decision-making horizons and preferences with regard to business strategies their portfolio firms may pursue.[60] As a result, it is possible that the specific make-up of investor syndicates in the industry has created a specific set of constraints imposed on managerial decision-making and the firms' strategic orientation.

## 3.  The syndicates: scale, characteristics and effects on firm behaviour

To examine the effects of ownership on managerial behaviour there are two empirical tasks. The first is to establish the nature of the ownership groups involved in the re-capitalisation boom of 1919–1920. Although an empirical contribution to the historical literature in its own right, this also provides a platform for the second empirical task which is the development of statistically testable hypotheses. Knowing the detailed composition of ownership groups allows the statistical results to be triangulated and judgements to be made about the suitability of the proxies used. These two tasks are dealt with in turn below.

### 3.1 Ownership and control characteristics

To examine ownership and control characteristics of the re-capitalised companies all available annual returns from the BT31 file at the The National Archives (TNA) were examined. The TNA has a policy of retaining a random sample of 1 in 5 company records and it was therefore appropriate to examine all surviving documents for firms that were known to be in existence, and to have been re-capitalised (as detailed in Worrall's and Tattersall's trade directories). The process produced a sample of 41 individual company archives. Within each, share registers, articles of association and annual returns (form E) were examined to identify the directors and significant shareholders in the re-capitalised companies, the scale of their cross-shareholdings, and the buy-sell and buy-hold behaviour of investing individuals and groups.

Table 1 shows the ownership details for the 41 firms. For each firm the table shows the paid up capital, the proportion of that capital owned by the directors, the proportion owned by significant (defined as 5% > ) blocks of outside investors, and the level and type of debt finance. Boards did not vary a great deal in size, typically consisting of five or six directors, so this data is not reported in Table 1 and the strength of insider control is measured using directors' share-ownership. The average total holding by directors' using the figures in Table 1 was 26.2%. As Table 1 shows, for five out of the 41 firms, the directors had outright control with combined holdings of greater than 50%.[61] In view of the size of these blockholdings and the pattern of ownership in residual shares, de facto control was likely to be even higher. Examples of inside blocks include Alexander Young and William Henry Heywood, two of the directors in Brunswick Mill, who jointly owned 31% on initial allotment; in Argyll, the directors owned 15.3%; Avon, 27.3%; Belgrave, 38.6%; Century Mill, 66.5%; Clover Mill, 35.7%, Delta, 28.3% and in Fern, the directors owned 22.8%.[62]

Most firms (29 out of 37 in Table 1 for which data was available) used debt finance of some description. Where debt was used, it represented 47% of the total (c.£4.25m debt compared to c.£4.72m equity for the 37 companies that had data on debt). As the equity of the firms was revalued for the purposes of the refloation, this represents a good estimate of the average leverage of the firms at the height of the boom. As the cases in Table 1 illustrate, loan finance predominated over structured debt (preference shares and debentures) and bank overdrafts. Indeed firms using bank finance represented a small minority of cases. Debt finance, as Keynes and others suggested, was important, but not specifically bank finance, reinforcing the view that the banks, when forced to intervene, were relatively new financial participants in the affairs of the industry when the crisis struck. Debt finance also varied considerably from firm to firm and may therefore have moderated different strategic responses at firm level during the crisis. This issue is returned to in the next subsection of the article.

Outside equity ownership meanwhile rarely amounted to significant influence. Only 13 out of the 41 companies in Table 1 had examples of significant outside ownership. For example, Francis Trippet, one of the directors of the Bolton Union Spinning Co., was also a director of City General Trust Ltd.[63] These connections may explain why Bolton Union represented a rare case of London-based investment, with significant investments from the

Table 1.    Re-capitalisation, block-holdings and financial characteristics of sample re-floated companies.

| Company | Date of Return[1] | Total paid up share capital (£) | % shares owned by directors | % shares owned by blockholders[2] | Loan capital (£) |
|---|---|---|---|---|---|
| 1. Ace Mill Ltd. | 14 April, 1921 | 240,000 | 37.7 | No sig. blocks | Mortgage: 150,000 |
| 2. Anchor Sp. Co. Ltd. | 24 January, 1921 | 37,500 | 74.6 | No sig. blocks | Loans: 146,635 |
| 3. Argyll Cotton Sp. Co. Ltd. | 28 April, 1921 | 150,000 | 15.3 | No sig. blocks | Loans: 149,320 |
| 4. Arrow Mill Ltd. | 26 June, 1920 | 150,000 | n.a. | 6.7 | Bank o/d: 45,000; Loans: 188,000 |
| 5. Asia Mill Ltd. | 19 January, 1921 | 160,000 | 17.9 | 25 | Loans: 72,562 |
| 6. Astley Mills Co Ltd. | 25 March, 1920 | 300,000 | 11.8 | No sig. blocks | Bank o/d: 104,000; Loans: 201,000 |
| 7. Athens Mill Co Ltd. | 8 March, 1920 | 120,000 | 19.1 | No sig. blocks | No debt |
| 8. Atherton Mills Ltd. | 27 October, 1920 | 250,000 | 2.4 | 7.6 | Loans: 299,000 |
| 9. Avon Sp. Co Ltd. | 11 February, 1920 | 150,000 | 27.3 | 38.3 | Loans: 26,000 |
| 10. Belgian Mills Co. | 4 August, 1920 | 70,000 | n.a. | n.a. | n.a. |
| 11. Belgrave Mills Co Ltd. | 20 October, 1920 | 20,000 | 38.6 | 27.5 | No debt |
| 12. Bolton Union Spinning Co Ltd. | 14 March, 1921 | 86,000 | 39.0 | 53.5 | n.a. |
| 13. Briar Mill Ltd. | 31 May, 1920 | 100,000 | 30.3 | No sig. blocks | Bank o/d: 80,253; Loans: 294,497 |
| 14. Broadway Sp. Co Ltd. | 25 May, 1920 | 90,000 | 34.1 | No sig. blocks | No debt |
| 15. Brunswick Mill Ltd. | 30 January, 1920 | 120,000 | 6.2 | No sig. blocks | Loans: 50,000 |
| 16. Butts Mills Ltd. | 9 June, 1921 | 375,000 | 15.4 | 7.5 | Bank o/d: 114,000; Debentures: 19,000; Loans: 257,000 |
| 17. Cairo Mill Co Ltd. | 25 April, 1921 | 175,000 | n.a. | No sig. blocks | Mortgage: 26,000 |
| 18. Cavendish Sp. Co Ltd. | 26 March 1920 | 176,920 | 7.7 | No sig. blocks | No debt |
| 19. Century Ring Mill Ltd. | 5 August, 1920 | 130,000 | 66.5 | No sig. blocks | n.a. |
| 20. Clover Mill Co Ltd. | 27 February, 1920 | 240,000 | 35.7 | No sig. blocks | Loans: 132,000 |
| 21. Commercial Mill Sp. Co Ltd. | 17 January, 1920 | 75,000 | 9.7 | No sig. blocks | n.a. |
| 22. Coppull Ring Sp Co. | 10 June, 1920 | 225,000 | 37.9 | 43.7 | Loans: 55,000 |
| 23. Coral Mills Ltd. | 30 December, 1919 | 150,000 | 0.0 | 6.1 | Loans: 59,000; Loans: 18,000; Mortgage: 60,000 |
| 24. Dawn Mill Co Ltd. | 29 April, 1920 | 100,000 | 17.3 | No sig. blocks | No debt |

Table 1.  (Continued).

| Company | Date of Return[1] | Total paid up share capital (£) | % shares owned by directors | % shares owned by blockholders[2] | Loan capital (£) |
|---|---|---|---|---|---|
| 25. Delta Mill Co Ltd. | 18 August 1920 | 150,000 | 28.3 | No sig. blocks | Loans: 166,000 Overdraft: 169,000 |
| 26. Duchess Sp. Co Ltd. | 24 March, 1920 | 60,000 | 36.2 | No sig. blocks | Loans: 71,368 |
| 27. Earl Mill Co Ltd. | 26 January, 1921 | 90,000 | 28.0 | No sig. blocks | No debt |
| 28. Elder Mill Ltd. | 14 May, 1920 | 61,125 | 12.3 | 49.9 | |
| 29. Falcon Mill Co. Ltd. | 24 September, 1920 | 190,000 | 10.9 | No sig. blocks | Loans: 142,000 |
| 30. Fern Cotton Sp. Co. Ltd. | 2 March, 1921 | 125,000 | 12.4 | 15.6 | No debt |
| 31. Fernhurst Sp.Co. Ltd. | 19 December, 1919 | 260,000 | 92.0 | No sig. blocks | Loans: 148,500 |
| 32. Glodwick Cotton Sp. Co Ltd. | 12 March, 1920 | 100,000 | 15.0 | No sig. blocks | Loans: 119,000 |
| 33. Gorse Mill Ltd. | 31 December, 1920 | 75,000 | n.a. | No sig. blocks | No debt |
| 34. Greenacres Cotton Sp. Co. Ltd. | 28 December 1919 | 125,000 | 14.4 | No sig. blocks | Loans: 152,000 |
| 35. Hartford Mill Ltd. | 21 October, 1920 | 130,000 | 31.0 | 8.7 | No debt |
| 36. Magnet Mill Ltd. | 29 December, 1921 | 76,630 | 0.0 | No sig. blocks | Loans: 109,000 Pref. shares: 37,000 |
| 37. Park Mill (Royton). | 11 February, 1920 | 36,000 | 11.2 | No sig. blocks | No debt |
| 38. Ruby Mill Co Ltd. | 19 May, 1920 | 31,552 | 0.0 | No sig. blocks | Loan. Deposit a/c: 27,000 |
| 39. Rutland Mill Ltd. | 25 June, 1918 | 48,000 | 1.9 | No sig. blocks | Loans: 153,000 |
| 40. Textile Mill Co Ltd. | 5 December, 1919 | 8,000 | 80.4 | 6.25 | Loans and interest: 185,000 |
| 41. Times Mill Co. Ltd | 29 April, 1919 | 32,000 | 65.7 | 16.9 | Loans: 234,000 |

Notes:
1 Refers to the date the source documents were filed at Companies House.
2 Significant block-holders are those who *individually* own 5% or greater of paid up share capital.
3 N.a. means not available.
Sources: Ace, *TNA*, BT 31/32360/162516; Anchor, *TNA*, BT 31/32438/168982; Argyll, *TNA*, BT 31/36914/165226; Arrow, *TNA*, BT 31/37696/16711; Astley, *TNA*, BT 31/32339/165099; Athens, *TNA*, BT 31/32335/160787; Atherton, *TNA*, BT 31/37693/162145; Avon, *TNA*, BT 31/38811/159919; Belgian, *TNA*, BT 31/32371/163568; Belgrave, *TNA*, BT 31/25035/158943; Bolton Union, *TNA*, BT 31/32419/166839; Briar, *TNA*, BT 31/36670/163570; Broadway, *TNA*, BT 31/32354/162152; Brunswick, *TNA*, BT 31/32378/163957; Butts, *TNA*, BT 31/38834-36/167722; Cairo, *TNA*, BT 31/39365/163619; Cavendish, *TNA*, BT 31/33811/165932; Century, *TNA*, BT 31/32338/161017; Clover, *TNA*, BT 31/36912/164330; Commercial, *TNA*, BT 31/37691/160540; Coppull, *TNA*, BT 31/35255/168122; Coral, *TNA*, BT 31/37277/161019; Dawn, *TNA*, BT 31/36384/161805; Delta, *TNA*, BT 31/36385/161972; Duchess, *TNA*, BT 31/32262/162803; Earl, *TNA*, BT 31/32261/162607; Elder, *TNA*, BT 31/32392/164696; Falcon, *TNA*, BT

Lancashire Cotton Syndicate, Barclays Bank and Horatio Bottomley, the MP and financial manipulator.[64] Indeed, outside of our sample, the only other Bolton spinning company for which we can establish significant external ownership, was Beehive which attracted a London investment group.[65] Manchester-based William P. Hartley, who had made money in preserves, invested in a portfolio of companies with investments in Asia, Duchess, Textile and Times. 'Gentlemen' investors were often based in Manchester, Liverpool and the Fylde coastal towns, but rarely in London or other non-Lancahsire metropolitan locations. Examples include William Sidebottom (Elder), James Chadwick (Fern), William Hartley Higham (Textile) and John Kenyon (Asia).[66]

Even then these outside investors were insignificant compared to the degree of inside control prevalent in the crisis-ridden Oldham section. Table 2 shows the number of directorships held by individuals identified from the returns of the 41 companies examined. This process identified seventeen individuals holding directorships in just under half of the 41 companies examined, but also including directorships in companies outside the sample and in a small minority of cases outside the cotton industry. Between them these 17 individuals were on the boards of 66 companies, mainly other cotton mills. Most of these individuals were also involved in the promotion of their companies in the recapitalisation booms and held some stock for resale post refloation. Promoter and share dealer Samuel Firth Mellor was a director of 18 companies.[67] Harry Tweedale, a stockbroker for Williams & Deacons Bank, was a director of Dale Mill and a founding director of Arrow Spinning Co. and Century Spinning Co. (in which he owned, or represented, 15.4% of the initial allotment of the stock). The pattern of interlocks reinforces the evidence of the influence of these promotional groups of insiders in the recapitalisation boom and the sunk nature of their investments. Their undiversified and risky position would be more likely to commit them to the industry, reducing the likelihood of exit.

These commitments led them, like Keynes, to call for the reconstruction of the industry. John S. Hammersley, who was also a director of several companies, advocated the financial restructuring of the industry, involving the variation of claim-holders' rights.[68] Unlike Keynes, therefore, he focused on ownership rather than the bank loans, capacity and short-selling problems. His scheme was based on cash for equity which, as the argument below suggests, was indeed necessary to rescue the industry. Compared to Keynes's argument, it is easy to see why it was unpersuasive. His scheme not only compensated the speculators for their failure, but it also presupposed there were new investors whose expectations about the industry's future were more optimistic than incumbent investors.[69]

Inside directors were in any case significant and typically long-term investors. For example, in the case of Anchor (1920), and Asia (1920), the original directors of these companies held the same, or increased, ownership shares, in 1934 and 1926, respectively.[70] Examination of *Statements in Lieu of Prospectus* indicates that the monies paid to directors who promoted their company could be substantial, and therefore they had no pressing incentive to sell further shares post issue. For example, Cecil Hilton and John Stuttard, who promoted Earl Mill and subsequently acted as directors, received £5000 each for their work as promoters.[71] Some outside investors exited completely and early. For example, Hartley, the preserve manufacturer referred to earlier, sold his entire holding of 28,000 shares in Asia Mill, on 21 July, 1921, 13 months after purchase.[72] Insiders made only partial disposals if at all, and such transactions usually involved stockbrokers such as Firth Mellor and Bunting. It is likely that the stockbrokers who were also directors simultaneously provided market liquidity in their own companies for potential buyers.[73] It is very difficult to believe that these stockbrokers were able to increase total liquidity for

Table 2.  Interlocking directorships within our sample of re-capitalised Lancashire spinning firms, 1919–1921.[1]

| Name of Director | Spinning Company directorships held |
|---|---|
| Edward Heaton Blackburn | Argyll Cotton Spinning Co. Ltd; Mona Mill Ltd; Peel Mills Co. Ltd; Raven Mill Ltd; Sun Mill Co. Ltd; Slack Mills Ltd. |
| Herbert Bleakley | Arkwright Cotton Spinning Co. Ltd; Arrow Mill Ltd; Century Ring Mill Ltd; Dale Mills Co. Ltd. |
| George Cottam | Argyll Cotton Spinning Co. Ltd; Hartford Mill Ltd; Mersey Mill Ltd; Atlas Mills Ltd. |
| Fred Dawson | Cavendish Spinning Company Ltd; Rayners Ltd; Minerva Spinning Co. Ltd; Astley Mills Co. Ltd; F.L. Bentley Ltd; Oldham Athletic Assoc. Football Club Ltd; Oldham Twist Co. Ltd; Hope Mill Co. Ltd; Chadderton Mill Co. Ltd; Copster Mill Co. Ltd; Melbourne Mill Co. Ltd; Malta Mill Co. Ltd; Ram Mill Co. Ltd; Bury Paper Tube Co. Ltd; Robert Stott Ltd; Robert Thatcher & Co. Ltd. |
| Joseph Deveney | Arrow Mills Ltd; Century Ring Mill Ltd; Slack Mills Ltd; Victoria Mill Ltd; Wellfield Mill Ltd. |
| Thomas Howe | Cavendish Spinning Company Ltd; Rayners Ltd; Minerva Spinning Co. Ltd; Astley Mills Co. Ltd; F.L. Bentley Ltd; Oldham Twist Co. Ltd; Hope Mill Co. Ltd; Chadderton Mill Co. Ltd; Copster Mill Co. Ltd; Melbourne Mill Co. Ltd; Malta Mill Co. Ltd; Ram Mill Co. Ltd; Robert Stott Ltd; Robert Thatcher & Co. Ltd. |
| Samuel Firth Mellor* | Argyll Mill Ltd; Broadway Spinning Co Ltd; Fernhurst Spinning Co Ltd; Gee Cross Mills Ltd; Gorse Mill Ltd; Greenacres Cotton Spinning Co. Ltd; Guide Bridge Spinning Co. Ltd; Hartford Mill Ltd; Marsland Mills Ltd; Mars Mill Ltd; Mersey Mill Ltd; Monton Mill Ltd; Orb Mill Co. Ltd; Peel Mills Co. Ltd; Princess Mill Co. Ltd; Rugby Mill Ltd; Stockport Ring Mill. |
| Herbert Mills | Cavendish Spinning Company Ltd; Rayners Ltd; Minerva Spinning Co. Ltd; Astley Mills Co. Ltd; F.L. Bentley Ltd; Oldham Athletic Association Football Club Ltd. |
| William Noton | Fern Cotton Spinning Co Ltd; Delta Mill Co. Ltd. |
| Frederick Simm | Arrow Mill Ltd; Century Ring Mill Ltd; Era Mill Ltd. |
| George Stott | Anchor Spinning Co. Ltd; Avon Spinning Co. Ltd; Fern Cotton Spinning Co. Ltd; Soudan Mills Co. Ltd; Kent Mill Ltd; Ace Mill Ltd. |
| Harry Tweedale* | Arrow; Dale |
| James Waller | Arrow; Dale; Union Ring Mill. |
| Bertram Whitehead | Cavendish Spinning Company Ltd; Minerva Spinning Co Ltd; Astley Mills Co. Ltd. |
| Edward Whitehead | Avon; Delta Mill Co. Ltd; Devon Mill Ltd; Gresham Mill Co. Ltd; Osborne Mill Co. Ltd. |
| Edwin Wilson | Argyll Cotton Spinning Co. Ltd; Equitable Spinning Co. Ltd; Monarch Mill Co. Ltd. |
| Alexander Young | Athens Mill Co. Ltd; Bolton Union Spinning Co Ltd; Brunswick Mill Ltd; Butts Mills Ltd; Falcon Mill Co. Ltd; Trencherfield Mills Co. Ltd. |

Notes: [1] Refers to directorships held by directors of spinning companies that re-capitalised between 1919–1921. * Samuel Firth Mellor and Harry Tweedale were stockbrokers.
Sources: Directorships of all directors are referenced in the following TNA files: Edward Heaton Blackburn, The Swan Mill, *TNA*, BT 31/40621/159990; Herbert Bleakley, Arrow, *TNA*, BT 31/32335/160744; Joseph Deveney, Arrow, *TNA*, BT 31/32335/160744; Samuel Firth Mellor, George Cottam and Edwin Wilson, Argyll, *TNA*, BT 31/36914/165226; William Noton, Delta, *TNA* BT 31/36385/161972; Fern, *TNA* BT 31/32371/163516; Frederick Simm, Arrow, *TNA*, BT 31/32335/160744; George Stott, Avon, *TNA*, BT 31/38811/159919; Harry Tweedale, Arrow, *TNA*, BT 31/32335/160744; Alexander Young, Bolton Union, *TNA*, BT 31/32419/166839; James Waller, Arrow, *TNA*, BT 31/32335/160744; Edward Whitehead, Avon, *TNA*, BT 31/38811/159919; Alexander Young, Bolton Union, *TNA*, BT 31/32419/166839; Herbert Mills, Fred Dawson, Thomas Howe, Bertram Whitehead, Cavendish, *TNA*, BT 31/33811/165932.

cotton shares, though there is some evidence that stockbrokers who were *not* directors were able to effect substantial liquidation of their holdings: for example, in 1928, Samuel Firth Mellor sold his entire holding of 38,700 shares (£24,187), in Gorse Mill to the Union Bank.[74] The fundamental feature of the Oldham Stock Exchange was its dependence on cotton shares: 'Cotton spinning companies continued to be the unique feature of the Oldham Stock Exchange throughout its time as an independent exchange'.[75] No other exchange quoted Oldham mill shares. The Manchester and London stock exchanges had substantially more liquidity, but the low volume of business and the increased risk because of poorer market intelligence made mill shares very unattractive. In any case, major stockbrokers at the Oldham exchange held multiple mill directorships, for example, James Henry Bunting and Kenneth Morris,[76] meaning that the fate of this exchange was inextricably linked to the fate of the industry. Consequently, the total number of shareholders was usually quite small and there were surprisingly few transactions, given they were quoted companies. An obvious problem was the absence of buyers after the collapse of the boom in 1920. Moreover, given the evidence from the share registers, the presence of controlling cliques of directors was in itself sufficient to impose conditions of market illiquidity.

This combination of low liquidity and significant individual holdings created a strong incentive for self-serving behaviour at the expense of the company and minority shareholders, that becomes stronger as control rights increase.[77] One option would be to obtain rents through payment of dividends since any further re-capitalisation and investment would shift future rents to minority investors.

There were relatively few examples of family block holders within our sample, though the holding in Coppull Ring Mill by the Hollas family was one exception. The Hollas's represented a significant textile interest and were effectively insider investors.[78] Similarly, George, Robert, and Thomas Braddock, and Eric and John Brierley jointly owned 17.6% and 12.7%, respectively of the stock in Avon Mill.[79] Variations in the importance of family blockholders include the Cheetham brothers, James and John, who were directors and jointly owned 25.3% of the stock in Anchor,[80] and the Mellor family (Samuel Firth, director) and his wife Annie (non-director), who jointly owned 32.7% of Hartford Mill.[81]

A final and very important feature was the striking continuity between these investor groups in the Oldham section and the operations of similar groups, sometimes involving the same individuals, in the pre-1914 period. A feature of previous booms, for example in 1907, was the involvement of Bunting in the mill promotion boom (Toms, 2002). Firth Mellor and Hammersley were also involved in putting together business groups through flotation and inter-locking directorships.[82] Another important continuity was the involvement of successor generations. So James Henry Bunting continued his pre-war apprenticeship whilst successive generations of the architects and mill-designers A.H. Stott and Sons continued their practice of investing in the mills they helped to build.[83] In short, the investors of the 1919–20 re-capitalisation boom were local, inter-connected, had intensive knowledge of the industry and were continuing well-established practice from before 1914. The connection to pre-war behaviour is important, insofar as the practices established then contributed to the subsequent failure of the industry.

The governance characteristics identified by this review of corporate level traits strongly emphasise the importance of investor syndicates within the context of the industry. Building on this evidence, we argue that controlling for debt, the firm's strategy, financial performance, and long term survival will be determined by the governance characteristics of investor syndicates. More specifically, we suggest that large and recapitalised firms with outside share owners (as opposed to closely controlled, non-quoted firms) were less likely to exit. Recapitalised firms faced higher fixed costs arising from the change in ownership structure in the form of depreciation charges, dividends and interest charges. These costs are not fixed in the strict sense; for example, dividends are highly discretionary but they are sunk in the sense that they must be paid at some point if investors are to recover their committed capital. As noted above, these investors were often directors closely linked to promotional groups who were overcommitted to the industry on the basis of their investments and interlocked board positions, thereby making it even more likely that recapitialisation would function as an exit barrier. Notwithstanding the influence of these and other directors, their control was not as complete as in a private firm and the availability of the option to sell implies that public firms would be more likely to exit.

For firms that remained in the industry, although systemic industry conditions prevented turnarounds in general, some firms were more financiallly successful than others. *Ceteris paribus*, because larger firms which had been recapitalised had potential access to greater financial resources, they were in a better position to dominate market niches or requip, where the directors chose to do so. However, such freedom of action would have been limited by pressure to pay dividends. Such pressures would have been higher where firms had recapitalised as investors holding such shares would require higher cash dividends to secure an equivalent return on their investments. To the extent that firms were leveraged through bank debt, it would be expected that, if Keynes was right, highly indebted firms would be less likely to exit. Empirical tests allow this argument to be tested against the contention that equity ownership was the driving force. In similar vein, as discussed above, banks had negligible involvement in 1920 but became closely involved subsequently and against their will as losses mounted, suggesting they had little knowldege of the industry and therefore were less likely to influence successful turnaround strategies. In restricting the free cash flow available to managers, they might have also limited the tendency of firms to pay dividends in response to investor pressure. These arguments lead to the following research hypotheses:

1. Controlling for leverage, large, recapitalised, publicly quoted firms were less likely to exit the industry.
2. Controlling for leverage, large, recapitalised, publicly quoted firms were more likely to be profitable.
3. Controlling for leverage, large, recapitalised, publicly quoted firms were more likely to pay high dividends.

The next section examines these complex relationships between corporate governance, strategy and performance using a statistical dataset.

### 3.2 Ownership characteristics and firm behaviour

The previous section indicated that some companies in our sample were controlled by a network of extensive cross-directorships, often involving stock brokers. Further, we also showed that directors of newly recapitalised firms were often substantial block holders. These findings facilitate the examination of the differential behaviour of firms within the industry in the 1920s and 1930s, with a particular focus on differences between governance arrangements, strategy and financial performance. We employ a sample of 147 spinning firms to test the hypotheses outlined in the previous section.

The sample is based on the first year of extensively available accounting and share price data taken from Frederick Tattersall's *Cotton Trade Review* from 1926 *et seq*, using all firms with available data. These data were used to examine first the determinants of the decision to exit and second the determinants of financial performance.

To examine the decision to exit, and the determinants of financial performance, data and financial information for the five-year period 1926–1931 was used in the following models:

$$EXIT = \beta_1 + \beta_2 RECAP + \beta_3 PUBLIC + \beta_4 LEV + \beta_5 SIZE + \mu \qquad (1)$$

$$APTC = \beta_1 + \beta_2 RECAP + \beta_3 PUBLIC + \beta_4 LEV + \beta_5 SIZE + \mu \qquad (2)$$

$$DIV = \beta_1 + \beta_2 RECAP + \beta_3 PUBLIC + \beta_4 LEV + \beta_5 SIZE + \mu \qquad (3)$$

Model (1) has a discrete dependent variable, the decision to exit (*EXIT*), and is specified as a Logit model. If a firm exits in the subsequent five years after 1926, *EXIT* is assigned a value of 1, and 0 otherwise. In model (2) the dependent variable is subsequent financial performance after 1926, defined as the ratio of accumulated profit/loss to total capital in 1931 (*APTC*). In general the higher this ratio the more successful the firm, and firms with positive ratios suffered no loss of capital in generally difficult trading circumstances and were able to pay dividends. The ratio is used as a proxy for turnaround success. In general, only firms with positive accumulated profits paid dividends, but because dividends also reduce the balance of accumulated profits, a third model was specified using the dividend rate (as a percentage of paid capital) as the dependent variable (*DIV*). Together these variables are proxies for relative success, at least from the financial perspective of the individual firm. Because the dividend variable is strongly left censored, model (3) is specified as a Tobit model. Model (2) is ordinary least squares.

The explanatory variables are common to all models and each is described in turn. The *RECAP* variable captures the fixed costs arising from governance structures. If the firm had recapitalised in the 1920 boom, it typically resold its shares to syndicates of outside investors at three times the price of non-recapitalised firms. Firms were classified 1 or 0 according to whether they had recapitalised or not. Because investors had an incentive to force the firm to remain in the industry on the basis of expected future recovery of the committed investment, the expected sign on the *RECAP* variable is negative. *RECAP* also potentially proxies for a second variable of interest, the presence of syndicate investor groups. To observe these effects separately, a further variable is required. The availability of active share price quotations was used to proxy for the presence of outside investors, including equity syndicates, as opposed to the insider quasi partnership investors where no such trading opportunities existed. Quoted firms, with therefore approximately wider share ownership were labelled as *PUBLIC* and assigned a value of 1, and 0 otherwise. As more closely controlled firms were under less pressure from outside investors to remain in the industry, and thus more likely to exit, the expected sign for the *PUBLIC* variable is positive.

In addition to these categorical variables, two further continuous variables were included. First the ratio of debt to total capital, or leverage (*LEV*) and second, to control for size the total value of balance sheet assets of the firm are used (*SIZE*). The *SIZE* variable might also proxy for the power of incumbent managers, as a function of the value of the assets under their control. *SIZE* was transformed logarithmically to achieve closer proximity to normality, whereas *LEV* was not transformed due to a significant number of zero variables.

As in many empirical governance studies, our data limitations do not allow us to research corporate governance as a process. As a result, we have to use governance proxies to describe the relationship between governance and organisational outcomes. In addition there are a number of specific caveats that should be borne in mind when interpreting the results. The first concerns preference shares, which might have impacted the relative voting power of large shareholders. Table 1 shows that of the 41 firms analysed in detail, few used preference shares. Of the 147 firms in the larger sample, only nine issued preference shares.[84] In all cases, these were issued prior to the 1919–1920 recapitalisation boom.[85] A further point is that it would have been interesting to specify a variable to test the effects of inside and outside ownership blocks. Unfortunately, the number of shareholder registers allowing the *precise* identification of this split was judged too small to allow tests of statistical significance. For this reason, some caution needs to be exercised in the interpretation of our RECAP variable. A final observation is that the age of firms might have had a bearing on our results. Thus, *ceterus paribus*, newer mills might be expected to be more profitable than older mills because of, for example, scale based advantages and the employment of modern technology. We included an age variable in our regressions but the results we report below did not change significantly.[86]

The results are presented in Tables 3–6. Tables 3 and 4 show descriptive statistics. Table 5 shows the classification of the 147 firms according to their strategy: turnaround success (APTC > 0), turnaround failures (APTC < 0) and exits. Table 6 shows the results for models (1), (2) and (3) above.

The *RECAP* variable is negative and strongly significant in model (1), showing that the presence of governance related fixed or sunk costs constitute an exit barrier. Table 5 confirms that relatively few recapitalised firms exited the industry. Where firms remained in the industry *RECAP* was associated with turnaround success, evidenced by the positive and significant coefficients in models (2) and (3). The *PUBLIC* variable is also negative in model (1) and significant, supporting the hypothesis that outside investor groups prevented exit. The data in Table 5 also show that a very high proportion (50/58, or 86%) of successful turnarounds were public companies. Although the *PUBLIC* variable is insignificant in model (2) it is positive and highly significant in model (3). Public

Table 3. Descriptive statistics.

|  | Min | Max | Mean | S.dev |
|---|---|---|---|---|
| ***Continuous variables:*** | | | | |
| *APTC* | − 6.696 | 2.079 | − 0.272 | 0.825*** |
| *DIV* | 0.000 | 25.000 | 3.630 | 5.580*** |
| *LEV* | 0.000 | 1.903 | 0.368 | 0.338*** |
| *SIZE* | 8.144 | 13.473 | 11.567 | 0.877** |
| ***Grouping variables:*** | | | | |
| *EXIT* | | | 0.224 | |
| *RE-CAP* | | | 0.476 | |
| *PUBLIC* | | | 0.776 | |
| S-Wilk p-value: | | | | |
| *** p < .01 | | | | |
| ** p < .05 | | | | |

Data definitions:
*APTC*: Accumulated profit to capital ratio, 1926–1931.
*DIV*: Dividend as a percentage of paid up capital.
*LEV*: Ratio of debt to total capital.
*SIZE*: natural logarithm of total assets.
*EXIT*: Dummy variable = 1 if the firm exits, = 0 otherwise.
*RE-CAP*: Dummy variable = 1 if the firm re-capitalised, = 0 otherwise.
*PUBLIC*: Dummy variable = 1 if the firm's shares are quoted, = 0 otherwise.

Table 4. Correlation matrix (independent variables).

| | RE-CAP | PUBLIC | LEV | SIZE |
|---|---|---|---|---|
| RE-CAP | 1.000 | | | |
| PUBLIC | −0.172** | 1.000 | | |
| LEV | 0.098 | −0.0230 | 1.000 | −0.059 |
| SIZE | −0.347*** | 0.165** | | 1.000 |

Spearman's Rho (below diagonal)/Pearson's co-efficient
(above diagonal) significance levels
*** p < .01
** p < .05

Data definitions:
*LEV*: Ratio of debt to total capital.
*SIZE*: natural logarithm of total assets.
*RE-CAP*: Dummy variable = 1 if the firm re-capitalised, = 0 otherwise.
*PUBLIC*: Dummy variable = 1 if the firm's shares are quoted, = 0 otherwise.

ownership, albeit by the syndicates, is therefore associated with firms staying in the industry and with turnaround success but this is manifested in the form of high dividend payments and not the accumulation of profits. In other words, syndicate investment acted as an exit barrier, helped stabilise cash flows, but undermined subsequent stages of the turnaround associated with new investment and repositioning.

Exit was positively but weakly related to high borrowing in model (1). Exiting firms had higher leverage than turnaround firms (Table 5), but the difference was marginal compared to firms unsuccessfully attempting turnarounds. In models (2) and (3) leverage was negatively and significantly related to turnaround success. In other words lenders exerted weak pressure on firms to exit and acted as a constraint for the firms that stayed in the industry and attempted turnarounds. Firms with relatively high debt were less likely to pay dividends. Jensen's (1986) FCF hypothesis suggests that opportunistic managers may try to appropriate FCF at the expense of minority shareholders, and the presence of fixed-claim holders may restrain this opportunism. There is some evidence from the data in Table 1 that debt holders did indeed constrain directors. The banks therefore did what they were supposed to do under the FCF hypothesis, even though for Keynes this wasn't enough.

Table 5. Descriptive statistics for strategic outcomes.

| STRATEGY | | VARIABLE | | | | | |
|---|---|---|---|---|---|---|---|
| | N | *APTC* | *DIV* % | *RE-CAP* N | *PUBLIC* N | *LEV* | *SIZE* £ |
| **Turnaround** | | | | | | | |
| − Success | 58 | 0.152 | 8.780 | 37 | 50 | 0.289 | 172,671 |
| − Fail | 56 | −0.282 | 0.435 | 20 | 43 | 0.408 | 141,392 |
| **Exits** | 33 | −0.999 | 0.000 | 13 | 21 | 0.436 | 112,631 |

Data definitions:
*APTC*: Accumulated profit to capital ratio, 1926–1931.
*DIV*: Dividend as a percentage of paid up capital.
*LEV*: Ratio of debt to total capital.
*SIZE*: natural logarithm of total assets.
*RE-CAP*: Dummy variable = 1 if the firm re-capitalised, = 0 otherwise.
*PUBLIC*: Dummy variable = 1 if the firm's shares are quoted, = 0 otherwise.

Table 6.  Regression models.

| Model | (1) Logit | (2) OLS | (3) Tobit |
|---|---|---|---|
| **Dependent variable** | **EXIT** | **APTC** | **DIV** |
| Independent variables: | | | |
| CONST | 11.386*** | −4.083** | −62.168*** |
| | 0.001 | 0.036 | 0.000 |
| RE-CAP | −1.406*** | 0.444** | 13.293*** |
| | 0.002 | 0.013 | 0.000 |
| PUBLIC | −0.955** | −0.072 | 6.936*** |
| | 0.042 | 0.612 | 0.005 |
| LEV | 0.843 | −0.589** | −11.397*** |
| | 0.155 | 0.014 | 0.000 |
| SIZE | −1.019*** | 0.334** | 4.504*** |
| | 0.001 | 0.037 | 0.000 |
| R-square[1] | 0.151 | 0.184 | 0.114 |
| Prob[2] | 0.000 | 0.000 | 0.000 |
| Residual S-Wilk | N/A | 0.000 | N/A |

Co-efficients are reported for each independent variable with respective p-values underneath. N = 147 for all models. In model (3) 95 observations are left-censored at 0. In models (1) and (2) p-values are based on White's (1980) heteroscedasticity consistent estimation matrix. All models were re-tested with serial deletion of inter-correlated variables and insertion of interaction variables. The results were robust to alternative specifications. Model (2) was re-tested using a non-parametric formulation (quantile regression). Model co-efficients signs remained unchanged and significance levels increased marginally for significant co-efficients in the OLS model.
[1]Psuedo in models (1) and (3), adjusted in model (2).
[2]> Chi in models (1) and (3), and > F in model (2).
Two-tailed significance levels: *** $p < .01$, ** $p < .05$.
Data definitions:
APTC: Accumulated profit to capital ratio, 1926–1931.
DIV: Dividend as a percentage of paid up capital.
LEV: Ratio of debt to total capital.
SIZE: natural logarithm of total assets.
EXIT: Dummy variable = 1 if the firm exits, = 0 otherwise.
RE-CAP: Dummy variable = 1 if the firm re-capitalised, = 0 otherwise.
PUBLIC: Dummy variable = 1 if the firm's shares are quoted, = 0 otherwise.

Finally *SIZE* had a significant and negative impact on exit and was positive and strongly significantly associated with turnaround success. Insofar as *SIZE* proxies for managerial power, the impact is the same direction as *PUBLIC*, supporting the view from the archival evidence that managerial groups were able to combine long run investment strategy with good knowledge of the industry. However, the speculation that enabled them to build business empires and appropriate associated rents in the pre-war period went badly wrong after 1920.

## 4.  Discussion and conclusions

Recapitalisation was not new in the Lancashire textile industry or, indeed, in other British industries. Macrosty, for example, demonstrated that large sections of British manufacturing, brewing, chemicals, iron and steel, and textiles, participated in similar schemes, often with subsequent dire financial performance during the early twentieth century.[87] However, the new and unique features of the boom in the Lancashire textile industry during the inter-war period were the scale of recapitalisation, the method of its financing, and the often disastrous involvement of external financial syndicates. Consequently, industrial reorganisation was totally untenable *without* government intervention.

Indeed, by the late 1920s, the Bank of England was increasingly concerned about the exposure of particular banks to the cotton spinning industry. According to Sayers, the Governor, Montague Norman, would 'have known that two if not three of the smaller banks, and at last two of the Big Five, were so deeply involved in Lancashire's financial mire that further deterioration and eventual exposure might have rocked the whole banking system'.[88] Attempts to improve the financial health of exposed banks via amalgamation met with only limited success. Consequently, direct intervention in the spinning industry by the Bank of England was necessary. In 1929, via the Bankers Industrial Development Corporation, the Bank of England financed the formation of the LCC. Between 1929 and 1931, the Bank advanced £920,000 to the LCC which it used to acquire approximately 10m spindles and 100 firms in the heavily depressed 'American' section. This amalgamation facilitated rationalisation of the industry and, by encouraging the formation of other combines, helped to eradicate ruinous price cutting.[89]

Keynes's assertion that capacity mattered is true and no one would dispute the problems caused by over-capacity and weak selling. However, we dispute the assertion that capacity was *all* that mattered and that recapitalisation was unimportant. Indeed, following from the above analysis the reverse was true: recapitalisation was a serious barrier to exit for some firms and to reorganisation by others. It was more significant than bank debt, even though, as has been demonstrated, bank debt performed its correct function of disciplining managers and associated insider groups. Over-capitalisation was serious without bank debt and would have become serious even without over-capacity, committing Lancashire firms to high fixed capital costs as overseas competitors entered export markets.

Changing capital structures, thereby undoing the mistakes of 1919–20, was therefore essential for the recovery of the industry. Even in the relatively weak legal framework of the 1920s, however, radical variation of ownership rights (writing-off the capital of a *whole* industry) was non-trivial. Not surprisingly perhaps, the only contemporaries calling for this solution were the speculators themselves, and they were unlikely to be received sympathetically by economists, policy makers or anyone else. The real irony is that, like Keynes, they recognised, through their own mistakes, the need for an end to *laissez-faire*.

This article has demonstrated that it is not possible to develop simple generalisations about the role of financial syndicates during the interwar years. Earlier scholarship revealed that many of the features of the Lancashire recapitalisation boom after 1919 were common to this and other industries, such as bicycles, brewing, and motor cars prior to 1914. An example was the practice of 'watering' (capitalising a company well above its asset value) and recycling the receipts from the purchase of a company to the previous shareholders.[90] However, in Lancashire, the involvement of external and local syndicates had undesirable results, though their financial environment was very different. External syndicates, for example White and Edgar, proved disastrous for ACMT and C&WCM, whose shares were quoted on the highly liquid London and Manchester stock exchanges. In contrast, local syndicates buying shares in Oldham companies became highly entrenched and prevented exit for the same reason the banks promoted weak selling – their inability to realise the value of their original investments through the highly illiquid Oldham exchange.

This case study suggests that a much broader business history enquiry is justified into the interactions between financial syndicates and business in general, which will help develop the 'circle of knowledge creation'.[91] For example, accounting analysis can demonstrate the precise impact of promoters and syndicates on particular companies: how big were the initial gains (and subsequent losses) in assets and share prices compared to a comparator group? How quickly did companies recover, and what factors were instrumental in this? Analysis of share registers can reveal the degree of 'stagging', which provides some indication of the severity of asymmetric information between promoters (vendors) and shareholders. Econometric analysis of share price data can reveal the illiquidity of stock markets and the range of survival strategies available to firms.

Finally, our findings have particular relevance to the development of theory and its application to industries in acute financial distress. The prior literature showcases the role of block-holders in promoting corporate restructuring, but this article suggests that liquid stock markets and/or exogenous solutions to the problem of sunk investment and embedded ownership rights are also important necessary conditions.

## Notes

1. The authors are grateful to participants at a seminar held at the 'New Business History' Conference, York (2012), for helpful comments on earlier versions of this article.
2. See, for example, Barley, *The Riddle*; MacGregor, "Rationalisation" and "Problems of Rationalisation"; Garside and Greaves, "Rationalisation"; Greaves, *Industrial Reorganisation*.
3. Keynes, *The Return to Gold*, 46–47.
4. Keynes, *The Return to Gold*, inaction of the banks, 605, cotton directors, 631, criticism of contemporary commentators, in Daniels and Jewkes, "The Post War Depression," discussion, 199.
5. De Jong, Higgins, and Van Driel, "New Business History?" 3–4, 7, 9.
6. For example, block ownership in corporate restructuring in the 1980s (Bethel and Liebeskind, "The Effects of Ownership Structure'), which in cases of performance decline tends to increase the frequency of asset reduction and lay-offs (Kang and Shivdasani, "Corporate Restructuring"). In contrast ownership claims can be an exit barrier when predicated on previously overinflated asset values (Filatotchev and Toms, "Corporate Governance'), sunk costs (Clark and Wrigley "Exit, the Firm and Sunk Costs"), and insider ownership (Filatotchev and Toms, "Corporate Governance").
7. Aguilera, Filatotchev, Gospel, and Jackson, "An Organizational Approach."
8. Filatotchev, Toms, and Wright, "The Firm's Strategic Dynamics"; Toms and Filatotchev, "Corporate Governance and Financial Constraints."
9. Calculated from Mitchell, *Abstract*; Robson, *The Cotton Industry*, statistical appendices.
10. Burnett-Hurst, "Lancashire and the Indian Market," 398.
11. Bowker, *Lancashire Under the Hammer*.
12. Daniels and Jewkes, "The Post War Depression," 182.
13. Keynes, *The Return to Gold*, 'rationalising process', 584; short time and financial exhaustion, 582, 590, 597, 602; disastrous long term solution, 588, 598; actual practice, 596–597.
14. Keynes, *The Return to Gold*, 598.
15. Keynes, *The Return to Gold*, 605.
16. Keynes, *The Return to Gold*, 603, 614.
17. Keynes, *The Return to Gold*, 603–604.
18. Keynes, *The Return to Gold*, 629–631.
19. MacGregor, "Rationalisation," 528.
20. Ryan and MacGregor, "Problems of Rationalisation," 359.
21. Keynes, *The Return to Gold*; Porter, "The Commercial Banks"; Bamberg, "The Rationalisation of the British Cotton Industry"; Marchionatti, "Keynes and the Collapse"; Bowden and Higgins, 'Short-time Working."
22. Keynes, *The Return to Gold*, 601; Bamberg, "The Rationalisation of the British Cotton Industry," 26–30.
23. Daniels and Jewkes, "The Post War Depression," 179.
24. Political and Economic Planning, *Report on the British Cotton Industry*, 59; Sayers, *The Bank of England*, 253.
25. Bamberg, "The Government," 308–309.

26. Bamberg, "The Government," 310.
27. Bamberg, "The Government," 310–312.
28. Saxonhouse and Wright, "Stubborn Mules," 89.
29. Lazonick, "The Cotton Industry," 396; Keynes, *The Return to Gold*, 578–637; Skidelsky, *John Maynard Keynes*, 261–263.
30. Dietrich, "The Plight"; Greaves, "Visible Hands."
31. Daniels and Jewkes, "The Post War Depression," 180–181; Political and Economic Planning, *Report on the British Cotton Industry*, 60.
32. Effect on prices, Daniels and Jewkes, "The Post War Depression," 181 on amalgamation; Political and Economic Planning, *Report on the British Cotton Industry*, 60.
33. Clay, *Report on the Position*, 64
34. Precise details are limited about the formation of the Beecham Trust. With the support of Sir Thomas Beecham, the pill magnate, White established the Trust in 1917, to carry on the business of financiers and merchants, with a capital of £300,000 in preference shares and £100,000 in ordinary shares, all of the latter being held by White. The company was liquidated in 1927 with assets of £134,467 against unsecured liabilities of £1,098,850, of which over £450,000 was owed to the Westminster Bank. White drew heavily on the Trust's funds for personal purposes and, on its winding-up, owed the Trust over £450,000. White died in 1927. *The Times*, 13 October, 1927, 5; *The Times*, 1 July, 1927, 5; *The Times*, 21 March, 1927, 5.
35. *The Economist*, 8 February, 1919, 188; *The Economist*, 29 March, 1919, 521. The Trust were also rumoured to be active purchasers of stock in De Beers. *The Economist*, 26 July, 1919, 140.
36. ACMT was registered in 1918 as a private company and converted into a public company in 1919. ACMT was formed to acquire the share capital of a number of cotton spinning/ cotton weaving companies, including, *inter alia*: Robert Hyde Buckley & Sons, Ltd; John Ashworth (1902), Ltd; Mill Hill Spinning Co, Ltd, and Horrockses, Crewdson & Co, Ltd. The company also owned controlling interests in a number of mills. *Stock Exchange Official Intelligence*, 1930.
37. *The Times*, 4 December, 1919, 24.
38. *Stock Exchange Official Intelligence*, 1939.
39. *Stock Exchange Official Intelligence*, 1930.
40. Vallance, *Very Private Enterprise*, 88–89.
41. For a review of White's business practices see Johnston, *Financiers and the Nation*, 94–96.
42. *Re Jubilee Cotton Mills Ltd*, [1923] 1 *Chancery*. 1, 31.
43. Johnston, *Financiers and the Nation*, 44.
44. C&WCM, was formed in 1920 by the amalgamation of Crosses & Winkworth Ltd, and other textile firms, for example, Ward & Walker, Lord Hampson & Lord (1919), Ainsworth Bros., Ltd. Subsequently, in 1922, C&WCM, established Crosses & Heatons' Associated Mills Ltd, an amalgamation of other Bolton-based spinning companies, including William Heaton & Sons, and the North End Spinning Co. Ltd (*Stock Exchange Official Intelligence*, 1930). Subsequently, it was reported that a group of London financiers had agreed terms with C&WCM to purchase the entire share capital of its subsidiary, John Bright & Brothers. *The Times*, 9 October, 1929, 21.
45. Edgar was also involved with White in the £9 million promotion of British Controlled Oilfields, a speculative venture that accumulated major losses for investors, leading to White's suicide in 1927. Johnston, *Financiers and the Nation*, 96.
46. Company Prospectus, *The Times* 16th March, 1920. From the information disclosed in the prospectus it is also possible to calculate that Sperling & Co. collected £300,000 in commission from the issue.
47. Company Prospectus, *Times* 16th March, 1920.
48. *The Times*, 26th May, 1920
49. *The Times*, 15 March, 1920, 24; *The Times*, 6 September, 1922, 15; *The Times*, 25 May, 1928, 20; *The Times*, 5 September, 1928, 19.
50. *Stock Exchange Official Intelligence*, 1931.
51. Filatochev and Toms, "Corporate Governance."
52. But see Higgins and Toms, "Financial Distress."
53. Frank and Goyal, "Testing the Pecking Order."
54. Filatotchev and Toms, "Corporate Governance."
55. Aghion and Bolton, "The Financial Structure."

56. Keynes, *The Return to Gold*, 631.
57. Director interlocks were extensive before 1914 and in the 1950s For pre-1914 evidence, see Toms, "The Rise of Modern Accounting" and "The English Cotton Industry"; for 1950s see Filatotchev and Toms, "Corporate Governance"; Toms and Filatotchev, "Corporate Governance."
58. Bolton was the centre of the fine section of the industry and was relatively untroubled by the problems of over-capacity prevalent in the Oldham-centred coarse sector. Contemporary observers recognised that during the 1920s, the depression that affected the Lancashire spinning industry was much more pronounced in Oldham compared to Bolton. An important reason for this was that foreign competition was most serious in the course-medium count trade in which Oldham traditionally specialised, compared to the fine and super-fine counts in which Bolton was pre-eminent. Clay, *Report on the Position*, 8–9; Political and Economic Planning, *Report on the British Cotton Industry*, 55–56, 58.
59. For example E.H. Stockton, the Chairman of the Manchester Chamber of Commerce pointed out that mills passing into the hands of any 'syndicate who have no knowledge of the conditions of an intricate industry is certain to lead to disaster'. *Oldham Chronicle*, 25th November, 1919. Keynes, *The Return to Gold*.
60. Hoskisson, Hitt, Johnson, and Grossman, "Conflicting Voices."
61. If the Braddocks are treated as outsiders in Arrow, this proportion falls to six out of 12.
62. Calculated from Brunswick Spinning Company Ltd., The National Archives (TNA) BT/31/32378/163957; Argyll Cotton Spinning Company Ltd., TNA, BT 31/36914/165226; BT 31/36915/165226; Avon Mill (1919), Ltd., TNA, BT 31/38811/159919; BT 31/38812/159919; Belgrave Ltd., TNA, BT 31/25035/158943; Century Ring Spinning Company Ltd, TNA, BT 31/32338/161017; Clover Mill (Rochdale) Ltd., TNA, BT 31/36912/164330; Delta Mill Ltd., BT/31/36385/161972; BT 31/36386/161972; Fern Cotton Spinning Company (1920) Ltd., TNA BT/31/32371/163516;
63. The Lancashire Cotton Syndicate Ltd, had a registered address in London, but was organised at least in part by local cotton mill managers. Alfred Holt was the Managing Director of the Syndicate and mill manager of Bolton Union Spinning Company. Bolton Union Spinning Company (1920) Ltd., TNA, BT/31/32419/166839.
64. Bottomley invested £26,000 (Share registers, Bolton Union Spinning Co, TNA, BT 31/32419/166839). For details of Bottomley's financial manipulations see Johnston, *Financiers and the Nation*, Ch.XI.
65. Beehive re-floated with a nominal share capital of 2 million two-shilling shares (£200,000). The annual return for this company in 1938 indicates that 23% of this stock was owned by the following London-based accounts: Midland Bank Nominees; Morrison Nominees; Barclays Bank Nominees; Branch Nominees; Control Nominees; Roycan Nominees, and one London based group not specified. Beehive Spinning Company Ltd., TNA, BT 31/42620/328092; BT 31/42621/328092.
66. Elder, *TNA*, BT 31/32392/164696; Fern, *TNA*, BT 31/32371/163516; Textile, *TNA*, BT 31/32270/153035; Asia Mill (Holdings) Ltd., TNA, BT 31/37696/167111.
67. John Bunting, of the same occupation was a director of about 20 mills (Farnie, "John Bunting," 506–509).
68. Hammersley, "Rationalisation: The Cotton Trade."
69. Higgins and Toms, "Financial Distress." As far as we can tell, the only contemporary economist who advocated a comparable scheme was Allen, who proposed that, in a scheme of rationalisation, the surviving firms should make a debenture issue and use the proceeds to acquire the capital of firms which were to close down. In these schemes, Allen proposed that the owners of the closed plants would receive a cash payment representing the pre-rationalisation value of their interest plus an additional sum equivalent to their capitalised share of the additional profit which the industry was expected to earn as a result of the scheme. Of course, as with the Hammersely scheme, Allen recognised that his proposal would only work with government intervention (Allen, "An Aspect of Industrial Reorganisation," 189).
70. Anchor, *TNA*, BT 31/32438/168982; Asia, *TNA*, BT 31/37696/167111.
71. Earl Mill, *TNA*, BT 31/32361/162607.
72. Asia Mill, *TNA*, BT 31/37696/167111.
73. These stockbrokers were sometimes responsible for substantial short-term sales of stock. Thus, for example Hood and Tweedale between them sold 30.3% of Century stock between

December 1919 and August 1920. Century Ring Spinning Company (1919) Ltd, TNA, BT 31/32338/161017;

74. Calculated from Gorse Mill, TNA, BT 31/32349/161673.
75. McKeown, *Oldham Stock Exchange*, 40–41.
76. McKeown, *Oldham Stock Exchange*, 29, 32.
77. Maug, "Large Shareholders."
78. Coppull Ring Spinning Company Ltd., TNA, BT 31/35255/168122. In Bolton, a prominent example of family control was provided by the reflotation of the Sir John Holden Mill Co. The Holden family owned 58.1% of the ordinary shares. This mill was liquidated in 1929 and became one of the founding mills in the Combined Egyptian (English) Mills Co. TNA, BT 31/32448/170236, Sir John Holden & Sons Ltd; Longworth, *The Cotton Mills*, 95–96.
79. Avon Mill (1919) Ltd., TNA, BT 31/38811/159919; BT 31/38812/159919.
80. Because these figures refer to family holdings, they will be smaller than the figures reported in Table 1 which refer to total blockholders. Anchor Spinning Company (1920) Ltd, TNA, BT 31/32438/168982.
81. Hartford Mill (1920) Ltd, TNA, BT 31/32314/158753.
82. Farnie and Gurr, "Design and Construction of Mills," 10.
83. For a biographical discussion of the activities of three generations of the Stott family, 1862–1937, see Farnie and Gurr, "Design and Construction of Mills," 15–18.
84. Tattersall's *Cotton Trade Review*
85. These were: Burns (1891); Fox (1911); Glen (1912), Goyt (1905); Laurel (1905); Magnet (1912); Majestic (1913); Park Road (1891), and Reyners (1912). We are grateful to a referee for indicating the caveats which are discussed in this section.
86. To develop a proxy for age a cut-off date of 1891 was used. This was the last mill building boom year of the nineteenth century and the next wave did not gain significant momentum until the period 1904–1907 (Toms, 'Finance and Growth'). Because almost all pre-1891 mills were still in operation in 1918 and there were relatively few mills built between 1891 and 1904, 1891 marks a useful watershed between the nineteenth century and twentieth century cotton mill. The age based dummy was marginally ($p < 0.1$) and positively related to financial performance in model 2 and insignificant in the other models.
87. Macrosty, *The Trust Movement*.
88. Sayers, *The Bank of England*, 319–320.
89. Bamberg, "The Government," 64–125; Hannah, *The Rise of the Corporate Economy*, 65; Political and Economic Planning, *Report on the British Cotton Industry*, 108–109.
90. Armstrong, "The Rise and Fall," 128–129.
91. De Jong, Higgins, and Van Driel, "New Business History," 4.

## Notes on contributors

David Higgins is Professor of Economics at Newcastle University Business School, University of Newcastle. His previous research has been on the Lancashire textile industry, economic performance and market structure.

Steven Toms is Professor of Accounting at Leeds University Business School, University of Leeds. His research has focused on the history of the Lancashire textile industry, business performance and accountability.

Igor Filatotchev is Professor of Corporate Governance and Strategy at Cass Business School, City University London, and Visiting Professor at Vienna University of Economics and Business. His research has focused on corporate governance effects on entrepreneurship and strategic decisions and the sociology of capital markets.

## References

Aghion, P., and P. Bolton. "The Financial Structure of the Firm and the Problem of Control." *European Economic Review* 33, no. 2/3 (1989): 286–293.
Aguilera, R., I. Filatotchev, H. Gospel, and G. Jackson. "An Organizational Approach to Comparative Corporate Governance: Costs, Contingencies, and Complementarities." *Organization Science* 19, no. 3 (2008): 475–492.

Allen, G. C. "An Aspect of Industrial Reorganisation." *Economic Journal* 55, no. 218/219 (1945): 179–191.

Armstrong, J. "The Rise and Fall of the Company Promoter and the Financing of British Industry." In *Capitalism in a Mature Economy*, edited by J. J. Helten and Y. Cassis, 115–138. Edward Elgar, 1990.

Bamberg, J. H. "The Government, the Banks and the Lancashire Cotton Industry, 1918–1939." Unpublished PhD thesis, University of Cambridge: Cambridge, 1984.

Bamberg, J. H. "The Rationalisation of the British Cotton Industry in the Inter-war Years." *Textile History* 19, no. 1 (1988): 83–102.

Barley, L. J. *The Riddle of Rationalisation*. London: George Allen & Unwin, 1932.

Bethel, J. E., and J. Liebeskind. "The Effects of Ownership Structure on Corporate Restructuring." *Strategic Management Journal* 14, no. S1 (2007): 15–31.

Bowden, S., and D. M. Higgins. "Short-time Working and Price Maintenance: Collusive Tendencies in the Cotton Spinning Industry, 1919–1939." *Economic History Review* 51, no. 3 (1998): 319–343.

Bowker, B. *Lancashire Under the Hammer*. London: Hogarth, 1928.

Burnett-Hurst, A. "Lancashire and the Indian Market." *Journal of the Royal Statistical Society* 95, no. 3 (1932): 395–440.

Clark, Gordon L., and Neil Wrigley. "Exit, the Firm and Sunk Costs: Reconceptualizing the Corporate Geography of Disinvestment and Plant Closure." *Progress in Human Geography* 21, no. 3 (1997): 338–358.

Clay, H. *Report on the Position of the English Cotton Industry*. London: Securities Management Trust Ltd, 1931.

Daniels, G., and J. Jewkes. "The Post War Depression in the Lancashire Cotton Industry." *Journal of the Royal Statistical Society* 91, no. 2 (1928): 153–206.

De Jong, A., D. Higgins, and H. Driel. "New Business History? An Invitation to Discuss." (2012). Available at September 2013: http://newbusinesshistory.files.wordpress.com/2012/06/new-business-history-july-6-2012.pdf

Dietrich, E. "The Plight of the Lancashire Cotton Industry." *American Economic Review* 18, no. 3, 469–476.

Farnie, D. "John Bunting." *Dictionary of Business Biography*. London: Butterworths, 1984.

Farnie, D. A., and D. A. Gurr. "Design and Construction of Mills." In *The Cotton Mills of Oldham*, 15–24, edited by D. A. Gurr and J. Hunt. Oldham: Oldham Education and Leisure, 1998.

Filatotchev, I., and J. S. Toms. "Corporate Governance, Strategy and Survival in a Declining Industry: A Study of Lancashire Textile Companies." *Journal of Management Studies* 40, no. 3 (2003): 895–920.

Filatotchev, I., S. Toms, and M. Wright. "The Firm's Strategic Dynamics and Corporate Governance Life-cycle." *International Journal of Managerial Finance* 2, no. 4 (2006): 256–279.

Frank, M. Z., and V. K. Goyal. "Testing the Pecking Order Theory of Capital Structure." *Journal of Financial Economics* 67, no. 2 (2003): 217–248.

Garside, W. R., and J. L. Greaves. "Rationalisation and Britain's industrial malaise: the interwar years revisited." *Journal of European Economic History* 26, no. 1 (1997): 37–68.

Greaves, J. L. "'Visible hands' and the Rationalisation of the British Cotton Industry, 1925–1932." *Textile History* 31, no. 1 (2000): 102–122.

Greaves, J. *Industrial Reorganisation and Government Policy in Interwar Britain*. London: Ashgate, 2005.

Hammersley, J. S. "Rationalisation: The Cotton Trade." *Lloyds Bank Limited, Monthly Review* 12 (1931): 47–56.

Hannah, L. *The Rise of the Corporate Economy*. London: Methuen, 1983.

Higgins, D. M., and S. Toms. "Financial Distress, Corporate Borrowing and Industrial Decline: The Lancashire Cotton Textile Industry, 1918–1938." *Accounting Business and Financial History* 13, no. 2 (2003): 207–232.

Hoskisson, R. E., M. Hitt, R. Johnson, and W. Grossman. "Conflicting Voices: The Effects of Institutional Ownership Heterogeneity and Internal Governance on Corporate Innovative Strategies." *Academy of Management Journal* 45, no. 4 (2002): 698–716.

Jensen, M. C. "Agency Cost of Free Cash Flow, Corporate Finance, and Takeovers." *American Economic Review* 76, no. 2 (1986): 323–329.

Johnston, T. *Financiers and the Nation*. 2nd ed. London: Methuen, 1935.

Kang, Jun-Koo, and Anil Shivdasani. "Corporate Restructuring During Performance Declines in Japan." *Journal of Financial Economics* 46, no. 1 (1997): 29–65.

Keynes, J. M. *The Return to Gold and Industrial Policy II*. Collected Works. Cambridge: Cambridge University Press, 1981.

Lazonick, W. "The Cotton Industry." In *The Decline of the British Economy*, edited by B. Elbaum and W. Lazonick, 18–50. Oxford: Oxford University Press, 1986.

Longworth, J. H. *The Cotton Mills of Bolton, 1780–1985: A Historical Directory*. Bolton: Bolton Museum and Art Gallery, 1986.

Macrosty, H. W. *The Trust Movement in British Industry*. London: Longmans, 1907.

MacGregor, D. H. "Rationalisation of industry." *Economic Journal* 37, no. 148 (1927): 521–550.

MacGregor, D. H. "Problems of Rationalisation: A Discussion." *Economic Journal* 40, no. 159 (1930): 351–368.

McKeown, J., Oldham Stock Exchange, 1926–1929. Unpublished MA thesis, Department of History, University of York, 2007.

Marchionatti, R. "Keynes and the Collapse of the British Cotton Industry in the 1920s: A Microeconomic Case Against Laissez-faire." *Journal of Post Keynesian Economics* 17, no. 3 (1995): 427–445.

Maug, E. "Large Shareholders as Monitors: Is There a Trade-off Between Liquidity and Control." *Journal of Finance* 53, no. 1 (1998): 65–92.

Mitchell, B. R. *Abstract of British Historical Statistics*. Cambridge: Cambridge University Press, 1962.

Political and Economic Planning. *Report on the British Cotton Industry*. London: Political and Economic Planning, 1934.

Porter, J. H. "The Commercial Banks and the Financial Problems of the English Cotton Industry, 1919–1939." *The International Review of Banking History* 9, no. 1 (1974): 1–16.

Robson, R. *The Cotton Industry in Britain*. London: Macmillan, 1957.

Ryan, J. "Problems of Rationalisation." *Economic Journal* 40, no. 159 (1930): 357–364.

Sayers, R. *The Bank of England, 1891–1944*, Vol. 1. Cambridge: Cambridge University Press, 1976.

Saxonhouse, G., and G. Wright. "Stubborn Mules and Vertical Integration: The Disappearing Constraint." *Economic History Review* 40, no. 1 (1987): 87–94.

Skidelsky, R. *John Maynard Keynes: The Economist as Saviour 1920–1937, Volume One*. London: Macmillan, 1992.

Toms, S. "The Rise of Modern Accounting and the Fall of the Public Company: The Lancashire Cotton Mills, 1870–1914." *Accounting Organizations and Society* 27, no. 1 (2002): 61–84.

Toms, S., and I. Filatotchev. "Corporate Governance, Business Strategy and the Dynamics of Networks: A Theoretical Model and Application to the British Cotton Industry, 1830–1980." *Organization Studies* 25, no. 4 (2004): 629–651.

Toms, S., and I. Filatotchev. "Corporate Governance and Financial Constraints on Strategic Turnarounds." *Journal of Management Studies* 43, no. 3 (2006): 407–433.

Toms, S. "The English Cotton Industry and the Loss of the World Market." In *King Cotton: A Tribute to Douglas Farnie*, edited by J. Wilson, 58–76. Lancaster: Carnegie, 2009.

Vallance, A. *Very Private Enterprise*. London: Thames & Hudson, 1955.

# Public Subsidy and Private Divestment: The Lancashire Cotton Textile Industry, *c*.1950–*c*.1965

David Higgins and Steven Toms

*University of Sheffield*
*University of Nottingham*

The Lancashire textile industry is often viewed with a great deal of sentimentality. This stems typically from either the lost greatness of the industrial revolution's Prometheus, or from sympathy for an industry that became dominated by old-fashioned attitudes and sadly set itself on a course of terminal self-destruction. That British entrepreneurs and governments did not take decisive remedial action during the spiral of decline after 1920 was, however, due as much to cold financial calculation as to mere emotion. It is to the former aspect that we turn below in a re-examination of Lancashire cotton as a classic case study of industrial decline.

The principal empirical question addressed in this article is to investigate why Lancashire entrepreneurs failed to make significant investments in technology or restructure the industry prior to the early 1960s. Previous studies on the decline of the Lancashire cotton textile industry have tended to focus on the interplay of firm structure, technology, and, more recently, financial performance.[1] It has also been suggested that decline was inevitable in a British industry dominated by old-fashioned attitudes and technologies and that divestment of capital and labour into newer industries should have been the objective of British government policies.[2] This article re-addresses these issues using evidence hitherto neglected. Specificall , the central concerns of the discussion are the profits, profit distributions, retention and reinvestment policies of firms. Unlike previous periods, what makes the 1950s and early 1960s especially interesting from this perspective is that the financial policies of firms were determined not only by private calculation, but also by government policy and the provision of public subsidies. It is the relationship between the private assessment of the future taken by the industry's entrepreneurs (as revealed by their divestment and investment activities) and the public assessment of the industry's future (as manifested by the provision of public subsidy), which is the central and novel theme of this article.

Analysis of divestment is particularly important because little is known about the dividend phenomenon within the general business history framework.[3] As far as public policy was concerned, in addition to the direct intervention of the 1959 Cotton Industry Act (hereafter, 1959 Act), whose effects have been extensively analysed,[4] there was also the effect of macro-economic policies on entrepreneurial behaviour at industry-level. Here, in conjunction with our own financial and archival analysis, we add to these contributions via a consideration of the impact of government taxation policies. Taxation and taxation adjustments to modify business behaviour are also neglected topics in business history. This is surprising, as taxation is an obvious reference point for the activities of lobby groups. Also, business history as a methodology is likely to offer useful insights, given the difficulties of conducting controlled experiments in tax variation faced by present-day regulators. In particular, the differential profit tax and investment allowance schemes of the 1950s offer potentially useful lessons to those seeking to modify the divestment strategies of corporate management groups and investors.[5]

The article is organised as follows. Section II briefly outlines why divestment had become such an important issue for this industry as a historical background to the problems facing it in the early 1950s. It then introduces theoretical relationships at three levels: first, capital markets and dividends, second, taxation and investment, and, finall , political lobbying and British government policy. Section III examines these relationships in turn with reference to the period prior to direct government intervention in 1959. Then section IV discusses the anticipated and actual outcomes of the 1959 Act. Case studies of corporate and political responses to the problems confronting British cotton textiles before and after the 1959 Act are incorporated into sections III and IV. Conclusions are drawn in section V.

## II

The essential problem facing Lancashire in the early 1950s remained the pre-war legacy of over-capacity. Years of prosperity and expanding world markets led Lancashire entrepreneurs to over-extend the capacity of the British cotton industry. In spinning, there were mill construction booms in 1905–7 and 1911–13, with installed capacity reaching its zenith in 1927.[6] Even before then, however, the market for Lancashire textiles had contracted dramatically and, as industry leaders came to accept, permanently. Resulting over-capacity meant that the fundamental problem was divestment, and this preceded and dominated the problem of investment and modernisation throughout the period. Removal of a significant amount of capacity with its associated costs was a precondition for any re-equipment that might have been desirable.[7]

Divestment was a problem specifically because of the ownership structure of the British cotton textile industry. For the typical entrepreneur, in the Lancashire variant of personal capitalism,[8] the priority was often the withdrawal of money capital rather than the retirement of physical capital. Thus fortunes earned in times of earlier prosperity were withdrawn or lost in subsequent slumps, whilst obsolete equipment was left in place.[9] From 1920 profit rates were generally low and risk perceptions increased with market uncertainty, again encouraging money divestment and discouraging plant re-investment. The over-capacity problem and loss of market share were iterative and further compounded difficulties. Nonetheless, Lancashire textiles remained a significant industry and traditionally the cotton industry was a strong political lobbying group. In the post-war decades when successive British governments sought to encourage growth through investment, it might have been expected that after the difficultie of the inter-war period new opportunities might await the industry. To address these issues, it is necessary to deal with three related propositions. These are, first, the relationship between investment and dividend policy, in particular the extent to which capital market demands for dividends diverted corporate cash fl w away from investment. Second, there is the relationship between government policy for the promotion of investment activity and the observed trends in Lancashire. Finally, there is the effectiveness of Lancashire as a lobbying group and the extent to which representatives were able to influence the policies of the government.

On the first set of relationships, recent research for the UK economy as a whole suggests that over-generous dividends remain important determinants of the problem of economic 'short-termism'.[10] As Lancashire firms had a particular tradition in previous generations of paying out large dividends to their owners, it might be expected that such priorities would undermine investment in subsequent periods.[11] Although some modern financial theorists doubt the relevance of this question on theoretical grounds,[12] there are many reasons why dividend policy is more usefully studied from the perspective of business history. Modern finance theory is predicated on a series of assumptions about modern capital markets, the most important of which, the efficient market hypothesis, remains fundamentally an empirical question.[13] Whilst for some theorists a totally efficient market is a logical impossibility even in modern conditions,[14] historically capital markets are inevitably characterised by higher transaction costs, the distortions of taxation, and lower transparency of managerial action and accountability.[15] In the British context, dividend policy is all the more significant as governance structures perpetuating the dominance of 'personal' capitalists and their associated absence of managerial hierarchies have been identified as possible determinants of the decline of the British economy.[16] If individual or family capitalists view businesses as part of their personal estates,[17] the 'voice'[18] of active shareholders might dominate the 'exit' control mechanism, thus precluding the emergence of an operationally efficient market.[19] Dividend policy can thus be a useful proxy for agency costs, moral hazard[20] and actual market efficien y. Finally, there is the issue of managerial behaviour. Whether the market is efficient or not, it does not also follow that managers will believe it to be, and hence will manipulate dividends to signal to investors their views concerning the future prospects for the company.[21] Especially in an environment characterised by increasing threats of takeover, dividend policy might be a short-run device to boost market confidence where other information signals are poor, or a longer run attempt to 'smooth' dividends to some constant proportion of profits, thereby reducing the investor's perception of uncertainty.[22] To summarise these issues with reference to Lancashire, the firs hypothesis examined is that in an efficient capital market, investment and restructuring were unaffected by the divestment activities of the owners of the British textile industry.

It is also expected that these relationships might be moderated by the second set of relationships, between taxation, government policy and investment. One mechanism of government policy is the administration of taxation rates to encourage capital investment. Another, related, example is the manipulation of the taxation system to discourage dividend payments. In these respects, the 1950s was a particularly interesting decade, as British governments, with these objectives in mind, manipulated the tax system to an unprecedented degree in successive budgets.[23] More direct intervention, such as the 1959 Act, might also be expected to modify investment and divestment activities. Moreover, in these conditions it is possible that governments might identify links between industry structure, divestment and a policy objective such as economic growth, and seek regulatory solutions. At national level, fiscal policy was a crucial issue during this period. By 1950, for example, tax revenue as a percentage of GDP was 39.2 per cent.[24] What has been of central concern is the importance of taxation policy to governments' management of the economy.[25] At the macro-level, a variety of studies have indicated that fiscal policy was a major factor underlying successive swings between 'stop' and 'go' during the 1950s and 1960s.[26] By comparison, the importance of swings in taxation policy for individual industries has been largely neglected. This discussion leads to a second hypothesis, that British government policy, specifically on taxes and subsidies, had no effect on the level of investment in cotton textiles.

Given the interactions between ownership and managerial groups implicit in the first hypothesis, and between government agencies and firms implicit in the second, it is sensible to examine political as well as financial variables. The latter are therefore subsumed within a political economy framework. For the purposes of the current analysis, this is defined as the interplay of power, the goals of those wielding power and the productive-exchange system, and is concerned with the origins and distribution of power in society. For present purposes, although changes in power and influence are held to be functions of changes in wealth, the term 'political economy' is used in a pluralist, non-Marxist sense, that is individual interests are not systematically reconstructed as class interests. Previous studies have examined the political/economic context of Lancashire's decline, and demonstrated the importance of political and cultural constraints on managerial action.[27] These have also suggested, although not fully analysed, splits within important Lancashire constituencies that undermined its effectiveness as a lobbying group.[28] A third hypothesis is therefore proposed: that these splits reduced the ability of the Lancashire cotton interest to secure tailored government intervention on its behalf.

As well as being worthy of investigation on an individual basis, these three hypotheses interact. To examine them specifically and collectively, an eclectic range of source material was therefore employed. Accounting data was obtained from the Cambridge University Companies Database (CUCD) for the period 1949 to 1965. For the purposes of this firs stage of the research, all companies involved in the spinning or manufacture of cotton before 1960 were selected. By definition these companies were all stock exchange quoted. Those companies with short series of data, that is, less than ten years or those that left the industry before 1960, were discarded. This left a sample of 41 companies. For each company and every available year of data, summary balance sheet and profit and loss account variables were collated. Accounting ratios for dividend pay-out were calculated. To examine linkages between the extent of divestment through dividends and reinvestment in plant and equipment, financial gearing, growth of capital employed and return on capital employed were also calculated.[29] From these data proxies for capital growth rates and risk variables were developed. Using these variables, hypothesised relationships were tested via statistical inference, using established models that tend to perform well in empirical testing.[30] The results are interpreted in conjunction with the narrative below. For a summary of models tested see the Appendix. Share price data for six of the largest cotton companies were obtained from Tattersall's *Cotton Trade Review* for the period 1950–63.[31] To document political responses to the economic and financial pressures suggested through inference, the board minutes of the largest and most important company, the Lancashire Cotton Corporation (LCC), Lancashire textile industry trade journals, and records of UK parliamentary papers and debates were examined.[32] The most significant findings from these varied sources are summarised in the next two sections.

## III

To address the three hypotheses set out in section II, the following discussion analyses empirical evidence for the period before 1959. First, via an empirical analysis of profits and dividends, the relationship between investment and divestment is considered and evaluated in the context of macro-economic influences. Second, in the light of corporate performance and its relationship to the wider economic environment, the impact of general fiscal investment incentives are examined. The combined effects of these economic and policy variables are analysed at the level of the individual firm, concentrating on the example of the LCC. Finally, as a precursor to the discussion of the 1959 Act in section IV, the effectiveness of the political response to the pressures on the British cotton textile industry is evaluated.

The most prominent features of Lancashire profits during the 1950s were volatility and decline. Conversely, dividend payments were characterised by a steady increase (Figure 1). Dividend pay-out ratios therefore also increased through time. As the chairman of the LCC, Sir John Grey, stated in 1952: 'In considering dividends our policy has always been to consider the vital needs of re-equipment, the necessity for maintaining a strong financial position, and to achieve stability on a reasonable dividend standard.'[33]

£'000s

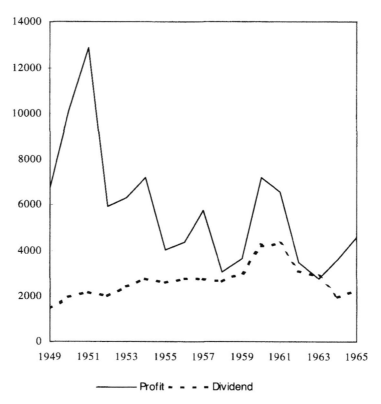

Figure 1.  Movement in profits and d vidends for a sample of lancashire textile firms, 1949–6

As this statement implies, there was a recognised conflict between steady dividends and re-investment. In the period 1952 to 1958 capital growth for sample companies averaged only 2.9 per cent per annum,[34] a relatively insignificant figure for an industry operating an old and, in some cases, fully depreciated physical capital base. To examine this relationship further, the dividend and investment requirement variables were regressed on the full cross-sectional sample of companies for the year 1958.[35] The results suggest that dividend policy was independent of capital requirement, the growth co-efficient being insignificant in all models tested. Financial risk, measured by capital gearing, had the expected effect of reducing dividends, although the results were not convincingly significant, and in any case most companies, having learned the lesson of the 1930s, were reluctant to borrow heavily.[36] In part, therefore, management groups may have been concerned to simply match the increases in dividend demanded by the capital market for all other industries.[37] Accordingly, for the period before 1959, the first hypothesis is accepted. Notwithstanding capital market inefficien y, dividend payments did not constrain investment.

However, the fluctuating and declining profits (Figure 1) of the 1950s must have acted as a disincentive by subjecting cotton companies to poor operating cash fl ws and high levels of risk. Variation in profits reflected instability of demand, a consequence of rising imports.

Between 1950 and 1960, cotton cloth imports increased more than twofold, from 287 million square yards to 728 million square yards.[38] Purchase tax also undermined the domestic market for textiles, particularly for the fine spinning companies otherwise more able to compete with cheap imports.[39] Very high costs of textile machinery during these years exacerbated the problems created by uncertain trading conditions. The effects of these market uncertainties should not be underestimated. Under such conditions the value of the option to make significant investment should trading conditions improve can be very significant, and the quantifiable benefits may need to be as much as twice the cost.[40] This problem had been created by failure to re-equip earlier and delays in re-equipment only made the problem worse, as the required costs increased further, creating an apparently permanent stalemate on the re-equipment issue.[41]

The effects of market uncertainties were undoubtedly serious impediments to investment, although in certain circumstances, as in the 1950s, these might reasonably be offset where governments offered grants or equivalent incentives through the tax system. Accordingly, British cotton industry representatives lobbied for the latter in the late 1940s.[42] In the 1950s prominent British government policy objectives were growth and investment, supported in specific industries by tailored intervention, and in the general case by fiscal incentives. Investment incentives were available to all industries, not just to Lancashire, and dividend distributions were penalised. To discourage such divestment, a differential profits tax was applied. Consequently, in many years of the 1950s, the rate of tax on distributed profits was as much as ten times the tax on undistributed profits.[43] At the same time, the government also adopted schemes of generous allowances on investment. For the most part these were provided as a deduction from taxable profits. Applying their arguments at an aggregate level, most commentators in the 1950s and 1960s concluded that the differential profits tax had a neutral impact on dividend payments and investment.[44] The effect for the economy as a whole was that companies paid a sharply declining proportion of their gross profits in taxation. Therefore, pay-out ratios calculated before tax showed greater fluctuation than those calculated after tax, and increases in dividends were funded primarily by reductions in overall taxation.[45]

However, when a similar analysis is applied to Lancashire, a very different picture emerges. As the trends in Figure 2 suggest, dividends were a smoothly rising proportion of pre-tax profits, but fluctuated more violently around a rising trend as a proportion of post-tax profits. This was because taxation remained at a high level relative to profits for Lancashire companies. Ratios of taxes to profits for Lancashire companies are contrasted with the national trend in Table 1. As the data show, the overall burden of direct taxes did not fall as quickly for Lancashire companies. This was in contrast to the national trend (Table 1). If the effective taxation rates for the rest of British industry were applied to cotton, the sample companies would have paid £9.7m less tax in the period 1950–61. Extrapolated to the cotton industry as a whole, this would have amounted to a cross subsidy from Lancashire textiles to the rest of the British economy in excess of the grants offered in the 1959 Act.[46] The second hypothesis, that this taxation regime was neutral, is therefore rejected.

The implications for investment were potentially significant. Investment allowances were given as deductions against taxable profits, and investment decision makers would have needed to make an assessment of the likelihood of achieving sufficient profits to take advantage of these allowances. In simple terms, a company with profits of £1m per year subject to corporate taxation at 50 per cent of profits could make investments in new fixed assets of £2m per year and avoid tax altogether. Marginal expenditure over £2m would not,

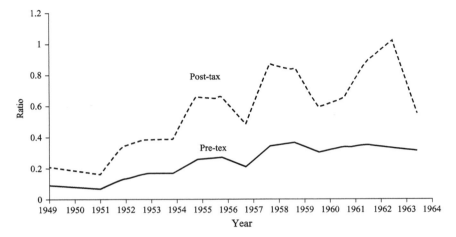

Figure 2.   Dividend pay-out ratios, 1949–64

Table 1.   Effective rates of taxation

| Period | Lancashire Cotton % | Whole Economy % |
|---|---|---|
| 1949–51 | 51.6 | 47.0 |
| 1950–52 | 52.7 | 48.4 |
| 1951–53 | 51.7 | 49.0 |
| 1952–54 | 49.7 | 47.1 |
| 1953–55 | 47.8 | 44.4 |
| 1954–56 | 47.2 | 42.6 |
| 1955–57 | 46.8 | 41.7 |
| 1956–58 | 46.1 | 40.3 |
| 1957–59 | 44.7 | 37.9 |
| 1958–60 | 42.1 | 36.3 |
| 1959–61 | 39.3 | 35.8 |

*Note*: Rate of tax is defined as the ratio of taxation charged in the profit and loss account to gross profits (before depreciation) falling to tax.
*Sources*: Lancashire Cotton is defined as the average ratio for our sample companies. Whole economy data taken from A. Rubner, 'British Differential Profits Tax', *Economic Journal*, Vol.74 (1964), p.349, Table III, column d.

however, be subject to any taxation-based incentive, and to a company like the LCC with uncertain profits and required capital expenditure in excess of £60m, there would be no benefit whatsoever in such a system of reliefs.[47] Indeed, where the requirements are such that new machines cannot be accommodated to the design structures of old buildings and therefore new factories are required as well, the effect would be to encourage replacement at the margin on the basis of current cash fl ws, rather than the root and branch restructuring that became increasingly necessary for Lancashire firms

Thus, the effects of declining and unstable profits illustrated in Figure 1 were greatly to reduce the value of tax relief available to Lancashire companies. As contemporary industry observers pointed out, tax, investment and corporate structure were closely inter-related.[48] For companies faced with the need to make significant investments in fi ed assets, the potential benefit of accelerated tax depreciation on such expenditure, especially where replacement costs were rising,[49] was very high. However, as with Lancashire in the 1950s, where profits were very low, or where companies made losses, the tax benefit of initial and investment allowances was low or non-existent.[50] At the same time, as noted already, companies elsewhere translated tax allowances into higher dividends that in turn informed capital market expectations. Managers of Lancashire firms responding to this pressure suffered from the disadvantages of the fiscal system without being able to share its advantages. Indeed, managers may in some cases have chosen to pay the higher distributed profits tax in order to create liabilities against which allowances on capital expenditure might be offset. In many more cases, the threat of large losses from market uncertainty may have been sufficient to suggest that the availability of tax depreciation as an immediate cash-fl w benefit on xpensive new assets might be jeopardised.

In similar, albeit accidental, fashion, the tax system penalised Lancashire in other respects. As pointed out above, in learning the lessons of history, cotton had become heavily dependent on equity finance. During the 1950s, however, the tax system offered important advantages to debt-financed firms through the differential treatment of loan interest and profits. [51]A further, but potentially very important, frustration to Lancashire entrepreneurs was the discriminatory effect of the system of allowances on investment in buildings. As a prominent Lancashire lobbyist, Hervey Rhodes MP, never tired of arguing, Lancashire desperately needed new buildings as a precursor to the installation of new machinery, yet tax incentives applied at much higher allowance levels for machinery than for buildings.[52]

Taking all of these issues together, at the level of the individual firm, external pressures and British government policy compounded the problem of investment and re-equipment. At the LCC, according to a series of published Chairman's Statements from Sir John Grey and Sir Frank Platt, the late 1940s and early 1950s were a period in which punitive taxes on corporate profits frustrated a genuine desire to invest.[53] In 1953/54, the company conducted a survey to establish the cost of rebuilding and reequipping the 52 mills under its control. This was estimated at over £62m, or more than three times the capital and reserves (and nearly fi e times as much as was made available to the whole British cotton industry for re-equipment in the 1959 Act). In addition, from the early 1950s onwards the company was forced to keep over £1m in a process and stock reserve - an insurance policy against fluctuations in raw cotton prices made necessary by the US government's policy of price support and the consequent moribund state of the Liverpool Futures Market.[54] Input price uncertainty, combined with the effects of import penetration and unstable demand in the home market, led to large unplanned increases and decreases in stock levels. For example, in the Annual Report for 1960, the Chairman, R.M. Lee, identified the need for stable markets as crucial to the future of the industry and pointed out that, although sales for that year were the highest since 1950, production was the lowest since 1945.[55] For these reasons especially, regardless of the disadvantages to individual firms, industry collective action through federal structures, such as the Yarn Spinners' Association (YSA), became impossible to discard voluntarily.

Despite the common strength of belief in such agreements, it is useful with reference to the third hypothesis to examine evidence of disunity within Lancashire. On the political level there is evidence that the Lancashire cotton interest was divided on the question of trade, particularly in constituencies where traditional liberal free trade values remained dominant.[56] This division was reflected in two sub-groups identifiable within British cotton textiles. The first considered import substitution to be the main threat to the industry.

Their demands were therefore associated with trade agreements and import controls. In particular, there were objections to duty-free Commonwealth imports and other concessions given to Japan and India, for fear that 'either might go communist' and that it is 'we in Lancashire who are suffering because of it'.[57] Emotive language coloured the attitudes of this group; the value of fiscal incentives was discounted in the face of Japanese 'dumping' and a suspicion that Whitehall had written off Lancashire.[58] The second group argued that improved efficien y was the only remedy. Their demands were therefore that British government policy should encourage greater verticalisation and investment in machinery via tax-based incentives.[59] Policies advocated by this group included the ending of punitive taxes on profits [60] They also condemned the way in which specific government policies favoured industries such as steel, motor vehicles, plastics and armaments, but not cotton.[61] These representatives also bemoaned the industry's inability to produce reliable statistics on the economics of cotton for government consumption and lobbying purposes.[62] A corollary of this problem is that it falls to the business historian to present, for the first time, the statistical evidence discussed above on the profit, d vidend and tax relationship.

At Westminster, the conflict between restructuring and import controls was obscured by the politics of the party machines. In the Conservative Party, the pressures of government placed the more protectionist-inclined Lancashire members in an awkward position, a point well illustrated by the 1955 debate on assistance to the cotton industry. Sufficient majorities in the 1950s underpinned a general policy, exemplified by Peter Thorneycroft as President of the Board of Trade, based on the principle of free trade and commitments to the Commonwealth and GATT. Significantl , this general line was underpinned by support for investment in other industries, an argument favoured by many Lancashire Conservatives from constituencies more peripheral to textile districts.[63] MPs for constituencies with large numbers of LCC mills, such as Lieutenant-Colonel Wentworth Schofield (Rochdale), Sir Harold Sutcliffe (Heywood and Royton) and Sir Ian Horobin (Oldham East), whilst making sympathetic speeches against the backdrop of the closure of 90 mills, all voted against a motion for action on Indian imports explicitly called for by the LCC management.[64] As Barbara Castle pointed out with considerable irony in the 1955 debate, 'members opposite . . . have obviously been tom between the desire to play down the problem of Lancashire to save the government's face, and the realisation that if they play it down too much they will be in trouble with their own supporters'.[65] For Labour and opposition MPs, such dilemmas were less keenly felt. Even MPs who argued within local circles that the trade issue was less relevant than that of industry structure and fiscal incentives, for example Ernest Thornton (Farnworth) and Hervey Rhodes (Ashton under Lyne), in the comfort of opposition, were able to argue at Westminster that the government ought to take measures against duty-free Indian imports. As a result of the political splits in Lancashire prior to 1959, it was the trade issue, not industry structure and re-equipment, that dominated. These splits were important, and help explain, as concluded elsewhere, that Lancashire was ineffective compared to the US cotton lobby at securing concessions.[66] Accordingly, the third hypothesis is rejected.

The above analysis has sought to explain why little direct political support was forthcoming before 1959 and the consequences of cotton textiles having to make do with the same investment incentives available to the rest of British industry. A result of setting subsidy proportionate to growth was also that an industry such as cotton textiles, that needed restructuring investment against a backdrop of uncertain and cyclical demand, could not benefit. Changed political circumstances in 1959, however, created a new opportunity for

Lancashire in the form of intervention via tailored subsidies. To explore the effectiveness of this mechanism further, as a contrast to the effects of tax allowances, it is to the grant system of the 1959 Act that we now turn in the next section.

## IV

The discussion below re-examines the hypothesised relationships in the previous section with reference to the period immediately following the 1959 Act. Once the British government had intervened, the taxation impact of general policy was altered in the light of new arrangements for subsidy. Divisions within the cotton lobby evidenced above also became less relevant once the Act was passed. Accordingly, the following discussion re-examines only the first two hypotheses in detail, and in considering the second examines the relationship between subsidy and investment. Capital market constraints as reinforced by the macro-economic climate are considered first. The effectiveness of government subsidies for restructuring and investment is then assessed. Finally, the sufficien y or otherwise of capital from private and government sources available to fund reinvestment, is considered, again from the perspective of the LCC.

As shown above, Lancashire cotton, like other industries, was able to satisfy the constraint of the capital market by steadily raising dividends through the 1950s, although, unlike other industries, in cotton this was funded from business cash fl w rather than tax breaks. The 1959 Act redressed the balance by providing new cash fl ws from subsidies. Figure 1 suggests there are good grounds for believing that the 1959 Act had a substantial impact on firms dividend and expenditure policies during the years 1959–61. In addition to the increase in dividend payments observable in this period, shareholders also benefited from the large capital repayments made by a substantial proportion of firms [67] The late 1950s saw a structural break in the pattern of divestment (Figures 1 and 2). This coincided with the 1959 Act and the lobbying period that preceded it.[68] Also the 1958 budget restored tax neutrality to the dividend decision,[69] so managerial decisions after that would tend to reflect British government policy only via the 1959 Act. The effect of government subsidy was thus an abandonment of 'smoothing' by managers when declaring dividends.[70] This may have been induced by the unpredictable impact the scheme had on after-tax profits, or by managers re-basing their decisions on cash fl w once the additional income stream from grants was anticipated.

The most surprising trend apparent from the data was that those companies with the greatest capital requirement were also those paying out the highest proportion of profits in dividends.[71] The result of government intervention, through committing companies to higher fi ed costs without guaranteeing stability of demand, was to increase capital market pressure on corporate cash fl w.[72] Thus the provision of re-equipment subsidies allowed modernising firms to pay higher dividends to shareholders, thereby compensating for their increased risk. Such policies were advocated by influential industrialists because modernisation, especially investment in vertically integrated, throughput production, would have committed firms to higher fi ed cost structures,[73] a very risky strategy in the face of market uncertainty.

Demands for high dividends also reflected share ownership. Analysis of weekly share price series in the period 1951–62 suggests that the capital market was inefficient [74] a view consistent with the manipulation of dividends to compensate for the perceived higher risk discussed above. Thin trading apparent in some cases would have made it difficult for shareholders to realise their investment and more likely to seek satisfactory returns from increases in dividends. The 'bird in the hand' safety of cash dividends might also have compensated investors for their greater risk at a time when profits in the British cotton textile industry were falling dramatically and when the costs of re-equipment were very high.[75] Even in companies with dispersed shareholdings, and therefore more tradable shares, management worried about take-over threats and saw dividends as 'protection money' payable in return for shareholder loyalty.[76] It is clear, therefore, that the capital market did act as a constraint on investment during the re-equipment phase after 1959. Dividend requirements now became a constraint on investment and the first hypothesis is rejected for this period.

As suggested above, the 1959 Act coincided with continuing uncertainty about demand. During the period of re-equipment, import penetration, a function of other important aspects of British government policy, for example quota agreements with key Commonwealth countries such as Hong Kong, increased from 27 per cent in 1958 to 43 per cent in 1963.[77] Commentators attributed the low levels of re-equipment consequent upon the Act to uncertainty about the import position in the early 1960s.[78] The uncertainty surrounding imports had a number of aspects. It was generally recognised that re-equipment involved the purchase of very expensive machinery which, given the allowances that had to be made for depreciation, could only be profitably employed if three-shift working was implemented. However, if there was an extension of shift working when the future level of demand for the British cotton industry's output was uncertain, this might mean that it would be unable to utilise its capacity fully.[79] A further problem was that the premiums paid to operatives to work a third (night) shift were so high as to make it unclear that re-equipment would so lower costs of production as to make the industry competitive.[80] However, given the uncertainty surrounding the future volume of imports, it was all the more imperative that firms which had re-equipped adopted three-shift working in order to recoup their capital expenditures as quickly as possible.[81] The destabilising effects of the 1960 boom and subsequent slump meant that new equipment was already lying idle.[82] Until the import position was cleared up many firms believed that the time allowed by the Act to submit applications for re-equipment was insufficient and there were calls for an even longer extension of the qualifying period.[83] Finally, the view was expressed that the cost advantage enjoyed by Far Eastern producers was so great that no amount of re-equipment would ever make Lancashire competitive.[84]

The effects of market uncertainty on investment were compounded by limitations of the legislation. One concern was that the re-equipment subsidy was far less generous than the scrapping subsidy, and that this might explain why there was a bigger takeup of the latter.[85] Over half of our sample companies shrank in terms of book value capital employed during the same period. This is surprising, given that most of the retired fi ed assets would have been at low carrying values and that subsidy was available for new plant acquisitions, or at even more generous levels for quitting the industry. Weaker companies lacked the cash fl w to fund dividends and thereby imitate the more successful companies. Moreover, the subsidy scheme interacted with tax investment allowances in the early 1960s so as to exclude re-equipping firms from the full available subsidy, thereby reducing the attractiveness of the scheme.[86] Another concern was that, as illustrated earlier by the financial position of the LCC, the size of the re-equipment subsidy was insufficient to justify large-scale re-equipment by firms [87] Given the rapid rate of technical progress, especially in the spinning section of the industry, even the most modem machinery would be rendered technically obsolete within fi e to six years and this, too, may have encouraged firms to be very cautious.[88] Finally, firms were reluctant to reequip because the destabilising effects of the 1960 boom meant that new equipment was already lying idle.

Another indirect aspect of British government policy cut against a vital organisational defence mechanism at a crucial moment. This was the abolition of the YSA by the Restrictive Practices Court in 1959. Without the YSA, 'which was the salvation of the industry' for limiting profit distribution above a fi ed percentage,[89] the dividend payments increases in the 1950s would have been even higher. Its abolition partly explains the structural break in dividend payment patterns in the period after 1958 (Figure 1).

Despite the availability of subsidy, the combined effect of the limitations of the Act and capital market constraints meant that the British cotton industry faced a capital shortage by 1961. Uncertain markets and higher dividend requirements drove up the cost of capital for Lancashire entrepreneurs, a problem compounded by the limitation of government assistance to the Act itself and inconsistencies with other aspects of government policy. Increased cost and a capital shortage prevented firms within the industry achieving concentration on a large scale. The LCC's 'Northern Plan' of 1962, to take over a large proportion of the industry by agreed acquisitions, failed due to an absence of sufficient capital within the company and the subsequent refusal of the quasi-government, Bank of England-sponsored, Finance Corporation for Industry (FCI) to provide assistance.[90] These negotiations also involved the Board of Trade and Barings Bank. The indifference of the former department must be judged by reference to the defined purpose of the FCI, which was to rehabilitate and develop businesses, in liaison with government departments, when this was in the national interest.[91] FCI reticence towards cotton contrasted with the large amounts lent to the British steel industry during the period 1947–65, and the large profits available to the investor in the steel industry as a function of government intervention were noted with some cynicism by relatively powerless lobbyists for the cotton industry.[92] The LCC scheme was the last attempt by the industry to re-structure itself from within. At the same time, it was an admission that it no longer possessed the financial resources to do so. Failure to secure direct intervention prior to 1959 exemplified the political weakness and increasing isolation of the Lancashire cotton interest. It is therefore easy to agree with the analysis of the political background to the intervention of 1959 by seeing the Act as essentially a knee-jerk response to industry lobbying from a British government temporarily faced with the need to protect small majorities in nine key Lancashire marginal constituencies.[93] A prevailing attitude of Whitehall indifference did not auger well for the potential success of this legislation, and the Act was indeed a failure when its achievement is compared to the scale of the task required. Prior to the introduction of the 1959 Act, the industry's own estimates of the total cost of re-equipping were in the range £78 million to £93 million.[94] Actual re-equipment expenditure following the Act was much lower than even cautiously inadequate *a priori* government estimates and also lower than the numbers cited in previous discussions of the 1959 Act.[95] Whereas the Board of Trade had estimated modernisation and re-equipment expenditures for the industry as a whole would total £6.5 million for the years 1960–62, the actual expenditure was only £1.94 million.[96]

Notwithstanding this apparent failure, as in the 1950s, it is important to assess British government policy in terms of its internal consistency and its congruence with the pressures facing the industry from elsewhere. Capital market inefficiencies, as manifested by the demand for dividends, constrained investment. In the 1950s, as we have shown, Lancashire contributed more than its share of taxation. On the basis of these findings, if the industry really had no long-term future, a rational government would have treated it as a 'cash cow' and allowed it to decline. Instead, the intervention of 1959 has the appearance of throwing good money after bad, or, for one last time, lining the pockets of the cotton investor.

## V

Immediately prior to the take-over of the LCC by Courtaulds in 1964, A.M Alfred, the Chief Economist at Courtaulds, argued that tax-free depreciation was perhaps twice as important as cash grants for the purposes of encouraging investment.[97] Lancashire's experience suggests that neither is adequate unless they are used consistently with other aspects of British government policy. As far as tax allowances are concerned, the use of investment allowances through the tax system is unlikely to stimulate turnarounds in declining industries where other forms of uncertainty are not first removed. In the 1950s, as one of the weakest competitive sectors, cotton also had one of the highest tax burdens. In terms of direct subsidies, the Act lacked cohesion with general government policy, dealing with structure but not markets. It also lacked internal consistency. As one commentator put it: 'The idea of a subsidy to reduce capacity in order to be eligible for a subsidy to increase it, has a faint fl vour of paradox to say the least.'[98]

The evidence presented here, however, is insufficient to judge British government policy as a whole, although it is fair to say that successive governments were unsupportive of Lancashire. Trade and investment policies were orientated towards all sectors, not just cotton. As the political analysis makes clear, a divided Lancashire was not a strong enough lobbying interest to secure other than the most limited of special favours. What is shown, nonetheless, is that Lancashire did suffer because general British government policy cut across the interests of the cotton industry in damaging ways, and in a fashion that was inconsistent with the limited specific policies that were offered. Further research by scholars in other industries might throw more light on the interplay of fiscal policy, capital markets and investment behaviour in this period.

Even so, the nemesis of over-extension and individualistic entrepreneurship from the days of free trade and growing markets played an important part. Free trade, once Lancashire's opportunity, now became a serious threat. Export and domestic market uncertainties based on cheaper overseas competition spilled over into the demands of the capital markets. Risk-averse investors required high dividends and thereby left the industry short of the capital it required for re-equipment. In contrast to the glory days before 1914 when economic strength underpinned the free trade philosophy of the 'Manchester School', the political economy of Lancashire in 1960 was best summarised by financial weakness and divided political representation. Either the philosophy of the Manchester School or the Lancashire cotton industry could survive, but not both.

## Appendix

The following variables were used in the tests described below:

$D_{it}$ — Dividend for firm i at time t
P — Profits  vailable as dividends to ordinary shareholders.
CE — Capital Employed.
GCE — Growth Rate of Capital Employed (annual compounded rate, t-6 ... t)
G — Gearing; ratio of long-term debt capital to total capital employed.

A series of tests were then applied to the data set. First, current dividends were modelled in relation to current year profits and prior year d vidend per equation (1).

$$\ln D_{it} = a + \beta \ln P_{it} + \gamma \ln D_{i(t-1)} + u_{it}$$

$$(1)$$

where current year's dividend for firm i (Dit), is explained in terms of current year profits (Pit) and the previous year's dividend (Di(t-l)). The inclusion of the lagged dividend term allows the computation of a long term dividend response elasticity to a change in profit, and facilitates the observation of managerial expectations (determined as the ratio $\beta/(1-\gamma)$, ie. the geometric progression, $\beta/(1+\gamma+\gamma^2+\ldots\ldots)$). Also, a high significance level for the lagged dependent variable provides evidence of managerial 'smoothing' of dividends. Hence, this contributes a potentially useful basic model of managerial behaviour. The model was tested for a cross-section of companies for each year between 1950 and 1964 (n>30 and <40 for all years; variation caused by dropping negative observations from the log transformed model). The results are reported in Table 1. In conjunction, average profits, dividends and the pay-out ratio were calculated for the whole sample and the aggregate trends shown in Figures 1 and 2.

The basic model (1) was then extended to include further variables for size (CE), growth (GCE) and financial risk (G) (models 1.1 and 1.2; Tables 2 and 3). Where additional regressors are employed as extensions to the Lintner model, certain weaknesses should be borne in mind. These are that there is a high degree of endogeneity due to the inclusion of a lagged dependent variable. Also, the resulting high $R^2$ co-efficient leaves little room for additional variables to add further explanatory power to the model. Therefore, a further model was tested in which the lagged dividend co-efficient as dropped.

$$D_i / CE_i = a + \beta\, GCE_i + \gamma\, G_i + u_i \qquad (2)$$

The general approach follows that of previous empirical work covering similar periods. For cotton textiles, on the basis of a likely structural break occurring due to government intervention in the legislation of 1959, each of the models 1.1, 1.2 and 2 were tested first for 1958 and then for 1963. The results are presented in Tables 2–4.

Table 2.  Determinants of dividend payments, 1950–64

|  | Pt | Dt-1 | Elasticity | R2 | F |
|---|---|---|---|---|---|
| 1950 | 0.103 | 0.951 | 2.102 | 0.976 | 604.1 |
|  | (2.688) | (21.529) |  |  |  |
| 1951 | 0.026 | 0.968 | 0.812 | 0.971 | 523.5 |
|  | (0.598) | (21.898) |  |  |  |
| 1952 | 0.099 | 0.896 | 0.952 | 0.977 | 602.8 |
|  | (3.595) | (22.66) |  |  |  |
| 1953 | 0.125 | 0.849 | 0.828 | 0.972 | 528.8 |
|  | (3.036) | (17.17) |  |  |  |
| 1954 | 0.036 | 0.975 | 1.44 | 0.972 | 554.7 |
|  | (0.743) | (17.51) |  |  |  |
| 1955 | 0.122 | 0.932 | 1.794 | 0.985 | 934.2 |
|  | (4.369) | (30.55) |  |  |  |
| 1956 | 0.097 | 0.815 | 0.524 | 0.892 | 123.2 |
|  | (1.023) | (8.098) |  |  |  |
| 1957 | 0.098 | 0.883 | 0.838 | 0.937 | 229.6 |

|      | $P_t$    | $D_{t-1}$ | Elasticity | R2    | F       |
|------|----------|-----------|------------|-------|---------|
|      | (1.096)  | (9.874)   |            |       |         |
| 1958 | 0.089    | 0.914     | 1.035      | 0.989 | 1150.02 |
|      | (3.228)  | (26.42)   |            |       |         |
| 1959 | 0.379    | 0.553     | 0.8479     | 0.894 | 118.3   |
|      | (5.354)  | (6.643)   |            |       |         |
| 1960 | 0.534    | 0.501     | 1.070      | 0.956 | 362.55  |
|      | (9.064)  | (7.896)   |            |       |         |
| 1961 | 0.301    | 0.7004    | 1.004      | 0.979 | 788.8   |
|      | (6.143)  | (13.07)   |            |       |         |
| 1962 | -0.019   | 3.788     | 0.007      | 0.973 | 408.9   |
|      | (0.296)  | (13.32)   |            |       |         |
| 1963 | 0.312    | 0.635     | 0.855      | 0.941 | 166.2   |
|      | (4.125)  | (6.495)   |            |       |         |
| 1964 | 0.378    | 0.665     | 1.128      | 0.952 | 139.7   |
|      | (2.614)  | (3.905)   |            |       |         |

*Note*: t statistics in parentheses.
*Sources*: Dividend and profit series der ved from CUCD.

Table 3.  Determinants of dividend payments, 1958

|                       | *(1.1)*   | *(1.2)*   | *(2)*         |
|-----------------------|-----------|-----------|---------------|
| Dependent variable    | $D_{it}$  | $D_{it}$  | $D_i/CE_j$    |
| Coefficient intercep  | −2.51     | 4.73      | 0.029         |
|                       | (0.795)   | (0.616)   | (7.903)       |
| P                     | 0.031     | 0.228     |               |
|                       | (1.69)    | (10.21)   |               |
| $D_{t-1}$             | 0.901     |           |               |
|                       | (12.42)   |           |               |
| CE                    | 0.0014    | 0.016     |               |
|                       | (1.089)   | (13.22)   |               |
| GCE                   | −0.067    | −0.54     | 0.0005        |
|                       | (0.172)   | (0.567)   | (1.171)       |
| G                     | −8.946    | −40.33    | −0.064        |
|                       | (0.521)   | (0.961)   | (3.401)       |
| Summary Statistics    |           |           |               |
| F                     | 1060.6    | 210.8     | 7.819         |
| $R^2$                 | 0.994     | 0.941     | 0.328         |

*Sources*: As Table 2.

Table 4. Determinants of dividend payments, 1963

|  | (1.1) | (1.2) | (2) |
|---|---|---|---|
| Dependent variable | $D_{it}$ | $D_{it}$ | $D_i/CE_j$ |
| Coefficient intercep | −1.215 | 1.241 | 0.022 |
|  | (0.295) | (0.107 | (8.15) |
| P | 0.051 | 0.399 |  |
|  | (1.06) | (3.429) |  |
| $D_{t-1}$ | 0.939 |  |  |
|  | (14.26) |  |  |
| CE | 0.0007 | 0.0196 |  |
|  | (0.417) | (6.747) |  |
| GCE | 2.07 | −1.047 | 0.0015 |
|  | (2.268) | (0.418) | (4.109) |
| G | 18.502 | −203.78 | −0.31 |
|  | (0.539) | (2.341) | (1.5) |
| Summary Statistics |  |  |  |
| F | 545.66 | 79.08 | 8.576 |
| $R^2$ | 0.989 | 0.916 | 0.356 |

*Sources*: As Table 2.

## Notes

We are grateful to the editors, two anonymous referees, Geoff Tweedale, and the participants at the Accounting, Business and Financial History Conference, Cardiff, September 1997, for helpful comments on earlier versions of this article.

1. Structure and technology issues, for example, are analysed in W.A. Lazonick, Competition, Specialisation, and Industrial Decline', *Journal of Economic History*, Vol.41 (1981), pp.31–8; idem, 'Industrial Organisation and Technological Change: The Decline of the British Cotton Industry', *Business History Review*, Vol.57 (1983), pp.195–236; these debates are summarised and contextualised in J. Singleton, 'The Decline of the British Cotton Industry Since 1940', in M.B. Rose (ed.), *The Lancashire Cotton Industry: A History Since 1700* (Preston, 1996); financial performance has been examined in D.M. Higgins, 'Rings, Mules, and Structural Constraints in the Lancashire Textile Industry, C.1945-C.1965', *Economic History Review*, Vol. XLVI (1993), pp.342–62; D.M. Higgins and J.S. Toms, 'Firm Structure and Financial Performance: The Lancashire Cotton Industry, c. 1884–1960', *Accounting, Business and Financial History*, Vol.7 (1997), pp.195–232.
2. J. Singleton, *Lancashire on the Scrapheap* (Oxford, 1991), pp.231–3.
3. R. Church, 'The Family Firm in Industrial Capitalism', *Business History*, Vol.35 (1993), pp.17–11.
4. C. Miles, *Lancashire Textiles: A Case Study of Industrial Change* (Cambridge, 1968), especially Chapter 4.
5. On recent advocacy of such changes to the tax structure, see W. Hutton, *The State We're In* (London, 1995), Chapter 6. On the use of historical investigation into their effects, see W.G. Christie and V. Nanda, 'Free Cash Flow, Shareholder Value, and the Undistributed Profits Tax of 1936 and 1937', *Journal of Finance*, Vol.49 No.5 (1994), pp.1727–55.
6. B.R. Mitchell and P. Deane, *Abstract of British Historical Statistics* (Cambridge, 1963), p. 186.
7. J.S. Toms, 'Growth, Profits and Technological Choice: The Case of the Lancashire Cotton Textile Industry', *Journal of Industrial History*, Vol. 1 (1998), pp.35–55.

8. Personal capitalism refers to the inhibiting effect of individual control of businesses on investment and growth, see A.D. Chandler, *Scale and Scope: The Dynamics of Industrial Capitalism* (Cambridge, MA, 1990); the Lancashire variant is outlined in J.S. Toms, 'Windows of Opportunity in the Textile Industry: The Business Strategies of Lancashire Entrepreneurs, 1880–1914', *Business History*, Vol.40 No.1 (1998), pp.1–25.

9. For pre-1914 examples of divestment policies, see J.S. Toms, 'Financial Constraints on Economic Growth: Profits, Capital Accumulation and the Development of the Lancashire Cotton Spinning Industry, 1885–1914', Accounting, *Business and Financial History*, Vol.4 No.3 (1994), pp.364–83; a post-1918 example was (later Sir) Frank Platt, who used profits from the 1920 flotation boom initially to finance early retirement; J. Bamberg, 'Sir Frank Platt', in D. Jeremy (ed.), *Dictionary of Business Biography* (London, 1984–86), p.6.

10. A.P. Dickerson, H.D. Gibson and E. Tsakalatos, 'Short-Termism and Under-Investment: The Influence of the Financial System', *Manchester School*, Vol.63 (1995), pp.351–67.

11. Toms, 'Financial Constraints', p.380.

12. Theoretically, the payment of a dividend has no effect on the market value of the company. By extension, dividend payments are unrelated to the investment requirements of a business. As far as shareholders are concerned, if a profit distribution is insufficient, additional dividend can be manufactured, in an efficient capital market, via the disposal of a proportion of the holding. In theory, it is argued, this 'irrelevance' proposition must be true since the present values of the investment projects of the firm are unaffected; M.H. Miller and F. Modigliani, 'Dividend Policy, Growth and the Valuation of Shares', *Journal of Business*, Vol.34 (1961), pp.411–33.

13. D.N. McCloskey, *Knowledge and Persuasion in Economics* (Cambridge, 1994), p. 154.

14. S. Grossman and J. Stiglitz, 'On the Impossibility of Informationally Efficient Markets', *American Economic Review*, Vol.70 (1980), pp.393–408.

15. W. Kennedy, *Industrial Structure, Capital Markets and the Origin of British Economic* Decline (Cambridge, 1987).

16. Chandler, *Scale and Scope*, pp.240–86; B. Elbaum and W.A. Lazonick (eds.), *The Decline of the British Economy* (Oxford, 1986).

17. Chandler, *Scale and Scope*, p.286.

18. A. Hirschman, Exit, *Voice and Loyalty* (Boston, 1970).

19. 'Operational efficien y' refers to the speed and accuracy of transaction processing, F. Fabozzi and F. Modigliani, *Capital Markets: Institutions and Instruments* (London, 1992), p.249.

20. See, for example, M. Rozeff, 'Growth, Beta and Agency costs as Determinants of Dividend Pay-out Ratios', *Journal of Financial Economics*, Vol.5 (1982), pp.249–59.

21. See, for example, R. Pettit, 'Dividend Announcements, Security Performance and Capital Market Efficien y', *Journal of Finance*, Vol.27 (1972), pp.993–1007.

22. For example, see J. Lintner, 'Distribution of Incomes of Corporations among Dividends, Retained Earnings and Taxes', *American Economic Review*, Vol.46 (1956), pp.97–113.

23. For a summary of tax differentials on distributed and undistributed profits, see *Political and Economic Planning, Growth in the British Economy* (London, 1960), p.123.

24. T.J. Hatton and A. Chrystal, 'The Budget and Fiscal Policy', in N.F.R. Crafts and D. Woodward (eds.), *The British Economy Since 1945* (Oxford, 1991), p.56.

25. S. Pollard, *The Development of the British Economy* (London, 3rd edn., 1983), pp.392–8; J. Tomlinson, 'British Economic Policy since 1945', in R. Floud and D.N. McCloskey (eds.), *The Economic History of Britain Since 1700, Vol.3: 1939–1992* (Cambridge, 1994).

26. J.C.R. Dow, *The Management of the British Economy, 1945–60* (Cambridge, 1964); R.W. Price, 'Budgetary Policy', in F.T. Blackaby (ed.), *British Economic Policy, 1960–74* (Cambridge, 1978).

27. For example, see M.B. Rose, 'The Politics of Protection: An Institutional Approach to Government–Industry Relations in the British and United States Cotton Industries', *Business History*, Vol.39 No.4 (1997), pp.128–50; and Singleton, *Lancashire on the Scrapheap*. The political economy framework used here is after M. Zald, 'Political Economy: A Framework for Competitive Analysis', in M. Zald (ed.), *Power in Organizations* (Nashville, 1970).

28. Rose, 'Politics of Protection', p.143.

29. Dividend pay-out was calculated as the ratio of dividend to profit before tax and to profit after tax. Financial gearing is the ratio of long-term borrowings to total capital employed.

Growth in capital employed is the annually compounded percentage change in capital employed. Return on capital employed is profit before interest and tax divided by capital employed. In all measures, capital employed is defined as shareholders' capital plus reserves plus long-term borrowings.

30. For the basic model (1) in the appendix, see Lintner, 'Distribution of Incomes', p.109. For an empirical example, see R. Alpine, 'Cross Section Regression Analysis of Profit and Dividends in the Brewing Industry, United Kingdom, 1951–1963', in P. Hart (ed.), *Studies in Profit, Business Saving and Investment in the United Kingdom, 1920–1963, Vol.2* (London, 1968), pp. 164–81. For extensions to this model (models 1.1, 1.2 and 2, Appendix), see T.M. Ryan, 'Dividend Policy and Market Valuation in British Industry', *Journal of Business Finance and Accounting*, Vol. 1 (1974), pp.415–28.

31. Tattersalls, Cotton Trade Review, 1952–62 inclusive. This gave a sample of six companies: Amalgamated Cotton Manufacturing Trust (ACMT), Crosses and Heatons, Fine Cotton Spinners and Doublers Association (FCSDA), Joshua Hoyle, Lancashire Cotton Corporation (LCC) and Rylands.

32. These records include Board Minutes and Annual Reports, Lancashire Cotton Corporation (LCC), Greater Manchester Record Office (GMRO); annual journals of the National Federation of Textile Works Managers' Associations (NFTWMA); Parliamentary Debates (Hansard), Fifth Series, London HMSO (hereafter PDH).

33. Lancashire Cotton Corporation, Statement by the Chairman, Annual Report and Accounts, 1952.

34. Calculated using the CUCD data set as the average compound growth rate of equity for all sample companies between 1952 and 1958.

35. To examine the relationship between dividend policy and capital requirement for the period prior to the 1959 Act, model (1), Appendix 1, was re-tested in turn with coefficients added for size, financial risk and capital requirement (proxied by the average growth rate in capital for the previous six years), models 1.1 and 1.2, together with model 2 for the year 1958 (appendix, Table 3).

36. The re-flotations of 1919–20 were largely financed by loans and overdrafts; S. Bowden and D.M. Higgins, 'Short Time Working and Price Maintenance: Collusive Tendencies in the Cotton Spinning Industry, 1919–1939', *Economic History Review*, Vol.LI No.2 (1998), pp.319–3; thus, by the 1930s, cotton, along with iron and steel, was the most indebted sector of the British economy, H. Sjogren, 'Financial Reconstruction and Industrial Reorganisation in Different Financial Systems: A Comparative View of British and Swedish Institutions during the Inter-War Period', *Business History*, Vol.39 No.4 (1997), p.90.

37. A. Rubner, 'The Irrelevancy of the British Differential Profits Tax', *Economic Journal*, Vol.74 (1964), pp.347–59.

38. Singleton, *Lancashire on the Scrapheap*, pp.116–17.

39. Accountant, 24 April, 1954, p.453; the damaging impact of Purchase Tax on the fine spinning sector is discussed in Higgins, 'Rings, Mules and Structural Constraints', pp.351–4.

40. R. McDonald and D. Siegel, 'The Value of Waiting to Invest', *Quarterly Journal of Economics*, Vol.101 (1986), pp.707–27.

41. Toms, 'Growth, Profits and Technological Choice'; D.M. Higgins and J.S. Toms, 'From the Age of Laissez Faire to the Age of De-Industrialisation: New Perspectives on the Decline of the Lancashire Cotton Textile Industry, 1880–1965', unpublished working paper presented at the Economic History Society Conference, University of Leeds, April, 1998.

42. M. Dupree (ed.), *Lancashire and Whitehall: The Diary of Sir Raymond Streat, Vol. 2* (Manchester, 1987); pp.186, 215, 226–7, 472–3.

43. Political and Economic Planning, *Growth in the British Economy*, p.123.

44. D. Walker, 'Some Economic Aspects of the Taxation of Companies', *Manchester School*, Vol.1954; I.M.D. Little, 'Higgledy Piggledy Growth', *Bulletin of the Oxford Institute of Economics and Statistics*, Vol.24 (1962), p.412; Rubner, 'The Irrelevancy of the British Differential Profits Tax'.

45. Rubner, 'British Differential Profits Tax', p.355.

46. Total government expenditure as a result of the 1959 Act was £24.7m, that is, scrapping grants £11.3m plus total eligible expenditure on re-equipment of £53m, with rate of grant applied to the latter at 25 per cent. C. Miles, 'Protection of the British Textile Industry', in W. Corden and

G. Fels (eds.), *Public Assistance to Industry: Protection and Subsidies in Britain and Germany* (London, 1976). Our figure of £9.7m, based on a sample of only the larger quoted companies, significantly under-estimates the total for the whole industry. Applying the tax differentials in Table 1 to 300 companies the size of the Oldham Twist Co. Ltd (a representatively capitalised company for the industry) assuming similar gross profits, gives a total of £33m. A conservative estimate for the whole industry would be £40–£50m.

47. Whilst intended as illustrative, these figures are broadly typical of those relevant to the LCC, as discussed subsequently. See also the numerical illustration in Dupree (ed.), *Lancashire and Whitehall*, p.226.

48. R. Robson, *The Cotton Industry in Britain* (London, 1957), pp.208–9.

49. Between 1950 and 1960, replacement costs of ring spindles and automatic looms more than doubled; Singleton, *Lancashire on the Scrapheap*, p. 151.

50. To give one example, in 1956 Jackson and Steeple made its largest capital investment of the decade, £207,000. With an effective rate of tax of 50 per cent, profits for that year were sufficient to reli ve only approximately £124,000, or 60 per cent of total expenditure.

51. Pollard, *Development of the British Economy*, p.393.

52. For example, PDH, 12 April 1954, Vol.256, pp.822–3; 2 May 1955, Vol.540, pp.1383–90.

53. GMRO/LCC, Annual Reports, Chairman's Statements, 1947–62.

54. *The Times*, 20 Jan. 1956, 15b. The support of the US government for its own producers provides many contrasts with the UK, see Rose, 'Politics of Protection'.

55. *The Times*, 22 Jan. 1960, 19d.

56. Rose, 'Politics of Protection', p. 143.

57. W.T. Shackleton, 'Government Trade Policy Criticised', *NFTWMA*, Vol. XXXV (1956), p.228.

58. J. Orme, The Future of Lancashire Textiles', *NFTWMA*, Vol. XXXIV (1955), p.113.

59. For examples of advocacy of this general argument, see G. McPherson, 'The Textile Trade's Problems: Improved Efficien y the Only Remedy', *NFTWMA*, Vol. XXXV (1956), p.241, and the specific solution via tax incentives, A. Green, 'Government Policy and the Textile Industry', *NFTWMA*, Vol. XXXV (1956), p.56. All of these advocates rejected arguments for import controls.

60. G. McPherson, 'The Outlook for the Textile Industry', *NFTWMA*, Vol. XXXIV (1955), p. 128.

61. H. Rhodes, 'Government Policy and the Textile Industry', *NFTWMA*, Vol. XXXV (1956), pp.58–9.

62. Ibid., p.58; Dupree (ed.), *Lancashire and Whitehall*, p.65.

63. For example, F.J. Erroll (Altrincham and Sale) PDH, 9 March 1955, Vol.538, p.517, William Shepherd (Cheadle), p.528, Richard Fort (Clitheroe), p.551. On the latter member, see also Dupree (ed.), *Lancashire and Whitehall*, p.774.

64. GMRO/LCC Annual Reports, Chairman's Statements; W.A. Burke, MP, PDH, Vol.538, pp.485–6; MPs' voting records on resolution for effective action to assist the cotton industry, pp.571–6.

65. By this Castle meant the resolutions of local Conservative Associations (for example, Middleton and Prestwich) and of local Chambers of Commerce (for example, Blackburn) calling on MPs to oppose government and support intervention on behalf of the cotton industry, PDH, Vol.538, pp.518–19.

66. Rose, 'Politics of Protection', p. 129.

67. In the period 1951–57, the median number of firms making capital repayments was three, with an average of £80,000 per firm. In the period 1958–61 this rose to 11.5 and £178,000 respectively (calculated from Tattersall's Cotton Trade Review, 1952–62).

68. The relatively low rates of capacity utilisation in the industry convinced many observers from the mid-1950s that some form of contraction was inevitable (Singleton, *Lancashire on the Scrapheap*, pp. 154–7).

69. Political and Economic Planning, *Growth in the British Economy*, p. 123.

70. In model 1, in the appendix, current year profit became a much more important explanatory variable and prior year dividend exhibits a corresponding decline in significance for the years immediately following the 1959 Act. For some years, such as 1959 and 1963, the model as a whole under-performs, produces unexpected coefficients (1962 profits), or shows significant deviation from the long-run profit/d vidend elasticity of one.

71. To test the relationship between dividend policy and capital requirement during the scrapping and re-equipment phases of the 1959 Act, models 1, 1.1, 1.2 and 2 were re-tested using 1963 as the base year; Appendix, Table 4. In contrast to the 1958 results (Table 3), there was a positive relationship between dividends and growth (Table 4, models 1.1, 1.2 and 2, and cf Table 3).

72. These issues are, of course, quite separate from the perceived inequitable effects of the Act on re-equipping firms. For example, those firms that remained had to pay a levy to compensate those firms leaving the industry. In addition, those firms which had re-equipped prior to the 1959 Act (and therefore had very few re-equipping plans in the short-term future) would have lost out to those firms which delayed re-equipping as long as possible in the hope that just such a scheme would be introduced.

73. A particularly vociferous exponent of this issue was A. Ormerod, 'The UK Cotton Textile Industry: Some Thoughts on Re-equipment', *NFTWMA*, Vol. XL (1961), pp.156–68.

74. Using the weekly share price data in Tattersall's for a single period lagged regression of log returns, three out of the six companies for which data was available, through serial correlation, demonstrated evidence of market inefficien y (t statistics for the lagged variable in parentheses): ACMT (0.14), Crosses and Heatons (0.16), Fine Spinners (1.34), Joshua Hoyle (2.59), LCC (2.47) and Rylands (2.31). In contrast to other studies, the expected result is that all statistics of serial correlation should be insignificant; E. Fama, 'The Behaviour of Stock Market Prices', *Journal of Business*, Vol.38 (1965), pp.34–105.

75. Ormerod, 'The UK Cotton Textile Industry', pp.156–68. Ormerod pointed out that, because of high fi ed costs, the effect of the Act was to transfer risk from the operatives to the holders of equity (p. 158).

76. Ormerod, *Industrial Odyssey*, pp. 154 and 198.

77. Rose, 'The Politics of Protection', p.130.

78. Ibid., p. x; Memorandum submitted by the Cotton Board, p.40; Q.222; Q.238; Memorandum submitted by Mr. Cartwright, p.71; QQ.399–400; Q.500; Memorandum submitted by Colonel Whitehead, p. 130.

79. Ibid. Q.395; Q.429.

80. Ibid. QQ.361–2; QQ.386–90. Estimates of the premium necessary to obtain workers for a night shift ranged from 36 to 40 per cent. Q.523; Q.656.

81. Ibid. QQ.562–5.

82. Ibid. QQ.328–31; QQ.402–3. Given the success of the scrapping schemes in 1959–60, there was a substantial increase in orders by merchants who feared that they would be unable to obtain supplies in the near future. By the time the industry's capacity had stabilised, there was a great deal of over-stocking, and orders dropped off very quickly from 1961.

83. Regulations laid down by the Board of Trade provided that, in order to be eligible for a re-equipment subsidy, firms in the spinning, doubling and weaving sections of the industry should place their orders no later than 8 July 1962. Because of the uncertainty in the industry and the delay in applying for re-equipment subsidies, this deadline was extended by a further year. Ibid., p.8; Q.282. Even this was thought insufficient, and there were calls for an even greater extension. Ibid., QQ.285–9. As it turned out, total expenditures which were eligible for the government subsidy amounted to £53.5 million, some £30-£40 million below what was originally anticipated; Miles, 'Protection of the British Textile Industry', p.191.

84. Ibid., Q.380; Memorandum submitted by Mr. Cartwright, p.91; Q.660; Q.758; Q.803.

85. Ibid. Q.216. In the reorganisation (scrapping) phase of the Act, two-thirds of the cost of scrapping machinery was to be borne by the government, the remaining one-third was to be borne by firms remaining in the industry. However, under the re-equipment phase, only 25 per cent of the costs of re-equipment were to be borne by the government, the remaining 75 per cent was to be borne by the firms themselves. The justification for this was that whereas the reorganisation phase would benefit all firms remaining in the industry, re-equipment subsidies would only benefit those firms that actually re-equippe

86. Inland Revenue Memorandum, reproduced in the *Accountant*, 29 Aug. 1959, outlined the interaction between subsidies and tax allowances. The net effect was a reduction in the value of re-equipment grant; Miles, *Lancashire Textiles*, p.77. For the impact on a particular firm where a 25 per cent grant was reduced to 7.5 per cent in *de facto* cash terms, see GMRO/LCC, Chairman's Statement, 1962.

87. Ibid., Q.222.
88. Ibid., QQ.371–2.
89. Open discussion, 'Functions and Problems of Management', *NFTWMA*, Vol. XXXIII (1954), p.113. Some commentators have gone further than this. Sutherland, for example, has argued that perhaps the most important feature of the YSA may have been that it produced evidence about the cotton spinning industry undermined the hope that the 1959 Act would have spectacular results; A. Sutherland, 'The Restrictive Practices Court and Cotton Spinning', *Journal of Industrial Economics*, Vol.8 (1959), p.61.
90. Profits declined as trading conditions worsened in 1962 (CUDC; GMRCO/LCC Annual Report and Accounts); for a record of the abortive negotiations, see GMRCO/LCC, Board Minutes, 13 Dec. 1962, 11 April 1963, 16 May 1963, 17 Sept. 1963, 17 Oct. 1963. For a more detailed discussion, see D.M. Higgins and J.S. Toms, 'Public Subsidy and Private Divestment', School of Management and Finance Discussion Paper, IX (1998) University of Nottingham, pp.21–4.
91. FCI, pamphlet, published by the organisation, March 1961, p.4.
92. Details of loans to the steel industry, ibid, p.3, FCI Report and Accounts, 1947–65, passim; for condemnation of large profits in that industry *vis-à-vis* cotton, see Rhodes, 'Government Policy and the Textile Industry', *NFTWMA*, Vol. XXXV (1956), p.58.
93. M.B. Rose, 'The Politics of Protection', p.142; Singleton, 'Decline Since 1940', pp.314–15.
94. These estimates have the following components: £40 million for re-equipment in spinning, £8 million for re-equipment in doubling, and between £30-£45 million for re-equipment in weaving. Board of Trade, Reorganisation of the Cotton Industry, Session 1958–59 (London, 1959), pp.5–6.
95. For example, Miles, 'Protection of British Textile Industry', cites eligible expenditure of £53.5m (p. 191). The maximum amount payable by the government could only be 25 per cent of this (that is, £13.38m) in the total period allowable by the Act, up to July 1964.
96. House of Commons, Fourth Report from the Estimates Committee, Session 1961–62, Assistance to the Cotton Industry (London, 1962), p.ix.
97. A.M. Alfred, 'Investment in the Development Districts of the United Kingdom and Discounted Cash Flow', *Journal of Accounting Research*, Vol.2 No.2 (1964), pp.174–82; in the comparison on p. 178, Alfred refers to Development Districts rather than the 1959 Act, but the point on tax allowances is equally valid; the comparison *vis-à-vis* Development Districts is interesting given the later investment strategy of Courtaulds (for details see Singleton, *Lancashire on the Scrapheap*, p. 165).
98. *Accountant*, 2 May 1959.

# Financial Institutions and Corporate Strategy: David Alliance and the Transformation of British Textiles, c.1950–c.1990

David M. Higgins and Steven Toms

*This article introduces and assesses a conceptual model of institutional and corporate change. In particular it seeks to integrate strategic choice and associated corporate structure with the role of the market for corporate control (MCC) as a governance mechanism. The model is illustrated using longitudinal case studies from the British textile industry with particular reference to the acquisition policy of David Alliance as he built up the Spirella Group and then used this as a vehicle to acquire, in turn, Vantona, Carrington Viyella, Nottingham Manufacturing Company and Coats Patons. These policies are contrasted with the acquisition strategies of the Lancashire Cotton Corporation (LCC) and Courtaulds and Imperial Chemical Industries (ICI). The evidence indicates that there was no relationship between the depth of the MCC and restructuring success, but to the extent that the market lacked depth, abnormal profits accrued to market-making entrepreneurs such as Alliance. There is evidence that decentralized market-led strategies were more successful than strategies based on the integration of production for the achievement of scale economies. Successful adoption of these strategies was also based on the acquisition of financial resources through appropriate network connections and associated political lobbying channels.*

## Introduction

A substantial literature has emerged on the post-1945 decline of the Lancashire textile industry.[1] Debates about industrial structure, technology, government policy, industrial relations and import quotas as causes of decline, first in Lancashire and then in textiles more generally, are well known. Even so, at the corporate level there were successes as well as failures. It is interesting therefore to examine strategies within this declining industry and evaluate reasons for differing outcomes. In this article the relative success of a previously neglected corporate grouping, what ultimately became Coats Viyella following a series of mergers largely orchestrated by David Alliance,[2] is contrasted with the relative failures of the Lancashire Cotton Company (LCC), Courtaulds and Imperial Chemical Industries (ICI). To identify critical strategic success factors, three elements are examined and contrasted. First, the accrual of profit and its distribution to interested parties as a consequence of takeover transactions, whether successful or not. Second, the methods used to access financial resources, contrasting local networks and city institutions as finance providers and exploring the associated success of political lobbying strategies. Third, the strategy based on the employment of those financial resources, specifically integration contrasted with decentralization, and consequent organization structure.

As suggested by this sequence, the aim is to show not only the traditional strategy and structure relationship, but also that strategy follows from ex ante resource endowment and the institutional mechanisms that determine such endowments. The approach extends the recent literature advocating these time-dependent strategy-governance approaches.[3] To inform a discussion of restructuring of the textile industry in this period, it is useful to focus on the evolution of one particular stock exchange provided institution, the market for corporate control (MCC). Indeed, there has been relatively little empirical or theoretical analysis of the origins of the MCC and in this respect the article also seeks to make an important contribution.[4]

To examine these relationships, the article uses a conceptual model based on the dynamic strategy-governance approach referred to above. It extends the approach by treating business organization and the MCC as the respective historical variables. Prior research on mergers and acquisitions in the financial economics field has treated the MCC as a given set of institutional variables.[5] Other research in the management and strategy literatures has also tended to examine the question of diversification through merger and acquisition,[6] and on the management of multi-business firms,[7] without too much reference to historical perspective. In the relatively few cases where a historical perspective has been adopted, the evidence suggests that these cross-sectional relationships reflect the time variant, and specifically the institutional relationships of corporate governance.[8] In this light the model and the case study analysis provide the opportunity to comment on these literatures.

The model is illustrated with reference to archives, both public and private, financial records, particularly balance sheets and stock market information, together with contemporary press articles. The article comprises five further sections. Section two presents the conceptual model and establishes associated research propositions. Section three provides background to the industry and the emerging agenda for corporate restructuring in the 1950s, including the failed attempt to restructure by the LCC in the early 1960s. Section four examines the cases of Courtaulds and ICI, and discusses the reasons why their attempts at rationalization failed. Section five analyses Alliance's strategy and how, first, he exploited the substantial profit opportunities offered by a passive (and illiquid) MCC; secondly, how he exploited financial networks and political lobbying opportunities to access further financial resources, and, finally, how he reinvested those profits to create a successful industrial grouping. Conclusions are presented in the final section.

## The Market for Corporate Control: A Conceptual Framework

The conceptual framework is shown in Figure 1 and has two dimensions. The first, the MCC, is represented on the horizontal axis. For the purposes of this article, the MCC is defined as the market for the control of a corporation in which such control is a valuable and tradable asset where value is driven by managerial performance. The ability of the MCC to function in this fashion is promoted by liquid share markets, transparent and flexible managerial labour markets, appropriate institutions of financial inter-mediation, promoting the realization of the collective value of the firm's assets.[9] In Figure 1, it is conceptualized as a continuum representing the degree of activity, ranging from very frequent takeover transactions occurring for a variety of motives, to an inert state where few if any such transactions occur. An active market requires liquidity in a market for ownership claims in firms, normally a share market. Where such institutional arrangements do not exist and the MCC is passive, ownership may still change but through bilateral negotiation rather than market inter-mediation. In Britain, the MCC was passive in the 1950s but subsequently became steadily more active. In terms of effective monitoring and other governance arrangements the MCC did not reach maturity in the UK until the 1980s, and there were important differences between the UK and the US.[10] The periodization of the study was adopted for this reason.

|  |  | Market for Corporate Control | |
|  |  | Active | Passive |
| Strategy and Organization | Centralized | Quadrant 4<br>High synergy<br>Rents accrue to target firm shareholders | Quadrant 2<br>High synergy<br>Rents accrue to managerial insiders |
|  | Decentralized | Quadrant 3<br>Low synergy<br>Rents accrue to target firm shareholders | Quadrant 1<br>Low synergy<br>Rents accrue to market makers |

**Figure 1**
A Conceptual and Analytical Model of Institutional and Corporate Change

A second element, represented on the vertical axis, evident from the behaviour of entrepreneurial and managerial groups during the period, was the adopted strategy-associated motives for building multi-plant or multi-business groups and the emergent organization structure. Because these strategies reflect managerial and entrepreneurial discretion, which is a function of the effectiveness of governance mechanisms, the vertical axis is primarily an empirical variable. Two broad generic strategies are first, to take over other businesses with a view to integrating them closely into the existing organization, for example exploiting scale and scope economies through vertical integration and related diversification. Such a strategy tends to promote centralization of control by management of the predatory firm. A second and opposite generic strategy is to take over other firms but to generate value by retaining separation or autonomy in the management of acquired assets. Cases might include unrelated diversification, buying up companies that are undervalued due to poor performance of incumbent management or market exit barriers, and realizing profits through asset stripping or accounting manipulations. In these cases a decentralized managerial strategy is more likely.

When these strategies interact with the institutional arrangements, it is possible to identify a historical diversity of industry models and forces that might govern adaptation and change. Where the MCC is passive and firms operate in a decentralized competitive market, an industrial district model may emerge, as in textiles (quadrant 1). Although this model has advantages,[11] incumbent firms may lack the resource base and credibility to expand. They may therefore seek private arrangements with capital providers and strategic alliances with similar firms. Such partnerships may facilitate extension of business scope and thereby promote vertical movement into quadrant 2. Institutional change, in the form of an active market for corporate control creates further possibilities. A firm operating in quadrant 1 for example may move into quadrants 3 and 4 depending on the strategic opportunity. Where target firms are under-valued by the market or where the MCC facilitates the removal of exit barriers, the logical move is to quadrant 3. Conversely, if the MCC provides firms with the opportunity to enter related markets more rapidly they will move into quadrant 4.

A further dimension of the model is the conceptualization of the MCC as a conduit for the distribution of financial surpluses and how such arrangements change through time. Two assumptions are necessary. First, that value is only created in the MCC where transactions create economies of scale or scope that previously did not exist; and, second, that asymmetric information leads to information costs and rent accrual resulting in a zero sum game. In an economy or industry characterized by a diverse resource base across a large number of firms and where the MCC is passive (quadrant 1), high abnormal returns (rents) accrue to the market maker, who is able simultaneously to set prices and supply the required liquidity. The extent to which abnormal returns are subsequently competed away depends on the rate at which other entrepreneurs replicate such activities, thereby deepening capital socialization and market liquidity, improving institutional monitoring, accountability structures and in general developing the MCC. Other things being equal, in an active market shares are fairly priced and bidding firm shareholders must pay a premium to secure control, implying an equivalent value transfer to target firm shareholders in the absence of synergy (quadrants 3 and 4).[12] Irrespective of these distributions between shareholder groups, managerial rents are low because a developed MCC provides efficient monitoring of managers. Conversely, if the MCC is passive, rents accruing to individuals with privileged information and managerial insider groups are more likely (quadrant 2). These can be characterized as returns for providing liquidity for shares that otherwise cannot be sold.

Further rents arise where resources are centralized in a single firm. Thus, economies of scope promote tacit knowledge within the organization thereby creating opportunities for the consumption of rent within the managerial hierarchy. Tacit knowledge is context specific and process driven, including organizational learning processes.[13] Managerial economies of scope by which business assets, including human capital assets, can be applied to more than one purpose, constitute entry barriers and create rents through the restriction of competition.[14] These assets provide synergies where the strategy is based on some degree of centralization (quadrants 2 and 4). The internalization of complex processes at the same time renders monitoring difficult by non-expert outside investors, which is compounded in a passive, opaque MCC (quadrant 2). In summary, therefore, quadrants 1 through 4 represent different patterns of profit and rent accrual to different groups according to the configuration of the MCC and the organization of the firm.

It is hoped that this model has wide utility for business historians and corporate strategists, particularly in the context of international business, and developing economies with emerging markets for corporate control. In the cases that follow, two particular propositions arising from the model are illustrated using case studies from the textile industry. First, with a centralizing strategy and a passive MCC, exemplified by the LCC in the 1950s, and Courtaulds in the 1960s and 1970s, gains from scale economies are likely to be consumed as managerial rents. Second, the rate of abnormal profits depends on MCC activity levels and when these are low such profits tend to accrue disproportionately to market-making individuals.

Before scrutinizing these propositions in more detail it is necessary to examine the background to the industry and then deal in turn with the failure of the LCC and Courtaulds in their attempts to restructure the industry before contrasting these with Alliance's successful strategy. To accompany these narrative sections, Figure 2 sketches the major shifts in the industry during the period using the parameters of Figure 1, and is referred to in the ensuing discussion.

## Attempts at Corporate Re-structuring during the 1950s

In 1945 the Lancashire cotton textile industry remained wedded to many of the essential features of the late nineteenth-century industrial district model. An important characteristic of this model was an extensive inter-locking directorship

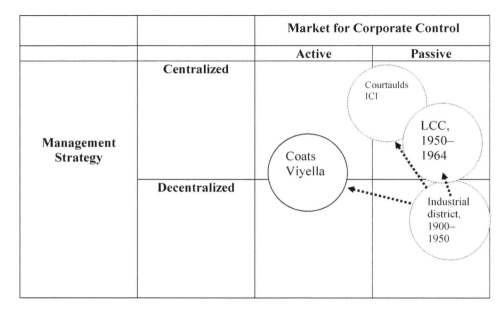

**Figure 2**
The Model Applied to Restructuring in the UK Textile Industry

structure.[15] Such interlocks were a substitute for the MCC and reflected market illiquidity in cotton company shares. In the 1890s' slump, cliques of directors were able to secure control of companies by accessing blocks of cheap shares.[16] In the boom of the 1900s these cliques benefited further by floating new companies and then re-floating existing mills in 1919–1920, to the cost of outside investors.[17] The pattern of entrepreneurial activity is significant because, as will be illustrated below, certain aspects were reproduced in the passive MCC of the 1960s.

The immediate consequence of these deals and interlocked board structures in the 1920s was to reduce the exit rate from an industry increasingly characterized by over-capacity.[18] The absence of an MCC meant there was no market mechanism whereby the least efficient firms could be taken over and closed down. Government intervention resulted in the creation of the LCC to fulfil this function. In the 1950s, when the loss of overseas export markets compounded the over-capacity problem, the LCC remained the principal vehicle for bilaterally negotiated takeovers between groups of interlocked directors. At the national level the pattern was similar. Transactions such as Clore's bid for Sears in 1953, the battle for British Aluminium in 1958, and the ICI bid for Courtaulds in 1961, contrasted with the gentlemanly, agreed mergers that remained prevalent in business combinations.[19] It was not until the boom in merger activity between 1968 and 1973 that such corporate control transactions became widespread, with 22 per cent of the top 200 listed firms in 1969 having been acquired by 1972.[20]

Table 1 shows a sample of takeover transactions involving textile firms during this period. To illustrate the discussion below, the table provides details of the purchase

**Table 1**

Acquisition Transactions: Textile Companies, 1953–1976

| Acquired company | Acquirer | Date | Sale proceeds (SP) £'000 | Book value (BV) £'000 | Market cap (MC) £'000 | Premium/ discount SP/BV | Premium/ discount SP/MC |
|---|---|---|---|---|---|---|---|
| Soudan | Cyril Lord* | 1953 | 864 | 723 | Nq | 1.20 | Nq |
| Asia | FCSDA* | 1954 | 357 | 379 | Nq | 0.94 | Nq |
| Maple | FCSDA* | 1954 | 464 | 501 | Nq | 0.93 | Nq |
| Roy | Shiloh* | 1953 | 46 | 124 | Nq | 0.37 | Nq |
| Park | Shiloh* | 1953 | 729 | 483 | Nq | 1.51 | Nq |
| Argyll | LCC* | 1954 | 229 | 250 | Nq | 0.92 | Nq |
| Durban/Eagle | LCC* | 1955 | 795 | 950 | 733 | 0.84 | 1.08 |
| Thos. Hoghton | D Alliance** | 1956 | 3 | 97 | 21 | 0.03 | 0.14 |
| Walton (Harry) Holdings | D Alliance** | 1957 | 66 | 245 | 40 | 0.27 | 1.65 |
| Rothwell | D Alliance** | 1962 | 1,044 | 1,337 | 783 | 0.78 | 1.33 |
| FCSDA | Courtaulds | 1964 | 14,000 | 16,853 | 13,556 | 0.83 | 1.03 |
| LCC | Courtaulds | 1964 | 23,000 | 24,040 | 21,851 | 0.96 | 1.05 |
| Renshaw | Spirella** | 1967 | 79 | 172 | Nq | 0.46 | Nq |
| W.T. Taylor | Spirella** | 1970 | 600 | 781 | Nq | 0.77 | Nq |
| Stott and Smith | Spirella** | 1970 | 350 | 420 | Nq | 0.83 | Nq |
| Fabricade | Spirella** | 1970 | 68 | 100 | Nq | 0.68 | Nq |
| British Northrop Loom | Spirella** | 1972 | 600 | 1,063 | Nq | 0.56 | Nq |
| Horrockses | Spirella** | 1973 | 1,350 | 1,991 | Nq | 0.68 | Nq |
| Vantona | Spirella** | 1976 | 4,600 | 7,829 | 3,833 | 0.59 | 1.20 |
| Carrington Viyella | Vantona** | 1983 | 19,060 | 40,900 | 16,339 | 0.47 | 1.17 |
| Nottingham Man. Co | Vantona Viyella** | 1985 | 200,000 | 122,431 | 175,000 | 1.63 | 1.14 |
| Coats Patons | Vantona Viyella** | 1986 | 734,000 | 601,200 | 553,000 | 1.22 | 1.33 |
| Averages | | | £m | £m | £m | | |
| 'Industrial district' mergers | | | 0.497 | 0.487 | na | 0.96 | na |
| Courtaulds | | | 18.500 | 20.447 | 17,704 | 0.89 | 1.04 |
| Alliance pre-1985 | | | 2.529 | 4.994 | 4.203 | 0.69 | 1.14 |
| Alliance 1985/86 | | | 467.000 | 361.816 | 364.000 | 1.43 | 1.24 |
| Totals | | | | | | | |
| 'Industrial district' mergers | | | 3.484 | 3.410 | | | |
| Courtaulds | | | 37.000 | 40.893 | | | |
| Alliance pre-1985 | | | 27.820 | 54.935 | | | |
| Alliance 1985/86 | | | 934.000 | 723.631 | | | |

*Notes*: *Industrial district mergers are all pre-1960 transactions not involving David Alliance.
\**Alliance firms listed, in addition to D. Alliance, are Spirella, Vantona and Vantona Viyella. Alliance 1985/86 averages are Nottingham Manufacturing and Coats Patons only, pre-1985 is all previous Alliance transactions. Nq = non-quoted firm.

*Sources*: SP and MC are taken from the *Stock Exchange Official Intelligence*, the *Financial Times* and for non-quoted Alliance firms, from CV papers. BV for quoted firms pre 1984 are taken from the Cambridge University Companies database, subsequent transactions and non-quoted firms are taken from individual company balance sheets deposited at Companies House.

consideration together with the book and market values for each firm. The table also shows the premium or discount arising on each transaction, defined as the difference between the book value and purchase consideration. Where the target was a quoted company, the premium or discount to the market price is also calculated. A major purpose is to contrast the transfers in value accruing to various shareholder groups between transactions arising from the 'industrial district' model, typified by LCC takeover transactions, and the transactions involving David Alliance. Averages are therefore calculated to contrast the levels of premium and discount arising from each group of transactions.

Table 1 includes a series of example transactions involving the LCC. Throughout the 1950s and early 1960s, the LCC management was concerned by the large number of small firms in the spinning industry, and the associated threat of undercutting, or 'weak selling', and its consequences for the LCC's market share. The problem was first raised in 1952 when two approaches were considered.[21] One of the solutions was that the LCC should close down a number of its older mills and take over a similar number of more efficient mills.[22] This strategy would simultaneously make the LCC's own production more efficient whilst reducing the number of its competitors. The second solution was that the LCC should assist in the formation of another large combine in the industry.[23] During the 1950s, the LCC had succeeded in taking over other firms on a piecemeal basis, usually by means of gentlemen's agreements through networks of connected directors, and involving acquisition premiums for firms with little economic rationale. Cyril Lord, the Fine Cotton Spinners' and Doublers' Association (FCSDA), and Shiloh pursued similar strategies.[24] In the absence of a MCC, such transactions depended on wealth transfers from LCC shareholders to target firm shareholders, providing an exit route for the latter in an otherwise illiquid market. As Table 1 suggests, the LCC was prepared to pay close to book values for its target firms on average, notwithstanding its strong perceptions of the surplus capacity problem, and the intention to close the acquired firms.

The need to acquire and then close down other spinning firms became more urgent from the later 1950s, when price-fixing through the Yarn Spinners' Association (YSA) was threatened by the Restrictive Practices Act. Abolition of the YSA meant the collapse of the industry's solidarity on minimum prices and a price-cutting free-for-all.[25] The LCC Board agreed to acquire a sufficient number of units in the industry which would permit it to remove redundant capacity thereby helping to maintain a balance between supply and demand.[26] In 1959, the Cotton Industry Act initiated a scheme to close down much of this capacity, notwithstanding the intentions of the LCC.[27]

The piecemeal acquisitions of the LCC in the 1950s fell well short of the scale of rationalization envisaged by the Cotton Industry Act. The principal reason was the passivity of the MCC, characterized by its gentlemen's agreements and interlocking directorates. Equally importantly, the LCC lacked the financial resources required to restructure the industry on its own.[28] Not surprisingly, therefore, the strategy of the LCC lacked ambition when compared with what was to follow, and had little to do with changing the management or strategies of the surviving firms; it was simply a question of capacity realignment.

By 1962 it had become apparent that the reduction in capacity brought about by the 1959 Act had been offset by a substantial rise in imports, and excess capacity was once again a problem.[29] The LCC board therefore again considered a programme of acquiring other mills, possibly in collaboration with other combines, thereby increasing the firm's dominance and allowing any losses from scrapping acquired machinery to be offset by spreading them over a much greater sales volume.[30] By November 1962, the managing director of LCC, John Whitehead, had received favourable responses to suggested takeovers from the chairmen of several firms.[31]

Such a merger would have been significant, but because of its scale the LCC lacked the required financial resources. As suggested by the regulatory changes of the 1950s and the 1959 Act, there was also a potential political aspect to any restructuring strategy. The lynchpin of the more ambitious plans of the 1960s was therefore again to request financial support from government sources, which unlike the 1959 subsidies available to all firms in the industry, would be channelled directly into the LCC's rationalization plan. To achieve this, the firm approached the Bank of England-sponsored Finance Corporation for Industry (FCI) to provide assistance.[32] Subsequent negotiations also involved the Board of Trade and Barings Bank. The indifference of the former department must be judged by its changed attitude in the 1970s (see below) and with reference the FCI's defined purpose, which was to rehabilitate and develop businesses, in liaison with government departments, when in the national interest.[33] FCI reticence towards cotton contrasted with the large amounts lent to the steel industry during the period 1947–1965, and the large profits available to the investor in the latter industry as a function of government intervention were noted with some cynicism by relatively powerless lobbyists for the cotton industry.[34] The LCC scheme was the last attempt by the industry to re-structure itself from within. At the same time, it was an admission that it no longer possessed the financial resources to do so.

Industry commentators frequently remarked that the uncertain trading environment of firms and their low levels of profitability meant that not only were firms themselves reluctant to invest but they also faced problems attracting external finance.[35] In contrast to the FCI, the Industrial and Commercial Finance Corporation (ICFC) had made loans available to other textile firms, such as Laura Ashley, Jaeger, Smith & Nephew, Viscose Investments, and Wood Bros. Some of these loans, such as those to Ashley and Wood Bros., fell clearly within the ICFC's nominal maximum loan amount of £200,000. Even in cases where they did not, such as with Jaeger and Smith & Nephew, the sums involved were insignificant compared to the amounts the LCC needed to finance its planned restructuring of the industry.[36] The LCC case appears to suggest that the industry was incapable of raising the finance necessary to restructure itself, thereby necessitating the intervention of Courtaulds and ICI. However, as argued below, the case of David Alliance demonstrates there were alternative means of generating the required financial resources.

## Courtaulds, ICI and Vertical Integration in the 1960s

The dominant event during the 1960s was the forward integration of outside firms such as Courtaulds and ICI into the Lancashire industrial district and the rapid concentration of the textile industry (Figure 2).[37] These firms integrated and centralized resources, and, importantly, relied on stock market support for their acquisition strategies. From this point on it is sensible to refer to the British textile industry, in which the Lancashire cotton textile industry becomes a dwindling sub-sector.

During the 1960s, as the MCC began to increase in activity, the textile industry was one of the most merger-intensive in Britain. Estimates suggest that 26 per cent of the cotton textile companies quoted in 1948 disappeared as a result of merger/acquisition by 1960, with the equivalent figure for many British industries averaging 20 per cent.[38] Between 1957 and 1969, 128 per cent of the increase in the five firm concentration ratio was due to mergers.[39] In terms of efficiency gains/losses from mergers, the consequences were generally negative. Estimates of the monopoly loss generated by each of the 'big four' in the year 1968–69 were as follows: Courtaulds, £4.83–7.43 million; Coats Patons, £3.06–4.05 million; Carrington Viyella, £0.78–1.65 million, and Tootal, £0.96–1.36 million.[40] Cowling *et al.* used a measure, 'k', to provide precise estimates of the efficiency gains/losses emanating from Courtauld's acquisition policy in textiles.[41] They reported that between 1963 and 1974 (the height of Courtaulds' acquisition policy), 'k' declined from 0.873 in 1963, to 0.732 in 1968, to 0.603 in 1974.[42] However, they warned that these *apparent* improvements in efficiency did not show that Courtaulds' acquisition policy was economically efficient, since efficiency improved because of productivity growth in man-made fibres *rather than* in textiles. Therefore improvements in productivity had little connection with Courtaulds' acquisition policy during this period and more to do with increasing product market power, which could be used to secure political influence.[43]

In the case of the LCC and FCSDA (Table 1), like the earlier 'industrial district' mergers, these acquisitions were priced at amounts close to the underlying book values of the assets acquired. The slight discounts in these cases contrast with the deep discounts achieved in many of the David Alliance takeovers discussed below. In contrast to the LCC's earlier takeovers in the underdeveloped MCC of the 1950s, Courtaulds used its own shares in exchange for shares in the LCC and FCDSA.

The acquisition strategies of Courtaulds and ICI were concerned with securing markets for their man-made fibres in the next stage of production but, in contrast to the market-led strategy of Alliance discussed below, did not consider the demands of the *ultimate* consumer. Even where integration meant the acquisition of firms producing the final end product (for example, Courtaulds' takeover of Highams, a major producer of bedding, and ICI's financing of Carrington Dewhurst, a specialist weaver),[44] fibre producers were still at least one stage removed from the final consumer. Forward integration into ready-made clothing and household textiles remained exceptional among textile producers and this separation from the *final* market subjected manufacturers to a number of disadvantages. Producers suffered magnified fluctuations in demand as merchants and retailers adjusted their inventories; they lost market share as some retailers resorted to imported fabrics and marketed products made from these fabrics under the same brand names as similar products made from UK cloth. Textile manufacturers also suffered from weak bargaining power vis-à-vis the large multiple retailers who could always import products. Finally, and perhaps most importantly, textile manufacturers did not use advertising and promotion effectively to influence final purchases.[45]

Meanwhile, the major retail groups were incapable of exercising sufficient leadership in responding to an evolving domestic market, which was placing greater emphasis on design, fashion, and style. Consequently, where long-term relationships did develop between forward-integrating textile companies and retailers, it was the latter that encouraged manufacturers to become specialized in producing standard garments and fabrics for the mass market. Retailers knew fairly clearly what they wanted, and passed the message down the line. Selling was largely a matter of quality, price and availability of variations on well-tried or classic fabrics. 'Novelty was at a discount.'[46] The development of close relationships between major retailers and textile producers reinforced the latter's concentration on mass-production of a limited range of textiles in order to secure maximum scale economies.[47] The fears of well-informed industry commentators, such as Alan Ormerod, that Britain could never compete in bulk-produced items were to be confirmed in the 1970s and 1980s. Extensive import penetration from low-cost producers resulted in an accelerated programme of mill closures, the rationalization of spinning and weaving capacity by Courtaulds, and ICI's hurried divestment of Carrington Viyella to David Alliance's Vantona group.[48]

During this period Courtaulds used highly centralized monitoring and bureaucratic control systems, which resembled a 'blizzard of paper' to those more used to traditional methods of operation in the textile industry.[49] Similarly in the fibres division of Imperial Chemical Industries new centralized financial control techniques were adopted as part of the integration process, and because these procedures were already employed elsewhere in the business, not necessarily because there were appropriate for textile production.[50]

As has been demonstrated, the LCC attempted (but failed) to effect a restructuring plan principally due to intra-network financial constraints and lack of political lobbying power. In addition, Courtauld's and ICI were able to use their accumulated resources earned outside the industry to implement their version of the LCC's plans, but ultimately this too proved a failure. The reasons were the strategy of integration and mass production and the associated neglect of customer needs, over-reliance on economies of scale, managerial hierarchy and bureaucratic control. These failures paralleled the abortive attempt at centralization by the LCC between 1929 and 1932. What was needed was someone with inside knowledge of the industry who also had access to an external financial and political network.

## David Alliance and the Transformation of the Industry

David Alliance's career as a textile entrepreneur began with his acquisition of Thomas Hoghton in 1956. This and subsequent transactions are detailed in Table 1 insofar as the archival evidence permits. The Hoghton transaction is illustrative of the returns available to a market maker in an otherwise non-existent market. The company had a market capitalization of £21,000, but Alliance needed just over £3,000 to secure control of 58 per cent of the A shares and 69 per cent of the B shares. His offer was only 24 per cent of the market price of the shares, suggesting poor liquidity and stagnant dividends for incumbent shareholders. In return for this investment he secured assets with book values of £97,000, most of which was working capital, that is, stock plus book debts, which were realized as he ran the company down between 1957 and 1960. This represented a very large return (in excess of 700 per cent) on a very small personal investment.[51] Although Alliance had to borrow at an interest rate of 24 per cent, the loan was quickly exceeded by asset realizations from the target company. Subsequent balance sheets show that he stripped the company's assets rather than 'turning it around'. The bank balance went from £31,000 overdraft in 1955 to £68,000 in the bank by 1959 as assets were sold off.

The outstanding features of the strategy were that, in the absence of liquidity in the MCC in the 1960s, Alliance could make very low offers to incumbent shareholders facing declining capital values. All target companies had low market to book ratios, usually less than unity (Table 1). Secondly, his use of 'pyramiding', securing control of more than 50 per cent of shares, but not making full bids, enabled him to access realizable values at low cost. The evidence in Table 1 suggests that the discounts of purchase consideration to book value achieved by Alliance were more substantial than those transactions involving the LCC. As demonstrated above, the reason was that in the LCC case deals were negotiated between groups of interlocked directors. Alliance was not part of this network and therefore had no requirement to trade on sentimentality or reciprocity and he made offers accordingly.

As a late entrant to the industry, Alliance had a much better appreciation than incumbents about how much more the assets he acquired could be made to 'sweat'. At the same time, unlike the managers of Courtaulds and ICI, Alliance's expertise was based on his direct and rapidly growing experience of the textile sector. In particular contrast, his understanding of the importance of leading brands was vital, and his acquisition strategy increasingly reflected a desire to control these.

At first sight, this would suggest Alliance might have offered a premium to acquire these intangibles, but this was not necessary. In a passive MCC characterized by illiquidity, beneficial exit options simply did not exist for incumbent shareholders and Alliance continued to acquire these resources at substantial discounts (Table 1). Alliance was not always able to offer below market price. However, in every case where there is evidence, Table 1 shows there was a clear pattern of bid price being below book value (Rothwell and other companies acquired by David Alliance/ Spirella) Such cases are suggestive of market illiquidity, and also that the earnings potential of assets deployed were less than realizable value from their disposal. In such conditions, asset stripping is an important strategic opportunity for equity groupings organized around market makers and entrepreneurs such as Alliance, and forms part of the return on investment for market creation.

This feature alone did not make Alliance unusual, because during the 1950s the LCC had already pursued the salient aspects of this strategy. Why, then, did Alliance's strategy differ, and prove more successful, than either of the strategies of the LCC or Courtaulds and ICI? Unlike the LCC, Alliance was able to secure funds to finance his acquisition policy. This was made possible by his ability to recycle capital from previous acquisitions into new investments and secondly through close links with Rothschild.[52] Ability to secure finance to fund diversification strategies was an important feature of the survival strategies of other textile firms.[53] Links with banks were also important in a passive MCC because many inactively traded shares were held in bank nominee accounts.

A further aspect of this networking strategy, and one where Alliance differed markedly from the LCC, was his success at exploiting political channels to secure business finance. In particular, he was able to exploit government industrial policy, which was based on creating competitive industrial groups ahead of Common Market entry.[54] Such funding, complemented by support from Rothschild, assisted greatly with his takeover of Horrockses in 1971 and his acquisitions of Stott & Smith and W.T. Taylor. This finance was pivotal to his strategy of levering large assets from a small personal financial base, thereby compounding high personal returns as well as creating funds for further takeovers. The Industrial Reorganisation Corporation (IRC)[55] made £1.3 million available to Alliance, which comprised an unsecured loan of £900,000 and 10 per cent convertible unsecured loan stock of £400,000.[56] The balance of the purchase price was provided from Spirella's own resources (see below).

Alliance benefited from changed political circumstances when acquiring this financial assistance. With the exception of the mergers between Coats Patons and West Riding Worsted and Woollen Mills (1968), and Allied Textiles and H.F. Hartley (1969), the IRC had no involvement in the textile sector until 1970.[57] Two events changed this. First, the government's intention to replace, from January 1972, the quota system governing textile imports with tariff protection and its recognition that the effectiveness of this change 'will depend on a high and rapid investment and modernization programme in the industry'.[58] Second, the publication in 1969 of the Textile Council's report on cotton and allied textiles, which recognized the unfavourable environment affecting British textile firms caused, in large measure, by the absence of tariff protection.[59] The report made a number of recommendations, including increasing the rate of investment grant in development areas: while 'recognising the special contribution that can come from smaller firms, we consider that some special incentive to invest may be required to enable the progress towards a transformed and re-equipped industry'.[60]

The government, however, was unwilling to entertain this recommendation because of its implications for regional policy and because it did not consider on public expenditure grounds that it 'would have been justified in singling out the industry for financial assistance on such a scale'.[61] Although the government recognized that the changeover to tariff would be of considerable advantage to the Revenue, the Balance of Payments, and the economy as whole, it was acutely aware that, if the industry did *not* invest there would be very strong pressure for quotas to be re-imposed.[62] A further complicating factor was that it was not considered practicable to help the industry by allowing it to exceed the ceiling on bank advances. In these circumstances, the IRC was thought to be the obvious institution to channel funds to small to medium sized firms wishing to merge.[63]

The new policy of financial support also reflected the outcome of negotiations between government agencies. The Ministry of Technology (MINTECH), the Paymaster General's Office and the Treasury recognized the serious difficulties facing the industry in its attempts to secure external finance. The President of the Board of Trade, for example, recognized that there was, 'a strong case for assistance because of the lack of confidence in the future prospects of the industry among the lending community'.[64] MINTECH 'attached most weight to the general lack of confidence in the future of the industry as the main obstacle preventing the industry raising the finance it needs'.[65] The view of some officials in Whitehall was that the poor creditworthiness of the industry was the primary cause of the shortage of finance to the industry.[66] Others thought that, 'the difficulties in obtaining finance for re-equipment were such that the modernization required to enable the industry to meet competition from imports in 1972 might be fatally delayed'.[67]

Even the proposal that the IRC should be the primary conduit through which government funds would be channelled to the industry was nearly scrapped,[68] providing further testimony to the extreme difficulties in generating *any* finance for the industry. Three problems in particular were identified when the IRC scheme for Lancashire was being conceived. First, it was originally thought that the rate of interest on these loans should be one percentage point higher than the bank rate. However, concern was expressed that this might not be attractive to the banking sector if the banks found that they could use all their available lending capacity to satisfy other customers. In addition, the rate of interest to be charged would have to bear some relation to that applied under other guaranteed facilities, for example overdrafts to nationalized industries.[69] The second problem was the term of these loans. MINTECH officials thought that a term of 10–15 years was the most suitable, but this 'placed a further question-mark against the likelihood that any part of the banking sector might provide the finance'.[70] In theory, given the length of term envisaged, the insurance companies might have been interested, but even this was doubted on the grounds that the pattern and timing of investment by textile firms would be unappealing, quite apart from issues surrounding transferability of assets. Alternatively, if the loan term were reduced to 5–7 years, to attract specialized parts of the banking sector, 'it would probably be impossible to arrange suitable guarantee terms at reasonable interest rates'.[71] The final obstacle was the amount of funds the IRC would have at its disposal. Officials at MINTECH had originally intended that the IRC should provide loans totalling between £30 million and £50 million.[72] The Treasury, however, argued that such sums represented a very large figure in relation to the IRC's total commitments to be earmarked for one industry, and that such proposals could generate pressure from other industries.[73] A complicating factor was whether any restriction should be placed on the size of firms eligible to apply for funds. MINTECH officials had considered lending to some of the largest firms, such as Viyella, and possibly other companies related to ICI, and the Paymaster General himself had indicated to Kearton (the Chairman of Courtaulds), that there would be no discrimination on grounds of size.[74] However, the Treasury was concerned about the reaction of businessmen if funds were made available to the largest firms; in fact, it believed that a more modest scheme involving sums of £10–20 million would be more prudent, but this could only be achieved if the largest firms were excluded.[75] Initially MINTECH objected to any restrictions being placed on the IRC's lending, but eventually it agreed to a funding limit of £10 million, which was feasible only if the five biggest firms were excluded.[76]

Over 40 applications were made to the IRC by firms engaged in cotton textiles, but only half of these were considered seriously.[77] The IRC finally authorized funds for a very limited number of projects under the cotton textile scheme. These were to Harwood Cash Ltd, the RFD Group (Perseverance Mill Ltd), Highams, and Vantona (Albert Hartley Ltd).[78] Alliance was in an especially favourable position to secure funds because the merchant bankers acting as financial advisers to the IRC, Rothschild,[79] were also bankers and financial advisers to Alliance! The £1.3 million made available to Alliance was described as being for 'restructuring a sector of the UK household textile industry'.[80] These funds were crucial in Alliance's acquisition of Stott & Smith, W.T. Taylor, John Ainscow (all of which operated in the towelling sector) and his purchase of Horrockses and Dorcas from the Slater Walker Industrial Group.[81] These acquisitions not only yielded significant wealth for Alliance (Table 1) but they were also instrumental in his restructuring of his own textile interest, which laid the basis for later (and more ambitious) acquisitions.

A further very important difference and success factor for Alliance was that, unlike Courtaulds' vertically integrated mass-production strategy for basic fibres and cloths, the acquisition of leading textile brands was a central feature. Following the IRC-funded acquisitions, Alliance effected a major restructuring of his business activities, separating his mail order from his textile interests.[82] After this restructuring, the revamped Spirella group was the vehicle Alliance used to launch even bigger and more ambitious takeover bids in UK textiles. In 1975, Spirella launched a takeover bid for Vantona. Advised by Rothschild, Spirella offered £1 of its own shares plus £1 cash or £1 nominal of a new 14 per cent 1990 unsecured loan stock, valuing Vantona at £4.6 million.[83] Again, Alliance acquired assets at less than book value, although he paid a premium on the quoted share price (Table 1). Also notable was that apart from strong complementarities between the two groups (Spirella was strong in towels, Vantona in sheets and bedspreads, and both were suppliers to Marks & Spencer), Vantona was a bigger company, with a turnover approximately 30 per cent greater than Spirella's in 1974.[84] In addition, the acquisition meant that the merged group became the UK's sixth biggest textile company (by turnover) or fifth biggest if Illingworth Morris (predominantly engaged in wool textiles) is excluded.[85]

Spirella (renamed Vantona), became the vehicle for further acquisitions in the 1980s, the leading case being the merger with Carrington Viyella (CV) in 1983. CV's attempts to find alternative suitors failed, as other textile interests were reluctant to diversify, or in the cases of Courtaulds and Tootal were already reducing their UK textile activities, leaving Alliance as the only bidder.[86] Meanwhile ICI, which owned 49 per cent of CV's equity, was concerned that the losses made by CV, £2.6 million in the half year to June 1982, were having a deleterious effect on its balance sheet.[87] As early as 1981, ICI had signalled that it wanted to get rid of its CV holding, writing the shares sharply down to their par value of 25p, and announcing it was not prepared to provide any further support for CV.[88] The banks were also in an uncomfortable position. National Westminster and Barclays in particular exerted pressure on CV to accept almost *any* deal. To secure the Vantona takeover, they agreed to reduce CV's crippling interest payments by converting £10 million of their loans into preference shares.[89] As a result of these difficulties, Vantona was able to acquire CV on very favourable terms. Advised by Rothschild, Vantona offered to acquire the whole of the issued ordinary share capital on the basis of two Vantona new ordinary shares of 20p each fully paid for every 25 CV existing ordinary shares of 25p each in issue, fully paid.[90] These terms valued CV at approximately £14 million, or around 8p a share, which was only fractionally above its all time low.[91] The total purchase price amounted to only 49 per cent of the book value of CVs assets. Such discounts were a defining characteristic of Alliance's transactions. Since 1956 he had acquired total assets with balance sheet values of £54.9 million at a cost of only £27.8 million.[92]

The merger with CV formed Vantona Viyella, and was quickly followed by the merger with Nottingham Manufacturing Co. (NMC) in 1985. The terms of this merger were three new ordinary shares of 20p each of Vantona for every four ordinary shares of NMC, which valued the latter at around £200 million.[93] This merger was particularly advantageous to Vantona because roughly half the purchase consideration was represented by NMC's cash (about £100 million), while Vantona had net debt of approximately £20 million.[94] Jacob Rothschild, who was on personal as well as business terms with Alliance and Djanogly (the Chairman of NMC), brokered the deal. Finally, in 1986, Vantona Viyella acquired Coats Patons (CP). Under the terms of the agreed offer Vantona Viyella exchanged ten new ordinary shares of 20p each for every 17 ordinary shares of 25p each in CP, apart from the 3.6 per cent of Coats Patons it already held. The offer valued CP at £734 million.[95] Once again, Rothschild was pivotal to the success of the deal: in the space of just a few hours on 10 February 1986, Alliance was able to raise £700 million to outbid Dawson International and secure CP.[96] The deal created Coats Viyella. Unlike previous takeovers, the NMC and CP transactions corresponded to the norms of a developed MCC. Alliance paid substantial premiums over market value which reflected rapid movements in the share price as the bid developed, and the discount to book value, which characterized previous transactions, was absent from these deals (Table 1).

Alliance usually acquired assets cheaply, but a further salient feature of his strategy was to employ them to good effect. The acquisition of companies with leading brands was a central feature of Alliance's acquisition strategy which developed alongside his mail-order businesses and which was in stark contrast to the typical merger/ acquisition activity of the 1960s based on rationalization and scale economies. Alliance's mail-order activities are important for two reasons: firstly, they indicate that Alliance had a very strong appreciation of the importance of marketing and, secondly, mail-order sales meant he was not so heavily reliant on the fashion dictates of the major multiple retailers. As a result of his mail order operations Alliance was able to influence the demand for fashion textiles *and* help satisfy this by supplying branded textiles. From 1970, when his mail order businesses were formally separated from his textile interests, Alliance's acquisition strategy was heavily focused towards leading brands. It is in this particular respect that Alliance revealed himself to be a true textile entrepreneur since, in stark contrast to the forward integration of Courtaulds and ICI, he recognized the demand-led characteristics of textile production. As Robinson suggested,

> the central function of the entrepreneur in a fashion industry is far less the efficient organisation of the production of a given commodity and much more the shrewd anticipation of the changing preferences of his clientele. In essence, what the entrepreneur offers for sale is his experienced judgement and willingness to take risks in the matter of design. The extraordinarily high rate of failure in such an industry is far more often due to erroneous style decisions and anticipations than to production inefficiencies.[97]

The acquisition of Horrockses-Dorcas by Spirella would mean it acquiring 'two of the best known brand names in this field'.[98] The purchase of John Ainscow (1970), and Stott & Smith (1970), gave Spirella access to the 'Beehive' and 'Chortex' brands, respectively, in towel manufacture. In 1975, Alliance acquired Vantona, which yielded further brand names such as 'Everwear' and 'Gaiety'.[99] In 1983, Vantona acquired Carrington Viyella which created a brand portfolio across a range of products: 'Dorma' for linens, 'Viyella', 'Van Heusen', 'Peter England' and 'Rocola' for shirts, as well as 'Driway' and 'Dhobi' coats.[100] Vantona Viyella's purchase of CP brought 'Jaeger', 'Country Casuals', 'Jean Muir', and 'Ladybird' under its control, and the acquisition of Tootal (1991) not only meant the acquisition of the 'Tootal' brands but other equally well known brands such as 'Trutex'.

These purchases made Vantona Viyella (subsequently Coats Viyella) the UK's major supplier of branded products across a wide range of apparel and household textiles, as well as an important supplier of civilian and military uniforms. In turn, these acquisitions redressed substantially the imbalance that had developed between the bargaining power of textile manufacturers and their principal retail buyers and nowhere was this most apparent than in the links between Coats Viyella and

Marks & Spencer. Effectively, Alliance's acquisition policy achieved two goals simultaneously: the acquisition of leading brands and the acquisition of key suppliers to Marks & Spencer. This placed Alliance at the centre of a Jewish business group, with Rothschild supplying the finance and Marks & Spencer supplying the market.

Even before Vantona began its ambitious takeover programme in the 1980s, Marks & Spencer already accounted for roughly 20 per cent of its sales.[101] Subsequent acquisitions intensified this relationship: for example, the acquisition of CV, which was known to be an important Marks & Spencer supplier, especially so in lingerie and shirts.[102] In 1984, Vantona acquired F. Miller, a Glasgow based clothing company, which sold 80 per cent of its output to Marks & Spencer.[103] NMC, acquired in 1985, supplied between 50 and 66 per cent of its output to Marks & Spencer. It was estimated that after the merger 33 per cent of the output of the combined group would be sold to Marks & Spencer.[104] Coats Patons, which supplied 10 per cent of its output to Marks & Spencer, was acquired in 1986.[105] Finally, it was estimated that the takeover of Tootal (1991) would mean that the enlarged company's share of Marks & Spencer's requirements for men's and women's garments would exceed 50 per cent.[106]

It is unsurprising therefore that, on the basis of such acquisitions, Alliance was able to redress the imbalance in bargaining power between the major retail groups and the textile manufacturers and increase the ability of the latter to improve the design, fashion and style content of their products. For example, it was said of the takeover of CV, 'if the emergence of a strong, financially secure supplier occurs as a result of this merger then the manufacturers will be able to meet their chain store customers on more equal terms. They might also be able to win back some of the trade lost to imports by becoming more fashion conscious than the big buyers would otherwise let them be'.[107]

## Conclusion

The above strategies provide interesting contrasts, illustrating how outcomes vary according to the evolution of the MCC. As suggested by the David Alliance case, where the MCC is passive, abnormal profits accrue to individual market makers, as evidenced by the large abnormal returns he was able to accrue on individual takeover transactions. This was most clearly demonstrated by his early acquisitions in the 1950s and 1960s. As the MCC developed in the 1970s and the 1980s, Alliance typically paid a premium over market price, although he continued to secure discounts over book value.

From the above discussion the foundations of Alliance's success are clear. First, he exploited the opportunity provided by a passive MCC to make large profits on early transactions. Acquisition discounts in the 1950s and 1960s contrast starkly with the earlier 'industrial district' takeovers (Table 1). Second, favourable access to the IRC accelerated this process and gave Alliance the opportunity to launch a series of ever-bigger acquisitions in the 1970s and 1980s. Underlining all of these transactions was the continued support of Rothschild. The net result was that textiles became one of the most attractive stocks in the 1980s, a far cry from its unpopularity in the preceding decades.

Alliance's success indicates that, besides internalization (Courtaulds' policy), and the scale and scope perspectives of Chandler and Lazonick,[108] which were heavily geared towards US experience, there remained an alternative strategic option to benefit from long-run industrial decline, based on the traditional *modus operandi* of the Lancashire entrepreneur. As the industrial district evolved in the late nineteenth century, new entrepreneurs emerged capable of building business groups by purchasing existing mills during slumps and floating new ones in booms. Centralized ownership contrasted with decentralized management.[109] Alliance's strategy was quite similar to this, with the exception of his use of the MCC, compared to the bilateral deals and share speculations of the earlier period, and was more effective in securing political support. Another difference was the construction of a vertical group, but on the lines of a marketing strategy, rather than integrated production.

Two aspects of his strategy were complementary: seeking out and acquiring under-valued companies and building up a portfolio of leading brands. Access to funds, using the connections of Rothschild, was not in itself sufficient because knowledge of the textile market, which Alliance helped transform into a highly fashion sensitive industry, was equally important. Rothschild's support of Alliance gave the latter a credible and favourable financial advantage over potential rivals. Alliance was also able to secure funding from the IRC at a time when the Treasury was acutely aware of how difficult it was for firms in the textile industry in general to secure funding from financial institutions, if less aware of the personal returns already accruing to Alliance.

Once again, the contrast with Courtaulds and ICI is striking. Managerial rents, particularly in the form of bureaucracy, made realizing mass production synergies difficult. The recession of the early 1980s comprehensively quashed any idea that Britain had any long term future in basic textile production, resulting in Courtaulds shedding 43,000 jobs in Britain[110] and ICI hastily selling off CV.

As far as the two propositions from section two are concerned we note, first, that with a centralizing strategy and a passive MCC, exemplified by Courtaulds in the 1960s and 1970s, gains from scale economies are likely to be consumed as managerial rents. For similar reasons, the company was unable to unlock the scope economies that the strategy literature suggests are more likely to exist where diversification is into related businesses.[111] Alliance's decentralized model worked better as a means of delivering the related diversification strategy, combining autonomous management with strategic fit and tight financial control.[112] Secondly, the rate of abnormal profits accruing to market makers depends on MCC activity levels and when these are low, abnormal profits are expected to be high. In such conditions, these gains might well accrue to the acquirers, as represented in this case by Alliance. Herein lies an exception to the general rule from cross-sectional studies, which conclude that defending shareholders gain and acquiring shareholders lose.[113] In general, the case provides a good illustration of the dynamic strategy-governance perspective of previous research and also illustrates the complementary importance of governance characteristics and financial relations in achieving turnaround strategies.[114]

## Acknowledgements

Earlier versions of this article were delivered to the ABH conference, 2004, and the Pasold Conference, 2004. We would like to thank the participants for their many useful comments.

## References

Ambrosini, Veronique, and Cliff Bowman. "Tacit Knowledge: Some Suggestions for Operationalisation." *Journal of Management Studies* 38, no. 6 (2001): 811–829.

Castanias, Richard, and Constance E. Helfat. "The Managerial Rents Model: Theory and Empirical Analysis." *Journal of Management* 27, no. 6 (2001): 661–678.

Chandler, Alfred. *Scale and Scope: The Dynamics of Industrial Capitalism.* Cambridge, MA: Belknap Press, 1990.

Coopey, Richard, and Donald Clarke. *3i: Fifty Years of Investing in Industry.* Oxford: Oxford University Press, 1995.

Cowling, Keith, Paul Stoneman, and John Cubbin *et al. Mergers and Economic Performance.* Cambridge: Cambridge University Press, 1980.

Farnie, Douglas, Nakaoka Tetsuro, John Wilson and Takeshi Abe, eds. *Region and Strategy in Britain and Japan: Business in Lancashire and Kansai, 1890–1990.* London: Routledge, 2000.

Filatotchev, Igor, and Steven Toms. "Corporate Governance, Strategy and Survival in a Declining Industry: A Study of UK Cotton Textile Companies." *Journal of Management Studies* 40, no. 4 (2003): 895–920.

Fishwick, Francis, and Robert Cornu. *A Study of the Evolution of Concentration in the United Kingdom Textile Industry.* Luxembourg: Commission of European Communities, 1975.

Franks, Julian, and Robert S. Harris. "Shareholder Wealth Effects of Corporate Takeovers: The UK Experience, 1955–1985." *Journal of Financial Economics* 23, no. 2 (1989): 225–249.

Goold, Michael, Andrew Campbell and Markus Alexander. *Corporate-Level Strategy: Creating Value in the Multibusiness Company.* New York: John Wiley & Sons, 1994.

Grant, Robert M., Azar P. Jammine and Howard Thomas. "Diversity, Diversification, and Profitability among British Manufacturing Companies." *Academy of Management Journal* 31, no. 4 (1988): 771–801.

Hague, Douglas, and Geoffrey Wilkinson. *The IRC: An Experiment in Industrial Intervention.* London: George Allen & Unwin, 1983.

Hannah, Leslie. *The Rise of the Corporate Economy.* London: Methuen, 1979.

Hannah, Leslie, and John Kay. *Concentration in Modern Industry: Theory, Measurement and the UK Experience.* London: Methuen, 1977.

Higgins, David, and Steven Toms. "Public Subsidy and Private Divestment: The Lancashire Cotton Textile History." *Business History* 42, no. 1 (2000): 59–84.

———. "Financial Distress, Corporate Borrowing and Industrial Decline: The Lancashire Cotton Textile Industry, 1918–1938." *Accounting, Business and Financial History Review* 13, no. 2 (2003): 207–232.

Hitt, Michael A., Robert E. Hoskisson, Richard A. Johnson and Douglas D. Moesel. "The Market for Corporate Control and Firm Innovation." *Academy of Management Journal* 39, no. 5 (1996): 1084–1119.

Jensen, Michael, and Richard Ruback. "The Market for Corporate Control: The Scientific Evidence." *Journal of Financial Economics* 11 (1983): 5–50.

Jeremy, David J. "Survival Strategies in Lancashire Textiles: Bleachers Association to Whitcroft plc, 1900–1980s." *Textile History* 24, no. 2 (1993): 163–209.

Kamien, Morton, Eitan Mueller and Israel Zang. "Research Joint Ventures and R&D Cartels." *American Economic Review* 82, no. 5 (1992): 1293–1306.

Lazonick, William. *Business Organisation and the Myth of the Market Economy*. Cambridge: Cambridge University Press, 1991.

Levitt, Barbara, and James G. March. "Organisational Learning." *Annual Review of Sociology* 14 (1988): 319–340.

Limmack, Robin. "Corporate Mergers and Shareholder Wealth Effects." *Accounting and Business Research* 21, no. 83 (1991): 239–251.

Littlewood, John. *The Stock Market*. London: Financial Times Pitman, 1998.

Manne, Henry G. "Mergers and the Market for Corporate Control." *Journal of Political Economy* 73, no. 2 (1965): 110–120.

Markides, Constantinos C. and Peter J. Williamson. "Related Diversification, Core Competencies and Corporate Performance." *Strategic Management Journal* 15, Special Issue (1994): 149–165.

Marshall, Alfred. *Principles of Economics*. London: Macmlllan, 1890.

Mass, William, and William Lazonick. "The British Cotton Industry and International Competitive Advantage: The State of the Debates." *Business History* 32, no. 4 (1990): 9–65.

Miles, Caroline. *Lancashire Textiles: A Case Study of Organisational Change*. Cambridge: Cambridge University Press, 1968.

———. "Protection of the British Textile Industry." In *Protection and Subsidies in Britain and Germany*, edited by Warne M. Corden and Gerhard Fels. London: Macmillan, 1976: 184–214.

National Economic Development Office (NEDO). Textiles Section. *Changing Needs and Relationships in the UK Apparel Market*. London: National Economic Development Office, 1982.

Nonaka, Ikujiro. "The Knowledge Creating Company." *Harvard Business Review* 69, no. 6 (1991): 96–104.

Ormerod, Alan. *An Industrial Odyssey*. Manchester: Textile Institute, 1996.

———. "The Decline of the UK Textile Industry: The Terminal Years, 1945–2003." *Journal of Industrial History* 6, no. 2 (2003): 1–33.

Palich, Leslie E., Laura B. Cardinal and Chet Miller. "Curvilinearity in the Diversification-Performance Linkage: An Examination of over Three Decades of Research." *Strategic Management Journal* 21 (2000): 155–174.

Pearcy, Jeff. *Recording an Empire: An Accounting History of Imperial Chemical Industries Limited, 1926–1976*. Glasgow: Institute of Chartered Accountants of Scotland, 2001.

Penrose, Edith. *The Theory of the Growth of the Firm*. Oxford: Oxford University Press.

Rhodes, Hervey. "Government Policy and the Textile Industry." *Journal of National Federation of Textile Works Managers Associations* 35 (1956): 58–60.

Roberts, Richard. "Regulatory Response to the Rise of the Market for Corporate Control in Britain in the 1950s." *Business History* 34, no. 1 (1992): 183–200.

Robinson, Dwight E. "The Economics of Fashion Demand." *Quarterly Journal of Economics* 75, no. 3 (1961): 376–398.

Roll, Richard. "The Hubris Hypothesis of Corporate Takeovers." *Journal of Business* 59, no. 2 (1986): 197–216.

———. *Firms, Networks and Business Values: The British and American Cotton Industries Since 1750*. Cambridge: Cambridge University Press, 2000.

Singh, Ajhit. *Take-overs: Their Relevance to the Stock Market and the Theory of the Firm*. Cambridge: Cambridge University Press, 1971.

Singleton, John. *Lancashire on the Scrapheap*. Oxford: Oxford University Press, 1991.

———. "The Decline of the British Cotton Industry Since 1940." In *The Lancashire Cotton Industry*, edited by Mary B. Rose. Preston: Lancashire County Books, 1996: 296–324.

Teece, David J. "Economies of Scope and the Scope of the Enterprise." *Journal of Economic Behaviour and Organisation* 1, no. 3 (1980): 223–247.

Teece, David J., Gary Pisano and Amy Sheun. "Dynamic Capabilities and Strategic Management." *Strategic Management Journal* 18, no. 8 (1997): 509–533.

Textile Council. *Cotton and Allied Textiles*. Manchester: Textile Council, 1969.

Toms, Steven. "The Supply of and the Demand for Accounting Information in an Unregulated Market: Examples from the Lancashire Cotton Mills." *Accounting, Organisations and Society* 23, no. 2 (1998): 217–238.

———. "Windows of Opportunity in the Textile Industry: The Business Strategies of Lancashire Entrepreneurs, 1880–1914." *Business History* 40, no. 1 (1998): 1–25.

———. "The Rise of Modern Accounting and the Fall of the Public Company: The Lancashire Cotton Mills, 1870–1914." *Accounting, Organisations and Society* 27, no. 1 (2002): 61–84.

Toms, Steven, and Igor Filatotchev. "Corporate Governance, Business Strategy and the Dynamics of Networks: A Theoretical Model and Application to the British Cotton Industry." *Organisation Studies* 25, no. 4 (2004): 629–651.

Toms, Steven, and John Wilson. "Scale, Scope and Accountability: Towards a New Paradigm of British Business History." *Business History* 45, no. 4 (2003): 1–23.

Toms, Steven, and Michael Wright. "Corporate Governance, Strategy and Structure in British Business History, 1950–2000." *Business History* 44, no. 3 (2002): 91–124.

Toms, Steven, and Michael Wright. "Divergence and Convergence within Anglo-American Corporate Governance Systems: Evidence from the US and UK, 1950–2000." *Business History* 47, no. 2 (2005): 267–295.

Van de Vliet, Anita. "A Ripping Yarn." *Management Today* (Aug. 1988): 41–45.

Zeitlin, Jonathan. "The Clothing Industry in Transition." *Textile History* 19, no. 2 (1988): 211–238.

## Notes

1 Miles, *Lancashire Textiles*; Mass and Lazonick, "The British Cotton Industry"; Singleton, *Lancashire on the Scrapheap*; Singleton, "The Decline of the British Cotton Industry"; Jeremy, "Survival Strategies in Lancashire Textiles"; Higgins, and Toms, "Public Subsidy and Private Divestment"; Rose, *Firms, Networks and Business Values*; Farnie *et al.*, *Region and Strategy in Britain and Japan*; Filatotchev and Toms, "Corporate Governance, Strategy and Survival in a Declining Industry"; Toms and Filatotchev, "Corporate Governance, Business Strategy and the Dynamics of Networks."

2 Van de Vliet, "A Ripping Yarn."

3 Toms and Wright, "Corporate Governance, Strategy and Structure"; Toms and Wilson, "Scale, Scope and Accountability"; Toms and Filatotchev, "Corporate Governance, Business Strategy and the Dynamics of Networks"; Toms and Wright, "Divergence and Convergence within Anglo-American Corporate Governance Systems."

4 For an empirical analysis, see Roberts, "Regulatory Response to the Rise of the Market for Corporate Control in Britain in the 1950s." The market for corporate control is based on the premise that there is a positive correlation between managerial efficiency and the market price of the shares of a company, and that low valuations facilitate the market purchase of managerial positions. Manne, "Mergers and the Market for Corporate Control."

5 For example, the research into the distribution of gains from mergers in the UK and the USA, see, respectively, Limmack, "Corporate Mergers and Shareholder Wealth Effects"; Jensen and Ruback, "The Market for Corporate Control: The Scientific Evidence."

6 For a recent review of this literature, see Palich *et al.*, "Curvilinearity in the Diversification-Performance Linkage., For an empirical UK survey see Grant *et al.*, "Diversity, Diversification and Profitability among British Manufacturing Companies."

7 Goold *et al.*, *Corporate-Level Strategy*.

8 Hannah, *The Rise of the Corporate Economy*; Toms and Wright, "Corporate Governance, Strategy and Structure"; Toms and Wright, "Divergence and Convergence within Anglo-American Corporate Governance Systems."

9 Hitt *et al.*, "The Market for Corporate Control and Firm Innovation."

10 Toms and Wright, "Corporate Governance, Strategy and Structure"; Toms and Wright, "Divergence and Convergence."

11 Marshall, *Principles of Economics*; Kamien *et al.*, "Research Joint Ventures and R&D Cartels."

12 Franks and Harris, "Shareholder Wealth Effects of Corporate Takeovers"; Jensen and Ruback, "The Market for Corporate Control"; Roll, "The Hubris Hypothesis of Corporate Takeovers."

13 Nonaka, "The Knowledge Creating Company"; Ambrosini and Bowman, "Tacit Knowledge: Some Suggestions for Operationalisation"; Levitt and March, "Organisational Learning."

14 Teece, "Economies of Scope and the Scope of the Enterprise"; Castanias and Helfat, "Managerial Rents"; Penrose, *The Theory of the Growth of the Firm*; Markides and Williamson, "Related Diversification, Core Competencies and Corporate Performance"; Teece *et al.*, "Dynamic Capabilities and Strategic Management."

15 Toms and Filatotchev, "Corporate Governance, Business Strategy and the Dynamics of Networks."

16 Toms, "The Supply of and Demand for Accounting Information"; Toms, "The Rise of Modern Accounting and the Fall of the Public Company."

17 Higgins and Toms, "Financial Distress, Corporate Borrowing and Industrial Decline."

18 *Ibid.*

19 Roberts, "Regulatory Response"; Littlewood, *The Stock Market*, 103.

20 Toms and Wright, "Corporate Governance, Strategy and Structure."

21 'The weakness created in the cotton industry by the existence of a large number of small units was generally recognised, and it was appreciated that any steps which could be taken to overcome this would be of benefit to the corporation and the industry as a whole.' LCC Board Minutes, 21 Feb. 1952.

22 *Ibid.* LCC Board Minutes, 25 Nov. 1955; LCC Board Minutes, 7 Dec. 1955.

23 LCC Board Minutes, 21 Feb. 1952. As it turned out, the LCC favoured the first option.

24 For example, when the Eagle Spinning Company was taken over by the LCC in 1956, J.B. Whitehead was a director of the former company for several years prior to being appointed to the LCC board as well in 1955. See Filatochev and Toms, "Corporate Governance, Strategy and Survival in a Declining Industry."

25 LCC Board Minutes, 11 Sept. 1958.

26 LCC Board Minutes, 18 July 1957.

27 For details of these schemes, see Miles, *Lancashire Textiles*.

28 Higgins and Toms, "Public Subsidy and Private Divestment".

29 "The UK Cotton Spinning Industry, August, 1962. Surplus Capacity." LCC Board Minutes, 20 Sept. 1962. Between 1958 and 1960, cotton yarn imports increased almost threefold. Authors' calculations from *Cotton Board Quarterly Statistical Review*.

30 'The LCC divided the cotton spinning industry into seven sections which included, *inter alia* small combines in the American and Egyptian sectors, vertical units, and large combines apart from the LCC.' LCC Board Minutes, 20 Sept. 1962. Evidence presented to the Board indicated that the cost of acquiring all the firms in section one would be around £11.5 million, and that the cost of acquiring 12 of the companies in section two would be approximately £11 million.

31 Clover Mill Ltd, Croft & State Spinners Ltd, A. & A. Crompton & Co. Royton Textile Corporation, Shiloh Spinners Ltd, and Jacksons (Hurstead) Ltd. LCC Board Minutes, 15 Nov. 1962.

32 Profits declined as trading conditions worsened in 1962 (CUDC; GMRCO/LCC Annual Report and Accounts); for a record of the abortive negotiations, see GMRCO/LCC, Board Minutes, 13 Dec. 1962; 11 April 1963; 16 May 1963; 17 Sept. 1963; 17 Oct. 1963.

33 FCI, pamphlet, published by the organization, March 1961, p. 4.

34 *Ibid*: Details of loans to the steel industry, p. 3, FCI Report and Accounts, 1947–1965, *passim*; condemnation of large profits in that industry vis-à-vis cotton, see Rhodes, "Government Policy and the Textile Industry," 58.

35 Miles, "Protection of the British Textile Industry," 191, 204; Textile Council, *Cotton and Allied Textiles*, 120.

36 Coopey and Clarke, *3i: Fifty Years of Investing in Industry*, 8, 44–47, 94. Moreover, compared to the 1950s, the proportion of the ICFC's funds invested in textiles declined from an average of 11.2 per cent in 1950–1959 to 6.9 per cent in 1960–1969. *Ibid.*, 410–411, Table A.16. It should also be stressed that the ICFC was largely concerned with manufacturing firms in the small and medium sized category, thereby ruling out the LCC's proposals.

37 The *principal* mergers/acquisitions were as follows: Courtaulds acquired the LCC and the FCDSA. ICI helped finance Viyella's takeover of Combined English Mills and the cotton textile groups of Clegg & Orr, Birtwistle, and Leigh, and was instrumental in the formation of Carrington Viyella (from the merger of Carrington & Dewhurst with Viyella International). Carrington Viyella was itself acquired by Alliance in 1983. Singleton, *Lancashire on the Scrapheap*, 216–228.

38 Singh, *Take-overs: Their Relevance to the Stock Market and the Theory of the Firm*, 20–30.

39 Hannah and Kay, *Concentration in Modern Industry*, 144. The five firm concentration ratio usually refers to the share of industry output (or sales) accounted for by the five largest firms. In this case *without* merger, the five firm concentration ratio would have decreased.

40 Cowling *et al.*, *Mergers and Economic Performance*, 46–48, Table 3.2. These estimates are based on a variety of assumptions governing the treatment of: advertising expenditure as a social cost; monopoly profits after tax, and whether changes in price and output following a merger are independent of each other.

41 'k' is defined as the total factor requirement per unit of output. Effectively, 'k' is inversely related to efficiency (the ratio of inputs to outputs). *Ibid.*, 59.

42 *Ibid.*, 297.

43 *Ibid.*, 301–302.

44 Fishwick and Cornu, *A Study of the Evolution of Concentration in the United Kingdom Textile Industry*, 39, 196.

45 *Ibid.*, 32–33.

46 National Economic Development Office (NEDO), *Changing Needs and Relationships*, 9; Zeitlin, "The Clothing Industry in Transition," 212–216.

47 NEDO, *Changing Needs and Relationships*, 8–10.

48 See, for example, Ormerod, "The Decline of the UK Textile Industry." By 2000, the British textile manufacturing industry was *entirely* dependent on imported yarn. *Ibid.*, 31.

49 Ormerod, *An Industrial Odyssey*.

50 Pearcy, Recording an Empire: An Accounting History of Imperial Chemical Industries Limited, 302–303.

51 Calculated as the continuously compounded ratio of realized capital, divided by invested personal capital, 1956–1960.

52 Coats Viyella (hereafter CV) papers (private collection of letters and internal company documents). Rothschild to Alliance, 1 Sept. 1964; 17 Nov. 1966; 7 Nov. 1970; 11 Nov. 1970;

Alliance to Rothschild, 14 Dec. 1967; 15 Nov. 1970. In fact, during the 1960s, Alliance had identified for Rothschild a sample of the best performing textile companies. Two of these companies, Stott & Smith, and W.T. Taylor were subsequently acquired by Alliance, using funds made available from the IRC and Rothschild. CV papers, Alliance to Rothschild, 19 Oct. 1962.
53 For example, Shiloh, Bleachers and Smith and Nephew. Filatotchev and Toms, "Corporate Governance."
54 CV papers, strategy report by A.W. Ward in May, 1971.
55 The IRC was established in 1966 to 'promote or assist the reorganisation or development of industry in the UK'. Hague and Wilkinson, *The IRC: An Experiment in Industrial Intervention*, 5.
56 *Hansard*, "Industrial Reorganisation Corporation (Investments)," 15 Nov. 1971.
57 Hague and Wilkinson, *The IRC: An Experiment in Industrial Intervention*, 257, 280.
58 National Archives (hereafter, NA), T326/1026, 19 March 1970, Painter to Armstrong.
59 Textile Council, *Cotton and Allied Textiles*, 128.
60 *Ibid.*, 126.
61 NA, T326/1026, 13 March 1970, paper from Vintner to Maude.
62 NA, T326/1026, "Summary: Financial Assistance for the Lancashire Textile Industry," 13 March 1970. It was estimated that the benefit to the Exchequer and the balance of payments from this change would be £6–9 million and £12–15 million, respectively. *Ibid.*
63 *Ibid.*
64 NA, T326/1026, "Financial Assistance to the Lancashire Textile Industry," Investment Incentives, 13 March 1970.
65 NA, T326/1026, Wilson to Maude and Mountfield, 3 April 1970.
66 NA, T326/1026, Painter to Armstrong, 19 March 1970.
67 NA, T326/1026, "Financial Assistance to the Lancashire Textile Industry," Investment Incentives, 13 March 1970. For similar statements see, for example, NA, T326/1026, "Summary: Financial Assistance to the Lancashire Textile Industry," 13 March 1970; ibid., Maude to Pinter, 16 March, 1970; ibid., "Note of a Meeting at the Treasury," 18 March 1970; ibid., "IRC Finance for the Lancashire Textile Industry: Paymaster-General's letter of 24 April," 12 May 1970.
68 NA, T326/1026, Cracknell to Painter, 13 April 1970.
69 NA, T326/1026, "Note of a Meeting at the Treasury," 18 March 1970.
70 *Ibid.*
71 *Ibid.*
72 NA, T326/1026, Vinter to Maude, 13 March 1970; Financial Assistance to the Lancashire Textile Industry, 13 March 1970; Painter to Armstrong, 19 March 1970.
73 NA, T326/1026, Meeting at the Treasury, 18 March 1970.
74 NA, T326/1026, Painter to Armstrong, 19 March 1970; Painter to Pliatzky, 16 April 1970.
75 NA, T326/1026, Painter to Armstrong 19 March, 1970; Meeting at the Treasury 18 March, 1970.
76 NA, T326/1026, "Assistance to the Textile Industry," 24 March 1970; "Financial Assistance for the Cotton Textile Industry," 13 April 1970; Painter to Pliatzky, 16 April 1970; Letter to Diamond, 24 April 1970; Pliatzky to Gedling and Mountfield, 12 May 1970; "IRC Finance for the Lancashire Textile Industry," 19 May 1970.
77 NA, T224/2264, Annual Report and Accounts of the IRC for the year 1970–1971, 8.
78 *Ibid.*
79 NA, T326/1348, 11 March 1971.
80 CV papers, Draft press release for publication, 30 Dec. 1970.
81 *Guardian*, 30 Dec.1970; Draft press release, Spirella Group Ltd/ Horrockses-Dorcas, CV papers; *Daily Telegraph*, 5 June 1970.

82 *Financial Times*, 28 Jan. 1970; Spirella Group Ltd, letter to ordinary shareholders, 28 Feb. 1970. Rothschild acted as adviser to Alliance on this restructuring. *Ibid.*

83 *Manchester Evening News*, 11 July 1975, 18.

84 Calculated from Fishwick and Cornu, *A Study of the Evolution of Concentration in the United Kingdom Textile Industry*, 219–220.

85 The rankings are based on sales figures for 1973. *Ibid.*, 216. Contemporary estimates indicate that the combined group was the UK's biggest producer, *Manchester Evening News*, 11 July. 1975, 18.

86 *Guardian*, 23 Dec. 1982. Other cash-rich companies, such as Dawsons and NMC, were unwilling to diversify out of knitwear. *Observer*, 17 Oct. 1982.

87 *Textile Weekly*, Sept. 1982.

88 *Financial Times*, 15 Oct. 1982.

89 *Times*, 5 Aug. 1982; *Daily Telegraph*, 16 Oct. 1982; *Guardian*, 16 Oct. 1982; *Times*, 19 Oct. 1982; *Financial Times*, 19 Oct. 1982.

90 Press announcement by N.M. Rothschild, 18 Oct. 1982.

91 *Daily Telegraph*, 19 Oct. 1982.

92 The sample in Table 1 is not exhaustive of Alliance's takeover transactions. Those excluded are typically the private firms where data is more difficult to obtain. Given the absence of liquidity in the shares of such companies, the discount effect noted here is probably understated.

93 Press release by N.M. Rothschild, *Observer*, 23 June 1985.

94 *Investors Chronicle*, 21 June 1985.

95 *Financial Times*, 11 Feb. 1986; *Times*, 11 Feb. 1986.

96 *Guardian*, 24 Feb. 1986; *Business*, June 1987, 88.

97 Robinson, "The Economics of Fashion Demand," 395–396.

98 Draft press release, acquisition by Spirella of Horrockses and Dorcas, 30 Dec. 1970, CV papers. Horrockses also dealt extensively with mail order companies.

99 *Manchester Evening News*, 11 July 1975, 18.

100 *Financial Times*, 16 Oct. 1982.

101 *Glasgow Herald*, 4 July 1984.

102 *Observer*, 17 Oct. 1982; *Times*, 16 Oct. 1982.

103 *Financial Times*, 24 Feb. 1984.

104 *Times*, 18 May 1985; *Sunday Times*, 23 June 1985; *Observer*, 23 June 1985. Of interest also is that Marks & Spencer owned 3 per cent of the ordinary shares issued by NMC in 1975. Fishwick and Cornu, *A Study of the Evolution of Concentration in the United Kingdom Textile Industry*, 182.

105 *Daily Mail*, 29 Sept. 1986.

106 *The Times*, 18 May 1991.

107 *Financial Times*, 19 Oct. 1982.

108 Chandler, Scale and Scope; Lazonick, Business Organization and the Myth of the Market Economy.

109 Toms, "Windows of Opportunity"; Toms, "Rise of Modern Accounting."

110 Zeitlin, "The Clothing Industry in Transition," 216.

111 Markides and Williamson, "Related Diversification, Core Competencies and Corporate Performance."

112 These features correspond to the structural factors for assessing strategic fit between parent and subsidiary as highlighted by Goold *et al.*, *Corporate-Level Strategy*.

113 Jensen and Ruback, "The Market for Corporate Control."

114 Filatotchev and Toms, "Corporate Governance, Strategy and Survival," make a similar case using the example of Lancashire textiles in the 1960s.

# Epilogue: Survival strategies in textiles

David Higgins and Steven Toms

**Windows of opportunity: 1960–2000**

One of the central themes in this book is the apparent requirement for the Lancashire textile industry to restructure. Much of the discussion has focused on the spinning and weaving stages of the productive value chain and the associated issue of technological choice. A second, interacting theme, is the volatility of profits and asset values, which dictated the supply of capital and potentially limited the options facing individual entrepreneurs, often forcing them into short-term solutions based on existing technology. The evidence demonstrates that the historical coincidences of these themes explain the long-run decline of the industry, particularly in the years immediately following the slump of 1920.

Notwithstanding the inherited weaknesses from the interwar period, there was no reason why the industry should have disappeared entirely. Isolated firms continue to function to the present day in Lancashire, including recent start-ups,[1] but the scale is minuscule compared to other advanced countries, for example, China, European Union (EU) states and the United States.[2] Why then, given its former dominance, has the contraction of the Lancashire textile industry been so dramatic?

A consistent theme throughout this book has been the opportunities and constraints presented to entrepreneurs by financial institutions and markets. Before 1939, access to finance for restructuring purposes was the dominant problem for Lancashire. After 1945, the progressive development of the market for corporate control facilitated reorganisation, such that, after 1964 in particular, large conglomerates dominated the industry. In the 1960s, the prospects for the industry were better than they had been for some time. There were three important reasons for this. First, as discussed in chapter 8, the 1959 Cotton Industry Act removed a great deal of old and surplus capacity. Second, responding to further political pressure and industry lobbying, the incoming Labour government instituted its pre-election Plan for cotton in 1964, aimed at limiting imports from Commonwealth competitors.[3] Finally, as demonstrated in chapter 9, the process of merger that had begun in the 1950s, accelerated in the 1960s, as the market for corporate control developed, whereby London financial markets were instrumental in the buying and selling of companies, allowing the remaining firms to operate on a larger scale. Firms that historically depended on local and regional pools of capital, as described in chapters 1 to 6, were now able, as part of larger conglomerate structures, to access the London Stock Exchange.

The old constraints on entrepreneurial behaviour, which had limited the scope for restructuring in the past, no longer existed. The absence of stock market finance, which prevented restructuring in the slump of the 1920s (chapters 6 and 7), was replaced by a sufficiency of funds in the mid-1960s that enabled the radical reorganisation of the industry.

Conglomerate firms with substantial resources could buy and sell firms as their strategy suited. At the same time, the rump of the traditional cotton industry began to lose its identity and independence. By the 1960s, cotton was one of the fabrics, along with woollens and synthetics, in the portfolio of the larger conglomerate firms, such as Courtaulds, the emergent Coats Viyella group and, for a time, Imperial Chemical Industries (ICI). Consequently, internal economies of scale and scope could now be accessed, creating the potential for competitive advantage based on technological investments and the efficient organisation of production. In their critique of the Lancashire cotton textile industry, Lazonick and Mass assumed that the vertically integrated US model was superior: it was a structure that Lancashire entrepreneurs naturally sought had they not been confronted by an immutably specialised system of production.[4]

The new circumstances of the early 1960s, therefore, provide an unlikely test of Lazonick's model.[5] The takeover of the rump of the Lancashire industry by synthetics giant Courtaulds was predicated on securing the supply chain and realising internal economies of scale through process integration. At the same time, the government announced measures designed to support Courtaulds' new investments in technology and expanded production using regional assistance grants and guaranteed stable demand conditions, using first import quotas and subsequently tariffs.[6] The strategy appears to have succeeded, at least for a time. Significant investment in new technology, such as open-end spinning and shuttle-less weaving, resulted in a 72.4 per cent increase in productivity in the period 1963–1973.[7] However, these measures proved insufficient to sustain the industry [8]

Lack of control over markets meant that for Lazonick, even large conglomerates were not integrated enough, and would have been successful had they integrated forward into marketing.[9] Barriers to such forward integration were not a new problem for Lancashire manufacturers, traditionally dependent on a network of merchants to source orders overseas. However, after 1945, the merchant and warehousing networks declined, bypassed by larger firms, and the survivors switched their expertise from exporting to importing as the balance of trade shifted.[10] Contemporaneously, as larger retailers secured greater market share on the high street, textile producers became increasingly dependent on securing orders from giants such as Marks & Spencer (M&S). Regulatory changes, such as the removal of resale price maintenance, underpinned this dominance.[11]

In the face of increased concentration in the retail sector, one possible strategy open to manufacturers was to build sufficient scale to exercise countervailing power. As chapter 9 has shown, by 1986, David Alliance had built up the substantial textile conglomerate, Coats Viyella, which in part, reflected this strategic objective. Increasingly, however, mainly because of their market attractiveness, Coats Viyella's takeovers were targeted at M&S suppliers. Ironically then, as Coats Viyella grew in size, its dependence on M&S increased.[12] Another consequence of lack of market control by producers was that poor communication between retailers, garment makers and fabric producers resulted in overproduction. Fabric producers, such as ICI, supplied garment makers on the expectation of M&S orders, which often subsequently failed to materialise.[13] Such overproduction then was a consequence of potentially lucrative retail contracts being passed up the value chain in a suboptimal manner.

The build up of large conglomerate groups coincided with an increased propensity of retailers to source supplies off shore, such that, as firms were taken over they were soon after closed down. In the case of Courtaulds, as Owen's recent book demonstrates, the consequences were wave after wave of restructuring, as successive executive teams attempted to extract value on behalf of stock market investors.[14] After Coats Viyella's takeover of Tootal in 1991, Singleton notes that along with Courtaulds, these two firms now 'reigned supreme over the wreckage of the traditional British textile industry'.[15]

By the 1980s, many of these large, diversified firms faced a new threat from financial markets. The so-called 'conglomerate discount', meant that low market valuations of sprawling groups of firms created pressures to break them up.[16] In response, Courtaulds demerged its textile business, leading to the creation of Courtaulds Textiles in 1989.[17] For these smaller successor firms of the post-conglomerate phase, countervailing power was no longer a viable strategy for dealing with the now entrenched buying power of retail organisations.

An alternative strategy, given such dominance, was for some textile producers to become satellites or even quasi-subsidiaries of the large retail chains. As a consequence, they lost control not only of their strategy but also of prices and volumes, which were now dictated by the retail stores. In return, the retailers were able to offer stability of demand, which was the crucial factor for survival, particularly where expensive investments in new technology were required. For several decades, up to the mid-1990s, many textile firms, including Coats Viyella and Courtaulds Textiles, survived through such arrangements with large retailers, most notably M&S.[18] These arrangements guaranteed demand suitable for longer production runs, thereby providing valuable insurances in view of the wider instabilities that had long characterised the market for cotton.

In the second half of the twentieth century, these instabilities reflected changing priorities of world trade institutions, which compounded the problems facing surviving textile manufacturers. As Beckert has argued, politics rather than markets determined the location and competitive advantage of national cotton textile industries.[19] Market stability and industrial restructuring were symbiotic: stability promoted investment and concentration, while greater concentration promoted political lobbying power. Notwithstanding, the putative superiority of the US model in the nineteenth century, as discussed in chapter 5, in the mid-twentieth century, vertical integration worked in the United States for precisely the same reason that it did not in Britain. The textile industry in the United States constituted a powerful lobby group that resulted in strong protection from imports and hence demand stability for US firms, which could make low-risk investments in new technology.[20] The US initiative that followed, to restrict imports via the Multi-Fibre Arrangement (MFA), led Europe to adopt similar quota-based protection measures in 1973.[21] Britain's entry into the European Common Market two years later provided similar protections.

However, the British textile industry and its access to markets were now dependent on the evolution of what became the EU and its trade policies.[22] These encouraged the location of textile production in Mediterranean countries, notably, Morocco. In the late 1970s and early 1980s, the textile conglomerates increasingly sourced the cotton and fabric element of their activities overseas, which also destroyed opportunities for specialist British firms, leading to 'the vanishing British cotton industry'.[23] For example, Courtaulds constructed Chelco in 1981 as a joint venture with Morocco's Office for Industrial Development and Moroccan private investors, and in 1988 had three factories selling to leading UK retailers.[24] The Moroccan model was to import raw fibres taking advantage of tax breaks and then re-export to Europe based on specifications laid down by a European partner.[25] As a result, outward processing and subcontracting for European firms led to a rapid expansion of textile capacity in countries like Morocco in the period 1987–1991.[26]

In this respect, what happened to the Lancashire textile industry was not unique. Fragmentation in global supply chains was a defining characteristic of the 'second unbundling' in which the information technology revolution facilitated the geographical separation of various manufacturing operations.[27] It has been estimated that 75 per cent of the clothing required by French and German suppliers is obtained overseas.[28] The consequence of these arrangements for the EU textile industry as a whole, and the United Kingdom in particular, was an increased tendency to move production offshore into cheap labour locations. Such relocations were more easily carried out in fibre production, including cotton and cheaper commodity-type textile outputs. Although much of these changes were carried out at the behest of increasingly powerful retail organisations, the long supply chains that resulted were not always in their best interests.

**Twenty-first-century survival strategies**

Although the forces identified in the previous 'windows of opportunity' section have affected most textile industries in advanced countries, the decline of British textiles has been much more pronounced. There are three principal features of this difference. The first is the overwhelming dominance of the retail sector in Britain. Other advanced countries have equally powerful retailers in terms of market concentration,[29] but in Britain, in part due to differences in regulation, retailers are more easily able to dominate the supply chain.[30] Zeitlin demonstrated that by the mid-1970s, 53.2, 7.5 and 5.2 per cent of the major clothing and textile outlets in the United Kingdom, Italy and France, respectively, were owned by multiple retailers. In contrast, the shares of 'independent' retailers were 8.7, 80.8 and 70.3 per cent, respectively, for the United Kingdom, Italy and France.[31]

A second feature – the willingness of dominant organisations, often retailers, to internationalise and segment the supply chain[32] – is connected to the third, the ideological commitment to free trade, and the determination of British policy makers to secure trade deals and international influence [33] The emphasis here has been on larger and influential sectors, notably financial services and defence, and including of course, access to cheaper overseas supplies for retailers.[34] Although these factors are present in other advanced economies, they have operated at a stronger and collectively significant level, insofar as British textile manufacturing has been concerned in the final decades of the twentieth century

In the face of such powerful forces, can the textile industry be resurrected? The dominance of retail and other large corporations, globalised supply chains and the commitment to free trade are strongly underpinned by lobbyist influences and ideology. However, in the United Kingdom at least, after the 2008 financial crisis, there is an increasing recognition that action is needed to rebalance the economy away from the financial sector and reindustrialise areas like North West England, that depended on traditional manufacturing industries.[35] In 2015, the Alliance Project Team (APT), sponsored by David (now Lord) Alliance, published a report for the Greater Manchester Combined Authority. It noted that textile employment was higher in Greater Manchester County, compared to other textile regions within the United Kingdom, especially so in the fields of technical/industrial textiles and household soft furnishings.[36] One feature, which deserves particular comment, is the report's emphasis on British provenance as a marketing device, including in rapidly growing overseas markets. For example, John Lewis is investing in 'Made in Britain' product lines, and Debenhams is launching a 'Made in Britain' campaign.[37] Large retailers have responded by developing British sourced ranges of clothing and home-wear, while design-led brands such as Burberry have successfully exploited demand for genuine British style abroad.[38] Requirements for British provenance in design-led marketing promote related requirements for UK sourced fabric production, including cotton, hence the recent reopening of a Lancashire cotton production facility at Tower Mill, Dukinfield in Greater Manchester

However, determining British provenance is potentially elusive: it need not mean that the design, material inputs, intermediate and final assembly are conducted within the United Kingdom. Unlike the United States, there is no compulsory legislation that requires products to be origin marked.[39] Before the outcome of the Brexit referendum in 2016, the United Kingdom's policy on origin marking was based on EU regulations, which made unlawful the application of 'Made in' to goods manufactured and traded within the Union. The Commission has consistently taken the view that compulsory origin marking was tantamount to a quantitative restriction (e.g. quota), which would thereby infringe Article 30 of the Treaty of Rome. Moreover, manufactures imported from outside the EU are entitled to 'free circulation' within the EU once they have satisfied necessary customs requirements (e.g. payment of duties).[40] Consequently, it is still possible for retailers to claim 'British' provenance without specifying what proportion of the good is made in Britain. Viewed from this perspective, it may be argued that the private brands of retailers, not country of origin, is more meaningful to consumers.

The emphasis on British provenance by major retailers such as Debenhams, John Lewis and M&S is indicative of greater efforts to 'on-shore' production, especially in the mid- to high-end segment of the textile market for which 'design' and 'fashion' are more important than price, per se. Such a trend may indicate a greater rebalancing of the relationship between manufacturers and retailers. For example, the uncertainty generated by accelerating globalisation has encouraged manufacturers to broaden their order books; use of computer-aided design technology has facilitated their ability to produce quickly a wider range of products without sacrificing scale economies.[41] Moreover, sourcing within the United Kingdom means that, in certain lines at least, the major retailers are no longer playing off domestic versus foreign manufacturers. One consequence of this rebalancing may be that manufacturers are better able to secure higher returns, which bodes well for investment.

Nonetheless, one feature of the manufacturer-retailer relationship, which remains potentially contentious, is which brand is used to promote the product. The academic literature on the Lancashire textile industry has long recognised conflict between 'makers' and 'sellers'. In the nineteenth and early twentieth centuries, specialised merchants imposed their own brands on exported textiles and played spinners and weavers off against each other.[42] As noted in chapter 8, this trend continued through retailers in the 1970s and 1980s. So long as retailers sell products with their own brands, it remains difficult for manufacturers to appeal directly to the public. Without significant forward vertical integration, such a strategy of direct selling risks antagonising the powerful retail organisations they depend on as their main customers. One solution to this zero-sum game is greater collaboration of firms within and between each stage of production to promote and sustain major brands. The Prato region in Italy is recognised as an exemplar in this respect.[43] According to the APT report:

> Places like Prato (despite the pressures to lower input prices and labour costs) have succeeded in building strong local networks, collaborative work and alliances between entrepreneurs, centres of innovation and designer/artisans – whose respective skills complement each other. . . . These factors have secured the success of the textiles sector in Prato. Italian textile companies have focussed upon ensuring the skills needed for the unique finishes and state-of-the art features that come at the end of the fabric and apparel production chain.[44]

The relevance of the Prato experience to the UK textile industry, *as a whole,* needs to be questioned: structural imbalances in the British economy in general, or the textile industry in particular, are unlikely to reverse on any significant scale. At the same time, niche-based manufacturers, like those in specialist fabrics for outdoor clothing and equipment referred to in the introductory chapter, and the brand-based clusters referred to in this epilogue, provide the potential for a limited revival. Such initiatives, like others featured in all the chapters of this book, will undoubtedly lead to successes at individual firm level, regardless of industry structure. As the chapters in the book have demonstrated, entrepreneurs have always responded rationally to opportunities when not unduly constrained by financial institutions and access to markets, or confounded by the often excessive instabilities arising from such dependencies. For a larger scale regeneration to occur, a significant rebalancing of power is required. Textiles, in Britain and the much of the world, is part of a strongly integrated value chain dominated by large retail concerns. The challenge for entrepreneurs and governments is how new 'windows of opportunity' can be created and exploited, such that collaborative networks can be built between relatively small manufacturers and the much larger and more powerful retail corporations.

## Notes

1. For example, Tower Mill, Dukinfield in Greater Manchester ('Restored cotton mill to drive rebirth of textiles industry', *Financial Times,* 7th August 2015). Elsewhere, new owners, such as Bill Beaumont, former captain of the England Rugby Union team, entered the industry to utilise the industry's skills base. Beaumont, a direct descendant of the founder of J. Blackledge & Son, which commenced weaving in 1914, established Bill Beaumont Textiles in Chorley. www.billbeaumont. co.uk/our-heritage/
2. In 2014, these locations accounted for the substantial majority of textile exports by value (Statista. com, 'Value of the leading 15 textile exporters worldwide in 2014', retrieved 13th September 2016).
3. 'Labour's Plan for Cotton', *Times,* 20th July 1963.
4. Mass and Lazonick, 'British cotton industry'.
5. Lazonick comments only briefly on this period, noting that the experiment failed due to insufficient integration between production and marketing. Lazonick, 'Cotton industry', p.39.
6. Ricks, 'Overview of government influence', pp.123–126
7. Shepherd, 'Textiles', p.30, notes a 72.4 per cent increase in productivity in the period 1963–1973.
8. Owen, *Rise and Fall of Great Companies.*
9. Lazonick, 'Cotton industry', p.39.
10. Chapman, 'Decline and rise of textile merchanting'; Farnie, 'Merchants as prime movers', p.47.
11. Mercer, 'Retailer–supplier relationships'.
12. Toms and Zhang, 'Marks & Spencer'. After a series of crises in its relationship with M&S, Coats Viyella abandoned contract clothing sales in 2001.
13. Buck, *More Ups than Downs,* p.90.
14. Owen, *Rise and Fall of Great Companies.*
15. Singleton, *World Textile Industry,* p.129.
16. Toms and Wright, 'Corporate governance, strategy and structure'.
17. Owen, *Rise and Fall of Great Companies,* pp.129–149.
18. Toms and Zhang, 'Marks & Spencer'.
19. Beckert, *Empire of Cotton.*
20. Singleton, 'Decline of the British Cotton Industry', p.312; Aggrawal and Haggard, 'Politics of protection'.
21. Aggrawal and Haggard, 'Politics of protection', pp.253–254, 265, 296.
22. 'Britain fights the battle of an earlier reality,' *Guardian,* 9th July 1992; Spinager, 'MFA phase out', p.3.

23. Blackburn, 'Vanishing UK cotton industry', p.52.
24. Toms and Zhang, 'Marks & Spencer'.
25. These partners included Mothercare and British Home Stores (not M&S). Other firms using a similar strategy included Benetton 'Profile of Morocco's Textile and Clothing Export Industry', *Textile Outlook International*, July 1994; Economic Intelligence Unit, *Mediterranean Textiles and Clothing*, p.92.
26. 'Profile of Morocco's Textile', *Textile Outlook International*.
27. Baldwin, 'Trade and industrialization,' pp.2, 6.
28. APT, *Repatriation of UK Textiles Manufacture*, p.72.
29. Gereffi, 'International trade and industrial upgrading', p.45
30. For example, as noted earlier, abolition of resale price maintenance (Mercer, 'Retailer–supplier relationships') and lack of regulation of supplier payment terms (APT, *Repatriation of UK Textiles Manufacture*, p.10).
31. Zeitlin, 'Clothing industry in transition,' p.212.
32. Toms and Zhang, 'Marks & Spencer'.
33. Berry, *Globalisation and Ideology*. Exposure to international markets of the United Kingdom, Germany and the United States has increased between the 1950s and the 1990s, but with the United Kingdom recording consistently higher levels throughout. Milner and Judkins, 'Partisanship, trade policy, and globalization', p.106.
34. In 2011, these sectors, along with advanced manufacturing, infrastructure, healthcare, education and creative industries, were listed as the UK priority sectors (United Kingdom Trade and Investment, 'Britain open for business').
35. Martin *et al.*, 'Rebalancing the UK economy'.
36. APT, *Repatriation of UK Textiles Manufacture*, pp.21–23.
37. Ibid., p.49.
38. For example, the M&S 'Best of British range' (*Drapers*, 22 Nov. 2013); APT, *Repatriation of UK Textiles Manufacture*; 'Burberry to invest at least £50m in new trenchcoat factory,' *Guardian*, 3rd November 2015.
39. Food is an exception. In the United States, origin marking allowing consumers to differentiate between domestic and foreign products began with the McKinley Tariff of 1890. Subsequently, this general provision was extended in the 1930s. Federal labelling requirements for textile and wool products, enforced by the Federal Trade Commission, require that most of these products have a label indicating the country of origin and the identity of the manufacturer. Ruyack, 'Origin marking requirements'; The Textile Fiber Identification Act, 1939 (Textile Act), 15 U.S.C. s.70 et seq; Wool Products Labeling Act of 1939 (Wool Act), 15 U.S.C. s. 68 et seq.
40. Zaimis, *EC Rules of Origin*, pp.87, 117.
41. Zeitlin, 'Clothing industry in transition,' pp.221–224.
42. See, for example, Clay, *Report on the Position*, p.39; Political and Economic Planning, *British Cotton Industry*, p.71; Higgins and Tweedale, 'Trade marks question'.
43. See, for example, Piore and Sable, *Second Industrial Divide*. One of the regions leading textile producers, Benetton, was ranked in the top 100 global brands by Interbrand in 2001. It was among but a handful of textile-associated names, such as Chanel, Gucci and Levis. http://museum.brand-home.com/docs/P0005_Brandvalue.pdf
44. APT, *Repatriation of UK Textiles Manufacture*, p.72.

## Bibliography

Aggrawal, V. and Haggard, S. (1984). 'The politics of protection in the US textile and apparel industries', in *American Industry in International Competition: Government Policies and Corporate Strategies*, eds. John Zysman and Laura Tyson. Cornell: University Press.
Alliance Project Team (2015). *Repatriation of UK Textiles Manufacture*, Manchester: Greater Manchester Combined Authority.

Baldwin, R. (2011). 'Trade and industrialization after globalization's 2nd unbundling: How building and joining a supply chain are different and why it matters'. NBER Working Paper, No. 17716, Cambridge, MA.

Beckert, S. (2014). *Empire of Cotton: A New History of Global Capitalism*. New York: Vintage.

Berry, C. (2011). *Globalisation and Ideology in Britain: Neoliberalism, Free Trade and the Global Economy*. Oxford: Oxford University Press.

Blackburn, J. A. (1982). 'The vanishing UK cotton industry'. *National Westminster Bank Quarterly Review* (November), 42–52.

Buck, D. (2001). *More Ups than Downs: An Autobiography* (Spennymoor)

Chapman, S. (1990). 'The decline and rise of textile merchanting, 1880–1990', *Business History 32*, 171–190.

Clay, H. (1931). *Report on the Position of the English Cotton Industry*. Confidential Report for Securities Management Trust. London: SMT.

Economic Intelligence Unit (1989). *Mediterranean Textiles and Clothing*. London: EIU.

Farnie, D. A. (2004). 'The role of merchants as prime movers in the expansion of the cotton industry, 1760-1990' in *the Fibre That Changed the World: The Cotton Industry in International Perspective*, eds. Farnie and Jeremy. Oxford: Oxford University Press, 15–56.

Gereffi, G. (1999). 'International trade and industrial upgrading in the apparel commodity chain'. *Journal of International Economics 48*(1), 37–70.

Higgins, D., and Tweedale, G. (1996). 'The trade marks question and the Lancashire cotton textile industry, 1870-1914'. *Textile History 27*(2), 207–228.

Lazonick, W. (1986), 'The cotton industry', in *The Decline of the British Economy*, eds. Bernard Elbaum, William Lazonick, and Michael H. Best (eds.). Oxford: Clarendon Press, 1986, p.39.

Martin, R., Pike A., Tyler, P., and Gardiner, B. (2016). 'Spatially Rebalancing the UK Economy: Towards a New Policy Model?'. *Regional Studies 50*(2), 342–357.

Mass, W., and Lazonick, W. (1990). 'The British cotton industry and international competitive advantage: The state of the debates'. *Business History 32*(4), 9–65.

Mercer, H. (2014). 'Retailer–supplier relationships before and after the Resale Prices Act, 1964: A turning point in British economic history?' *Enterprise and Society 15*(1), 132–165.

Milner, H. V., and Judkins, B. (2004). 'Partisanship, trade policy, and globalization: Is there a left–right divide on trade policy?' *International Studies Quarterly 48*(1), 95–120.

Owen, G. (2010). *The Rise and Fall of Great Companies: Courtaulds and the Reshaping of the Manmade Fibres Industry*. Oxford: Oxford University Press.

Piore, M. J., and Sabel, C. F. (1984). *The Second Industrial Divide: Possibilities for Prosperity*. New York: Basic Books.

Political and Economic Planning. (1934). *Report on the British Cotton Industry*. London: Political and Economic Planning.

Ricks, D. (1984). 'An overview of government influence,' in *The Global Textile Industry*, ed. Brian Toyne. London: Allen & Unwin.

Ruyack, R. (1974). 'United States country of origin marking requirements: the application of a Nontariff barrier'. *Law and Policy in International Business 6*(2), 485–531.

Shepherd, G. (1983). 'Textiles', in *Europe's Industries: Public and Private Strategies for Change*, eds. Geoffrey Shepherd, Francois Duchêne, and Christopher Saunders. London: Frances Pinter.

Singleton, J. (1996), 'Decline of the British Cotton Industry since 1940', in *The Lancashire Cotton Industry: A History Since 1700*. Preston: Lancashire County Books.

Singleton, J. (2013). *The World Textile Industry*. Abingdon: Routledge.

Spinager, D. (1988). 'Textiles beyond the MFA phase out'. CSGR Working Paper No. 13/98, University of Warwick, Coventry, England.

Toms, S., and Wright, M. (2002). 'Corporate governance, strategy and structure in British business history, 1950-2000'. *Business History 44*(3), 91–124.

Toms, S., and Zhang, Q. (2016). 'Marks & Spencer and the decline of the British textile industry'. *Business History Review 90*(01), 3–30.

United Kingdom Trade and investment (2011). 'Britain open for business: the next phase'. www.ukti.gov.uk/uktihome/aboutukti/aimsobjectives/corporatestrategy.html

Zaimis, N. (1992). *EC Rules of Origin*. London: Chancery Lane Publishing.

Zeitlin, J. (1988). 'The clothing industry in transition: International trends and British response'. *Textile History 19*(2), 211–237.

# Index

For Product Safety Concerns and Information please contact our EU
representative GPSR@taylorandfrancis.com
Taylor & Francis Verlag GmbH, Kaufingerstraße 24, 80331 München, Germany

www.ingramcontent.com/pod-product-compliance
Ingram Content Group UK Ltd.
Pitfield, Milton Keynes, MK11 3LW, UK
UKHW051832180425
457613UK00022B/1214